PAUL *and the* JEWS

PAUL *and the* JEWS

A. Andrew Das

LIBRARY OF PAULINE STUDIES

Stanley E. Porter, *General Editor*

© 2003 by A. Andrew Das

Hendrickson Publishers, Inc.
P.O. Box 3473
Peabody, Massachusetts 01961-3473

ISBN 1-56563-676-7

Printed in the United States of America

Second Printing—May 2005

Library of Congress Cataloging-in-Publication Data

Das, A. Andrew.
    Paul and the Jews / A. Andrew Das.
      p. cm. — (Library of Pauline studies)
    Includes bibliographical references.
    ISBN 1-56563-676-7 (pbk. : alk. paper)
    1. Paul, the Apostle, Saint—Views on Judaism. I. Title. II. Series.
    BS2655.J4D37 2004
    261.2′6′092—dc22
                          2003018247

To my parents,

Ajit and Rebecca Das

TABLE OF CONTENTS

ACKNOWLEDGMENTS

IN FIRST grade at a small private school in Indianapolis, I used to sit next to Lenny Birnbaum. During our free periods we enjoyed an occasional game of cards or checkers. He was bright, witty, an incredible card player. Lenny was also Jewish. We sometimes talked about our religious beliefs. He explained to me that Jews do not believe in Jesus. This was the first time it really dawned on me that people do differ in their religious beliefs. I am hoping with this book to further the conversation, now as an adult.

I am grateful to Professor Stephen Westerholm, Professor Frank Matera, and especially to Professor Paul J. Achtemeier, who graciously reviewed the manuscript and offered critical suggestions for improvement. Thanks are due to my wife, Susan, the love of my life, for her support of this project and for her help, especially while raising three very small children—a toddler and twin babies. I have dedicated this book to my parents, Ajit and Rebecca Das. My mother painstakingly reviewed the entire manuscript for style, and I expect that readers will benefit immensely from the clarity that she helped bring to the work. Finally, I am thankful to Patrick Alexander, former academic editor at Hendrickson Publishers, who approached me for this book within the Library of Pauline Studies, and also to Stanley Porter, the series editor, who has also reviewed the manuscript. I bear the responsibility for what remains.

My hope is that readers will find in these pages a sensitive topic treated with honesty and compassion. I find myself sympathetic with those with whom I am in disagreement—particularly those who think they have found a way past the stumbling block Jesus poses for Jews when Christians identify him as the Jewish Messiah, a Messiah who seems to loom large across the pages of the apostle. I hope and pray that we, Jews and Christians, will continue to find ways to come together as fellow interpreters and as fellow human beings to further the discussion even when we may not always agree.

ABBREVIATIONS

GENERAL

ca.	circa
ch(s).	chapter(s)
ed.	editor, edited by, edition
frg.	fragment
Heb.	Hebrew
LXX	Septuagint
MT	Masoretic Text (of the OT)
NT	New Testament
NS	new series
OT	Old Testament
trans.	translated by
v(v).	verse(s)

BIBLE TEXTS, VERSIONS, ETC.

LB	Living Bible
NRSV	New Revised Standard Version

OLD TESTAMENT PSEUDEPIGRAPHA

Ascen. Isa.	*Mart. Ascen. Isa. 6–11*
2 Bar.	*2 Baruch (Syriac Apocalypse)*
1 En.	*1 Enoch (Ethiopic Apocalypse)*
2 En.	*2 Enoch (Slavonic Apocalypse)*
Jub.	*Jubilees*
L.A.B.	*Liber antiquitatum biblicarum* (Pseudo-Philo)
Mart. Ascen. Isa.	*Martyrdom and Ascension of Isaiah*
Pss. Sol.	*Psalms of Solomon*
T. Ab.	*Testament of Abraham*
T. Dan	*Testament of Dan*

T. Reu.	*Testament of Reuben*
T. Sim.	*Testament of Simeon*

DEAD SEA SCROLLS AND RELATED TEXTS

1QHª	*Hodayot*ª or *Thanksgiving Hymns*ª
1QpHab	*Pesher Habakkuk*
1QM	*Milḥamah* or *War Scroll*
1QS	*Serek Hayaḥad* or *Rule of the Community*
1QSa	*Rule of the Congregation* (Appendix a to 1QS)
4QMessAp	*Messianic Apocalypse*
4QMMT	*Miqṣat Maʿaśê ha-Torah*
4QpNah	*Nahum Pesher*
4QPsᶠ	*Apocryphal Psalms*
11QMelch	*Melchizedek*
11QTª	*Temple Scroll*ª
CD	Cairo Genizah copy of the *Damascus Document*

PHILO

Abr.	*De Abrahamo*
Congr.	*De congressu eruditionis gratia*
Decal.	*De decalogo*
Deus	*Quod Deus sit immutabilis*
Ebr.	*De ebrietate*
Fug.	*De fuga et inventione*
Her.	*Quis rerum divinarum heres sit*
Ios.	*De Iosepho*
Leg. 3	*Legum allegoriae* III
Legat.	*Legatio ad Gaium*
Migr.	*De migratione Abrahami*
Mos. 1, 2	*De vita Mosis* I, II
Mut.	*De mutatione nominum*
Opif.	*De opificio mundi*
Post.	*De posteritate Caini*
Praem.	*De praemiis et poenis*
Prob.	*Quod omnis probus liber sit*
QG 1	*Quaestiones et solutiones in Genesin* I
Sacr.	*De sacrificiis Abelis et Caini*
Somn. 1	*De somniis* I
Spec. 1, 2, 3, 4	*De specialibus legibus* I, II, III, IV
Virt.	*De virtutibus*

Josephus

Ant.	*Jewish Antiquities*
Ag. Ap.	*Against Apion*
J.W.	*Jewish War*
Life	*The Life*

Mishnah, Talmud, and Related Literature

b.	Babylonian
m.	Mishna
t.	Tosefta
Ker.	*Kerithot*
Qidd.	*Qiddušin*
Sanh.	*Sanhedrin*
Šabb.	*Šabbat*

Apostolic Fathers

1 Clem.	*1 Clement*
Herm. *Vis.*	Shepherd of Hermas, *Vision*
Ign. *Rom.*	Ignatius, *To the Romans*

New Testament Apocrypha and Pseudepigrapha

Acts Pil.	*Acts of Pilate*
Gos. Pet.	*Gospel of Peter*
Let. Pet. Jas.	*Letter of Peter to James*
Ps.-Clem. Rec.	*Pseudo-Clementine Recognitions*

Ancient Christian Writings

Eusebius
  Hist. eccl.   *Historia ecclesiastica*
Irenaeus
  Haer.   *Adversus haereses*
Justin
  1 Apol.   *Apologiai*
Lactantius
  Inst.   *Divinarum institutionum libri VII*
Orosius, Paulus
  Hist. adv. pag. *Historiae adversus paganos*

Tertullian
   Apol.   *Apologeticus*

ANCIENT NON-CHRISTIAN WRITINGS

Aristotle
   Rhet.   *Rhetorica*
Cicero
   Flac.   *Pro Flacco*
   Tusc.   *Tusculanae disputationes*
Dio Cassius
   Hist.   *Historia romana*
Epictetus
   Diatr.   *Diatribae (Dissertationes)*
Horace
   Sat.   *Satirae*
Juvenal
   Sat.   *Satires*
Martial
   Epigr.   *Epigrammata*
Persius
   Sat.   *Satirae*
Plato
   Rep.   *Republica*
Plutarch
   Am. prol.   *De amore prolis*
   Quaest. conv. *Quaestionum convivialium libri IX*
Strabo
   Geogr.   *Geographica*
Suetonius
   Claud.   *Divus Claudius*
   Dom.   *Domitianus*
   Jul.   *Divus Julius*
   Tib.   *Tiberius*
Tacitus
   Ann.   *Annales*
   Hist.   *Historiae*
Theon
   Progymn.   *Progymnasmata*
Valerius Maximus
   Facta   *Facta et dicta memorabilia*
Xenophon
   Anab.   *Anabasis*
   Mem.   *Memorabilia*

SECONDARY SOURCES

AB	Anchor Bible
ABD	*Anchor Bible Dictionary.* Edited by D. N. Freedman. 6 vols. New York: Doubleday, 1992
AGJU	Arbeiten zur Geschichte des antiken Judentums und des Urchristentums
AnBib	Analecta biblica
ANTC	Abingdon New Testament Commentaries
BDF	Blass, F., A. Debrunner, and R. W. Funk. *A Greek Grammar of the New Testament and Other Early Christian Literature.* Chicago: University of Chicago Press, 1961
Bib	*Biblica*
BJRL	*Bulletin of the John Rylands University Library of Manchester*
BNTC	Black's New Testament Commentaries
CBQ	*Catholic Biblical Quarterly*
CRINT	Compendia rerum iudaicarum ad Novum Testamentum
CTM	*Concordia Theological Monthly*
EKKNT	Evangelisch-katholischer Kommentar zum Neuen Testament
ExpTim	*Expository Times*
FBBS	Facet Books, Biblical Series
FRLANT	Forschungen zur Religion und Literatur des Alten und Neuen Testaments
HBT	*Horizons in Biblical Theology*
HNT	Handbuch zum Neuen Testament
HTKNT	Herders theologischer Kommentar zum Neuen Testament
HTR	*Harvard Theological Review*
HUCA	*Hebrew Union College Annual*
IBC	Interpretation: A Bible Commentary for Teaching and Preaching
ICC	International Critical Commentary
Int	*Interpretation*
JBL	*Journal of Biblical Literature*
JBLMS	Journal of Biblical Literature Monograph Series
JETS	*Journal of the Evangelical Theological Society*
JRS	*Journal of Roman Studies*
JSJSup	Journal for the Study of Judaism in the Persian, Hellenistic, and Roman Periods: Supplement Series
JSNT	*Journal for the Study of the New Testament*
JSNTSup	Journal for the Study of the New Testament: Supplement Series
LCL	Loeb Classical Library

LSJ   Liddell, H. G., R. Scott, and H. S. Jones, *A Greek-English Lexicon.* 9th ed. with revised supplement. Oxford: Oxford University Press, 1996
MM   Moulton, J. H., and G. Milligan. *The Vocabulary of the Greek Testament.* London: Hodder & Stoughton, 1930. Reprint, Peabody, Mass.: Hendrickson, 1997
MSJ   *The Master's Seminary Journal*
NCB   New Century Bible
NICNT   New International Commentary on the New Testament
NIGTC   New International Greek Testament Commentary
NovT   *Novum Testamentum*
NTS   *New Testament Studies*
OBT   Overtures to Biblical Theology
OTP   *Old Testament Pseudepigrapha.* Edited by J. H. Charlesworth. 2 vols. Garden City, N.Y.: Doubleday, 1983
PL   Patrologia latina [= Patrologiae cursus completus: Series latina]. Edited by J.-P. Migne. 217 vols. Paris, 1844–1864
Presb   *Presbyterion*
PRSt   *Perspectives in Religious Studies*
RBL   *Ruch biblijny i liturgiczny*
SBLDS   Society of Biblical Literature Dissertation Series
SBLSymS   Society of Biblical Literature Symposium Series
SD   Studies and Documents
SJLA   Studies in Judaism in Late Antiquity
SNTSMS   Society for New Testament Studies Monograph Series
SP   Sacra pagina
SR   *Studies in Religion*
TDNT   *Theological Dictionary of the New Testament.* Edited by G. Kittel and G. Friedrich. Translated by G. W. Bromiley. 10 vols. Grand Rapids: Eerdmans, 1964–1976
Them   *Themelios*
TJ   *Trinity Journal*
TLZ   *Theologische Literaturzeitung*
TZ   *Theologische Zeitschrift*
WBC   Word Biblical Commentary
WUNT   Wissenschaftliche Untersuchungen zum Neuen Testament
ZNW   *Zeitschrift für die neutestamentliche Wissenschaft und die Kunde der älteren Kirche*
ZTK   *Zeitschrift für Theologie und Kirche*

∽ 1 ∾

PAUL AND THE JEWS:
A NEW STARTING POINT

THE APOSTLE Paul describes a telling incident in his Letter to the Galatians. In what must have been a calculated move on his part, he went up to meet the Jerusalem apostles, taking along an uncircumcised man. He laid before the acknowledged leaders of the church the gospel he preached among the Gentiles, with the uncircumcised Titus as exhibit A. All might have gone well except that certain "false believers" "slipped in" to the private meeting "to spy on the freedom we have in Christ Jesus, so that they might enslave us" (Gal 2:4), but "we did not submit to them even for a moment, so that the truth of the gospel might always remain with you [Gentile Galatians]" (2:5). Later, after Peter had arrived at Antioch and was eating with Gentile Christians there, certain people came from James in Jerusalem. Peter immediately withdrew from the table "for fear of the circumcision faction," and "the other Jews" joined Peter in his withdrawal (2:12). Paul stood up and opposed Peter to his face. At both Jerusalem and Antioch, people loyal to Judaism and its central rite of circumcision opposed Paul's circumcision-free mission to the Gentiles. They sensed in his teachings elements that seemed to compromise the essence of the Jewish faith. The zealous persecutor of Christians ironically became himself the focal point for Jewish zeal. After the dust settled from the conflicts at Jerusalem and Antioch more than a hundred years later, a Jewish Christian author reflecting on Paul would label him "the enemy man," a destroyer of Judaism.[1] Many Jews through the centuries would have agreed.

The reaction is understandable when one comes across a passage such as 1 Thess 2:14–16. Paul says that the Jews

> killed both the Lord Jesus and the prophets, and drove us out; they displease God and oppose everyone by hindering us from speaking to the Gentiles so

---

[1] The author of the *Letter of Peter to James* (2:3–5) claims to be part of a group observant of the law of Moses. The author goes on to speak of *two* missions to the Gentiles, one by Peter and the other by Paul, "the man who is my enemy," who preached a "lawless and absurd doctrine." Further, it was Peter's mission that was the first to the Gentiles; cf. Acts 8–11.

that they may be saved. Thus they have constantly been filling up the measure
of their sins; but God's wrath has overtaken them at last.

The Jews are "Christ killers." While this would become a common label
among second-century Christians for the Jews, its roots go back to the very
first decades of Christianity. Paul adds that the Jews have been filling up the
measure of their sins and so God's wrath has overtaken them at last. Elsewhere he writes:

> Beware the dogs, beware of the evil workers, beware of those who mutilate the
> flesh. For it is we who are the circumcision, who worship in the Spirit of God
> and boast in Christ Jesus and have no confidence in the flesh. (Phil 3:2–4)

While in these verses Paul may be opposing Jewish teachers who were
themselves also followers of Jesus Christ, does not the vicious rhetoric lend
itself better against the circumcised who do *not* boast in Christ? The
uncircumcised who believe in Christ have *taken the place* of Jews as the true
circumcised. Circumcision is a matter of indifference, as Paul explains in his
Letter to the Galatians: "For in Christ Jesus neither circumcision nor
uncircumcision counts for anything; the only thing that counts is faith working through love" (Gal 5:6). In case his recipients do not realize the full
impact of the statement, Paul repeats it: "For neither circumcision nor
uncircumcision is anything" (6:15). In 4:21–31 the apostle speaks of two
women, Sarah and Hagar, who bore offspring for the Jewish patriarch Abraham (cf. Genesis 16, 21). These two women represent two covenants. The
Jews were historically descended from Sarah, Abraham's wife. In a surprising twist Paul associates the Jewish covenant, which included the sacred
Law ("Mount Sinai"), with Hagar, Abraham's slave woman banished into the
wilderness of Arabia. In Paul's thinking, Mount Sinai, the holy site where
God had given the Jewish people the Law, "corresponds to *the present Jerusalem,
for she is in slavery with her children.*" Paul's language may again be taken as in-
dicting ethnic Jews in general ("present Jerusalem," "Mount Sinai," "children of slavery" / "Hagar" vs. "children of promise" / "the free woman").

The same apostle can speak of a church, inclusive of Gentiles, that appears to have swallowed up entirely the historical prerogatives of ethnic
Jews. In Gal 3:15 Paul surprisingly insists that Abraham's promised "seed"
was grammatically singular, unlike the corporate sense of the Hebrew original in Genesis. His implication is that corporate Israel is no longer Abraham's proper heir. By the end of Galatians 3 Paul transforms the promise of
a corporate Israel from the Hebrew Scriptures into a new corporate body of
those united by their shared faith in Jesus Christ, the sole legal beneficiary
of Abraham's promises. The promises to Abraham benefit only those who
are "in Christ" by their faith or trust in him. First Corinthians 10:1–13 narrates the story of Israel's stumbling in the wilderness, that is, the "Israel according to the flesh." Paul explains that the story of Israel's stumbling was
ultimately intended for the benefit of his Gentile Christian readers (10:6, 11).

The events of Israel's past prefigured *Christian* experience. Believers in Christ are thus the beneficiaries of Israel's promises. Biblical texts that once referred to ethnic Israel are redirected toward the church.[2]

Alongside the rite of circumcision at the heart of Jewish identity was the practice of Moses' Law. The Law had historically distinguished the Jewish people and their religion from antiquity. Paul, a former zealot for the Law, ironically proclaims that "all who rely on the works of the law are under a curse" (Gal 3:10; cf. 1:14). Moses' Law, he claims, is a "law of sin and death" (Rom 8:2). The Law was only a temporary measure in the history of humanity (Gal 3:19, 23–24). Now that Christ has come, the role of the harsh disciplinarian has ended (3:25). Christ is the "end" of the Mosaic Law and/or its "goal" and was what it had been proclaiming all along (Rom 10:4–8). Unfortunately, the Jews missed the goal. They did "not succeed in fulfilling that law" (9:31) and are "enemies of God" (11:28). "Indeed, to this very day whenever Moses is read, a veil lies over their minds" (2 Cor 3:15). Paul's message at times seems to fan the flames of anti-Judaism. In a generation that lives after the *Shoah,* the mass murder of Jews in concentration camps, it may seem that Jewish readers of Paul through the centuries have been right—his message of redemption is unredeemable; his "good news" is really bad news.

Other readers of Paul have noted a different, perhaps contradictory trajectory in his thought. He also refers to the Law's commandments as "holy and just and good" (Rom 7:12; 8:2). He claims to uphold the Law's continuing relevance (Rom 3:31; 1 Cor 9:8; 14:21). He cites the Law as an abiding and normative moral code that must be fulfilled, even by Christians (Rom 13:8–10). Salvation remains to the Jew "first" and then to the Greek (1:16–17). According to Paul, the Jewish people maintain a position of priority in God's plan: "They are Israelites, and to them belong the adoption, the glory, the covenants, the giving of the law, the worship, and the promises; to them belong the patriarchs" (9:4–5). "Then what advantage has the Jew? Or what is the value of circumcision? Much, in every way" (3:1–2). Paul even anticipates a day when "all Israel will be saved" (11:26). Is this the same apostle who had just claimed that the people of Israel are "enemies of God"? Is Paul's message redeemable after all?

Some have considered Paul an utterly contradictory thinker. Perhaps this is a sign of the frustration that many have experienced in trying to make sense of these diverging strands in his thought. Is it really conceivable that he would contradict himself so thoroughly and so often, even within a single paragraph or sentence? It may be that these contradictory emphases are the product of a complex line of reasoning rather than actual inconsistencies, although such a proposition would need to be supported. What follows will

---

[2] E.g., whereas the prophet Hosea foresaw a brighter future for the people of Israel (Hos 2:25 LXX [2:23 MT]), in Rom 9:25 Paul transforms the prophecy into a vision of the Gentiles who would one day join the church; see ch. 4, below.

4   *Chapter 1*

seek and examine the logic behind these apparently divergent strands of thought in the apostle's relationship with his Jewish heritage.

Paul says that he was "a Hebrew born of Hebrews," a Pharisee, and zealous for the Law of Moses (Phil 3:5–6). He had excelled in Judaism beyond his contemporaries (Gal 1:14). An accurate understanding of first-century Judaism is therefore crucial in interpreting Paul's statements about the Jews, their Scriptures, and their traditions. Unfortunately, those immersed in the interpretation of Paul, the former Pharisee, have in the past projected onto Judaism an understanding derived more from the apostle's writings than from a study of Judaism itself. In other words, Pauline interpretation has sometimes led to a very negative understanding of first-century Judaism. Even today some scholars remain convinced that the grace-oriented Paul, who taught God's love, was opposing Jewish legalists trying to earn their way into heaven by their good works.[3] This remains a common way of understanding first-century Judaism in many churches and pulpits as well. This popular notion of Judaism accurately reflects the consensus among NT scholars prior to the last quarter of the twentieth century.

For almost a hundred years, NT specialists drew upon, whether consciously or not, the research and writings of one man—Ferdinand Weber, who published in 1880 a famous work on early rabbinic Judaism.[4] Before Weber, nineteenth-century Christian scholars had been eager to show in their writings how Judaism had pointed forward to Christianity. Christianity was thus the legitimate fulfillment of what Judaism, or at least its Scriptures, had predicted. Weber's approach supplanted the fulfillment schema.[5] He contended that rabbinic Judaism was fundamentally a legalistic religion. God had granted the people a covenant relationship, which Israel had promptly broken in the wilderness. All that was left for them was the weighing of the scales. Individuals enjoyed a place in the world to come only if their good deeds outweighed the bad on the divine scales. Although a Jewish individual might benefit from the treasury of merits earned long ago by the patriarchal ancestors of Israel, the accounting of individual deeds remained strict. Weber contended that, for some Jews, the system led to self-righteous boasting and that, for others, it led to despair and uncertainty over whether a person had accumulated enough good deeds before the holy and righteous God, whom the Jews viewed as remote and inaccessible.

Precedence for Weber's description may be traced to Martin Luther and the sixteenth-century Reformation. Luther rejected what he perceived

---

[3] See Thomas R. Schreiner, *The Law and Its Fulfillment: A Pauline Theology of Law* (Grand Rapids: Baker, 1993); and Seyoon Kim, *Paul and the New Perspective: Second Thoughts on the Origin of Paul's Gospel* (Grand Rapids: Eerdmans, 2002).

[4] Ferdinand Weber, *System der altsynagogalen palästinischen Theologie* (ed. Franz Delitzsch and Georg Schnedermann; 1880); revised in 1886 as *Die Lehren des Talmuds*. Schnedermann revised Weber's book in a second edition under a third title, *Jüdische Theologie auf Grund des Talmud und verwandte Schriften,* in 1897.

[5] George Foot Moore, "Christian Writers on Judaism," *HTR* 14 (1921): 228–37.

as the Roman Catholic Church's insistence on indulgences and good works as the means of earning one's way into heaven. He found in the apostle Paul's writings a similar struggle. In Luther's reading, Paul was likewise contending against "works righteousness," that of the Jews. Of course, Martin Luther was also known for other, darker statements concerning the Jews. In *On the Jews and Their Lies* in 1543 he argued at length for razing their homes, seizing their sacred books, and burning down their synagogues.[6] Throughout his writings, he spoke of the Jews' "claim to be God's people by reason of their deeds, works, and external show" "in the same way as our papists, bishops, monks, and priests."[7] Not surprisingly, Ferdinand Weber, a German Lutheran, was advancing a way of approaching Paul and the Jews that had at its root Luther's perennial struggle against works righteousness.[8]

At the end of the nineteenth century, many scholars objected to Weber's description of Judaism as sorely inaccurate and based on an inadequate study of the primary sources. George Foot Moore critiqued Weber at length.[9] Several Jewish scholars voiced their objections. The dissent was drowned out by a chorus of voices from within the ranks of Christian biblical scholars, especially German Lutherans, who were drawing upon Weber's work as the standard for good scholarship on Judaism. Furthermore, many of these scholars were famous and influential in their own right. Wilhelm Bousset, a renowned scholar at the beginning of the twentieth century, drew upon Weber's work, and Bousset's writings remained in print longer.[10] Bousset conveyed Weber's legacy to his own student, Rudolf Bultmann, who would become arguably the most influential biblical scholar of the twentieth century. Bultmann defined "Jewish legalism" as "a piety

---

[6] Martin Luther, "On the Jews and Their Lies, 1543," in vol. 47 of *Luther's Works* (Philadelphia: Fortress, 1971), 268–69.

[7] Ibid., 175. Luther compares Jewish works righteousness to that of the pope (and the devil) on pp. 162–63 as well.

[8] Hans J. Hillerbrand ("Martin Luther and the Jews," in *Jews and Christians: Exploring the Past, Present, and Future* [ed. James H. Charlesworth; New York: Crossroad, 1990], 134) writes, "Since the repudiation of all forms of works righteousness formed the pivotal core of Luther's theology, his repudiation of the Jews—as a theological entity—was categorical. The Jews were exemplars of false religion, as were Catholics, Turks, and Anabaptists." For other post-Holocaust Lutheran scholarly reflection on Luther and the Jews, see Heiko A. Oberman, *The Roots of Anti-Semitism in the Age of Renaissance and Reformation* (trans. James I. Porter; Philadelphia: Fortress, 1983). Note also Ken Schurb's fine-tuning of Oberman's reading of Luther in "Luther and the Jews: A Reconsideration," *Concordia Journal* 13 (1987): 307–30. E. P. Sanders (*Paul and Palestinian Judaism: A Comparison of Patterns of Religion* [Philadelphia: Fortress, 1977], 55) describes the divide that took place between German-speaking scholars who were relying upon Weber and several English-speaking scholars who dissented.

[9] Moore, "Christian Writers on Judaism," 197–254.

[10] Wilhelm Bousset, *Die Religion des Judentums im neutestamentlichen Zeitalter* (Berlin: Reuther & Reichard, 1903). A revised edition of his volume appeared in 1925.

which endeavors to win God's favor by the toil of minutely fulfilling the Law's stipulations."[11] In this system, "the idea of reward and punishment becomes the motivation, but also—and this is the characteristic thing for Judaism—that the obedience man owes to God and to His demand for good is understood as a purely formal one; i.e. as an obedience which fulfills the letter of the law, obeying a law simply because it is commanded without asking the reason, the meaning, of its demand."[12] Bultmann's students then championed the synthesis, as did several articles in the widely used *Theological Dictionary of the New Testament,* edited by Gerhard Kittel and Gerhard Friedrich.[13]

Wilhelm Bousset was only one trajectory from Weber. In 1874, about six years before Weber's classic work, Emil Schürer published his *Lehrbuch der Neutestamentlichen Zeitgeschichte.* Schürer intended this work to introduce students to the aspects of Jewish history from 175 B.C.E. to 70 C.E., a period crucial for the interpretation of the Christian NT. He extensively revised and enlarged the book in 1886–1890 as *Geschichte des jüdischen Volkes im Zeitalter Jesu Christi,* translated into English as *History of the Jewish People in the Age of Jesus Christ.* Though a very useful work that remains popular and is still in print, Schürer's revision drew upon Weber as a key source and equated Judaism with legalism. In a section entitled "Life under the Law," he explained that God would reward or punish the Jews strictly on the basis of their deeds:

> But what were the motives, whence sprang this enthusiasm for the law, what the means whereby it obtained this enormous sway over minds? To answer briefly: it was *faith in Divine retribution,* and that a retribution in the strictest juristic sense. The prophetic idea of the covenant, which God had entered into with the chosen people, was apprehended in the purely juristic sense; the covenant was a legal one, by which both the contracting parties were mutually bound. The people to observe the law given them by God, exactly, accurately and conscientiously: while God was also bound in return to pay the promised recompense in proportion to their performances. And the obligation held good not only with respect to the nation as a whole, but to every individual; performance and recompense always stood in corresponding relation to each other. He who did much had to expect from God's justice the bestowal of much reward; while on the other hand every transgression entailed a corresponding punishment.[14]

---

[11] Rudolf Bultmann, *Theology of the New Testament* (trans. Kendrick Grobel; 2 vols.; New York: Charles Scribner's Sons, 1951–1955), 1:11.

[12] Ibid., 1:11–12.

[13] Gerhard Kittel and Gerhard Friedrich, *Theological Dictionary of the New Testament* (trans. G. W. Bromiley; 10 vols.; Grand Rapids: Eerdmans, 1964–1976), originally published as *Theologisches Wörterbuch zum Neuen Testament.*

[14] Emil Schürer, *A History of the Jewish People in the Time of Jesus Christ.* 2.2 (trans. Sophia Taylor and Peter Christie; 1890; repr., Peabody, Mass.: Hendrickson, 1994), 90–91. See § 28 (pp. 90–96, 120–25) for further dark descriptions of Jewish legalism and externalism.

According to Schürer, this belief in a just and exact rewarding of deeds led to an "externalism." All Jewish religious and moral life revolved around the external fulfillment of legal stipulations in order to merit God's reward. Two Christian rabbinic scholars, Hermann Strack and Paul Billerbeck, wrote a lengthy commentary on the NT in the light of later rabbinic literature early in the twentieth century.[15] Commentators would frequently refer to Schürer's and Strack and Billerbeck's works in order to help interpret the NT in the light of its Jewish context. For instance, those who read R. C. H. Lenski's popular commentary series were introduced to the synthesis as mediated through Schürer, Strack, and Billerbeck. Such views then filtered down from academia into pulpits and Bible classes, the audience for whom Lenski intended his series. Lenski regularly speaks of "the Jews with their moralistic, self-righteous use of the Mosaic code of law" or "legal works-righteousness" in contrast to Christians with their religion of grace.[16]

Jewish scholar after Jewish scholar—Samuel Sandmel, Solomon Schechter, Claude Montefiore, Louis Finkelstein, Jacob Lauterbach—repeatedly and to no avail urged Christian scholars to look firsthand at the primary sources left behind by the Jewish authors of the first and second centuries and to recognize the error of the Weberian picture. The situation would finally change when the dissent came from within the ranks of Christian NT scholars. In 1977 a NT specialist named E. P. Sanders, himself indebted to these Jewish predecessors, reviewed the primary sources and demonstrated that Weber's synthesis was a caricature. Judaism was not the legalistic religion that Christian scholars following Weber had described it to be.[17]

Sanders drew attention to passages in the rabbinic Mishnah from 200 C.E., a compilation of the oral traditions and interpretation of the Torah from earlier generations. In several places the Mishnah reflects first-century discussions. Mishnah *Sanhedrin* 10:1 says, "All Israelites have a share in the world to come." The passage then goes on to speak of those excluded from this general rule as only the most egregious and blatantly unrepentant sinners in Israel's past. In other words, only those who had deliberately acted in defiance of the God of Israel were excluded from a place in the world to come. Ordinary Israelites could be confident of their place in that future world because of God's election of the people of Israel. They need not despair of their place in a divine plan enacted long ago to include them.

Certainly these rabbis spoke of laws, rules, and regulations. These regulations may even seem overwhelming and strange to the modern,

---

[15] Hermann L. Strack and Paul Billerbeck, *Kommentar zum Neuen Testament aus Talmud und Midrash* (4 vols.; Munich: C. H. Beck, 1924–1928).

[16] R. C. H. Lenski, *The Interpretation of St. Paul's Epistle to the Romans* (Lutheran Book Concern, 1936; repr., Peabody, Mass.: Hendrickson, 2001), 238, 180.

[17] Sanders, *Paul and Palestinian Judaism*. See esp. Sanders's review of the history of scholarship on this question, pp. 33–59.

uninitiated reader. Sanders must remind the modern reader of laws that people obey every day and that are embedded in the very fabric of society. No one would consider stopping at a red traffic light an instance of legalism. Meats purchased in a store have passed regulatory codes through an inspection process. Citizens of industrialized countries usually must possess certain governmental forms of personal identification as well as licenses for their vehicles. No one would likely conclude as a result that the average Westerner is "legalistic." These are simply the laws that structure life in a particular society. The same may be said of the laws of Moses. The fact that the laws of Moses were derived not from a human source but from divine legislation would have been a greater incentive for a Jew to observe these laws. A first-century Jew would also have appreciated that these laws were designed to serve as a reminder of the special relationship that he or she enjoyed with the Creator of the universe.

An Israelite would not despair should his or her performance of the Law fall short of the Mosaic standard. The Law included various means of restoring a broken relationship with God. Sanders pointed to the system of sacrifices and atonement. The laws concerning such would comfort and encourage consciences troubled by sin. Even after the Romans destroyed the temple in 70 C.E. during the first Jewish revolt, the Jews were not deterred from their observance of the Law. The rabbis substituted the study of temple laws for the actual sacrifices that were central to their religion. God did not require of people what was physically impossible, only what was realistically attainable. The mere intent to perform a biblical law, even if not carried out, would satisfy the legal requirement, according to the rabbis. Sanders coined the term "covenantal nomism" to describe this perspective. God's gracious election and covenant relationship with the people, along with the merciful provision of sacrifice and atonement for failure, enveloped and formed a framework around the Jews' observance of the Law's requirements, the embedded "nomism."[18]

As a result of Sanders's study, most NT scholars have abandoned the view that a fundamentally petty legalism characterized the religion of first-century or rabbinic Judaism. Such a view does not adequately account for the unique relationship of Israel with the God who had elected them as a special people. The notion that all but the most unrepentant sinners in Israel would find a place in the world to come simply does not conform to the Weberian description of Judaism. After Sanders reviewed rabbinic Judaism, he turned to several Jewish documents from the Second Temple period through the end of the first century. These documents demonstrated the same, generally gracious pattern of religion. No longer could Jewish legal-

---

[18] Sanders defines "covenantal nomism": "Briefly put, covenantal nomism is the view that one's place in God's plan is established on the basis of the covenant and that the covenant requires as the proper response of man his obedience to its commandments, while providing means of atonement for transgression" (ibid., 75).

ism be the proper foil for the apostle Paul's critique of the Mosaic Law. A proper Christian understanding of first-century Judaism and of the beginning of the rabbinic movement, the foundations for normative Judaism, would go far toward improving Jewish-Christian relations after centuries of caricature.

Once the Weberian fog had lifted, scholars began to see more clearly that Paul was never really confronting Jewish works righteousness. Romans 2 critiques Jewish confidence on the basis of mere *possession* of the Law. Paul seeks to disturb that comfort by reminding the hypothetical Jew that he or she must also obey that Law. To borrow a phrase from Dietrich Bonhoeffer, perhaps Paul would have labeled the problem "cheap grace." Certainly nothing in Romans 2 suggests that the Jews were trying to earn their way into heaven by their good works. Likewise Gal 3:15–21 speaks of a Law that simply came 430 years after God's gracious dealings with Abraham and thus was never intended to save in itself. Not a word in the passage suggests Jewish legalism. Pauline specialists were forced to look afresh at Paul's problem with the Law: what is it that he saw as problematic about the Mosaic Law if he was not confronting Jewish legalism? A heated discussion began that rages on even today.

Out of the discussion a dominant approach has emerged that some believe deserves the status of a new paradigm; it is auspiciously labeled "the new perspective on Paul and the Law." The scholar James D. G. Dunn has been its most ardent and articulate champion. Dunn took Sanders's scholarship in a new direction. The starting point was Sanders's premise that Judaism was a gracious religious system grounded in God's election and favor toward the people. No Jew would have had to obey God's Law perfectly. The provisions of sacrifice, repentance, and atonement guaranteed that an individual could experience life in the world to come even if he or she were less than absolutely meticulous in the observance of all that God had commanded. Such a construal of Judaism resonated for Pauline specialists with Paul's own description of himself as "blameless" in Phil 3:2–9. Along with his autobiography in Galatians 1, where he boasts that he had excelled in Judaism well beyond his peers, the apostle does not appear to be a man who had been burdened by pangs of conscience, angst, and guilt as would allegedly be typical of a formerly Law-observant Jew from the traditional standpoint. Perfect obedience of the Law was simply never an issue for Paul or for anyone in his day. First-century Jews would have clung to a gracious and merciful system of religion grounded in a God who had chosen and elected Israel.

Sanders had been content to say that what Paul found problematic about Judaism was that it was not Christianity; Judaism was not based on faith in Christ. Dunn found this less than satisfying. As Dunn read through the writings Paul left behind, he noted the recurrent ethnic dimension of Paul's reasoning. Paul juxtaposes Jew with Gentile or Greek quite regularly in the very passages in which he is talking about Moses' Law and the issues

this Law raised for Paul's missionary work among Gentiles. Dunn concluded that Paul's problem with the Mosaic Law must therefore relate to its
ethnic features. The Jews had treated the Law as a boundary marker in identifying a special people who enjoyed God's grace. The Gentiles would have
to submit to circumcision, Sabbath, and dietary regulations if they wanted to
be included among God's people and thereby be guaranteed a place in the
world to come. In Dunn's reading of Paul, the apostle faulted the Jews on
just this point. The Jews had failed to understand that the Scriptures had always pointed toward the inclusion of the Gentiles in God's plan. God's
grace was never just for the nation of Israel but was ultimately intended for
the non-Jew as well. It was a misunderstanding that had resulted in the Jews'
excessive pride in their ethnic identity because of their exclusive possession
of the Law. The Jews were wrongly forcing the Gentiles to live like Jews.[19]
Consequently, Paul draws differently the boundaries identifying God's
people. The boundary marking God's people is not circumcision, Sabbath,
or any other ritual from the Mosaic Law but rather an existence "in Christ."
As the Law itself testified, God had planned all along to include all the
peoples of the world. The Gentiles did not need to observe the aspects of the
Law that distinguished Jews from Gentiles, that is, the "works of the Law," if
they wanted to experience God's favor. Dunn concluded that whenever
Paul speaks positively of the Law, it is the Law understood apart from Jewish ethnic identity or boundary markers. Whenever Paul speaks negatively
of the Law, he has in mind primarily these ethnic boundary markers.

After a long period during which many interpreters of Paul's critique
had viewed first-century Jews as crass legalists, Dunn represented a very different approach. Dunn's approach was indeed a "new perspective on Paul
and the Law."[20] No longer did Paul's critique of the Law have anything to
do with people not being able to obey the Mosaic Law as perfectly as God
required. The critique was entirely of Jewish ethnic presumption. The new
perspective that Dunn introduced offers several advantages sustaining a
more positive Jewish-Christian interfaith relationship. Not only did Dunn

---

[19] Some would wrongly say that his opponents were "judaizing" and thus were
"Judaizers." Such a use of the term "judaizing" is improper since the word referred
to those who adopted a Jewish way of life for themselves, not to those advocating or
compelling such a lifestyle. See James D. G. Dunn, *The Epistle to the Galatians*
(BNTC 9; Peabody, Mass.: Hendrickson, 1993), 9 n. 2; and Shaye J. D. Cohen, *The
Beginnings of Jewishness: Boundaries, Varieties, Uncertainties* (Hellenistic Culture and
Society 31; Berkeley: University of California Press, 1999), 175–97. Christians have
historically employed the label "Judaizers" as a pejorative term.

[20] Advocates of the new-perspective approach also include N. T. Wright, *Climax of the Covenant: Christ and the Law in Pauline Theology* (Minneapolis: Fortress,
1991); Francis Watson, *Paul, Judaism, and the Gentiles: A Sociological Approach*
(SNTSMS 56; Cambridge: Cambridge University Press, 1986); Michael Cranford,
"Abraham in Romans 4: The Father of All Who Believe," *NTS* 41 (1995): 71–88;
idem, "The Possibility of Perfect Obedience: Paul and an Implied Premise in Galatians 3:10 and 5:3," *NovT* 36 (1994): 242–58.

work with an understanding of Judaism that included a gracious and approachable God and that avoided the caricature of busy, anxiety-ridden Jews trying to earn their way into heaven on the divine scales, he was able to maintain a positive perspective on the Mosaic Law in Paul. Paul does not discard the Law as the relic of a past era. The Law is actually good in and of itself. The Mosaic Law remains the sign of an elect people that includes Gentiles and of a giving Lord, albeit whose blessings are realized only by faith in the *Jewish* Messiah, Jesus Christ.

More traditional biblical scholars have resisted the "new perspective" paradigm, as fruitful as it may be for Jewish-Christian interfaith dialogue, because of its inability to account for key passages where the apostle does appear to be speaking of humans as unable to accomplish what the Law demands. In other words, while Dunn and important predecessors such as Krister Stendahl[21] have certainly advanced the modern understanding of Paul by highlighting the often intensely ethnic dimension to the apostle's reasoning, these advances must be reconciled with the strengths of the traditional reading. The possibility must also be entertained that these two approaches are not mutually exclusive. Paul may very well be critiquing the Law on the basis of the difficulty of doing the works that it requires. Upon further, more detailed examination, subsequent scholarship has also criticized Sanders's global characterization of "common Judaism" as covenantal nomism. Sanders grossly generalized the complexities of Second Temple Judaism. The Jews held God's grace, God's mercy, and repentance in a lively tension alongside the necessity for people to do God's Law. The shape of this tension varies from writing to writing and from genre to genre. The emphasis may fall toward one extreme or the other.[22] How one resolves

---

[21] Krister Stendahl, *Paul among Jews and Gentiles* (Philadelphia: Fortress, 1976).

[22] I argued at length for this modification of Sanders's view of Judaism in A. Andrew Das, *Paul, the Law, and the Covenant* (Peabody, Mass.: Hendrickson, 2001), 12–69. Independently, Friedrich Avemarie took a similar approach to rabbinic literature (*Tora und Leben: Untersuchungen zur Heilsbedeutung der Tora in der frühen rabbinischen Literatur* [TSAJ 55; Tübingen: J. C. B. Mohr (Paul Siebeck), 1996], esp. his conclusions on pp. 575–84). Certain passages in Second Temple and rabbinic Judaism do advocate strict observance of the Law as a means to gaining the reward of a place in the world to come. Recently a group of specialists in the literature of Second Temple Judaism have corroborated my approach and that of Avemarie; see the essays in D. A. Carson, Peter T. O'Brien, and Mark A. Siefrid, eds., *The Complexities of Second Temple Judaism*, vol. 1 of *Justification and Variegated Nomism* (Grand Rapids: Baker, 2001). The essayists offer a more nuanced view of the literature in question but do not return to the pre-Sanders caricature of Judaism as a religion of crass works righteousness and gross legalism. The essayists generally recognize the importance of election, covenant, sacrifice, and repentance in the Jewish systems of thought that they discuss, even while reexamining the extent and role of God's grace. Greater and more sustained attention in the volume to the matter of strict and perfect obedience in Judaism would have been helpful since it is the denial of perfect obedience to the Law in Judaism that forms the basis for the new perspective reading of Paul. Further, the authors of the volume do not always recognize the

these questions will naturally figure in one's understanding of Paul's relationship with, and opinion of, other Jews who did not choose to join the early Christ movement.

Few have realized, however, that an approach to Judaism as a religion inclusive of God's grace and mercy may lead to a very different reading of Paul than that offered by Dunn. If Paul is a formerly strict Pharisaic Jew, as the apostle himself claims, then a proper understanding of first-century Judaism presents the best background to the apostle's own position. Sanders's covenantal nomism distinguished between the embedded nomism, the strict rules and regulations God handed down from Mount Sinai to be accomplished, and the overarching gracious framework that included the full narrative of a God who had entered into a relationship with the people of Israel and their ancestors, rescued them from their enemies and slavery, and then protected them in the wilderness and in subsequent generations. Even in scholarly discussions critical of Sanders, the tension remains between the strict demand of the Law and God's mitigating grace and mercy.

This tension in Judaism may be taken in a different direction than the path Dunn took. When Jesus Christ revealed himself to the future apostle, Paul realized that Judaism did not offer a viable path to salvation; the path to a right relationship with God was only in Christ. In Paul's reasoning, the gracious elements in Judaism were never efficacious for salvation of themselves and apart from the suffering, death, and resurrection of Jesus Christ. The Mosaic Law had never provided salvation in and of itself. Performance of its regulations involved empty human deeds, and nothing more, apart from the proper framework of grace in Christ, Abraham's seed. Consequently, if the works required by the Mosaic Law were never the means to salvation, then the Law's own distinctions between Jew and Gentile would not be the basis for identifying those who have a place in the world to come. If this understanding of Paul is correct—and what follows will advocate and work from this "newer perspective"—the denial of any saving value in the Law's works will provide a crucial plank in reconstructing Paul's view of the Jewish people. In other words, while the Jews did not approach the Law le-

---

significance of the tension they themselves highlight in Judaism (and Paul) between salvation by God's grace and a judgment according to works. Occasionally, when an essayist finds works and obedience extolled as necessary in Jewish literature, the essayist assumes a degree of works righteousness in spite of the presence of God's grace and mercy (e.g., Craig Evans's essay). The interplay between grace and demand is complex in both Judaism and Paul and need not equate to earning a place in the world to come entirely by one's own efforts. The apostle specifically qualifies the divine origin of human works in relation to salvation (Phil 2:12–13). Are not Jewish authors in his day capable of similar reasoning? Also, some of the essayists deem efforts to "stay in" the Jewish community, such as Law observance, instances of works righteousness. If so, should Christian acts of piety and avoidance of sin, all of which help maintain status within their community of faith, be analogously labeled as works righteousness? Greater sophistication in the analyses of these matters would have been helpful.

galistically, Paul's critique of the Law as based on works is a consequence of the transition in his thinking from one conception of grace to another.

The association of grace with Christ in Paul's thought may very well have been accompanied by a denial of Jewish ethnic privilege or election. An exploration of whether Israel maintains a special place as an ethnic people in God's plan or whether Jewish identity has been swallowed up by a new Christian identity within the church will therefore be necessary. If Israel does maintain a special relationship with God, what is the nature and value of that relationship?[23] Further, as Paul's reasoning led him away from associating God's grace with the Jewish institutions of election, sacrifice, or covenant, the apostle might very well have viewed the Law as likewise ineffectual or ceasing with the coming of Christ. This possibility leads to several further questions that deserve attention: Does the Law function positively for Paul? To what extent should Christians observe the Law, or does it even continue to function as a norm for Christians?[24] The chapters that follow will address the extent to which Paul's association of God's grace with Christ sent ripples through his entire system of thought.

Since Paul explicitly discusses the Mosaic Law, the distinction between Jews and Gentiles/Greeks, justification, and the relationship between the church and its Jewish roots in his letters to the Galatians and the Romans, the bulk of what follows will concentrate on those two letters. At the same time, one of the advances in Pauline scholarship this last century has been the recognition that Paul was a situationally driven thinker. He never formulated abstract, systematic doctrine, although Romans in particular has been culled for its doctrinal statements. The historical situation behind a letter must be developed before one can begin to resolve Paul's approach to the Mosaic Law or the Jews in that letter.[25] Only when the situation he was addressing has been properly reconstructed will a nuanced and fair reading of Paul's view of Judaism, its election, and its Law be possible.

In reconstructing the situation of the letter to the Galatians, many scholars have concluded that Paul was not critiquing Judaism as such. If he was engaged in an intense dispute with fellow missionaries in the service of Jesus Christ, his critical comments would most likely be directed against his rival peers rather than against Jews in general. Many recent Pauline specialists aver that to take Paul's statements as a blanket condemnation of the Jews is a gross misinterpretation.[26]

---

[23] Chs. 4 and 5, below, will tackle these issues.

[24] I did not treat in *Paul, the Law, and the Covenant* the passages that could lead to a potentially more positive view of the Law. Ch. 6, below, will briefly expand what I previously argued, and ch. 7 will develop my understanding of the Law's continuing role in Paul's theology.

[25] See ch. 2, below.

[26] For the strongest recent expression of this view, see J. Louis Martyn, *Galatians* (AB 33A; New York: Doubleday, 1997).

At the same time, any reading of Paul that is sensitive to the situations within the churches to which these letters were addressed must also recognize that the Pauline churches were among the earliest within the Christ movement. Had the first followers of Christ separated from the Jewish synagogues? Was Pauline Christianity still a movement of Judaism, or had there been some separation? Some have suggested that the followers of Christ in Rome were still meeting alongside other Jews for worship. The Galatian Christians may have attended synagogue worship or known people who did. The interpretation of Paul's correspondence would be decisively influenced by the question of whether his audiences were worshiping *within* or interacting with the Jewish assemblies.[27]

Chapter 2 will therefore reconstruct the concrete situation at Galatia by means of the clues hidden within the letter. In the mid-twentieth century, many scholars supposed that the apostle was combating more than one rival group. Eventually, by the end of the last century, scholars reached an almost unanimous consensus that the contents of the letter may be explained on the basis of a single rival group at work in the Galatians' midst. Recent developments have challenged that consensus. At the same time, at the end of the last century, specialists began to realize that Paul's Letter to the Galatians reflects an apocalyptic worldview that decisively shaped his reasoning with respect to Judaism and the Jewish Law. A review of the debate over the situation of the Galatian letter—especially the role of the Mosaic Law, faith in Jesus Christ, and Paul's apocalyptic worldview—will offer an excellent test case for the newer perspective sketched here. The way Paul treats notions such as the Mosaic covenant, atoning sacrifice, and the place of the Jewish people as God's elect will help illumine whether the apostle considers Judaism's gracious elements efficacious or saving.

Paul's Letter to the Romans addresses many of the same topics as his Letter to the Galatians. The Mosaic Law and the place of Jews and Christians among God's elect are prominent within the discussion. And once again, the letter appears to be aimed toward the concrete situation of the Roman congregation. Contrary to the optimism that characterized study of the Galatian situation, no one can claim that a similar consensus has been reached on the situation at Rome. Many scholars have leaned toward a particular reconstruction in the last several decades: Paul was addressing the tensions within a mixed congregation of Jewish and Gentile Christians over matters of distinctive Jewish practices. Nevertheless, books frequently appear with such titles as *The Romans Debate* or *The Mystery of Romans.* Chapter 3 will therefore delve into these matters by beginning with the origins of Jews and Christians in Rome. For the first Christians in Rome, the evidence is not limited to the biblical material but includes information from the Roman historians. Chapter 3 will develop a hypothesis regarding the situation at

---

[27] See the discussion of Mark Nanos's proposals in chs. 2 and 3, below.

Rome and then test it against a recent and very different proposal, which would situate the Roman Christians within the Jewish synagogues rather than within their own assemblies. The chapter will conclude with the potential implications of the situation within the Roman congregation as well as Paul's advice to the congregation for Jewish-Christian relations.

The clues used to reconstruct the situation at Rome lie primarily in Romans 14 and 15, but a discussion of the implications for Jewish-Christian relations requires a review of what Paul has written earlier in the letter on these very topics. Romans speaks at length about the role of the Jews and the Gentiles in God's plan and their relationship to each other, especially in Romans 9–11 as well as in the first three chapters of the letter. Indeed, Paul draws upon the language of the Jewish Scriptures for God's elect people in describing Christians, and yet he does not deny a place for ethnic Jews in God's plan. The vast majority of ethnic Jews, however, have not assented to Paul's claims regarding Jesus as the Messiah.

The precise role of the Messiah for the future of Israel within Paul's letters is a matter of intense contemporary debate, and again, a resolution to these modern debates will decisively shape what one may conclude about the role of ethnic Jews in God's saving plan for the world to come. For instance, if Jesus Christ were God's operative path to salvation only for the Gentiles, then the Jews might be able to approach God through the Mosaic Law. If Paul has assumed a two-covenant model and if his position is to influence modern perspectives, then modern Jewish-Christian relations would be very different than if Paul thinks God saves *all* people through faith in Christ. In other words, the framework of grace for the Jews as an elect people may be effective after all. This question—whether the Jews remain an elect people and what this entails—is the topic of ch. 4.

Chapter 5 will take the matter of ethnic Israel one step further in order to consider whether the Jews maintain a position of *priority* in God's plan for the world. Paul seems to speak of Jewish priority in Romans 9–11, but students of the apostle have questioned whether the Jews occupy a privileged position anywhere else in his letters. In the last several years a growing number of scholars have concluded, on the basis of a careful examination of Paul's use of pronouns to distinguish Christian Jews from Christian Gentiles in Galatians, that Paul prioritizes the Jewish people in that letter as well. Paul appears to be making the claim that the Gentiles are enjoying their blessings in Christ as a result of what God has done and is continuing to do for the Jewish people. At the same time, other passages within the undisputed Pauline corpus appear to rule out a privileged place for ethnic Israel. The most notorious anti-Jewish passage is 1 Thess 2:14–16, where Paul speaks of the destruction that has finally, rightfully come upon the Jewish people. Such sentiments, if as truly dark as they initially seem, would undermine anything positive the apostle has said about the Jews elsewhere. The question, then, is how to explain these diverging trajectories in Paul's comments with respect to Jewish priority in God's plan for the world.

Chapters 3 to 5 revolve around the issue of Israel's election. If the gracious election of a people was of no benefit apart from what God has done in Christ, what is the value of the Law bequeathed to the Jewish people through Moses? Paul's position on the Law has been just as disputed as his view of ethnic Israel's status as God's elect. Again, one group of passages speaks very negatively about the Law while others speak positively. In the first century, the Jews viewed the Law as leading to life for the Jewish people. Paul alludes to that tradition (Rom 7:12; 8:2), but ultimately his thinking on the Law was shaped by an awareness of the decisive apocalyptic change of eras created by Christ's entry onto the stage of human history. From the point of view of this new age in Christ, Paul contends that God never intended the Law to function as an instrument of salvation. At the same time, such a contention does not necessarily imply that the Law ceases to function within Christian existence (although many Pauline specialists have argued that Paul thinks the Law no longer remains in effect). Certainly, if the Law were to remain in effect for the Christian, it would have to be understood in light of the momentous, transforming events of Christ's life, death, and resurrection.

Each of the following chapters will therefore tackle a unique set of problems within the body of Pauline scholarship. Once the most probable readings of the apostle have been established, the various strands of Paul's thought will be drawn together into a coherent account of his stance toward the Jewish people. This will not be the definitive, final answer on Paul's view of his fellow Jews. Scholars will undoubtedly continue to debate Paul's view of the Law and of Judaism because of the sheer breadth and complexity of these topics. Nevertheless, a careful reading of Paul that is ever cognizant of the various positions scholars have taken as well as of the supporting evidence for their positions should lead to the most probable interpretation. As modern Jews and Christians seek positive and constructive ways to relate to each other, the question must finally be asked: Does the apostle's stance toward his people foster anti-Semitism or do his writings lead to a renewed appreciation of the Jewish faith and its heritage?

∽ 2 ∾

THE CRISIS IN GALATIA: SALVATION IN CHRIST AND THE MOSAIC LAW

> But even if we or an angel from heaven should proclaim to you a gospel contrary to what we proclaimed to you, let that one be accursed! As we have said before, so now I repeat, if anyone proclaims to you a gospel contrary to what you received, let that one be accursed! (Gal 1:8–9)

BARELY A few verses into Paul's Letter to the Galatians, the apostle lashes out with striking, harsh language. Anyone who proclaims a gospel message different from Paul's will most certainly suffer the wrath of God! Let that person be anathema! This outburst of curses at the beginning of the letter is not the last time that we will encounter such language. Within the context of a discussion of circumcision, a practice for which the Jews were often slandered and ridiculed, Paul blurts out, "I wish those who unsettle you would castrate themselves!" (Gal 5:12).[1] This biting comment gives us a glimpse into the identity of those who have incited the apostle to such seething fury. The objects of Paul's rage appear to be associated in some way with Judaism. The entire letter represents an ongoing discussion of the relationship between the young Christ movement and its Jewish heritage. Galatians thus offers a test case for whether Paul sees saving value in the gracious elements of Judaism, that is, in its covenant(s) and elect identity. At the same time, the Jewish Law given through Moses, the Torah, is at the center of the discussion. Ultimately one must ask precisely what Paul finds problematic about the Law and why he believes the Law cannot save.

THE SITUATION IN GALATIA: "YOU" AND "THEY"

Although Paul's letter unfortunately offers only one side of the conversation with the Galatians, a reconstruction of the Galatian situation is still possible.

---

[1] See the references to circumcision in Menahem Stern, *Greek and Latin Authors on Jews and Judaism* (3 vols.; Fontes ad res judaicas spectantes; Jerusalem: Israel Academy of Sciences and Humanities, 1974–1984).

Paul is remarkably consistent throughout the letter in employing the second-person-plural pronouns ("you") in clear contrast to third-person-plural pronouns ("they," "those people," "some"). This distinction is the key to unlocking the situation of the letter and indicates that there are two separate groups. If we read through the letter and observe what Paul says about "you" as opposed to "them," the identity of these two groups begins to come into focus, together with Paul's point of contention.

Paul addresses his Galatian readers with the second-person "you," and his comments offer a glimpse into the Galatians' identity. In Gal 4:8 he identifies the recipients of his letter as former Gentiles, or non-Jews: "Formerly, when you did not know God, you were enslaved to beings that by nature are not gods." They had been enslaved to pagan idols. The Galatians had "welcomed" him "as an angel of God, as Christ Jesus" himself (4:14). The apostle describes himself in 4:19 as a mother who has given and is giving birth to them as his children. In 1:6, however, he "is astonished that you [Galatians] are so quickly deserting the one who called you in the grace of Christ." Apparently it has only been a short while since he was "formerly" preaching a "gospel" message to them, and already a new situation has arisen (1:6–9; 4:13).[2] Paul is concerned lest they "turn back again to the weak and beggarly elemental spirits" (4:9). The Galatians are entertaining a position that would represent a return to the same sad condition of slavery to the false gods and idols from which they had been rescued by Paul's message.

Paul refers to another group, which he distinguishes from the Galatians by the use of third-person pronouns. In 1:7 he speaks of "some who are confusing you and want to pervert the gospel of Christ." In 5:12 he wishes that "those who unsettle you would castrate themselves." In 6:13 he says, "Even the circumcised do not themselves obey the law, but they want you to be circumcised so that they may boast about your flesh." Galatians 5:12 and 6:13 clearly connect the third-person group with the rite of circumcision; "they" are advocating the circumcision of the Galatians.[3]

---

[2] The Greek word in 4:13 for "formerly" (πρότερος) can also mean "first" (of two prior visits), but see MM 554; BDF §62, p. 34; C. F. D. Moule, *An Idiom Book of New Testament Greek* (Cambridge: Cambridge University Press, 1959), 98; Plato, *Rep.* 522a; Xenophon, *Mem.* 3.8.1; *Anab.* 4.4.14; Herm. *Vis.* 3.3.5; John 6:62; 9:8; 1 Tim 1:12–13. Paul nowhere identifies two separate visits prior to the letter; Martyn, *Galatians,* 421. Rather, he is contrasting the Galatians' condition "formerly," when he had been with them, and "now" as he writes.

[3] Paul clearly considers the third-person group to be his opponents or rivals. His language is polemical. These people may be labeled Paul's "opponents" or "rivals" as long as the reader is cognizant that this is language influenced by Paul's own perspective within the letter. These people likely did not view themselves as Paul's opponents. George Howard (*Paul—Crisis in Galatia: A Study in Early Christian Theology* [2d ed.; Cambridge: Cambridge University Press, 1990], 8–9, cf. 11) points to Paul's comment in Gal 5:11 that he is *not* still preaching circumcision as evidence that some may have claimed that Paul was in support of their own message of circumcision; see also Jerry Sumney, *"Servants of Satan," "False Brothers," and Other*

At various points in Paul's letter, it appears that the "they" group, who were advocating circumcision, were not content to stop there but were promoting adherence to the entirety of the Mosaic Law. Paul does not directly address the matter of circumcision until ch. 5 of the letter. In preparation for his comments, he lays a careful foundation in an extensive discussion about the value of the Mosaic Law. He identifies the Galatians in 4:21 as those "who desire to be subject to the law." Likewise Paul's comments in 3:1–5 indicate that the Galatians are considering adopting a more comprehensive approach to the Mosaic Law. Paul reprises the harsh language with which he began the letter: "You foolish Galatians!" He then asks, "Who has bewitched you?" One cannot fail to hear the note of polemic against his rivals, the "bewitchers." Paul asks if the Galatians had received God's Spirit by doing the works the Law requires or by "believing what you heard," which perhaps may be better translated, "the message that evokes faith." The bewitchers were apparently urging the Galatians to consider the works prescribed by the Mosaic Law as the key to unleashing the power and possession of God's Spirit. Another clue that Paul's rivals were advocating a more comprehensive approach to the Mosaic Law is the reference in 4:10 to the Galatians' "observing special days, and months, and seasons, and years." The Jews celebrated Sabbaths, new moons, seasons of Pentecost and Passover, and sabbatical years. Paul's audience would thus be adopting a Jewish liturgical calendar that ironically corresponded to the pagan calendars of their past.[4]

Opponents of Paul (JSNTSup 188; Sheffield, England: Sheffield Academic Press, 1999), 145–46, 158–59. The interpretation of Gal 5:11 remains contested, and it is also possible that the "opponents" may not have known Paul at all. Mark D. Nanos (*The Irony of Galatians* [Minneapolis: Fortress, 2002], 124–25) has suggested that Paul is writing his letter *anticipating* how it will be read in the presence of this other group.

[4] Troy Martin ("Apostasy to Paganism: The Rhetorical Stasis of the Galatian Controversy," *JBL* 114 [1995]: 437–61) thinks they are returning to paganism because of the difficulty of the circumcision requirement. But the Galatians' desire to be under the Law in Gal 4:21 suggests otherwise. Martin would counter that 4:21–5:6 addresses the Teachers rather than the Galatians. Paul's careful distinction elsewhere in Galatians between "you" Galatians and the outside group in the third person is problematic for his rejoinder. Also, Martin does not recognize that Paul *figuratively* equates the adoption of Jewish practices with their former paganism. Similarly in 5:12, Paul equates circumcision figuratively and ironically with castration, a pagan practice especially prominent among the adherents of the mother goddess cult in Galatia; see Hans Dieter Betz, *Galatians* (Hermeneia; Philadelphia: Fortress, 1979), 270; Susan M. Elliott, "Choose Your Mother, Choose Your Master: Galatians 4:21–5:1 in the Shadow of the Anatolian Mother of the Gods," *JBL* 118 (1999): 661–83. The Galatians were not actually returning to pagan practices such as castration or their former calendars, but the Jewish rituals they were considering were virtually equivalents, at least from the point of view of Paul's rhetoric. Finally, Paul otherwise treats the Galatians as a homogeneous group, as Martin himself points out, and yet elsewhere in the letter the issue is an entertaining of Law observance, not paganism.

It is difficult to imagine how Paul's opponents could advocate Jewish circumcision without also promoting Law observance in general. Circumcision was the most difficult and formidable aspect of the Mosaic Law for a non-Jew. To be circumcised entailed a certain stigma in Greco-Roman society since everyone would recognize the circumcised man or boy in pagan company at the baths or during athletic competitions in the gymnasia.[5] Many Jews sought to conceal circumcision rather than endure ridicule.[6] Although Strabo, the first-century B.C.E. historian and geographer, spoke well of Moses' religion, he considered circumcision a later superstitious corruption of the Jewish faith. He pejoratively described circumcision as a mutilation of the glans penis.[7] Josephus, the first-century Jewish historian, reported that Apion derided circumcision as well.[8] Because of the exposure of the glans penis, the circumcised male appeared to the Greek and Roman "to be in a perpetual state of sexual arousal."[9] Jewish literature may be reacting against this perception in its assertion that circumcision actually excised the passions.[10] Further, lower-class Jewish youths would not have had the same opportunities in the gymnasia for social advancement as other youths. In many cities patterned on the Greek model throughout the empire, citizenship depended on the training to be an ephebe, which included an exercise component in the gymnasium.[11] Sympathetic Gentiles would have had no problem observing virtually any aspect of Moses' Law, but circumcision was another matter. It required the ultimate commitment. The procedure

---

[5] On circumcision as the distinctive mark of Jewish males, see Cohen, *Beginnings of Jewishness,* 39–49; and John M. G. Barclay, *Jews in the Mediterranean Diaspora: From Alexander to Trajan (323 B.C.E.–117 C.E.)* (Edinburgh: T&T Clark, 1996), 438–39.

[6] See, e.g., Martial, *Epigr.* 7.82; Suetonius, *Dom.* 12.2; *Jub.* 15:33; 1 Macc 1:11–15; 2 Macc 4:9, 12–14; Josephus, *Ant.* 12.5.1, §§ 240–241. For additional references, see Robert G. Hall, "Arguing Like an Apocalypse: Galatians and an Ancient *topos* outside the Greco-Roman Rhetorical Tradition," *NTS* 42 (1996): 440–41.

[7] Strabo, *Geogr.* 16.2.37; 16.4.9. Paul himself, echoing the sentiments of many non-Jews, speaks of circumcision as a sort of castration (Gal 5:12). Περιτέμνω, "to circumcise," was used for the mutilation of body parts, including the severing of body parts such as the nose or ear. When speaking of the mutilation/circumcision of the genitals, the verb would be further qualified (e.g., τῶν αἰδοίων). The privative ἀπερίτμητος meant "unmaimed" (Plutarch, *Am. prol.* 3 [2:495c]). See Steve Mason, "Paul, Classical Anti-Jewish Polemic, and the Letter to the Romans," in *Self-Definition and Self-Discovery in Early Christianity: A Study in Changing Horizons* (ed. David J. Hawkin and Tom Robinson; Studies in the Bible and Early Christianity 26; Lewiston, N.Y.: Edwin Mellen, 1990), 188–91.

[8] Josephus, *Ag. Ap.* 2.13 §137.

[9] Troy Martin, "Whose Flesh? What Temptation? (Galatians 4.13–14)," *JSNT* 74 (1999): 87–89.

[10] Philo, *Spec.* 1.9.

[11] Bruce Winter, *Seek the Welfare of the City: Christians as Benefactors and Citizens* (First Century Christians in the Graeco-Roman World; Grand Rapids: Eerdmans, 1994), 146–52; Robert G. Hall, "Circumcision," *ABD* 1:1027–29.

was painful and only partially reversible and would be socially compromising in the midst of a Gentile world. A willingness to undergo circumcision would signal a clear intent to live by the other, less painful and stigmatizing aspects of the Law as well.[12]

Additional evidence that Paul's rivals were advocating full observance of the Mosaic Law may lie in the use of the Jewish Scriptures throughout his letter. Repeatedly the sacred texts that Paul cites support the opposite position of the one he is otherwise advocating. For instance, in Gal 3:10 Paul's own point is that "all who rely on the works of the law are under a curse." In support Paul quotes Deut 27:26: "Cursed is everyone who does not observe and obey all the things written in the book of the law." The Deuteronomy passage encouraged, by the threat of curse, observance of the Law. The curse was threatened for *not doing* the Law. Paul, on the other hand, says that people who rely on and *do* the Law are under a curse. Paul appears to be forcing the passage to support the opposite of what it actually says. Why would he have bothered with such a problematic text for his case in the first place? The passage more likely was not part of his own repertoire but was rather a proof text employed by the "they" against whom he is contending.

The same dynamic manifests itself in Gal 3:12. Paul quotes Lev 18:5: "Whoever does the works of the law will live by them." The point of the scriptural quote is totally at odds with the apostle's own point at the beginning of v. 11: "Now it is evident that no one is justified before God by the law." Does not the Law itself promise life for those who do its works, according to the very passage Paul cites in v. 12? Why would he use such a poor text in support of his own position? Again Paul appears to be reinterpreting a passage employed by his rivals. Even the citation in v. 11 fits this pattern. Paul quotes Hab 2:4: "The one who is righteous will live by faith." While the apostle's own interpretation of Hab 2:4 is clear in light of Gal 3:6's reference to Abraham's *believing* "faith," the Jews of Paul's day understood Hab 2:4's "faith" as *faithfulness*. According to the Masoretic Text of the Hebrew Scriptures, the individual in Hab 2:4 stood as a faithful contrast to the arrogant person who was not upright. The *faithful one* would thereby endure the difficult and trying times in which he or she lived. A passage from the Dead Sea Scrolls, left by the Qumran community, interpreted Hab 2:4 as the community's *faithfulness* in acting in accordance with their founding Teacher's interpretation of the law (1QpHab 7:5–8:3). The LXX, a translation of the original Hebrew text, interpreted Hab 2:4 as referring to *God's faithfulness* to promises. Paul has reinterpreted a passage typically taken to refer to faithfulness as a reference to believing faith instead.[13]

---

[12] In fact, Paul treats "those of the circumcision" synonymously with "those of the law" in Rom 4:12, 16.

[13] Another instance would be Paul's quotation of the language of Ps 143:2 in Gal 2:16. He avoids mentioning Ps 143:8's reference to the "way" in which one should walk or v. 10's doing the "will" of God. Elsewhere in the Psalms, the way in

The Jews of Paul's day esteemed the patriarch Abraham from the biblical book of Genesis as the premier example of faithfulness to the Law. Abraham manifested his faithfulness not only by obeying God's command to circumcise in Genesis 17 but also by observing the Law of God long before it would be given in written form through Moses. According to the second-century B.C.E. apocryphal document Sirach (44:20), "He kept the law of the Most High, . . . and when he was tested he proved faithful." *Jubilees,* another second-century B.C.E. work, concurred that Abraham kept the Law before it was written (23:10; cf. 16:28). *Jubilees* 24:11 adds, "And all of the nations of the earth will bless themselves by your seed *because your father obeyed me and observed my restrictions and my commandments and my laws and my ordinances and my covenant.* And now, obey my voice, and dwell in this land." In 1 Macc 2:52, a document in the Apocrypha also written before the time of Christ, Mattathias reminded his sons, "Was not Abraham found faithful [πιστος] when tested [in his willingness to obey God's command to sacrifice Isaac (Genesis 22)], and it was reckoned to him as righteousness [εἰς δικαιοσύνην]?"[14] This tradition continued after the time of Christ. In the late-first-century apocalyptic work *2 Baruch,* Abraham possessed the unwritten law and fulfilled its works (57:1–2). The Mishnah (200 C.E.), the written record of the rabbinic oral laws, says, "And we find that Abraham our father *had performed the whole Law* before it was given" (emphasis mine) (*m. Qidd.* 4.14).

The figure of Abraham would have suited well the perspective of Paul's opponents. Not only was he a model of Law-observant faithfulness; he was also a convert from paganism. He had abandoned the idolatry of his ancestors and had become a follower of the one true God when that God had beckoned. Abraham's conversion culminated in his circumcision. Philo, a first-century contemporary of Paul, treated Abraham as an individual on a journey from a pagan origin toward perfection in the one true God. Along the way, according to Philo, he had to be circumcised in order to bring the passions and lusts of his flesh under subjection. Paul's opponents may likewise have promoted Abraham as a model of Gentile conversion and perfection through circumcision from the flesh's desires. In the same way, the Galatian Gentiles should observe the Law and be circumcised in order to excise the passions of the flesh.[15]

One ought not marvel, then, that Abraham figures so heavily in Paul's Letter to the Galatians. The patriarch was the faithful recipient of God's command to be circumcised and perhaps had obeyed the entire Law in its earlier,

---

which one should walk and the will of God are identified with the Mosaic Law (Ps 18:22–24; 40:9; 119:1).

[14] Similarly Pr Man 8: "You, therefore, O Lord, God of the righteous, have not appointed repentance for the righteous, for Abraham and Isaac and Jacob, who did not sin against you." In *T. Ab.* 10:13 a voice comes down from heaven, attesting that up to that point "Abraham has not sinned."

[15] Philo, *Spec.* 1.9.

unwritten form. So in Gal 3:15–17 and 4:21–31 Paul has to work back through the Genesis narratives of Abraham. In the process the apostle is forced to say some surprising things in response.[16] In Gal 4:21–31 the Law, signified by "Mount Sinai," is associated not with Isaac, the child of promise in Genesis 16–22, but with Ishmael, the child of slavery. The Law of Moses, given to Isaac's descendants according to the Pentateuch, suddenly is a Law given to the slaves descended from Hagar and Ishmael instead. Why the radical reversal of what the Scriptures actually claim unless Paul is reacting to his rivals' use of the very same texts? The pattern recurs too frequently within the letter to be a mere coincidence.[17] Repeatedly Paul responds to passages from the Jewish Scriptures that promote observance of the Mosaic Law. Paul's opponents were therefore drawing upon the Scriptures to inculcate not only circumcision but also full observance of the Mosaic Law.

FURTHER IDENTIFYING THE "THEY" GROUP

Most scholars would further identify the "they" group in Galatia as Jewish *Christians.* "Christian" is an anachronistic term after two thousand years of ecclesiastical development. Scholars debate the degree of continuity between Paul and the Judaism of his day, but he is writing before the key events leading to the painful divorce that would place Jews and "Christ-believers" on separate paths. One might ask, on the other hand, whether the seeds for this later divorce are present in part already in Paul's writings. In any case, the label "Christian" does require qualification.[18]

---

[16] Nor are the surprises limited to Gal 3:15–17 with its discussion of a singular seed as opposed to the collective seed of Gen 17:8 (or Gal 4:21–31 for that matter). Note the sudden mention of "descendants of Abraham" in Gal 3:7 after Paul explicates Gen 15:6 in Gal 3:6. Paul appears to be answering a question that the Gen 15:6 quote had never raised: "Who are truly Abraham's children?" Galatians 3:7's sudden reference to "descendants of Abraham," along with the unusual discussion of Abraham's children in 4:21–31, suggests that "descendants of Abraham" is the terminology of Paul's opponents. They had offered circumcision and the Law as means to become descendants of Abraham and thereby benefit from the promises. See J. Louis Martyn, "Covenant, Christ, and Church in Galatians," in *The Future of Christology: Essays in Honor of Leander E. Keck* (ed. Abraham J. Malherbe and Wayne A. Meeks; Minneapolis: Fortress, 1993), 138–41.

[17] Paul sometimes employs his own scriptural texts in response to his opponents' texts. E.g., Gal 3:13's citation of Deut 21:23, with its reference to curse, appears deliberately designed to answer the curse invoked by Paul's opponents in their use of Deut 27:26 (in Gal. 3:10). See also Isa 54:1 (cf. Isa 52:1) in Gal 4:27. Paul's own use of Scripture bears the pattern of response to scriptural texts employed by the outsiders.

[18] Most scholars continue to use the term "Christian" for these first followers of Christ. Those who see Christianity as a movement still within the larger Jewish community often employ the label "Christ-believing." The extent of interaction between Paul's addressees and the synagogues is debated.

The apostle's condemnation of "another gospel" message proclaimed by "those people" in Gal 1:6 suggests that the rivals consider themselves Christians, that is, Christ-believing. Paul favors the term "gospel" (εὐαγγέλιον) in his writings for the saving message about Jesus Christ, as did other early Christian authors.[19] He would certainly never countenance dignifying his opponents' message with the term "gospel," only to have to turn around and immediately qualify that it is really not, unless the opponents had already adopted "gospel" as a label for their own message.[20] Paul's rivals must have been declaring some sort of Christ message. Such a message would suggest Jewish Christians.[21] Galatians 2:15–16 offers additional proof that Paul is interacting with a form of Jewish Christianity. He speaks of "we Jews by birth" affirming a justification by faith in Christ within a section of the letter that many scholars identify as its thesis. Such an affirmation would hardly befit advocates of a non-Christian form of Judaism. In Gal 6:12 Paul identifies the opponents as people who were seeking to avoid being persecuted *for the cross of Christ* by encouraging the Galatians to be circumcised. They sought to maintain adherence both to the cross of Christ and to Jewish ethnic identity.

Mark D. Nanos, an important Jewish voice in modern Pauline scholarship, has found the arguments in favor of identifying the "they" group as Jewish Christians far from compelling.[22] He prefers identifying the "they" group as *non*-Christ-believing Jews. He points out that the word "gospel" is by no means a technical term for the message about Christ. This word group, whether employed in a verbal or a nominal form, simply meant "good news" or "glad tidings" (εὐαγγέλιον), and the word group would have been familiar to both Jews and Gentiles. The Greek translation of Isaiah employed the "gospel" or "good news" word group (e.g., 52:7–10). The Jews in Paul's era opposed the imperial "good news" of the empire with their own "good news" as they drew upon Isaiah's prophecy.[23] Since inhabitants of the Roman Empire commonly used the "good news" word group, Nanos suggests that Paul may very well have been ironically playing on the meaning of the word in Gal 1:6–9: Others have brought their own form of "good news" to the Galatians, a good news that is different from the good news about Christ and really is not good news at all. Their good news was, rather, a perversion of the good news about Christ. In fact, this competing message had nothing to do with Christ.

---

[19] E.g., Mark 1:1; Rom 1:1. See the discussion of Gal 2:15–16 to follow.

[20] Paul would certainly consider the Galatian outsiders *his* opponents, but they may have viewed their Law-observant message as a supplement and compatible with Paul's previous teaching. They would be simply correcting an oversight, albeit a critical one, on Paul's part.

[21] In 2 Cor 11:4, 22–23 Paul similarly confronts a Jewish Christian message as a "different gospel" (ἕτερον εὐαγγέλιον).

[22] Nanos, *Irony*.

[23] See *Pss. Sol.* 11:1; 11QMelch 2:15–24; 4QMessAp frg. 2:2.12; and Nanos, *Irony*, 290–91.

Although Nanos has highlighted several weaknesses in the way most scholars read Gal 1:6–9 and offers a persuasive reading of his own, one area that deserves further scrutiny is the identification by commentators on Galatians of the *singular* use of the noun "gospel" (εὐαγγέλιον) as a technical term for *the* glad tiding or message of Christ.[24] Nanos points out that his reasoning with respect to the "good news" word group in general applies also to the singular "gospel" or "glad tiding." He cites, however, only one undisputed instance from Jewish literature.[25] While Nanos openly admits that the singular "gospel" (εὐαγγέλιον) is rare in Greek literature apart from early Christian influence, the NT writings regularly employ the singular form of the noun with reference to the proclamation of Christ. The unusual and consistent use of the singular noun within early Christianity poses a problem for Nanos's approach and indicates that "gospel" was a chosen designation by the early believers in Christ for their message. The opponents' message most likely referred to Christ, contra Nanos, since Paul is applying the early Christian designation for Christ's message and then is seeking to question its validity as a label for their message.

Nanos has not directly addressed the evidence that Gal 2:15–16 appears to provide for identifying the rivals as Jewish Christians.[26] He does contend that those who slipped into the meeting of apostolic leaders at Jerusalem in 2:1–10 were non-Christ-believing Jews.[27] He is not sure whether the "circumcision" group involved in the Antioch incident in 2:11–14 were Christ-believing or not. Galatians 2:15–16 may represent Paul's continued response to Peter in the situation he describes in 2:11–14, or these verses may represent Paul's own reflections *after* the Antioch incident for the benefit of the Galatians. Those who have classified Paul's letters on the basis of ancient rhetorical theory are not certain whether 2:15–21 is a continuation of Paul's description of the Antioch incident or is a new section within the letter (a *propositio* perhaps, a statement of what is agreed and disagreed upon by the parties in the dispute).[28] Galatians 2:15–16a therefore clarifies what is

---

[24] See, e.g., Martyn, *Galatians,* 310–12; and Dunn, *Galatians,* 9–10, 41. Dunn finds the exclusive use of the singular of the noun "gospel" (εὐαγγέλιον) throughout the NT as the clincher.

[25] Nanos (*Irony,* 296 n. 41) identifies Josephus, *J.W.* 2.17.4 §420. He also cites Philo and Paul's Thessalonian correspondence, but Nanos's Philo citations use verbal forms and not the singular form of the noun. Nor is there any reason to question that the "gospel" Paul speaks of in the Thessalonian correspondence remains a proclamation about Christ's significance (e.g., 1 Thess 1:3–4; 3:2).

[26] This is a surprising omission, since Nanos appears otherwise aware of Dunn's reasoning for Jewish Christian opponents in Galatia and Dunn points to these verses (*Galatians,* 10). Certainly Gal 2:15–16 represents the position of those described in the preceding verses.

[27] Nanos, *Irony,* 150–52.

[28] Stanley E. Porter outlines the various positions in "Paul of Tarsus and His Letters," in *Handbook of Classical Rhetoric in the Hellenistic Period, 330 B.C.–A. D. 400* (ed. Stanley E. Porter; Leiden: E. J. Brill, 1997), 541–47.

agreed upon either by all the parties in vv. 11–14 or by "Jews" in general quite apart from specific reference to vv. 11–14 (note Paul's phrasing). The "Jews" in question are Jewish Christians since v. 16a affirms faith in Christ: "we know that a person is justified not by the works of the Law but [ἐὰν μή] through faith in Jesus Christ."[29] When Paul begins in v. 15 with "We . . . Jews . . . know," he is indicating a shared affirmation acceptable to other Jewish Christians. Paul outlines in vv. 16–21 key ideas, including the relationship between faith in Christ and the works of the Law, that he will develop further in the course of the letter. Paul does not, however, phrase what "we . . . Jews . . . know" in an unambiguous fashion. Paul's ambiguity suggests an intra-Christian dispute with clear implications for the Galatian situation.[30] Certainly if the Galatian Gentile Christians are in conversation with non-Christ-believing Jews, Paul's firm declaration of what Jews believe about Christ would be debatable, and yet Paul assumes what "we . . . Jews . . . know" as a premise for his line of thought in what follows. The premise would need to be qualified or defended if stated in the context of non-Christ-believing Jews.

In Gal 6:12 Paul claims that those who are promoting circumcision are seeking to avoid persecution for the cross of Christ. While most scholars recognize this verse as evidence that those promoting circumcision were Christ-believers, Nanos has offered an explanation in support of his own reading.[31] The Galatian Gentile Christians were claiming "equal and full rights with Jewish people."[32] The problem was that the Galatian Christians were uncircumcised and might be viewed by the larger pagan world as not fully and properly integrated into the Jewish community. The Jewish communities throughout the empire enjoyed the privilege of practicing their faith and avoiding pagan celebrations and the imperial cult, but non-Jews resented and sometimes challenged this privilege.[33] So the Jewish community would have felt pressure from non-Jews to encourage the Gentile Galatians to become full members of the Jewish religion and community by circumcision. Uncircumcised Gentile Christians claiming the rights and privileges of the Jewish community would have led to a situation that might jeopardize the religious privileges the Jews were enjoying. The "influencers" in Galatia, to use Nanos's preferred terminology, wanted to avoid the perse-

---

[29] One may also translate "faith in Jesus Christ" as "the faith *of* Jesus Christ." See Richard B. Hays, *The Faith of Jesus Christ: The Narrative Substructure of Galatians 3:1–4:11* (2d ed.; Grand Rapids: Eerdmans, 2001). If one adopts this translation, Paul specifies in the following clause of Gal 2:16 that the faith of Christ is still associated with faith *in* Christ. The overall line of reasoning here would remain unaffected.

[30] The following section will return to the ambiguity of Paul's formulation in Gal 2:15–16.

[31] Nanos, *Irony,* 221–24, 257–71.

[32] Ibid., 265.

[33] Ibid., 260 (citing Josephus).

cution that the Gentiles' adherence to Paul's message of the cross of Christ could bring to the Jewish community. In the words of Gal 6:12: "It is those who want to make a good showing in the flesh that try to compel you to be circumcised—only that they may not be persecuted for the cross of Christ." The influencers did not themselves agree with this message of Christ.

Nanos has provided an understanding of Gal 6:12 that would fit well with his overall hypothesis that non-Christian Jews were encouraging Christian Gentiles to be circumcised. Nanos contends that the Gentile Christians in Galatia were claiming Jewish rights and privileges without being circumcised or being members of the Jewish community. The Gentile Christians were avoiding pagan religious activities and the imperial cult to honor the God of Israel. So the influencers were encouraging the Galatian Gentile Christians to become Jews. The influencers probably were teaching the Galatians how Abraham received the covenant of circumcision, and this covenant included the obligation to observe Moses' Law. Undoubtedly the influencers taught the Galatian Gentiles from the Jewish Scriptures. Paul simply reminds the Galatians that they were a "new creation" where neither circumcision nor uncircumcision counts for anything (5:12; 6:15).

Nanos has pointed to the Jewish community's fear of persecution from the larger pagan world if the Jews did not properly enforce their group's boundaries.[34] The Jewish influencers feared persecution for the cross of Christ precisely (and ironically) because they did not share faith in Christ. Nanos's interpretation of Gal 6:12, however, does not adequately account for Paul's mention of persecution several times earlier in the letter. In each case, he refers to the persecuting activity of ethnic Jews and not non-Jews. In 1:13 Paul narrates how he, as a non-Christian Jew, formerly persecuted the church of God and violently tried to destroy it. The fear of just such persecution from other ethnic Jews led Peter to withdraw from fellowship with the Gentile Christians at Antioch in 2:12. In 4:21–31 Paul contrasts the child born according to the flesh from the slave woman, the present Jerusalem, with the child born according to the Spirit from the free woman, the Jerusalem above, and in v. 29 the child born according to the flesh "persecuted the child who was born according to the Spirit." Paul speaks in 6:17 of the marks of Jesus that he bears in his body, marks that likely correspond to the list in 2 Cor 11:24–25 of the punishments he received from fellow Jews. In view of the entirety of Paul's letter, the danger of persecution in Gal 6:12 stems from the Jewish community itself rather than from the outside world.

---

[34] It is not entirely clear to me why the Galatian Gentile Christians' claim to share in Israel's heritage would require their circumcision for the sake of the safety and preservation of the Jewish community when Nanos (Mark D. Nanos, *The Mystery of Romans: The Jewish Context of Paul's Letter* [Minneapolis: Fortress, 1996]) maintains that there were uncircumcised God-fearers clinging to, and accepted by, Diaspora synagogues in Rome and elsewhere. Why would the Gentile Christ-believers in Galatia compromise the safety and status of the Jewish community whereas Gentile God-fearers at Rome did not?

Nothing in Gal 6:12 identifies or alludes to a situation of hostility from the pagan world surrounding the Jewish community, and Paul never signals that those who fear persecution "for the cross of Christ" are *not* themselves Christians. If the influencers feared persecution from other Jews, then the influencers themselves would be Jewish *Christians* rather than non-Christian Jews. Paul says that the influencers would suffer persecution for the cross of Christ if they did not compel the Gentile Christians to be circumcised. This threat of persecution because of the cross of Christ is logically prior to their advocacy of circumcision. The influencers are advocating circumcision for the specific purpose of avoiding the danger of persecution that has resulted from their adherence to the cross of Christ. If the influencers did not believe in Christ, they would suffer no danger of persecution from fellow Jews if they failed to compel the Galatian Christians to be circumcised. Merely engaging in conversation with Christ-believing Gentiles would not cause other Jews to doubt the influencers' loyalties to Judaism. The situation would differ for Christ-believing Jews who were straddling the line between the Jewish community and an uncircumcised Gentile Christian community. Other members of the Jewish community could accuse Jewish Christians of apostasy for appearing to advocate by their association a belief system that had abandoned Judaism's central rite of circumcision. Such Jewish Christians would have keenly felt the pressure by others in the Jewish community to demonstrate their allegiance to Judaism. In response, they would no doubt have vigorously campaigned for circumcision among their friends in the Gentile Christian community.[35] Paul's boasts of the persecution he received for his adherence to the cross of Christ in 6:17 serve as a foil for other Jewish Christians who, from his vantage point, were seeking to avoid persecution for their adherence to the cross of Christ.[36]

Nanos's approach has much for which it may be commended. For instance, J. Louis Martyn, a leading Galatians scholar, has highlighted the de-

---

[35] Nanos (*Irony*, 222) critiques this approach to the letter as positing "Christ-believing Jews who transparently lack sufficient loyalty to the norms of the Christ-believing coalition so as to avoid suffering for what they believe in, the crucified Jesus, which conviction, at the same time, forms the basis for the concerted effort that the influencers make toward the addressees in order to preserve the interest of those who share this faith in the face of pressure from those who do not." The problem with Nanos's critique is that he (ironically) does not sufficiently recognize that this is polemical language. The influencers believed that Gentile Christian identity must be accompanied by adherence to the Law of Moses. For Paul, this is a denial of the new state of affairs that Christ has brought about for the Gentiles. The influencers are effectively denying Christ's work. It is *Paul's* claim that they lack sufficient loyalty to the norms of the Christ-believing coalition (as he understood it). The influencers themselves would have viewed the situation differently.

[36] Interpreters through the centuries have found the Christian identity of the influencers the more natural reading. It is also the simpler reading since it does not require the positing of an additional group not mentioned within the text: pagan authorities.

rogatory reference to "the present Jerusalem" in 4:25. He believes that Paul is combating a form of Jewish Christianity that would foist upon the Gentiles Law observance. Martyn explains that Paul has never included non-Christ-believing Jews in his prior references to "Jerusalem" in the letter. The point may be debated in the instance of 2:1–10 as Nanos has shown, but if one grants Martyn's reasoning, then the condemnation of "the present Jerusalem" in 4:25 would implicate the Jerusalem *church*. Yet Paul has belabored the point that the Jerusalem church agreed with his gospel message in 2:1–10. Only the outsiders who slipped into the apostolic meeting disagreed. So does Paul's blanket condemnation of the Jerusalem church include the apostles or their many followers who would have agreed with Paul on the "gospel"? Nanos's approach might be able to offer a solution to this problem for Martyn's reading. The Jerusalem apostles would be members of "the Jerusalem above" along with others who affirm a faith based on what God has done (2:15–16). On the other hand, the implications of Nanos's position are rather dark for Jewish-Christian relations. Paul employs some terribly harsh language against those who advocate "castration" (circumcision) and against a "present Jerusalem . . . in slavery" with Hagar (rather than being Sarah's offspring). If one adopts Nanos's approach, Paul would be directing this language against non-Christ-believing Jews, his very own people.[37]

Paul is therefore most likely directing his critique against Jewish Christians in the Galatians' midst. One cannot read Paul's harsh statements throughout the letter as a polemic against the Jews as an ethnic people. When Paul wishes his rivals would "castrate themselves," he is addressing not Judaism or all Jews (Paul was a Jew) but rather a situation in early Christianity where certain Jewish Christians were advocating circumcision of Gentile Christians. It was an intra-Christian struggle! Although this would dampen some of the force of Paul's statements regarding the Jews, his logic as he responds to his rivals' message likely still has implications for his understanding of Judaism. The language Paul employs remains harsh and dark.[38]

---

[37] This is an unfortunate implication, in my opinion, of Nanos's perspective. He would counter that Paul is not derisively labeling all Jews but only those who did not agree with his own perspective that Gentile Christ-believers enjoy equal status with the Jews among God's elect people. Such a group, however, would surely include the majority of the Jews of Paul's day, if not since.

[38] As Richard B. Hays (review of J. Louis Martyn, *Galatians*, *RBL* 3 [2001]: 63–64) comments: "Can Martyn really maintain at the end of the day that Galatians, as he reads it, does not lead inevitably to an anti-Jewish, supersessionist Christian theology? . . . He impressively shows that the polemic of the letter is targeted not against Jews but against rival Jewish-Christian evangelists, and he argues that Galatians 'is not an anti-Judaic text.' . . . Nonetheless, the letter's slanderous statements about the Law and its radical negation (on Martyn's reading) of the election of Israel seemingly leave no room for the continuing existence of a Law-observant Jewish people." (Cf. J. Louis Martyn, "The Covenants of Hagar and Sarah: Two Covenants and Two Gentile Missions," in *Faith and History: Essays in Honor of Paul W. Meyer* [ed. John T. Carroll, Charles H. Cosgrove, and E. Elizabeth Johnson; Atlanta: Scholars

THE HEART OF THE CONFLICT

In the context of the public reading of the letter, by Gal 2:15–16 Paul has exposed those listening to what he has written, whether the Gentile Galatians or their Jewish Christian teachers, to a broad array of early Jewish Christian viewpoints. Paul clearly does not consider all of these positions legitimate. In 2:1–14 he has articulated his own Jewish Christian position, in opposition to others, on whether Gentile Christians should observe the Law of Moses. At the private meeting with the Jerusalem apostles, "false brothers . . . slipped in to spy on" the proceedings.[39] Paul points out that Titus was not "compelled to be circumcised," even though the intruders were advocating a position on circumcision parallel to the rivals in Galatia (note the nod to the Galatians' situation in v. 5). In 2:3–5 Paul employs for the Jerusalem meeting descriptive terminology similar to what he uses for the Galatian situation throughout the rest of the letter (slavery/freedom, 4:1–9, 21–31; 5:1; compulsion, 2:14; 6:12; truth, 2:14; 4:16; 5:7).[40] Likewise Paul's description of "the circumcision faction" in 2:12b points toward the Galatian Jewish Christian teachers.[41] His description of the conflict at Jerusalem targets a particular faction in early Jewish Christianity that parallels the group Paul opposes in Galatia. The apostles, on the other hand, represent in 2:1–14 a mediating position between Paul and the Jewish Christians advocating that the Gentiles observe the Law. The apostles recognized Paul's ministry to the uncircumcised with the right hand of "fellowship" alongside their ministry to the circumcised (2:7–9). None of the apostles (as Paul reported the meeting) suggested that the Gentiles needed to be circumcised and obey the Mosaic Law. The following incident at Antioch in 2:11–14 shows that the

---

Press, 1990], 188–89). Hays would argue that there is greater continuity between Paul's message and the people of Israel than Martyn allows, but the problem of Paul's violent language remains (e.g., "curse," "bewitched," "castrate").

[39] Verses 4–5 describe the same event as v. 2, a "private" event (κατ᾽ ἰδίαν) into which certain people "slipped in" (παρεισῆλθον).

[40] On the parallels between the "false brothers," "the circumcision faction" of 2:12, and the Galatian teachers of the rest of the letter, see Martyn, *Galatians,* 217–18; and Philip F. Esler, *Galatians* (New Testament Readings; London: Routledge, 1988), 131.

[41] "The circumcision faction" in v. 12b is linked by "and" to "the other Jews" (NRSV), or "the rest of the Jews," in v. 13. "The other Jews," on the other hand, refers to the Jewish Christians at Antioch (note the mention of Barnabas). "The circumcision faction" most likely refers, then, to Jewish Christians. It most probably should be identified with "certain people from James" in v. 12; Peter Stuhlmacher, *Das paulinische Evangelium* (FRLANT 95; Göttingen: Vandenhoeck & Ruprecht, 1968), 106 n. 1. Vincent M. Smiles, *The Gospel and the Law in Galatia: Paul's Response to Jewish-Christian Separatism and the Threat of Galatian Apostasy* (Collegeville, Minn.: Liturgical Press, 1998), 90–91, writes that if "certain people from James" and "the circumcision faction" do not refer to the same people, then the reference to "the circumcision faction" would be unusually abrupt.

Jerusalem leadership may have differed with Paul, however, on the question of mixed table fellowship when Jewish and Gentile Christians came together to eat. In the instance of mixed table fellowship, the Gentiles should yield to Jewish practice and not vice versa. Paul blurs the difference between the issue of circumcision and that of mixed table fellowship and interprets Peter's actions at Antioch as compelling "the Gentiles to live like Jews."[42]

Galatians 2:15–16 flows naturally out of the preceding discussion. A few interpreters have even considered vv. 15–21 a continuation of Paul's speech at Antioch. He addresses Peter in v. 14: "If you, though a Jew, live like a Gentile and not like a Jew, how can you compel the Gentiles to live like Jews?" Verse 15's "We ourselves are Jews by birth and not Gentile sinners" could therefore be a continuation of Paul's speech, or it could function as the beginning of a new section in the letter.[43] Even if vv. 15–16 signal a turn toward the Galatian situation itself, as is probably the case if the verses are transitional, they cannot be severed from vv. 1–14. The "We . . . Jews" of vv. 15–16 must include not only the Jewish Christians represented by Paul's own position but also the other Jews represented within vv. 1–14: Peter, Barnabas, "the circumcision faction"/"men from James," as well as the Jewish Christian teachers in Galatia (alluded to in v. 5).[44]

Paul articulates what "we . . . Jews" all "know" and affirm in v. 16a as follows: "we know that a person is justified not by the works of the law *but* [ἐὰν μή] through faith in Jesus Christ." One can take the phrasing in this verse as expressing two mutually exclusive means of being justified, whether by faith in Christ or by the works of the Law. Such a mutually exclusive interpretation would certainly reflect Paul's own position. On the other hand, 2:16a could be translated and understood very differently: "we know that a person is not justified by the works of the Law *except* [ἐὰν μή] through faith in Jesus Christ." One *is* justified by the works of the Law when that obedience is accompanied by faith in Christ.[45] The opponents who were advocating Law observance in Galatia would surely have understood the shared affirmation in 2:16a in this fashion. It is precisely the ambiguity in the formulation—that it can express

---

[42] Esler (*Galatians,* 136–40) goes so far as to suggest that the Jerusalem position would require that the Gentiles be circumcised. See, for further discussion, A. Andrew Das, "Another Look at ἐὰν μή in Galatians 2:16, *JBL* 119 (2000): 529–39.

[43] The reference to "judaizing" in v. 14b's question corresponds to Jews "by birth" (φύσει) in v. 15's answer (D. J. Verseput, "Paul's Gentile Mission and the Jewish Christian Community: A Study of the Narrative in Galatians 1 and 2," *NTS* 39 [1993]: 53–54). Verseput represents the minority view that does not see a break after 2:14.

[44] Likewise v. 17 must be understood inclusively of the forms of Jewish Christianity represented in 2:1–14 as well. The subject of the "we" has remained unchanged since v. 15: "we [Jews by birth]." Paul places the Jews in the same category that the Jews had applied to the Gentiles: "sinners." " 'Even we' Jews 'were found' in the light of the gospel to be 'sinners' no less than the Gentiles" (Smiles, *Gospel and Law,* 149).

[45] See also Das, "Another Look."

both a complementary and an antithetical relationship between the Law's works and faith in Christ—that forces Paul to restate matters in clearly antithetical terms by the end of the verse in order to rule out a justification by the works of the Law. The broad spectrum included within "We . . . Jews"—the Jewish Christians represented throughout 2:1–14 as well as in Galatia—could accede to this affirmation simply because it was ambiguous on whether the observance of the Law is a factor in justification.

Why would Paul draw upon such a shared affirmation—a person is not justified by the works of the Law except/but rather through faith in Christ—if it did not unambiguously support his own position? One possibility is that Paul's opponents were using the same affirmation in their teaching. Like the Jewish Scriptures, this statement would represent shared common ground in early Christianity. Paul cannot ignore the expression but simply reinterprets it as a statement regarding justification by faith in Christ alone. The Jewish Christian affirmation provides a shared starting point with Paul's opponents and the Galatians for the apostle's own conclusions. As Paul's wrestling with the Scriptures shows, this would not be the last time he would have to reinterpret the evidence his opponents were using in support of their position.

Paul's rivals are advocating in their Christ-plus-Law approach an understandable and attractive viewpoint. After all, did not the Jewish Scriptures enjoin people to observe the Mosaic Law? Is not the Mosaic Law God's Law? Paul hesitates to admit as much in his response. In Gal 3:19–20 he writes, "Why then the law? It was added because of transgressions, until the offspring would come to whom the promise had been made; and it was ordained through angels by a mediator. Now a mediator involves more than one party; but God is one." The apostle distances the Law from its ultimately divine origin (cf. 3:21). The Law is inferior because it came through the multiplicity of angels and by a mediator. If the Scriptures promote the observance of the divine Law, Paul's rejection of Law observance for the Gentiles is difficult initially to comprehend.

In Gal 5:13–6:10 the apostle addresses how Christians are to live. His instructions on Christian living, however, are sandwiched between two passages that attack the demand by the opponents that the Galatians be circumcised (5:1–12; 6:13–18). Paul's positive instructions are likely a response, then, to the rivals' guidance for the Christian life through the Mosaic Law. They appear to have been advocating the path of the Mosaic Law as a far more concrete and practical approach to Christian living than Paul's gospel message. Those looking for direction on how to live as Christian people need only observe the precepts established long ago in God's own law. Perhaps the rivals faulted Paul for not adequately instructing the Galatians in the Law's precepts for living.

For Paul the key to the Christian life is not the observance of the Law but the guidance of God's Spirit. In Gal 5:22–23 the Spirit will produce in the Christian an appropriate fruit. Yet for those seeking a christianized version of the concrete demands of the Mosaic Law, Paul's positive construal is tantalizingly vague. Paul points to the fruit of the Spirit: love, joy, peace, patience, kindness, generosity, faithfulness, gentleness, and self-control. From the apostle's standpoint, these nine attributes of the fruit of the Spirit may not be as detailed or as structured as the Mosaic Law in all its legislative array, but anyone who lives according to the Spirit will be doing what the Law had been promoting all along. They will be fulfilling the Law (5:13–14). They will be living according to what Paul calls in 6:2 "the law of Christ." Throughout the letter up to this point, the word "Law" (νόμος) always refers to the Mosaic Law. It is unlikely, then, that the reference to "the law [νόμος] of Christ" in 6:2 should be understood without any connection to the Mosaic Law. To express the thought of 6:2 more precisely, Christians will indeed be living according to the Mosaic Law, but—and this is the crucial difference—it is the Law as expressed through the example of Christ. In the hands of Christ, the Law expresses itself in a very different manner. Even as the Law had brought curse and death to Christ (3:13), now Jesus Christ takes hold of and powerfully transforms the Law itself.[46] This transforming power of Christ is none other than the Spirit.

It should be clear by now that Paul is concerned not only with how one enters into a right relationship with God, as 2:15–16 indicates, but also with the implications for the ongoing life in Christ that follows.[47] In 3:1–5, if the Galatians received the Spirit initially through the preaching of Christ crucified, why then do they now seek the Spirit through the works of the Law? Having begun with the Spirit, they are now ending with the flesh and with the Law and its works. The presence of the Spirit, however, should demonstrate once and for all that they are in a right relationship with God, quite apart from the Law and its demands, and that they have power available for their Christian lives. Thus Paul's letter very naturally culminates in the moral advice of Galatians 5 and 6. Even as the Galatians have been justified apart from the works of the Law through faith in Christ (2:15–16a), the subsequent Christian life in the Spirit is based on faith in Christ and not on the Mosaic Law. This crucial point distinguishes Paul's message from that of his Galatian rivals.

---

[46] The function of the Mosaic Law in the Christian life will be the subject matter of chapter 7. For now, "the law of Christ" must be left at the level of a provocative suggestion. Certainly 6:2 must be interpreted in light of 5:13–14, where Paul speaks of Christians' "fulfilling" the Law and not trying to "do" it.

[47] With Paul's concern in Galatians 5 and 6 with the Christian life ("staying in" to use Sanders' terminology), some scholars do not think Paul is concerned with "getting in" to a right relationship with God. Paul's discussion does not permit an either-or. The mother-giving-birth language Paul uses for his and his opponents' ministries in 4:19, 21–31 makes better sense if getting into a right relationship with God is also at issue; see Martyn, "Covenants of Hagar and Sarah," 170–84. Likewise in 3:23–29 Paul emphasizes that the Galatians are coheirs with Christ and thus recipients of the promised Spirit (4:6). They have received the Spirit on the basis of their relationship with God through Christ and not by their doing of the Law and its works.

PAUL'S APOCALYPTIC PERSPECTIVE

The power of the Spirit is, from Paul's standpoint, an aspect of the world still to come. Paul's entire viewpoint is dominated by apocalyptic categories that describe otherworldly realities hidden behind the realities of this world. He speaks of the Spirit as the Christian's down payment on the world to come (Rom 8:23; 2 Cor 1:22). In the presence of the Spirit, a new apocalyptic reality has invaded the cosmos. The Spirit's arrival in the work of Christ has shattered the old dominion of the Law. The apostle's problem with the Mosaic Law ultimately stems from his apocalyptic vantage point.

Galatians does not conform to the literary genre of the apocalypse.[48] No angelic mediator appears on the stage to reveal the hidden secrets of God. On the contrary, the apostle received his revelation directly from God. Paul does not provide a narrative of his heavenly journeys or showcase the epochs of history alongside a glimpse of the ages to come. Nevertheless, he shares the worldview of the apocalypses and has enjoyed similar otherworldly experiences.

> I know a person in Christ who fourteen years ago was caught up to the third heaven—whether in the body or out of the body I do not know; God knows. And I know that such a person—whether in the body or out of the body I do not know; God knows—was caught up into Paradise and heard things that are not to be told, that no mortal is permitted to repeat. (2 Cor 12:2-4)

Paul had visited the realm of the third heaven whether in or out of the body. He there heard things that cannot be shared. Even as a heavenly reality stands beyond the earthly, he affirms an era still to come.

> For this we declare to you by the word of the Lord, that we who are alive, who are left until the coming of the Lord, will by no means precede those who have died. For the Lord himself, with a cry of command, with the archangel's call and with the sound of God's trumpet, will descend from heaven, and the dead in Christ will rise first. Then we who are alive, who are left, will be caught up in the clouds together with them to meet the Lord in the air; and so we will be with the Lord forever. (1 Thess 4:15-17)

The apostle had a clear vision of what the future holds. The Lord could come at any moment, like a thief in the night (1 Thess 5:2). Since this world is soon passing away, Paul instructs the Corinthians to live as though the time is short.

---

[48] Scholars have developed a technical definition for apocalyptic writing: "A genre of revelatory literature with a narrative framework, in which a revelation is mediated by an otherworldly being to a human recipient, disclosing a transcendent reality which is both temporal, insofar as it envisages eschatological salvation, and spatial, insofar as it involves another, supernatural world" (John J. Collins, ed., *Apocalypse: The Morphology of a Genre* [Semeia 14; Missoula, Mont.: Scholars Press, 1979]).

I mean, brothers and sisters, the appointed time has grown short; from now on, let even those who have wives be as though they were not rejoicing, and those who buy as though they had no possessions, and those who deal with the world as though they had no dealings with it. For the present form of this world is passing away. (1 Cor 7:29–31)

Even if one should die before Christ's climactic return, Paul points to the confident hope of a resurrected body and new life.

Do you not know that all of us who have been baptized into Christ Jesus were baptized into his death? Therefore we have been buried with him by baptism into death, so that, just as Christ was raised from the dead by the glory of the Father, so we too might walk in the newness of life. For if we have been united with him in a death like his, we will certainly be united with him in a resurrection like his. (Rom 6:3–5)

For as all die in Adam, so all will be made alive in Christ. But each in his own order: Christ the first fruits, then at his coming those who belong to Christ. Then comes the end, when he hands over the kingdom to God the Father, after he has destroyed every ruler and every authority and power. . . . Listen, I will tell you a mystery! We will not all die, but we will all be changed, in a moment, in the twinkling of an eye, at the last trumpet. For the trumpet will sound, and the dead will be raised imperishable, and we will be changed. For this perishable body must put on imperishability, and this mortal body must put on immortality. (1 Cor 15:22–24, 51–53)

Before the trumpet heralding the full arrival of the world to come, Christians are caught up in a struggle between this present world and the dawning new age. All creation groans in travail, eagerly expecting the consummation of the coming age (Rom 8:19–23).

Paul's apocalyptic worldview manifests itself in his Letter to the Galatians as well. After contrasting his opponents' urging of circumcision with his own boast in the cross of Christ, he writes in Gal 6:14–15,

May I never boast of anything except the cross of our Lord Jesus Christ, by which *the world* has been crucified to me, and I to *the world*. For neither circumcision nor uncircumcision is anything; but a new creation is everything!

Paul speaks of two different worlds. By participating in Christ's death through faith and baptism, Christians are taken from one world and its reality into another. Circumcision and uncircumcision, on the other hand, are part of the old reality that is passing away. Martyn, who first illumined the apocalyptic patterns in Galatians, explains that circumcision and uncircumcision are a pair of opposites characteristic of the old world.[49] Classical Greek thought understood the elements of the universe as pairs, whether earth and water, fire and air, or earth and air, fire and water. So when the present age is abolished by a oneness and identity in Christ in Gal 3:27–28,

---

[49] J. Louis Martyn, "Apocalyptic Antinomies in Paul's Letter to the Galatians," *NTS* 31 (1985): 410–24.

there is neither Jew/Greek, slave/free, male/female. "For all of you are one in Christ Jesus." Yet even while the new world has dawned in Christ Jesus, the old world is waging a war against the incoming reality.

> Live by the Spirit, I say, and do not gratify the desires of the flesh. For what the flesh desires is opposed to the Spirit, and what the Spirit desires is opposed to the flesh; for these are opposed to each other. (5:16–17)

In effect, a *new* pair of opposites comes into existence as the elements of the invading world do battle against the elements of this present age. The old world is waging its last stand. This explains the new and striking pairs of opposites in 4:21–31 associated with the two Jerusalems, the one below and the one above. One child is born in slavery and the other in freedom. One is in the flesh; the other is in the Spirit. The new creation in the Spirit is at war with the world of the flesh. As Paul opens the Letter to the Galatians (1:3–4),

> Grace to you and peace from God our Father and our Lord Jesus Christ, who gave himself for our sins to set us free from *the present evil age,* according to the will of our God and Father, to whom be the glory forever and ever.

The Law had functioned to divide the present age into Jew and Gentile, a pair of opposites, those with the Law and those without the Law. Although the Law-observant male could thank God that he was not born a woman, a slave, or a Gentile, these very distinctions, according to 3:28, are done away with in the oneness that is in Christ. A new reality, a new creation has dawned. The true antidote to the urges of the flesh, then, is not the Law, an ally of the flesh, but the power of the new age, the power of the Spirit.

PAUL'S CRITIQUE OF THE LAW: INITIAL OBSERVATIONS

According to Paul, something radically new took place in Christ's death on the cross, a moment in time freighted with apocalyptic and decisive power. The Law, on the other hand, is just one of the weak and beggarly forces of this world. If one could enter a right relationship with God through the Mosaic Law, then all that God did in Christ was pointless (Gal 2:21). Christ died for nothing. "For if a law had been given that could make alive, then righteousness would indeed come through the law" (3:21). What is it about the Law that renders it incapable of mediating righteousness and salvation? Why couldn't the Law have ushered in the dawn of a new era with Christ and the Spirit? Alongside his positive construal of Christ's powerful work, Paul develops a stinging critique of the Law, especially in 3:10.

Galatians 3:10 forms what the ancients called an enthymeme, a logical argument in which one of the premises is missing because it should have been obvious to the original readers.[50] The stated premise is, "Cursed is

---

[50] Aristotle, *Rhet.* 1.2.13 (1357a); 2.22.3 (1395b); 3.18.2, 4 (1419a); Epictetus, *Diatr.* 1.8.1–4; Quintilian, *Institutio Oratoria* 5.14.24; 5.10.3; Theon, *Progymn.* 3.104–

everyone who does not observe and obey all the things written in this book of the law." Paul concludes, "All who rely on the works of the law are under a curse." The premise that needs to be supplied by the reader to complete the argument is, "All who rely on the works of the law do not observe and obey all the things written in this book of the law." People simply are not capable of doing all that the Law requires and thus fall under its curse. This fundamental human inability is central to Paul's critique of the Law.

Modern scholarship resists the notion that the Jews ever viewed the Mosaic Torah as impossible to obey in all that it required.[51] Whereas Paul himself may be claiming in 3:10 that the Mosaic Law is difficult to obey perfectly, Pauline interpreters have offered alternative understandings of this verse that conform to the more optimistic perspective on the Law among the other Jews of his day. Among the more prominent approaches to 3:10, some interpreters have concluded that the verse refers to Israel's corporate fate in exile and says nothing about individual disobedience to the Law.[52] It is difficult, however, to see how the fate of the nation as a corporate whole can be considered abstractly apart from the conduct of its individual members. The sins of individual Israelites accrued to Israel as a whole. Deuteronomy 27, the passage Paul cites, exhibited just such a tension between the corporate fate of Israel and individual accountability. Deuteronomy 27:26 was the twelfth in a series of curses (27:15–26). Two of the twelve curses were for sins committed "in secret" (vv. 15, 24). Four more were for private sexual sins (vv. 20–24). No one would publicly move a boundary marker in violation of the Law (v. 17). A blind man would never be able to testify that he had been led astray (v. 18). When the Levites, in conclusion, pronounced the curse and the community responded in affirmation during the ceremony envisioned in Deuteronomy 27, the community was guaranteeing that sins committed by individuals in secret would not bring about God's vengeance on the community as a whole (e.g., the story of Achan in Joshua 7). God would curse the guilty criminal, and the community would no longer be responsible.[53] Deuteronomy 27:26 was therefore situated at the end of a paragraph concerning the retributive divine curse that fell upon *individual*

---

109 ("The 'Progymnasmata' of Theon: A New Text with Translation and Commentary," [trans. James R. Butts; Ph.D. diss., Claremont Graduate School, 1986; Ann Arbor, Mich.: University Microfilms International, 1986], 198–201).

[51] See Sanders, *Paul and Palestinian Judaism*, ch. 1.

[52] Wright, *Climax of the Covenant*, 147; James M. Scott, " 'For as Many as Are of Works of the Law Are under a Curse' (Galatians 3.10)," in *Paul and the Scriptures of Israel* (ed. Craig A. Evans and James A. Sanders; JSNTSup 83; Sheffield, England: JSOT Press, 1993), 214 n. 89.

[53] Elizabeth Bellefontaine, "The Curses of Deuteronomy 27: Their Relationship to the Prohibitives," in *A Song of Power and the Power of Song* (ed. Duane L. Christensen; Winona Lake, Ind.: Eisenbrauns, 1993), 260, 262, 267; see also Albrecht Alt, "The Origins of Israelite Law," in *Essays on Old Testament History and Religion* (Oxford: Basil Blackwell, 1966), 115.

lawbreakers for secret sins in the midst of the corporate community. Like-wise Deuteronomy 29–30 shifted back and forth between individual and corporate accountability. The fate of corporate Israel depended directly on the deeds of its individual members. The sinful conduct of individual Israel-ites would eventually reach a critical mass, and the exile that these chapters threatened for violation of the Law would finally take place.

Paul may very well be adopting the stance that the people of Israel are in a sort of exile on the basis of Deut 27:26 in its context.[54] Some Second Temple Jews certainly contemplated a continuing exile, but others consid-ered the end of the exile in progress (Bar 4:36–37; 5:5–9), the exile ended (Jdt 4:1–5; 5:17–19; Josephus, *Ant.* 4.8.46 §314; 10.7.3 §§112–113; 11.1.1 §§1–4), or a new exile possible (*m. ʾAbot* 1:11). Paul's opponents in Galatia were among those who held a more optimistic view and did not consider the exile of the Jewish people to have continued, likely because of Israel's devo-tion to the Law of Moses since their return. It is Paul who is positing the darker motifs of exile in Scripture as proof of Israel's current plight and his more pessimistic estimation of the human ability to obey the Law God had given to Moses.[55] An absence of exilic patterns of thought on the part of those influencing the Galatian congregation would help explain Paul's em-

---

[54] See James M. Scott, "Paul's Use of Deuteronomic Tradition," *JBL* 112 (1993): 645–65. See also Scott's dissertation, which contended for exilic allusions in Gal 4:1–7 (*Adoption as Sons of God: An Exegetical Investigation into the Background of* ΥΙΟΘΕΣΙΑ *in the Pauline Corpus* [WUNT 2/48; Tübingen: J. C. B. Mohr (Paul Siebeck), 1992], 121–86). For Jewish texts espousing a continuing exile, see Scott, "'For as Many'"; and the series of essays in James M. Scott, ed., *Exile: Old Testament, Jewish, and Christian Conceptions* (JSJSup 56; Leiden: E. J. Brill, 1997). Recently Susan Eastman has drawn attention to Paul's use of the verb βασκαίνω ("bewitch") in Gal 3:1, a word employed in the covenantal curses of Deut 28:53–57 ("The Evil Eye and the Curse of the Law: Galatians 3.1 Revisited," *JSNT* 83 [2001], 69–87). (The LXX uses the word elsewhere only in Sir 14:6, 8.) Eastman concludes that Christ absorbs the curse while on the cross (Gal 3:13), a deliverance that functions as the content of the message of faith (ἀκοὴ πίστεως) in 3:2, 5. Paul's argument echoes Deuteronomy 28 with its own series of blessings (Gal 3:6–9) and curses (3:10–12).

[55] I argued this in Das, *Paul, the Law, and the Covenant,* 153–55. Mark A. Seifrid ("The 'New Perspective on Paul' and Its Problems," *Them* 25 [2000]: 8–12; *Christ, Our Righteousness: Paul's Theology of Justification* [New Studies in Biblical Theology 9; Downers Grove, Ill.: InterVarsity, 2000], 21–25) has independently come to the same conclusion. He rightly points out that Second Temple Jewish literature held varying conceptions of Israel's exile and its duration, if at all (see also D. A. Carson's comments, on the basis of Bryan's essay, in "Summaries and Conclusions," in *The Complexities of Second Temple Judaism,* vol. 1 of *Justification and Variegated Nomism* [ed. D. A. Carson, Peter T. O'Brien, and Mark A. Seifrid; Grand Rapids: Baker, 2001], 546–47 n. 158. I have not been able to locate the Bryan reference). In Rom 11:20 Paul revisits Israel's condition and speaks of branches that have been broken off be-cause of unbelief. The present rejection of the Messiah has brought about a new exile for the majority of the Jewish people who do not affirm the Christian Messiah. On the beginning of a new exile, see also Seifrid, *Christ, Our Righteousness,* 168–69. For more on Paul's messianic train of thought in Rom 9–11, see ch. 5, below.

phasis in response that "the present Jerusalem" is actually in slavery with her children (Gal 5:25).

Another popular way of explaining Gal 3:10 asserts that perfect obedience is not an issue in this verse. Paul is using a technical term, "works of the Law," that refers especially to the works required by the Law that distinguish the Jews from Gentiles—works such as circumcision, Sabbath observance, and food laws.[56] The primary (but not exclusive) focus of the phrase would be on those laws that act as national and ethnic boundary markers of Jewish identity. Galatians 3:10 could be paraphrased, "Those who rely on their Jewish ethnic identity are under a curse." Those relying on their ethnic heritage would be guilty because they have denied that God's plan included uncircumcised Gentiles as well. By insisting on the "works of the Law," the Jews, in their nationalistic zeal, would be sinfully excluding the Gentiles from God's people.[57]

This "new perspective" on Paul and the Law rightly underscores how the apostle considers the Law to be the unique possession of the Jews (e.g., Rom 2:12). The phrase "works of the Law" is undeniably associated with Jewish ethnic identity in Rom 3:27–29. On the other hand, to grant that the Law is the unique and special possession of the Jewish people does not rule out the understanding that this Law must also be obeyed strictly and in its entirety. Dunn, the premier advocate of the "new perspective," has pointed to Gal 2:16 as an instance of "works of the Law" highlighting Jewish ethnic distinctiveness, but Paul continues in 2:21, "for if justification comes through *the law,* then Christ died for nothing." Paul's statement in 2:21 regarding justification parallels his claim a few verses earlier that no one is justified by the "works of the Law." Paul therefore restates his critique of "works of the Law" in v. 16 in terms of the Law itself in v. 21. Likewise in v. 19: "For through the law I died to the law, so that I might live to God." The elaboration in the ensuing verses seems to have more to do with the Law as a whole than with a focus on only the aspects of the Law that distinguish Jew from Gentile.[58] Paul's point is that the Law *as such* cannot justify. A better approach would begin not with the boundary-marking features of the Law but with the Law in its entirety. Obedience to the Law requires obedience in all

---

[56] James D. G. Dunn, *Romans 1–8* (WBC 38A; Dallas: Word, 1988), lxxi–lxxii, 186–87, 190–94; "Paul and Justification by Faith," in *The Road from Damascus: The Impact of Paul's Conversion on His Life, Thought, and Ministry* (ed. Richard N. Longenecker; Grand Rapids: Eerdmans, 1997), 96–97.

[57] James D. G. Dunn, *Galatians,* 172; *Jesus, Paul, and the Law: Studies in Mark and Galatians* (Louisville: Westminster John Knox, 1990), 231.

[58] Heikki Räisänen objects to Dunn's claim that the Jews misunderstood the law in overly ethnic terms according to Galatians 3: "It is altogether impossible to read chapter 3 as an attack on just a particular *attitude* to the law. Why should the death of Christ have been necessary to liberate men from an attitude of theirs?" ("Galatians 2.16 and Paul's Break with Judaism," in *Jesus, Paul, and Torah: Collected Essays* [trans. David E. Orton; JSNTSup 43; Sheffield, England: JSOT Press, 1992], 122).

that it commands, which would certainly include the aspects of the Law that distinguish the Jews from the Gentiles. Conversely, to do part of what the Law requires, such as circumcision or keeping Sabbath, entails obeying the whole Law. Thus Paul can move very naturally from a review of his critique of Peter at Antioch to a discussion of the Law itself. The apostle sees no point in forcing the Gentiles to live like Jews under the Law since the Law does not offer a right relationship with God (vv. 15–16).

Paul claims in Gal 3:10 that everyone who relies on "the works of the law" is under a curse. Another clue that Paul's phrase "works of the Law" cannot be limited just to the aspects of the Law that distinguish the Jews as an ethnic people comes from the passage Paul cites. Deuteronomy 27:26 was situated in a portion of Deuteronomy, chs. 27–30, that condemned all sorts of legal violations—illicit sexual relations, misleading the blind, changing borders, following other gods, even withholding justice from widows and orphans. The summary verses in 27:26, 28:1, 15, 58, 61; 30:10 consistently emphasize obedience to all that God commanded in the Law. The language was comprehensive; the Law is an organic whole that must all be obeyed. Nowhere was Deuteronomy focused on just the laws that distinguish Israel from other nations. Even in the more immediate context of the verses that preceded 27:26, the commands often concerned sins committed in secret (27:15–26). In fact, the prohibitions in this passage usually corresponded to similar prohibitions elsewhere.[59] Deuteronomy 27:15–26 had simply extended the threatened curses to situations where the sin took place in private. Since 27:26, the verse Paul cites, concluded a section hardly concerned with prohibitions that distinguish Israel as an ethnic people, it is difficult to see why Paul's conclusion about "works of the Law" in Gal 3:10 should be limited to the features of the Law that function as boundary markers for the people of Israel.

The Qumran manuscripts 4QMMT offer a rare independent witness in Hebrew to Paul's phrase "works of the Law" (מעשי תורה). The Qumran phrase refers to all that the Law required. Whenever an individual chose to depart from the community's understanding of God's Law on a particular point, that member had apostasized. From the community's perspective, to neglect *any* aspect of the Law would bring into play the curses of Deut 27–30 and the need for separation from the community (as Dunn himself showed). The phrase "works of the Law" always referred primarily to what the Law required in general and in its entirety. Only secondarily did it focus on particular boundary-defining strictures.[60] Because the focus was primarily

---

[59] E.g., compare v. 16 with Exod 20:12; 21:17 and Lev 19:3; 20:9. Compare v. 17 with Deut 19:14, v. 18 with Lev 19:14, and v. 19 with Exod 22:20–23; 23:9; Lev 19:33–34; and Deut 1:17; 10:18–19; 24:17–18. See Bellefontaine's discussion in "The Curses of Deuteronomy 27" for the remaining curses; as well as Gerhard Wallis, "Der Vollbürgereid in Deuteronomium 27, 15–26," *HUCA* 45 (1974): 50–51.

[60] James D. G. Dunn ("4QMMT and Galatians," *NTS* 43 [1997]: 147–53; "Paul and Justification by Faith," 98) reverses the rightful emphases.

upon the Law as a whole, the particular laws the phrase referred to can vary from one conflict situation to another. In the face of a wrongful departure from the entirety of God's Law, the specific laws that have been violated must come to the fore and serve as a mark of separation.[61] The *Rule of the Community* (1QS) at Qumran confirms this more inclusive interpretation of 4QMMT. The *Rule of the Community* called members to "return to the law of Moses according to *all* that he commanded" (1QS 5:8; italics added). In 1QS 5:21 individuals were examined upon entry into the community with respect to their "works of the law," whether they had been careful "to walk according to *all* these precepts" (see also 1QS 6:18; italics added). The precepts included the "avoidance of anger, impatience, hatred, insulting elders, blasphemy, malice, foolish talk, and nakedness" (1QS 5:25–26; 6:24–7:18). Circumcision, observance of the Sabbath, and the food laws were only the starting point. These passages from Qumran would, then, parallel Paul's own use of the phrase "works of the Law" in Gal 3:10 for more than just the ethnic or boundary-marking components of the Law.[62]

The traditional approach to Gal 3:10 remains the most viable understanding.[63] Paul has simply omitted the premise that he considered would

---

[61] 4QMMT's heading indicates that it addresses "*some* of the works of the Law." "Works of the Law" must therefore go beyond those aspects in dispute within the document to include the entirety of the Law; Ben Witherington III, *Grace in Galatia: A Commentary on Paul's Letter to the Galatians* (Grand Rapids: Eerdmans, 1998), 176–77; see also Michael Bachmann, "4QMMT und Galaterbrief, התורה מעשי und ΕΡΓΑ ΝΟΜΟΥ," *ZNW* 89 (1998): 91–113. Joseph A. Fitzmyer, ("Paul's Jewish Background and the Deeds of the Law," in *According to Paul: Studies in the Theology of the Apostle* [Mahwah, N.J.: Paulist, 1993], 23) has likewise noted the "broad outlook" of this document. Nothing suggests the restriction of the phrase to only certain boundary-marking aspects of the Law. Fitzmyer repeatedly emphasizes throughout his article that "works of the Law" at Qumran must be taken as the works that the Law requires in a general sense (pp. 19–24). Timo Eskola ("*Avodat Israel* and the 'Works of the Law' in Paul," in *From the Ancient Sites of Israel: Essays on Archaeology, History, and Theology* [ed. T. Eskola and E. Junkaala; Helsinki: Theological Institute of Finland, 1998], 185) notes that the "works" mentioned in 4QMMT regard the laws pertaining to priestly ceremonies that distinguished the community's practices from Jerusalem's. He concludes, "They were items which became separating factors between the Qumran priests and the priests of the Temple. This is why it is possible to reach a conclusion as to the significance of the works of the law for the rebellious priests. For them it was a matter of being obedient to the word of God. Works of the law signified perfect obedience to and fulfillment of the precepts of the *Torah*."

[62] For a recent, thorough review of the Qumran evidence for the phrase "works of the Law" that independently comes to a similar conclusion regarding the meaning of the phrase, contra Dunn, see Jacqueline C. R. de Roo, "The Concept of 'Works of the Law' in Jewish and Christian Literature," in *Christian-Jewish Relations through the Centuries* (ed. Stanley E. Porter and Brook W. R. Pearson; JSNTSup 192; Sheffield: Sheffield Academic Press, 2000), 116–47.

[63] For a critique of other attempts to explain this text with a new-perspective paradigm (including Sanders's own approach), see Das, *Paul, the Law, and the Covenant,* 145–70.

be obvious to his readers: no one perfectly obeys the Law. Paul elsewhere makes it clear that all people are guilty of sin (e.g., Rom 3:10–12, 23). If the Galatians desire to observe the Law, they will place themselves under its curse for inevitable failure.

RETHINKING AN ELECT COVENANT PEOPLE

Pauline interpreters have searched so diligently for alternative explanations of Gal 3:10 because Jewish literature from Paul's day rarely exhibited any pessimism about the possibility of satisfactorily obeying God's Law. Certain elements of Paul's reasoning are inexplicable from a Jewish standpoint. Did not the Law, a testimony in itself of God's love for an elect and chosen people, already offer provision for sin? It is not entirely clear why perfect obedience to the Law would be a problem for a Jew such as Paul. One could disobey God's Law and then simply make atonement for sin and failure even as the Law itself instructed. The obligations of the Mosaic Law were always embedded within a body of writings that testified to God's grace and love. To comprehend Paul's thinking on the Law, it is vital to determine where and how the elements of divine grace and mercy in Judaism are operative in Galatians—that is, *if* they are operative.

Galatians is one of the few letters in which Paul talks about the Jewish covenant, and he gives the distinct impression of not being entirely comfortable with the concept. Paul first employs the Greek word for "covenant" (διαθήκη) in Gal 3:15, and he uses the term to refer not to the Jewish covenant but to a last will and testament. "Last will and testament" was precisely what this word would mean to non-Jews such as the Galatians. When the Jewish Scriptures were translated into Greek, this word was used to translate the Hebrew word for "covenant" (בְּרִית). No sooner has Paul introduced the concept of "last will and testament" (διαθήκη) in v. 15 than he shifts in v. 17 to using the same word for the Abrahamic "covenant." Paul seems intent initially on distancing the word from the Jewish concept of a covenant, only to return to that concept rather joltingly in the very next breath. Paul's tinkering with the meaning of the Greek word signals that he is not entirely comfortable with what it signifies in Galatia. The language of covenant would point decisively toward God's relationship with Abraham in Genesis 17, which included circumcision as its sign. "Covenant" was likely the preferred lingo for Paul's opponents.[64]

The play on words is not the only signal that Paul is uncomfortable with the Jewish concept of covenant. It was common in first-century Judaism to connect, or even to equate, the Abrahamic covenant with the later covenant and Law given to Moses at Mount Sinai. The provisions of the

---

[64] Martyn, "Covenant, Christ, and Church," 141–45.

Mosaic Law were regularly viewed as an extension of the Abrahamic covenant; the Abrahamic and the Sinaitic covenants were really one covenant.[65] The Jews therefore claimed that Abraham was obeying the Mosaic Law already in his day.[66] By speaking in vv. 15–18 of the Mosaic Law as if it were an illegal codicil to the last will and testament—which is really the Abrahamic covenant—Paul can drive a wedge between the two historic events. He completely divorces the Mosaic Law at Mount Sinai from the Abrahamic covenant. His discomfort with the term "covenant" stems, then, from its close association with the requirements of the Law. For Paul, the Abrahamic covenant is based entirely on God's gracious promise with no mention of circumcision. The apostle further departs from the covenantal understanding of Judaism when he speaks of the singular "seed." Far from acknowledging a special people as the beneficiaries of God's covenantal dealings with Abraham, Paul envisions only one beneficiary of God's covenant: Jesus Christ. The history of God's saving work seems to skip from Abraham to Christ. A very different covenant people exist in Christ, a people incorporated by faith and baptism into Christ, *the* "seed" (3:15–18, 27–29).[67]

Paul's discomfort with the Jewish concept of covenant manifests itself one last time in Gal 4:21–31 when the one Abrahamic covenant of 3:15–17 suddenly becomes two covenants. Ishmael received a covenant just as Isaac received his covenant. In yet another bold departure from the Genesis accounts, Paul makes no mention of circumcision, probably the most notable aspect of the Abrahamic covenant in Genesis 17. He presents a series of harsh antitheses, with the children of the slave woman and bondage on the one side and the children of the free woman and the promise on the other. One child is begotten according to the flesh; the other, according to the

---

[65] The Mosaic Law and the covenant were considered two sides of the same coin. Thus, e.g., Sir 39:8, "the law of the Lord's covenant" (see also 28:7; 42:2; 44:19–20; 45:5), and *Pss. Sol.* 10:4, "the law of the eternal covenant." The *Mekilta* from the third century C.E. likewise affirms, "By covenant is meant nothing other than the Torah" (*Bahodesh* 6; on Exod 20:6). Note the undifferentiated use of the term "covenant" (contra Paul). For additional references, see Annie Jaubert, *La notion d'alliance dans le judaïsme: Aux abords de l'ère chrétienne* (Patristica sorbonensia 6; Paris: Cerf [Editions du Seuil], 1963), 457–58; James D. G Dunn, "What Was the Issue between Paul and 'Those of the Circumcision'?" in *Paulus und das antike Judentum* (ed. Martin Hengel and Ulrich Heckel; Tübingen: J. C. B. Mohr [Paul Siebeck], 1991), 295–317, esp. 299.

[66] See Sir 44:19–20 and *2 Bar.* 57:2; so also Philo, *Abr.* 275–276; *Jub.* 11–23; *m. Qidd.* 4.14; *b. Yoma* 28b.

[67] On the participatory mode of Paul's argument, see A. Andrew Das, "Oneness in Christ: The *nexus indivulsus* between Justification and Sanctification in Paul's Letter to the Galatians," *Concordia Journal* 21 (1995): 173–86. Paul's use of a singular "seed" runs counter to the collective understanding of "seed" in Judaism (and presumably the Jewish Christianity in Galatia). On the "seed of Abraham" as an important motif in Jewish thought, see *Jub.* 16:17, 1 Macc 12:21; *Ps.-Clem. Rec.*, 1.33.3; 1.34.1.

Spirit. Shockingly, Paul identifies the child of flesh and slavery with the present Jerusalem and Mount Sinai in opposition to the heavenly Jerusalem. The Mosaic Law stands on the same side of the divide as Hagar, Abraham's slave. Paul's opponents may have objected, after hearing 3:15–18, that he had ignored the covenant God made with Moses at Mount Sinai. Surely the Sinaitic covenant was based on God's dealings with Abraham. So Paul returns in 4:21–31 to the connection between Law and covenant. This time he draws a contrast between *two* Abrahamic covenants, one of which is associated with the Mosaic Law. Paul finally grants an association between the Mosaic Law and an Abrahamic covenant. Unfortunately for his opponents, theirs is the wrong covenant, the covenant of slavery. Paul speaks similarly elsewhere of the Mosaic covenant. In 2 Corinthians 3 he contrasts the lesser glory of the Mosaic covenant of death with the greater glory of the "new covenant" in Christ.[68]

The Mosaic covenant with its Law was the basis of Jewish identity. The giving of the Law was a sign of Israel's election and special place before God. Early Jewish Christianity was in agreement that the Law and its works were incapable of creating a right relationship with God apart from faith in Jesus Christ (Gal 2:15–16). Paul explains that those who would benefit from God's election of Abraham do so only by being incorporated into the singular seed Jesus Christ by the same faith as Abraham (3:6–9, 15–18, 28–29). Only those in Christ are children of Abraham and members of the assembly of the Lord (1:2, 13; 3:26, 29). The Mosaic Law, which had defined an elect ethnic people, now stands equated with Hagar, the slave woman who is bearing children into slavery (4:24–25). In this radical move, Paul equates God's elect not with the Jewish people per se but with believers in Christ.

Likewise Gal 6:15–16 attests that ethnic Israel's election has been radically redefined:

> For neither circumcision nor uncircumcision is anything; but a new creation is everything! As for those who follow this rule—peace be upon them, and mercy, and upon the Israel of God.

Circumcision, previously the sign of an elect people, now is inconsequential in and of itself. The apostle goes on to speak of "the Israel of God." Some interpreters think that Paul is pronouncing God's peace and mercy upon the same group, namely, the Israel of God.[69] At the end of a letter blasting circumcision as an entrance requirement into God's people, with 6:11–16 as the final parting shot, the apostle would be closing with a rhetorically pow-

---

[68] For a detailed discussion of this passage, see Das, *Paul, the Law, and the Covenant,* 76–94. See also the critique of Scott Hafemann's work, on which my analysis was based, offered by Sigurd Grindheim ("The Law Kills but the Gospel Gives Life: The Letter-Spirit Dualism in 2 Corinthians 3.5–18," *JSNT* 84 [2001]: 97–115). In Grindheim's analysis of 2 Corinthians 3, the Mosaic covenant functions only to condemn people to their deaths. Only the new covenant in Christ offers people life.

[69] E.g., Martyn, *Galatians,* 574–77.

erful redefinition of the Israel of God. In Isa 54:10 the prophet speaks of both "peace" and "mercy," an otherwise unusual combination, within the context of God's impending "new creation" of Israel. All three elements recur in Gal 6:15–16, suggesting an allusion to the prophet, but Paul speaks of a "new creation" where there is neither circumcised nor uncircumcised (6:15).[70] Paul prepared for the inclusive "Israel of God" in 6:16 by his reference to "the Jerusalem above" that is, for the Galatian Gentiles, "our mother" (4:26, 28–29). Jew and Gentile have been brought together once and for all in Christ (3:29) as the true children of Abraham (3:6) and Sarah, "the free woman" (4:30–31). God's election of Israel has been redefined in terms of the church, inclusive of both Jewish and Gentile believers.

Other scholars think that the Greek wording of Gal 6:15–16 (καί) distinguishes two separate groups of people and should be translated simply as "and" or "even":[71] Grace and mercy be upon all who follow this rule as well as ("and") upon the Israel of God. If Paul had intended to convey that "the Israel of God" is the same group as the immediately preceding "those who follow this rule," he would have omitted the unnecessary "and"/"even." The "and" suggests that the groups are distinct. In that case, although Jew and Gentile are united in Christ (3:29), Paul still recognizes that the one gospel manifests itself in a distinct mission to Jews as Jews and in a mission to Gentiles as Gentiles (2:7). Indeed, some would maintain that the mission to the Gentiles is dependent on God's rescue of the Jews from their condition "under the Law."[72] Paul thus continues to distinguish between Jews and Gentiles. If Paul is distinguishing between two separate groups, "the Israel of God" would once again be a redefined Israel; it would be the Jews who believe in the one gospel of Jesus Christ.[73] The implication would be that the circumcision party and those who preached "another gospel," that the Gentiles need also to obey God's Law, are among those now excluded from "the Israel of God." Those Jewish Christians would not be included in God's blessings (1:8–9; 2:4–5). Throughout the letter Paul has denigrated and condemned his opponents' insistence on circumcision as necessary to salvation in Christ, quite contrary to the "rule" of 6:15. The Israel of God would

---

[70] G. K. Beale, "Peace and Mercy upon the Israel of God: The Old Testament Background of Galatians 6,16b," *Bib* 80 (1999): 204–23.

[71] E.g., Betz, *Galatians,* 322–23; Peter Richardson, *Israel in the Apostolic Church* (SNTSMS 10; Cambridge: Cambridge University Press, 1969), 74–84, esp. 82–83.

[72] Terence L. Donaldson ("The 'Curse of the Law' and the Inclusion of the Gentiles: Galatians 3. 13–14," *NTS* 32 [1986]: 94–112) is the leading advocate of the position that Paul consistently distinguishes "we" Jews from "you" Gentile Galatians. In other words, a distinct "Israel of God" within the same context as an apparent relativizing of the significance of circumcision is not abrupt after all in light of the consistent distinctions earlier in Paul's letter. See, however, the critique of Donaldson's position in ch. 5, below.

[73] The mission to the Gentiles and the mission to the circumcised in 2:9 are both outworkings of one and the same gospel.

consist of the Jewish Christians who adhered to the true, Pauline under-standing of the gospel of Christ.[74] Whether or not "the Israel of God" refers to a church inclusive of Jews and Gentiles or to ethnic Jews alone, Paul has redefined Israel in such a way that ethnic Israel per se has been excluded apart from faith in the gospel message about Christ.

The last element of God's grace and mercy in Judaism is the provision of atonement for failure to observe the Law, but Paul nowhere admits any redeeming value to atoning sacrifice. Paul offers only one solution to the plight of those who fail to observe God's Law. When the Law pronounces a curse upon those who fail to obey it in its entirety in 3:10, Paul's answer comes in v. 13: "Christ redeemed us from the curse of the law by becoming a curse for us." One looks in vain for any reference to the atoning sacrifices of Judaism or to a reconciliation with God apart from Christ. The very situa-tion of curse under the Law is rectified by Christ's action and not by sacri-fice or by any other means. Paul then quotes Deut 21:22–23 about the hanging of a corpse on a tree after execution. The Deuteronomy text was interpreted by the Qumran community (see 11QT[a] 64:6–13; 4QpNah 1:17–18) as referring to crucifixion. Paul may be aware of such an interpre-tation when he sees in Deut 21:22–23 a reference to Christ on the cross. Likewise Christ was born "under the law, in order to redeem those who were under the law" (Gal 4:4–5).[75] In effect, the gracious elements of Juda-ism have been redefined in terms of grace centered on the person and work of Jesus Christ. That leaves the regulations of the Mosaic Law as a series of mere demands and obligations with no provision for failure. Paul under-stands in terms of Christ's redeeming work the life-giving and gracious ele-ments typically associated with the Law, an understanding that leads to a more pessimistic view of the Law than would be common among other Jews in his day.

Martyn has pointed to the quotation of Deut 21:22–23 in Gal 3:13 as the clue to comprehending Paul's placement of Christ and the Torah in such a sharp antithesis. As is obvious from his conflicts with Law-observant Jew-ish Christians, the sharp antithesis was not the only position available to him when he became a follower of Christ. Martyn believes that before his con-version Paul had persecuted the Jewish followers of Jesus Christ because he was convinced that a crucified Messiah was incompatible with Judaism since the Law pronounced a curse upon anyone who hung on a tree, that is, who was crucified (Deut 21:22–23). Paul had understood Jesus Christ to be an individual accursed by the Torah of God rather than the Messiah (cf.

---

[74] The advantage of this interpretation is that "Israel" would refer to the Jews alone, as it does all throughout Romans 9–11 (as even Martyn recognizes, who would otherwise maintain that "Israel of God" in Gal 6:16 is inclusive of Gentile believers).

[75] The word "redeem" (ἐξαγοράζω) in both 3:13 and 4:5 links the two verses. It is commercial language used especially for the emancipation of slaves; cf. 5:1.

1 Cor 1:23).[76] Upon meeting the resurrected Jesus Christ, the Torah and Christ remained antithetical in Paul's reasoning but were inverted when he concluded that the problem was not with Christ but with the Torah.

Galatians 3:13 may not be the key to Paul's antithetical approach to Christ and the Torah as Martyn thought. First-century Jews would not necessarily have concluded from Deut 21:23 that the crucified were cursed by God. The Jewish and Jewish Christian scholars Aquila and Theodotion translated the Hebrew of Deut 21:23 (קִלְלַת אֱלֹהִים) into Greek as "an affront to God," and Symmachus and the Mishnah (*Sanh.* 6.4; also *Targum Onqelos*) translated the phrase as "one who curses God" rather than as one who is cursed by God. The Jews of Paul's day had not concluded that Saul and Jonathan were cursed by God in 2 Sam 21:12. Nor had the Jews concluded that the eight hundred crucified by Jannaeus a little over a century before were cursed (Josephus *Ant.* 13.14.2 §380). Similarly, the Jews did not view the many unjustly crucified by the Romans as cursed by God.[77] As Terence Donaldson has pointed out in his important work *Paul and the Gentiles,* a Jewish Christian might have reconciled the Torah and Jesus Christ by demonstrating that Jesus was actually innocent and undeserving of such a punishment (cf. Deut 21:22). A first-century Jew might have concluded that the Romans martyred Jesus on the cross. Donaldson has noted that Paul had been a zealot for the Law before his conversion (Gal 1:14) and so he would surely have sought to reconcile Christ and the Torah if possible. Many of his opponents took that approach. Deuteronomy 21:22–23 would not in itself have forced him to maintain the sharp antithesis.[78]

Donaldson has contended that the pre-Damascus Paul, like those present in the Galatians' midst, had promoted a law-observant form of Judaism requiring circumcision (Gal 5:11).[79] Paul the convert and apostle arrived at the position that God's people are those who have placed their faith in Christ rather than those who adhere to the Torah and circumcision. Faith in Christ, not adherence to the Torah, functions as the boundary marker for

---

[76] Martyn, *Galatians,* 162.

[77] C. M. Tuckett, "Deuteronomy 21,23 and Paul's Conversion," in *L'apôtre Paul: Personnalité, style, et conception du ministère* (ed. A. VanHoye; Leuven: Leuven University Press, 1986), 347–48.

[78] Terence L. Donaldson, *Paul and the Gentiles: Remapping the Apostle's Convictional World* (Minneapolis: Fortress, 1997), 170–71.

[79] Ibid., 276–83. It is not entirely clear that there is adequate evidence that the pre-Christian Paul, or others for that matter, proselytized Gentiles as Donaldson contends. See Scot McKnight, *A Light among the Gentiles: Jewish Missionary Activity in the Second Temple Period* (Minneapolis: Fortress, 1991); and Martin Goodman, *Mission and Conversion: Proselytizing in the Religious History of the Roman Empire* (Oxford: Oxford University Press, 1994). The pre-Christian Paul need not have proselytized to have had an interest in Abraham (Galatians 3; Romans 4). Observance of the Torah marked God's elect people, and Abraham was the model pagan convert to the God and Law of Judaism. Paul simply maintained, with many of his peers, the requirement for circumcision in order to be a member of God's people, the Jews.

the people who enjoy God's favor and salvation.[80] And so Paul faulted many of his Jewish Christian peers in Galatians 2 for what he perceived to be an inconsistency when they promoted the Law as necessary for enjoying God's favor alongside faith in Christ. What God has done in Christ is powerful and sufficient for the salvation of all humanity and requires no supplement. The zealot for the Law had become a zealot for Christ.

GALATIANS IN REVIEW

When Paul wrote his letter to the Galatians, he was confronting a situation that arose shortly after his departure. Jewish Christians had entered the congregation and were promoting among the Gentile Galatians a gospel message that included Law observance along with faith in Christ as the basis for Christian existence. Paul's concern was that by placing the Law alongside faith in Christ, the rivals essentially denied the power and efficacy of Christ's saving work. For Paul, something radically new and awesome had taken place with Christ's death and the arrival of the Spirit. The very Spirit the Galatians already possessed was their key to the Christian life. The Law was simply a series of obligations or bare commands that cannot save. According to Gal 4:21, the Law, in the sense of its broader witness as Scripture, had always pointed forward to the new reality that would dawn in Christ and the Spirit. As Paul searched for God's grace and mercy in Judaism and its Scriptures, he found the person and work of Jesus Christ.

When Paul saw Jesus on the road to Damascus, it became perfectly clear to him that the apocalyptic age of the Messiah had already dawned. The revelation of God's Messiah substantially altered the way the apostle viewed the Judaism he inherited from his ancestors. If it is faith in Christ that incorporates a person into this new reality, then the Mosaic Law does not have saving significance in and of itself. Paul says this in Gal 2:21 and 3:21. The Law must be understood now in terms of Christ or, better, in the hands of Christ (6:2). By this "Law of Christ" the Christian will now live.

The Letter to the Galatians has provided a useful starting point for a comprehensive approach to Paul's views on such matters as the election of Israel, the Abrahamic and Sinaitic covenants, and the Mosaic Law. The apostle's reasoning on these matters will figure in his overall understanding of the place of the Jewish people in the divine plan. Since Paul treats many of the same topics in his other letters, especially in his Letter to the Romans, the investigation must proceed to Rome—the next stop.

---

[80] Donaldson, *Paul and the Gentiles,* 172–73, 284–85.

⊰ 3 ⊱

THE SITUATION AT ROME:
THE LAW-OBSERVANT AND
THE NON-LAW-OBSERVANT

> Welcome one another, therefore, just as Christ has welcomed you,
> for the glory of God. For I tell you that Christ has become a servant
> of the circumcised on behalf of the truth of God in order that he
> might confirm the promises given to the patriarchs, and in order
> that the Gentiles might glorify God for his mercy. (Rom 15:7–9a)

FOR CENTURIES people considered the Letter to the Romans the apostle's
most thorough treatment of Christian doctrine and belief. Paul cogitated at
length on such heady topics as sin, grace, salvation, justification, and the
sanctified life and in the process offered fodder for later systematic treatises
on Christian doctrine. In the last several decades, scholars have begun to
approach Romans differently since Paul's other letters have proven to be
motivated by, and aimed toward, very specific local situations in the congregations they address. The Letter to the Galatians, far from being an abstract
expression of Paul's thinking, addresses the concrete situation of Jewish
Christian evangelists who had entered into the Galatian Gentile churches.
The First Letter to the Thessalonians consoles and advises a young congregation shortly after the apostle had departed when death intervened
and prevented several members from witnessing Christ's imminent return
(1 Thess 4:13–18).[1] Paul's First Letter to the Corinthians combats divisions
within the congregation (1 Cor 1:10).[2] Likewise the Letter to the Philippians
may be pointed toward the dispute between two women in the congregation
(Phil 4:2–3).[3] Paul's message in each letter appears tailored to the situation

---

[1] See John M. G. Barclay, "Thessalonica and Corinth: Social Contrasts in
Pauline Christianity," *JSNT* 47 (1992): 49–74.
[2] Ibid.; Margaret M. Mitchell, *Paul and the Rhetoric of Reconciliation: An
Exegetical Investigation of the Language and Composition of 1 Corinthians* (Louisville:
Westminster John Knox, 1991).
[3] Thus David E. Garland, "Composition and Unity of Philippians," *NovT* 27
(1985): 141–73. Nils A. Dahl independently came to the same conclusion in his

within a particular church. So when Paul writes, "Welcome one another" in Rom 15:7, the question naturally is whether a situation has arisen at Rome to which the apostle is privy.

Scholars have struggled with the details of the situation behind Romans. Central to the "Romans debate" has been the context of Paul's admonition "Welcome one another." Romans 15:7–9a follows on the heels of his instructions to the "strong" and the "weak" (14:1–15:6). Although a minority think that the apostle's instructions are too general to identify a specific group as the "weak," most students of the letter think the "weak" are Law-observant Christians. One scholar has even contended that the "weak" are non-Christian Jews. Paul may very well, then, be addressing a particular situation in Rome as well. In a letter brimming with references to Judaism, its Law, and its customs and ways, how one reconstructs the situation of the letter would have profound implications for understanding Paul's relationship with the Jews and Judaism.

ROME, JUDAISM, AND THE FIRST CHRISTIANS

Along with Antioch on the Orontes in Syria, Alexandria in Egypt, and Corinth in Greece, Rome was one of the four most important cities in the Mediterranean world of the first century C.E. Tradition traces Rome's founding to the descendants of Aeneas, Romulus, and Remus in 753 B.C.E. Originally a shepherd's village and an offshoot of Alba Longa, Rome surpassed the other towns because of its position on the ford of the Tiber River. By the sixth century the various shepherd settlements on the now famous hills had coalesced to form a single city. For a time Rome was ruled by kings. Eventually it became a republic ruled by two consuls elected annually by the people. By 275 B.C.E. Rome ruled all of Italy. During the remainder of the third century, Rome waged war on Carthage and began to acquire provinces: the island of Sicily to the south in 241, the island of Sardinia to the west in 238, and Spain in 206. During the second century B.C.E. Rome's influence and interventions expanded to encompass the entire Mediterranean area. In 148 Macedonia, the homeland of Alexander the Great, just north of Greece, became a Roman province, and in 146 the great Greek city of Corinth was destroyed when the Aegean Confederacy fell to the Roman general Lucius Mummius Achaicus. Rome renamed the Greek homeland as a province in honor of the conquering general (Achaia).

Instability marked the end of the second century and beginning of the first: slave wars, class struggle, and dictatorship. But by 60 B.C.E. Rome was in the hands of the triumvirate of Pompey, Crassus, and Julius Caesar.

---

essay "Euodia and Syntyche and Paul's Letter to the Philippians," in *The Social World of the First Christians: Essays in Honor of Wayne A. Meeks* (ed. L. Michael White and O. Larry Yarbrough; Minneapolis: Fortress, 1995), 3–15.

Pompey had conquered the eastern shores of the Mediterranean, including Judea and Jerusalem in 63 B.C.E. The triumvirate eventually broke up, and Julius Caesar gained control of Rome, only to be assassinated in 44 B.C.E. In the wake of Caesar's death, Octavius and Mark Antony vied for power until Antony's defeat at the battle of Actium in September 31 B.C.E. The long and wearying years of tumult and violence had finally settled down by 27 B.C.E., when the senate conferred upon Octavius the title "Augustus" ("the venerable one"; in Greek, "Sebastos"). Augustus reigned until 14 B.C.E., during a period known as the Pax Augusta, a time of remarkable and unparalleled peace within the land. This was the golden age of Latin literature, the era of Virgil, Horace, and Livy. After Augustus's death Tiberius ruled from 14 to 37 C.E., a time that coincided with Jesus' adolescence and adulthood and the earliest church in Jerusalem. The emperor Gaius Caligula reigned from 37 to 41, during the early years of the Christian church and the time in which Paul was a new convert and apostle. Claudius ruled from 41 to 54, and Nero from 54 to 68. The reigns of Claudius and Nero are crucial to the discussion of Paul's Letter to the Romans. Events transpired during their reigns that decisively shaped the Roman Christian community, a community that had its origin among the Jews in Rome.

The emerging power of the city of Rome attracted foreigners along with their customs and cults. Already in 161 B.C.E. and twice thereafter, Judas Maccabee, the revolutionary Jewish leader who had helped win Judea's independence from the Greek rulers in the East, is reported to have sent envoys to the Roman senate. The Romans responded by officially acknowledging the new Jewish state (1 Macc 8:1–32; 2 Macc 11:37). Rome was already expanding into the east and undermining the old Greek states, the legacy of Alexander the Great, by granting recognition and occasional military assistance to their enemies. The earliest known reference to Jews in Rome concerns events in 139 B.C.E. Valerius Maximus reports that the Romans "forced the Jews, who tried to contaminate Roman customs with the cult of Jupiter Sabazius, to return to their own homes."[4] The Romans may have mistaken the sound of "Yahweh Sabbaoth," the Jewish God, for a more familiar-sounding "Jupiter Sabazius." The largest influx of Jews into Rome took place in 62 B.C.E. when Pompey brought Jewish slaves to Rome from his conquest of the eastern Mediterranean and Palestine.[5] Many of these slaves or their descendants would eventually earn their freedom.[6] Even before the influx under Pompey, however, a well-established and sizable Jewish community likely existed in Rome. Cicero, the great rhetorician and statesman, indicates that the Jews

---

[4] Valerius Maximus, *Facta* 1.3.3 (first century C.E.), as cited in Stern, *Greek and Latin Authors,* 1:358–60 (§§ 147a, 147b); see, for a discussion, Harry J. Leon, *The Jews of Ancient Rome* (rev. ed.; Peabody, Mass.: Hendrickson, 1995), 2–4. The passage may also be interpreted in terms of a Maccabean delegation.

[5] Josephus, *Ant.* 14.4.5 §77; *J.W.* 1.7.7 §155.

[6] See Philo, *Legat.* 23.155–57.

were sending money to Palestine before 59 B.C.E., and as he defended Flaccus, he was annoyed with large crowds of Jews in his audience.[7] It is unlikely that this politically influential crowd consisted only of freed slaves from Pompey's conquests a few years earlier. Jewish support for Julius Caesar in the subsequent civil wars contributed to their rising status.[8] A grateful Caesar exempted the Jews of Rome from a ban on associations.[9] His favorable administrative actions may have influenced Roman policy toward the Jews.[10] The Jews, perhaps more than any other group, mourned his death, a testimony to their positive relationship.[11]

Philo, the first-century Jewish scholar in Alexandria, writes that during Augustus's era the Jews, including many former prisoners of war, inhabited a large area on the other side of the Tiber River in Rome.[12] Estimates place the burgeoning Jewish population in Rome from fifteen thousand to fifty thousand by the early first century C.E., with the majority of the estimates clustered toward the higher number.[13] The Jewish historian Josephus claims that eight thousand Roman Jews accompanied a Jewish delegation from Palestine to appear before Augustus.[14] Under Tiberius in 19 C.E., four thousand Jews of draftable age were deported, an event of such magnitude that it left a ripple effect all through the historians of the period.[15] Four thousand young men of draftable age suggests a substantially larger Jewish population in Rome. Such a population would most certainly have gathered in assemblies. The Roman Jews named their assemblies, or synagogues, in honor of contemporary figures who served as benefactors to their community. Their names—the Synagogue of the Hebrews (perhaps the oldest of the synagogues), of Augustus, of Agrippa, of the Herodians, and of the Volumnians (the procurator of Syria at the time of Herod the Great)—indicate the existence of at least five synagogues in Rome by the mid-first century C.E.[16]

---

[7] Cicero, *Flac.* 28.67–69.

[8] Josephus, *Ant.* 14.10.1–8 §§185–216.

[9] Josephus, *Ant.* 14.10.8 §§213–216; Suetonius, *Jul.* 42.3.

[10] See Josephus, *Ant.* 16.6 §§160–178. Tessa Rajak ("Was There a Roman Charter for the Jews?" *JRS* 74 [1984]: 107–23) warns that this possibility should not be overstated. There is no real evidence for a Roman charter for the Jews under Julius Caesar or at any other time. Julius Caesar's exemption from the ban on associations applied only to the Jews of Rome. Josephus typically exaggerates the significance of favorable, more limited Roman actions as if they applied to Jews universally.

[11] Suetonius, *Jul.* 84.5.

[12] Philo, *Legat.* 23.155; likewise also Juvenal, *Sat.* 3.12–16.

[13] For an estimate nearer to fifty thousand, see Leon, *Jews of Ancient Rome,* 15, 257.

[14] Josephus, *Ant.* 17.11.1 §§299–303; cf. *J.W.* 2.6.1 §80.

[15] Suetonius, *Tib.* 36; Josephus, *Ant.* 18.3.5 §§81–84; cf. Tacitus, *Ann.* 2.85.

[16] By the second and third centuries, there were at least thirteen synagogues in Rome. See the helpful discussion in Peter Richardson, "Augustan-Era Synagogues in Rome," in *Judaism and Christianity in First-Century Rome* (ed. Karl P. Donfried and Peter Richardson; Grand Rapids: Eerdmans, 1998), 17–29.

Other synagogues could well have existed, the remains of which have been lost. The presence of so many synagogues suggests a substantial Jewish population in Rome.

The origins in Rome of the first believers in Christ are shrouded in mystery. Christianity most likely began as a movement within the synagogues. Later third- and fourth-century ecclesiastical traditions point to Peter as the founder of the Roman church in 42 C.E.[17] The traditions that Peter as well as Paul were the "founders" of the Roman Christian community most likely stem from their martyrdoms in Rome and the possession of their mortal remains by the Roman church.[18] By the time he writes to the Romans, Paul has not yet visited the congregation and mentions that the church had already been in place "for many years" (Rom 15:23). The ecclesiastical traditions do not offer viable evidence that Peter was indeed the founder of the Christian congregation at Rome. The traditions appear to be offering a theory on where Peter may have gone after he left Jerusalem for the period of time recorded in Acts 12:17. By Acts 15 he had returned for the Jerusalem council in 49 C.E. (cf. Gal 2:7–9). In his letter Paul never hints at any earlier activity by Peter in Rome (15:20–23). Luke's Acts does not connect Peter with the Roman church. Luke instead suggests that the church originated with "visitors from Rome" who were present in Jerusalem at the major pilgrimage feast of Pentecost in Acts 2:10. These sojourners were converted and subsequently returned home.[19] These early converts to Christianity would, then, have taken the message of the Jewish Messiah Jesus back to Rome. If Christianity in Rome began just after Pentecost, Paul's reference to an established church in Rome "for many years" would make sense.

CLAUDIUS'S EDICT EXPELLING THE JEWS

If Christianity in Rome did indeed begin shortly after Pentecost, it left little trace of its existence prior to the late 40s C.E., several years later. The second-century historian Suetonius offers a glimpse into the life of the early Roman "Christians." In his biography of the Caesars, Suetonius mentions that Claudius "expelled the Jews who were making constant disturbances at the instigation of Chrestus" (*Claud.* 25.4). Suetonius may have confused the

---

[17] Eusebius, *Hist. eccl.* 2.14.6; 2.25.5–8; Irenaeus, *Haer.* 3.1.1. These traditions are further circumstantial evidence of the ultimately Jewish origin of Roman Christianity.

[18] Ign. *Rom.* 4:3; Irenaeus, *Haer.* 3.1.1, 3.3.2.

[19] On the other hand, the suggestion must remain tentative. James S. Jeffers (*Conflict at Rome: Social Order and Hierarchy in Early Christianity* [Minneapolis: Fortress, 1991], 12) contends that the word for "visitor" (ἐπιδημῶν) can also refer to a resident alien (see Acts 17:21), and that the word in Acts 2:5 for "one who dwells" (κατοικῶν) in Jerusalem may also be a technical term for a resident alien in the city.

name Christus, or Christ, with Chrestus. Christus was virtually unknown as a proper name in Rome at the time, and the two names were pronounced the same way. Chrestus, on the other hand, was a very common name for slaves and freedmen in Rome. Harry J. Leon, in his important study on the Jews in Rome, lists 550 Jewish names; Chrestus, though common elsewhere, is not in the list.[20] It is difficult to imagine that a current or former slave could have caused such an uproar within the Jewish community in Rome. Nor is there any corroborating evidence for a Jewish rabble-rousing extremist at Rome named Chrestus. Had the Jewish community been disturbed by an otherwise unknown figure, Suetonius would likely have written instead "at the instigation of *a certain* Chrestus" *(impulsore Chresto quodam).*[21]

The confusion of the names Chrestus and Christus would continue well into the following centuries. One of the major Greek manuscript witnesses to the NT text, the Sinaiticus, spells "Christian" in Acts 11:26; 26:28 and 1 Pet 4:16 *Chrēstianos* (Χρηστιανός).[22] Even when the proper spelling was well known, the defenders of Christianity lamented that their opponents enjoyed misspelling the word for Christian *Chrestianus* in order to imply to their readers that the founder of Christianity, this new "superstition," bore the name of a common slave.[23] Suetonius's report implies that "Chrestus" was present in Rome, which would be an absurd statement if referring to Jesus Christ. One explanation is that "the notorious confusion displayed in the words *impulsore Chresto* suggest a contemporary police record. It is well known that Suetonius merely reproduced his sources without attempting to evaluate them carefully."[24] The confusion by Suetonius is understandable since he does not otherwise reveal any knowledge about the person and life of Christ in *Nero* 16.2.[25] Writing seventy years after the events, he may have mistakenly assumed that Christ had actually been pres-

---

[20] Leon, *Jews of Ancient Rome*, 93–121. Rainer Riesner (*Paul's Early Period: Chronology, Mission Strategy, Theology* [Grand Rapids: Eerdmans, 1998], 165) adds that no evidence exists even outside Rome for a Jew ever being named Chrestus. This poses a problem for Stephen Benko's theory that "Chrestus" must have been an extremist ("zealot") leader in the Jewish community of Rome at the time ("The Edict of Claudius of A.D. 49 and the Instigator Chrestus," *TZ* 25 [1969]: 406–18).

[21] F. F. Bruce, "Christianity under Claudius," *BJRL* 44 (1961): 316.

[22] For deliberate play with the spelling, see Benko, "Edict of Claudius," 410.

[23] Thus Justin, *1 Apol.* 4; Tertullian, *Apol.* 3; Lactantius, *Inst.* 4.7. See also William L. Lane, "Social Perspectives on Roman Christianity during the Formative Years from Nero to Nerva: Romans, Hebrews, *1 Clement*," in *Judaism and Christianity in First-Century Rome* (ed. Karl P. Donfried and Peter Richardson; Grand Rapids: Eerdmans, 1998), 205. Suetonius's spelling may have been a deliberate aspersion; thus Riesner, *Paul's Early Period,* 165.

[24] Lane, "Roman Christianity," 204–205.

[25] Cf. Tacitus, *Ann.* 15.44, who is better informed; Irina Levinskaya, *The Book of Acts in Its Diaspora Setting,* vol. 5 in *The Book of Acts in its First Century Setting* (ed. Bruce W. Winter; Grand Rapids: Eerdmans, 1996), 179 n 53. Levinskaya (pp. 179–181) further contends, on the basis of the manuscript evidence, that one cannot be certain that Tacitus knew the correct spelling of "Christ" or "Christian."

ent. The brevity and ambiguity of the "Chrestus" comment also permits reference to the "Christ-movement" in Rome, the advocates of "Chrestus," rather than to the presence of Christ.[26]

The most plausible understanding of Suetonius's reference, then, is that there had been an uproar in the Jewish community in Rome as a result of those promoting "Chrestus" or Christ. Apparently some in the Jewish community were opposing others who accepted Jesus as Messiah, and the conflicts were severe enough to warrant an imperial banishment of the Jews from Rome. Acts 18:2 offers corroborating evidence: Paul in Corinth "found a Jew named Aquila . . . who had recently [προσφάτως] come from Italy with his wife Priscilla, because Claudius had ordered all the Jews to leave Rome." The couple had been forced to leave Rome because of an edict of Claudius regarding the Jews. Acts indicates that there had been similar conflicts between advocates of Christ and synagogue Jews during this period elsewhere (13:42–52; 17:1–9).

The fourth-century writer Orosius (*Hist. adv. pag.* 7.6.15–16) dates to 49 C.E. the expulsion under Claudius to which Suetonius refers. Orosius claims that he found the date in Josephus's history, but Josephus's extensive extant works nowhere mention the expulsion under Claudius, let alone its date.[27] Orosius's date, however, is corroborated by further considerations. First, Acts 18:2 independently suggests the date 49 C.E.[28] Although scholars vary in their assessments of Acts' historical accuracy, Paul's period in Corinth in Acts 18, when he met Aquila and Priscilla, can be fairly precisely dated.[29] During Paul's eighteen-month stay in Corinth, according to 18:12–17, he met the proconsul Gallio. An inscription permits scholars to date Gallio's tenure in Achaia and Corinth in all probability to the summer of 51 C.E.[30] Priscilla and Aquila's departure from Rome in 49 C.E., Orosius's date, would neatly dovetail with Paul's meeting the couple in Corinth not

---

[26] Riesner, *Paul's Early Period,* 166.

[27] The source of Orosius's information may have been Julius Africanus (who drew upon Josephus); see Kirsopp Lake, "The Chronology of Acts," in *The Acts of the Apostles,* part 1 of *The Beginnings of Christianity* (ed. F. J. Foakes Jackson and Kirsopp Lake; Grand Rapids: Baker, 1979), 5:459; and Riesner, *Paul's Early Period,* 184–85.

[28] On the independence of Orosius and Acts, see Riesner's argumentation in *Paul's Early Period,* 182–86. Acts 18:2 does not cite a 49 C.E. date, but the date is derived by means of the Gallio inscription (see the following discussion)

[29] For a more critical assessment of Acts' historicity, see Paul J. Achtemeier, *The Quest for Unity in the New Testament Church* (Philadelphia: Fortress, 1987), esp. 67–74. For an excellent defense of Acts' historicity, see Colin Hemer, *The Book of Acts in the Setting of Hellenistic History* (ed. Conrad H. Gempf; Winona Lake, Ind.: Eisenbrauns, 1990). Abraham J. Malherbe (*The Letters to the Thessalonians* [AB 32B; New York: Doubleday, 2000], 55–71) and Riesner (*Paul's Early Period,* 29–31, 412–15) argue that this particular section of Acts has proven especially reliable when compared with Paul's own letters or the extrabiblical evidence.

[30] Jerome Murphy-O'Connor, "Paul and Gallio," *JBL* 112 (1993): 315–17; Riesner, *Paul's Early Period,* 207.

long thereafter.[31] Second, 47–52 C.E. was a time in Claudius's reign when he was actively engaged in a campaign to curb the growth of foreign cults and to reestablish the old Roman religious rites.[32] The Jewish expulsion would not be out of character with Claudius's actions during these years.

Several scholars have supposed that Claudius expelled all the Jews from Rome. This is certainly a valid way of translating Suetonius's text *(Iudaeos impulsore Chresto assidue tumultuantis Roma expulit):* "Since the Jews were constantly making disturbances at the instigation of Chrestus, he expelled them from Rome." If Claudius expelled all the Jews from Rome, then certainly the Jewish Christian presence would have been severely diminished, forcing a complete social restructuring of the Roman Christian community.[33] But the assumption of a complete expulsion of the Jews under Claudius is fraught with insurmountable problems. The Roman historian Tacitus nowhere mentions an expulsion of the Jews in his record of this period *(Ann.* 12). Nor does Josephus mention it.

The only corroborating evidence for an expulsion of Jews from Rome is Acts' reference to the arrival of Priscilla and Aquila in Corinth from Rome. Dio Cassius, another Roman historian, likewise nowhere mentions the mass expulsion to which Suetonius refers, but he does record an earlier action by Claudius to ban the Jews from meeting. Dio Cassius indicates that Claudius took this action because he *could not* expel them *(Hist.* 60.6.6). The Jews in Rome, a population likely near forty to fifty thousand, were simply too numerous to be expelled. By way of contrast, the historians all record the massive operation when the emperor Tiberius expelled four thousand Jewish men of draftable age in 19 C.E.[34] If tens of thousands of Jews had been expelled, one would expect that such an event would have left an even greater imprint in the pages of the historians, but such is not the case. The Romans were constantly expelling people, whether astrologers, fortune-tellers, or cult leaders. The senate would agree to a decree of expulsion and then the commanders of the army would or would not enforce it. Expulsions were haphazard affairs.[35] Tacitus in his *Annals* records a telling instance: "The expulsion of the astrologers from Italy was ordered by a drastic and *impotent* decree of the senate"

---

[31] On the other hand, if the couple had not gone directly to Corinth from Rome, the date of their departure from Rome prior to these additional travels may be earlier than the late 40s. An earlier dating would not dovetail as well with Orosius.

[32] Lake, "Chronology of Acts," 460; Lane, "Roman Christianity," 205. Riesner, *Paul's Early Period,* 194–201.

[33] The classic exposition of this view is Wolfgang Wiefel's "The Jewish Community in Ancient Rome and the Origins of Roman Christianity," in *The Romans Debate* (ed. Karl P. Donfried; rev. ed.; Peabody, Mass.: Hendrickson, 1991), 85–101.

[34] Josephus, *Ant.* 18.3.5 §§83–84; Tacitus, *Ann.* 2.85; Suetonius, *Tib.* 36; Dio Cassius, *Hist.* 57.18.5.

[35] Tacitus, *Hist.* 1.22 (astrologers); Ramsay Macmullen, *Enemies of the Roman Order: Treason, Unrest, and Alienation in the Empire* (Cambridge: Harvard University Press, 1966), 125–26, 132–33.

(emphasis mine).[36] "Administrative action required both policy and the will to act on it. Rome's will to act in such cases was motivated by civil disturbances or the lobbying of concerned parties (e.g., informants)."[37]

Josephus's omission of an expulsion of the Jews under Claudius is very telling for other reasons as well. Although not presenting Claudius in the best light, Josephus nevertheless characterizes Claudius as supportive of the Jews. The Jewish ruler Agrippa I was raised in Rome and socialized with the future emperors Gaius and Claudius (*Ant.* 18.6.1 §§143–146; 18.6.4 §§165– 166). Agrippa I undertook perilous negotiations with the Roman senate in order to gain its endorsement of Claudius as the new emperor (*Ant.* 19.4.1 §§236–247; cf. 19.5.1 §§274–275). Josephus relates that Claudius issued edicts confirming Judean rights in the empire and Jewish civic status in Alexandria (*Ant.* 19.5.2 §§278–291; cf. 19.6.3 §§302–311). Josephus even narrates how Claudius overruled his governors in favor of the Jews (*Ant.* 15.11.4 §407//20.1.2 §§7–14; *J.W.* 2.12.7 §245//*Ant.* 20.6.3 §136).[38] A mass expulsion of the Jews, had such an incredible event taken place, would have contradicted Josephus's overall portrayal of Claudius and required some explanation. For the benefit of his Roman audience, Josephus's habit was to explain away as the fault of other groups what might reflect badly on the Jews. So Josephus would not only have had to explain away such an expulsion in light of his depiction of Claudius; he would also have wanted to exonerate the Jews lest such an expulsion offer an obvious counterexample to his favorable portrayal of his own people.[39]

Scholars have been left to explore other approaches to the history of the period since a mass expulsion of all Jews from Rome under Claudius cannot be substantiated apart from the Suetonius account. Furthermore, the Suetonius text itself need not be translated in such a way as to suggest such a large-scale action. Suetonius may be saying that it was those Jews involved in the "Chrestus" disturbance who were expelled from Rome ("He expelled from Rome the Jews constantly making disturbances at the instigation of Chrestus").[40] In other words, Suetonius's reference to the expulsion of "the

---

[36] Tacitus, *Ann.* 12.52 (Jackson, LCL).

[37] James C. Walters, *Ethnic Issues in Paul's Letter to the Romans: Changing Self-Definitions in Earliest Roman Christianity* (Valley Forge, Pa.: Trinity Press International, 1993), 43.

[38] Steve Mason, " 'For I Am Not Ashamed of the Gospel' (Rom. 1.16): The Gospel and the First Readers of Romans," in *Gospel in Paul: Studies on Corinthians, Galatians, and Romans for Richard N. Longenecker* (ed. L. Ann Jervis and Peter Richardson; JSNTSup 108; Sheffield, England: Sheffield Academic Press, 1994), 265; Benko, "Edict of Claudius, 407–8.

[39] On Josephus's pattern of exoneration of the Jews in general, see Steve Mason, *Josephus and the New Testament* (2d ed.; Peabody, Mass: Hendrickson, 2003), 55–145.

[40] William L. Lane, *Hebrews 1–8* (WBC 47; Dallas: Word Books, 1991), lxiv–lxv; idem, "Roman Christianity," 204; E. Mary Smallwood, *The Jews under Roman Rule: From Pompey to Diocletian* (SJLA 20; Leiden: E. J. Brill, 1976), 216.

Jews" may very well have referred to a small-scale action involving only the ringleaders of the conflict.

Likewise, although Luke asserts in Acts 18:2 that "all the Jews" had been expelled from Italy (!), he often employs the word "all" in his narratives in a nonliteral, exaggerated sense.[41] The expelled group in Acts 18:2 would simply have been all those involved in the conflict to which Claudius's edict had been directed, and the verse need not have implied that every Jew in Italy was expelled. Luke may also be referring to the wording of the edict itself rather than to the execution of the edict. Such an action on Claudius's part, even if much more limited than a mass expulsion, could still have violently disrupted the population of Christians in the Roman synagogues.

The expulsion of the Jews under Claudius to which Suetonius refers should not be confused with another, earlier action by the emperor.[42] In Dio Cassius's record of the year 41 C.E., Claudius ordered the Jews "not to hold meetings." The historian adds that it was impossible for Claudius to expel the Jews because of their number, a statement at odds with Suetonius's claim that an expulsion did happen. These two assertions are contradictory only if they refer to the same event.[43] Claudius's actions toward the beginning of his reign in 41 C.E. quite often favored the Jews. For instance, his establishment of a system of redress for adherents of the Jewish religion in Alexandria in 41 C.E. may have generally strengthened the status of Jews throughout the empire.[44] A mass expulsion of the Jews early in his career as emperor would have been at odds with his policies. Although Orosius's dating of the expulsion to 49 C.E. is based on a source other than Josephus, this other source does not appear to be Acts 18. Orosius and Acts 18 are both independent witnesses to an expulsion in 49.[45] Some scholars have therefore theorized that since Claudius's ban on meetings in 41 did not work, he took

---

[41] See, e.g., Acts 2:5, 47; 3:9, 11, 18; 4:21; 5:11, 34; 8:1, 9–10; 9:35; 10:12, 22, 41; 19:10. Robert G. Hoerber ("The Decree of Claudius in Acts 18:2," *CTM* 31 [1960] 692–93) suggests that if πάντας ("all") is in the predicate position, Acts 18:2 would never have referred to the totality of all the Jews in Rome (as that would require the attributive position).

[42] Levinskaya, *Book of Acts,* 174.

[43] Along with the difference over an expulsion, Suetonius claims that there were Jewish tumults; Dio speaks only of the potential of tumult. Suetonius says that Claudius acted against the Jews, but Dio that he acted against Jewish institutions. Dixon Slingerland notes these differences and adds, "In reality, until it has been demonstrated that [Dio Cassius and Suetonius] refer to the same event, no disagreement exists between the two accounts. In other words, such argumentation is circular" ("Acts 18:1–17 and Luedemann's Pauline Chronology," *JBL* 109 [1990]: 688–90).

[44] Against the theory that Jews had enjoyed legal privileges since Julius Caesar, see Ben Witherington III, *The Acts of the Apostles: A Socio-rhetorical Commentary* (Grand Rapids: Eerdmans, 1998), 541–44.

[45] See Riesner, *Paul's Early Period,* 182–86.

the more drastic measure in 49 of expelling Jews from Rome because of their quarrel over "Chrestus," or Christ. Such a reconstruction would agree with Aquila's and Priscilla's "recent" arrival in Corinth from Rome, which cannot be dated as early as 41.[46] If this interpretation of the Suetonius record of Claudius's decree is correct, the implication is that the Roman Christians had not severed their ties with the Jewish synagogues before the expulsion. Jews, both Christian and non-Christian, had been associating with each other in the synagogues. Suetonius represents the dispute as an intra-Jewish conflict. If Claudius expelled only the ringleaders in the conflict, then most certainly the Jewish advocates of "Chrestus" who had caused the stir at Rome among the Jews would have been among those expelled. The Jewish Christian presence in Rome would have been decimated.

After drawing the attention of the Roman imperium, the Jewish synagogues would likely have taken measures to distance themselves from the emerging Christian movement.[47] Certainly relations between Christbelievers and non-Christ-believing Jews with(in) the synagogues, strained prior to the Claudian edict, would have worsened as a result of the edict. "The edict in effect drove a wedge between [Christ-believers and non-Christian Jews in Rome] by dramatically communicating—especially to non-Christian Jews—that it would be in their best interests to go their separate ways."[48] If Roman Christians had previously been indistinguishable from ordinary synagogue members, where would Christians worship after the Jewish expulsion necessitated a split? Although Claudius's edict likely expelled the Jewish Christian instigators and perhaps a few of the more prominent Gentile Christian God-fearers involved in the conflict, no doubt other Gentile Christians would have remained behind.[49] The Christians who had been left behind after the expulsion would become the core of a new church in Rome. For the first time Christianity in Rome would become a Gentile phenomenon. No longer would Christians have been welcome to meet in the Jewish synagogues. They would have had to form their own house churches.

---

[46] Riesner (ibid., 176–79) provides additional evidence as to why Dio Cassius and Suetonius cannot be referring to the same event.

[47] Too much discussion of the Roman situation has remained fixated on the return of Jewish Christians to Rome after the expiration of the expulsion edict. A more plausible reconstruction of the situation at Rome prior to Paul's letter must account for the immediate aftermath of the expulsion of Jewish Christians.

[48] James C. Walters, "Romans, Jews, and Christians: The Impact of the Romans on Jewish/Christian Relations in First Century Rome," in *Judaism and Christianity in First-Century Rome* (ed. Karl P. Donfried and Peter Richardson; Grand Rapids: Eerdmans, 1998), 178. On the possible expulsion of Gentile God-fearers in the conflict, see Walters, *Ethnic Issues*, 58–59.

[49] For an excellent overview of the issues and evidence for God-fearers, see McKnight, *Light among the Gentiles,* 110–15; also Alan F. Segal, *Paul the Convert: The Apostolate and Apostasy of Saul the Pharisee* (New Haven: Yale University Press, 1990), 93–96.

By the time Christian Jews such as Aquila and Priscilla returned to Rome after 54 C.E., the Roman church would have existed apart from the synagogues for over five years. "Because the self-identity of these Christians was not shaped in a Jewish context they were less likely to conform to Jewish practices. Roman Christianity lacked significant 'Jewish' presence for about five years, until the death of Claudius (54 C.E.)."[50] A minority of Roman Christians had learned of Christ in the synagogues as God-fearers several years before, but the majority would now be Gentiles who joined the movement after the separation from the synagogues. A Christian population that had originally consisted primarily of Jewish believers would now be losing its Jewish character and would be faced with the problem of its Jewish origin. New converts who had never associated with the Jewish religious assemblies would not have had the same appreciation for Judaism as the earlier members of the church. This would have raised new issues for Roman Christianity, not the least of which would have been the role of the Jewish Law and the Jewish heritage. Tensions would have arisen over Jewish customs and identity. Gentiles who previously associated with the synagogues before the expulsion might have preferred a Law-observant lifestyle as God-fearers whereas newer members likely cared little for such practices and perhaps scorned them. Christian churches would no doubt have faced an identity crisis as new Christ-believers joined their ranks. The fact that Paul's letter addresses the relationship between Christianity and its Jewish heritage is hardly surprising.

The separation process, which began in the synagogues as the aftermath of the Claudian edict, likely continued as the Jews distanced themselves from the Christians. Whereas Suetonius does not distinguish the Jewish followers of "Chrestus" from other Jews under Claudius in 49 C.E., "Christians" were apparently a distinct and recognizable group to many in Rome by the time of Nero's persecution.[51] Such a rapid change from 49 to 64 C.E. most likely was the result of the Jews' lobbying to distance themselves from the Christians after the Claudian edict. The Jews would have wanted to avoid further negative attention from the imperium. The persecution of Christians under Nero may even have been a side effect of this attempt at differentiation. At the time of Nero's persecution of the Christians, the Jews had strong ties to the imperial court. Nero was married from 62 to 65 C.E. to Poppaea Sabina, a God-fearer who according to Josephus would have been sympathetic to Judaism.[52] During this period two Judean embassies were successful with Nero even though they made requests contrary to Roman interests. Josephus traces these results to Poppaea's mediation (*Ant.*

---

[50] Walters, *Ethnic Issues,* 60.

[51] Suetonius, *Nero* 16.2. "Nero's persecution presupposes that Roman administrators could distinguish between Christians and Jews when sufficiently motivated to do so" (Walters, *Ethnic Issues,* 62).

[52] Josephus, *Ant.* 20.8.11 §195.

20.8.11 §195; *Life* 16). Jewish influence in the court may have helped lead to the targeting of Christians as distinct from Jews or at least distinct from *legitimate* Jews.[53] Although the believers in Christ at Rome were not called "Christians" until 70 C.E., they were likely recognized by many in Rome as a group distinct from the Jews in the mid-sixties C.E. during this period of intense persecution.[54]

THE EVIDENCE OF PAUL'S LETTER

What has been sketched so far is a hypothetical reconstruction, based on what little external evidence is available, of the composition of the Roman Christian congregations. The critical test for any theoretical reconstruction is its ability to incorporate Paul's Letter to the Romans.[55] Some scholars question whether Paul's letter offers clear and sufficient evidence for a specific reconstruction of the Roman situation and of the identity of the "weak" and the "strong."[56] When Paul addressed specific situations in the various churches he founded, he generally identified the situations more directly than he did in Romans. He had never visited the Roman congregation. Perhaps the content of his letter reflects circumstances in Paul's own life and ministry at this turning point in his apostolic career after his work in the East was completed (Rom 15:18–24) rather than circumstances in Rome. He had completed the collection for the Jerusalem saints and was preparing to deliver it (15:25–28). The apostle to the Gentiles was anxious about the reception of the collection at Jerusalem. This collection embodied Paul's hopes for the unity of Jewish and Gentile Christians (15:30–33). Jerusalem's acceptance of the gift would ensure that there would remain one Christian church and not two. A positive reception of the Gentiles' gifts would legitimate the status of the Gentile churches founded by Paul.

The view that the letter reflects only Paul's own concerns is problematic on a number of counts. In the first place, Paul indicates in Romans 16 that he knew at least twenty-seven people in Rome. He would therefore

---

[53] Smallwood, *Jews under Roman Rule,* 217–19; Stephen Benko, *Pagan Rome and the Early Christians* (Bloomington: Indiana University Press, 1984), 14–21, esp. 20.

[54] Acts 11:26; Tacitus, *Ann.* 15.44; Suetonius, *Nero* 16.2; *1 Clem.* 5:1; 6:1.

[55] Dixon Slingerland's excellent essay ("Chrestus: Christus?" in *The Literature of Early Rabbinic Judaism: Issues in Talmudic Redaction and Interpretation* [ed. Alan J. Avery-Peck; New Perspectives on Ancient Judaism 4; Lanham, Md.: University Press of America, 1989], 133–44) demonstrates that the external evidence for a reconstruction of the Roman church's situation is not as conclusive as one would prefer. Hypotheses must necessarily remain tentative, but Slingerland does not account for the potentially strong corroborating force of Paul's letter itself.

[56] E.g., Wayne A. Meeks, "Judgment and the Brother: Romans 14:1–15:13," in *Tradition and Interpretation in the New Testament* (ed. Gerald F. Hawthorne and Otto Betz; Grand Rapids: Eerdmans, 1987), 290–300.

have possessed some knowledge of the Roman church through his con-
tacts.[57] Indeed, specific knowledge of the situation at Rome may be evident
at several points in the letter: Paul commends the Romans' faith (1:8), matu-
rity (15:14), and obedience as "known to all" (16:19). In 6:17 he refers to the
"teaching" the Romans had received. Paul is confident that his instructions
in 15:14–15 are serving only as "a reminder" for the addressees. Likewise in
16:17 he speaks of the teaching they have learned. Some commentators
even think that Paul's instructions in 13:6–7 regarding taxes are responding
to a developing situation in Rome at the time.[58] Such passages cumulatively
indicate that Paul has at least some knowledge of the situation within the
Roman church.[59] Nevertheless, Paul's general indirectness with respect to
the Roman situation is understandable since he had not been there before.
His policy had been one of noninterference in the churches founded by others, and this policy would certainly have included a Roman congregation
that he had never visited (15:20–22; 2 Cor 10:13–16). The Letter to the
Romans would therefore represent a departure from his usual policy, and
this alone may account for the tactful reserve.

Some scholars have thought that Paul is only generalizing to the
Romans comments originally targeted to the more specific situation elsewhere at Corinth, but the differences between such key pasages as 1 Corinthians 8–10 and Romans 14–15 suggest diverging situations. Paul does not
mention food offered to idols in Romans as he does in 1 Cor 8:1, 4, 7, 10
and 10:19. In Romans he does not emphasize "knowledge" as he does 1 Cor
8:1–11. Paul does not refer in Romans to the "conscience" as he does in
1 Cor 8:7, 10, 12; 10:25, 27–29. Paul's admonition to "welcome" or "accept"
one another in Rom 14:1, 3; 15:7 (twice) is not found in 1 Corinthians. The
difference between the strong and the weak in Romans centers on faith
(Rom 14:1, 22, 23 [twice]), but faith is never an issue in 1 Corinthians 8–10.
Nor do the Corinthian "weak" consider meat to be "common" or "unclean"
(κοινός) as do the Roman "weak."[60] Paul says nothing about idol meat in

---

[57] Paul's knowledge of the Roman situation is rendered more likely by the
general recognition of Romans 16 as an integral part of the letter; see esp. Harry
Gamble Jr., *The Textual History of the Letter to the Romans: A Study in Textual and Literary Criticism* (SD 42; Grand Rapids: Eerdmans, 1977).

[58] James D. G. Dunn, *Romans 9–16* (WBC 38B; Dallas: Word, 1988), 759. In
these verses Paul is drawing upon conventional Jewish wisdom and early Christian
tradition (see, e.g., 1 Pet 2:13–17; Wis 6:3–4). These traditions do not, however,
offer advice regarding taxation. Paul's comments in this regard therefore appear to
have been motivated by his knowledge of an issue specific to Roman Christianity.

[59] For additional argumentation that Paul has some knowledge of the Roman
situation, see James C. Miller, *The Obedience of Faith, the Eschatological People of God,
and the Purpose of Romans* (SBLDS 177; Atlanta: Society of Biblical Literature, 2000),
116–18.

[60] Mark Reasoner, "The Theology of Romans 12:1–15:13," in *Romans,* vol. 3
of *Pauline Theology* (ed. David M. Hay and E. Elizabeth Johnson; Minneapolis: Fortress, 1995), 288–89 n. 5; Dunn, *Romans 9–16,* 795; John M. G. Barclay, "'Do We

Romans even as he mentions other specifics to the Romans that do not figure in his discussions with the Corinthians. He mentions, for instance, eating vegetables (Rom 14:2) and observing days (Rom 14:5), both of which appear aimed at the Roman situation. Romans 14:1–15:6 occupies a prominent position as the climax of Paul's exhortations to this community. Surely such a positioning in Paul's letter is based on the community's needs. The fact that Paul aligns himself with "the strong" in 15:1 demonstrates that he is aware of the issues and the parties involved at Rome.[61]

Furthermore, the unique aspects of the discussion in 1 Corinthians reflect similar emphases elsewhere in 1 Corinthians germane to the community. For instance, the Corinthians were puffed up with knowledge and were not bothered in their consciences by horrendous sins. One might similarly conclude from Romans 15 that foods that were "common" or "unclean" had been a stumbling block preventing some members of the church from welcoming or accepting others. Such a conclusion is strengthened by the extensive discussion of the Mosaic Law throughout the rest of the letter. Paul's Letter to the Romans, used carefully and critically, may therefore be of use in reconstructing the situation at Rome. Some have objected that the apostle's language admits of a more general application beyond a specific dispute over Jewish customs.[62] On the other hand, Paul may have phrased his discussion of Jewish customs in such a way as to be paradigmatic for other similar divisions among the Christians.[63] Or he may be attempting to proceed with tact by speaking more generally and obliquely since he has neither founded nor visited this church.[64]

Granted the exodus from Rome of Christian Jewish leaders after Claudius's edict in the wake of the conflict over "Chrestus," the question is whether the rest of the Christian Jews were expelled along with their leaders.[65] In other words, were there both Jews and Gentiles among the Roman Christians, or just Gentiles? The Letter to the Romans may offer the answer. In Rom 1:5–6 Paul refers to Jesus Christ as the one "through whom we have received grace and apostleship to bring about the obedience of faith *among all*

Undermine the Law?" A Study of Romans 14.1–15.6," in *Paul and the Mosaic Law* (ed. James D. G. Dunn; Tübingen: J. C. B. Mohr [Paul Siebeck], 1996), 287–308; Meeks, "Judgment and the Brother," 293.

[61] Barclay, " 'Do We Undermine the Law?' " 288–89; contra Meeks.

[62] Meeks, "Judgment and the Brother."

[63] E.g., Paul speaks of the weak who "observe the day" (Rom 14:5–6). Even if this refers to the Sabbath, "Paul's oblique approach puts no Roman group in the spotlight" (J. Paul Sampley, "The Weak and the Strong: Paul's Careful and Crafty Rhetorical Strategy in Romans 14:1–15:13," in *The Social World of the First Christians: Essays in Honor of Wayne A. Meeks* [ed. L. Michael White and O. Larry Yarbrough; Minneapolis: Fortress, 1995], 42). The chapters permit broader application even if pertaining primarily to Jewish customs.

[64] Thus Barclay, " 'Do We Undermine the Law?' " 289.

[65] I am using the terms "Jewish Christian"/"Gentile Christian" and "Christian Jew"/"Christian Gentile" interchangeably throughout this work.

the Gentiles for the sake of his name, *including* yourselves who are called to belong to Jesus Christ."[66] In 1:13 he writes, "I want you to know, brothers and sisters, that I have often intended to come to you (but thus far have been prevented), in order that I may reap some harvest among you as I have among the rest of the Gentiles" (καὶ ἐν ὑμῖν καθὼς καὶ ἐν τοῖς λοιποῖς ἔθνεσιν). When Paul addresses the Roman audience and then refers to "the rest" of the Gentiles, the most natural reading is that Paul is thereby implying the Gentile identity of the Roman audience.[67] He goes on to write in vv. 14–15, "I am a debtor to Greeks and to barbarians, both to the wise and to the foolish— hence also my eagerness to proclaim the gospel to you also who are in Rome." Paul says nothing of Christian Jews in Rome in these verses either.[68] Romans 6:17–22 provides strong evidence that the apostle is writing to a Gentile audience: Paul recalls for his readers their former sinful lives as heathens. They were slaves to "impurity" or "uncleanness" (τῇ ἀκαθαρσίᾳ) and "lawlessness" (ἀνομίᾳ). Although Jews are sinful as well and certainly transgress the law when they disobey it (2:17–28), the apostle never characterizes the Jews in his writings as "lawless" and "unclean." It is the Gentiles whose former ways may properly be characterized as "lawless" and "unclean" (cf. 2:14). In 11:13 Paul speaks directly to his audience and identifies them as "you Gentiles."[69] He never offers a corresponding "you Jews" (similarly 11:17–18, 24). Perhaps the most likely potential instance of "you Jews" is

---

[66] Another translation of Paul's wording would suggest that he is writing to the called *among* the Gentiles; the addressees need not themselves be Gentiles. The passage could refer to geographical location rather than ethnic makeup; C. E. B. Cranfield, *A Critical and Exegetical Commentary on the Epistle to the Romans* (2 vols.; ICC; Edinburgh: T&T Clark, 1975–1979), 1:68; see also Rom 15:15–16. On the other hand, in a letter so concerned with the ethnic distinction between Jew and Gentile, the ethnic interpretation of the verse is more probable than the geographical. Furthermore, Cranfield is unable to explain the καί ("also"), which implies that "the Roman Christians are *part of*—not just 'in the midst of'—the Gentiles of v. 5" (Douglas J. Moo, *The Epistle to the Romans* [NICNT; Grand Rapids: Eerdmans, 1996], 54 n.79).

[67] Cranfield (*Romans,* 1:20) contends Paul is stating that he hopes to bear fruit in Rome even as he has throughout the rest of the Gentile world. He is not necessarily implying that the Roman church is Gentile. Paul is using the word as an ethnic designation for non-Jews throughout the letter rather than as a designation for territory or nations. See, e.g., Rom 2:14, 24; 3:29; 9:24, 30; 11:11–13, 25; 15:9–12, 16.

[68] Mason ("'For I Am Not Ashamed of the Gospel,'" 271) thinks the reference to barbarians in Rome too insulting. Paul must be speaking of the "remainder" of the Gentiles beyond the Greek world in Spain. Mention of Spain, however, does not come until much later in the letter.

[69] As Stanley K. Stowers (*A Rereading of Romans: Justice, Jews, and Gentiles* [Fontes ad res judaicas spectantes; New Haven: Yale University Press, 1994], 288–89) points out, "The *menoun* with *de* after *hymin* makes it almost impossible to understand Paul as turning to one group within the letter's audience (the gentile portion) rather than to the letter's audience as a whole." He explains (p. 288), "The part of the sentence set in contrast by *menoun* corrects any mistaken impression that the discussion of Israel's future has no place in this letter so wholly addressed to gentiles and the gentile situation."

2:17–29, but interpreters have identified these verses as a rhetorical address since the section conforms to the ancient genre of a diatribe, in which fictive addressees were standard fare.[70] On the other hand, diatribal features are completely lacking in 11:13's address to "you Gentiles."[71]

Interpreters generally recognize Romans 16 as part of the original letter.[72] Since this chapter mentions a few Christian Jews, many have concluded that there must have been a significant Jewish presence in the Roman Christian congregation at the time. Paul's Jewish coworkers, Prisca and Aquila (Acts 18:2), are present. They no doubt share Paul's view that the Law is not necessary for Christian salvation. Peter Lampe in his important study of Romans 16 cites three names from this chapter that are paralleled in the Jewish inscriptions from Rome—Maria, Rufus, and Julia—but he points out that these names could equally refer to Gentiles. Indeed, they probably were Gentiles since Paul does not call them his "compatriots."[73] Interpreters usually list Andronicus and Junia (v. 7) and Herodion (v. 11) as Jewish. They are all identified as "compatriots" (συγγενεῖς), and Paul has already referred to his fellow Jews by means of the same word earlier in 9:3. On the other hand, this Greek word (συγγενής) ordinarily means "relative" or "kin" and not "fellow national." The six non-Pauline occurrences of συγγενής in the NT all mean "family member." Whereas the context of Rom 9:3 suggests "compatriot," nothing in Romans 16 requires a departure from the usual meaning of the word as "relative."[74] Paul has been metaphorically employing terms of familial affection all through the chapter. He speaks of "my beloved" (ἀγαπητόν μου) in vv. 5, 8, 9, and 12, "brother"/"sister" in vv. 14, 15, and 17, "fellow worker" in vv. 3, 6, 9, and

---

[70] On the other hand, Douglas A. Campbell ("Determining the Gospel through Rhetorical Analysis in Paul's Letter to the Roman Christians," in *Gospel in Paul: Studies on Corinthians, Galatians, and Romans for Richard N. Longenecker* [ed. L. Ann Jervis and Peter Richardson; JSNTSup 108; Sheffield, England: Sheffield Academic Press, 1984], 325–31), in an important cautionary note, has responded that diatribal rhetoric never addresses an entirely imaginary interlocutor with no connection to a context. Nevertheless, to specify members of the church as Jewish overextends Campbell's evidence. The Romans may simply be attracted to, or interested in, Jewish customs without actually being Jewish.

[71] In 4:1 Paul refers to Abraham as "our ancestor according to the flesh," but after 2:27–29 this could apply to Gentile Christians as well, and the verse may also be translated as an interrogative, with Richard B. Hays ("Have We Found Abraham to Be Our Forefather according to the Flesh? A Reconsideration of Rom 4:1," *NovT* 27 [1985]: 76–98): "Have we found Abraham to be our forefather with respect to the flesh?" Thus Paul specifies in 4:11–12 that he is the forefather of both the circumcised and the uncircumcised who believe.

[72] See Gamble, *Textual History of the Letter to the Romans;* Dunn, *Romans 9–16,* 884–85; Karl Paul Donfried, "A Short Note on Romans 16," in *The Romans Debate* (ed. Karl P. Donfried; rev. ed.; Peabody, Mass.; Hendrickson, 1991), 44–52.

[73] Peter Lampe, "The Roman Christians of Romans 16," in *The Romans Debate* (ed. Karl P. Donfried; rev. ed.; Peabody, Mass.: Hendrickson, 1991), 224–25.

[74] Mason, "For I Am Not Ashamed of the Gospel," 259.

12, and "mother" in v. 13. Paul is using such "affectionate language" "to build bridges" with the Roman congregation.[75] Even if one could be certain of the Jewish identity of more people than the potential handful listed in Romans 16, their numbers were so few that Paul felt comfortable addressing the Roman Christians as non-Jews.[76] Cumulatively, the evidence warrants a description of the Roman congregation as almost exclusively Gentile.[77]

Although Paul addresses his audience as Gentiles, it is difficult to account for the contents of this letter apart from the influence of Judaism in Rome. What would necessitate such an extended discussion of the Mosaic Law, justification by faith, circumcision, and God's faithfulness to Israel? These are precisely the sorts of issues that do *not* figure in Paul's letter to the Gentile Thessalonians, a congregation affected very little, if at all, by a Jewish Christian constituency. Paul even claims that his Roman readers are, in whole or in part, "people who know the law" (Rom 7:1; cf. 15:4), and he offers an extended discussion of the fate of ethnic Israel in chapters 9–11. Whereas the scriptural passages Paul cites in his Letter to the Galatians appear to be largely those already in use by his opponents or passages employed by Paul to counter his opponents' texts, he assumes that his Roman addressees will be able to follow his reasoning as he freely draws upon and discusses the scriptural heritage of the Jews. Paul assumes that his Roman audience knows the Scriptures. This knowledge of the Jewish Scriptures (including perhaps even the "mercy seat" [ἱλαστήριον; NRSV: "sacrifice of atonement"] in 3:25) can only be accounted for if the Roman Gentile Christians have been in conversation with, and have learned from, those who had participated in Jewish worship and who had been instructed in the LXX translation of the Jewish Scriptures.[78] The LXX was not otherwise known in Greco-Roman circles.[79] Church tradition corroborates that Roman Christianity was ultimately indebted to the Jewish community for its knowledge of the Scriptures:

> It is established that there were Jews living in Rome in the times of the apostles, and that those Jews who had believed [in Christ] passed on to the Romans the tradition that they ought to profess Christ but keep the law. . . .

---

[75] As Mason points out (ibid., 260).

[76] Even granting the greeting of Jewish Christians in Rome, Stanley Stowers points out that this would hardly be decisive in determining the addressees of the letter: "Ancient letters frequently send salutations to individuals who are not the encoded readers" (*Rereading of Romans,* 33).

[77] Other arguments bandied about in the debate are less conclusive. E.g., Paul speaks of Israel in the third person in 9:3–5, a fact that suggests to some a Gentile audience. But he also speaks of Gentiles in the third person in 9:24, 30; 11:11–12, and his own people in 9:3–5 do not believe in Christ (10:1–2; 11:23, 28, 31). The Israelites in question are not potential Jewish Christian addressees. These verses therefore offer little help in identifying the addressees.

[78] For a critical review of the "mercy seat" identification in Rom 3:25, see Das, *Paul, the Law, and the Covenant,* 132–42.

[79] John J. Collins, *Between Athens and Jerusalem: Jewish Identity in the Hellenistic Diaspora* (2d ed.; Grand Rapids: Eerdmans, 2000), 6.

One ought not to condemn the Romans, but to praise their faith; because without seeing any signs or miracles and without seeing any of the apostles, they nevertheless accepted faith in Christ, although according to a Jewish rite *[ritu licet Judaico]*.[80]

Ambrosiaster's description confirms that the Gentile Roman church had its origin within a Jewish Christian context.

Romans 14–15 suggests that a contingent within the Roman congregation, the "weak," was seeking to keep Jewish customs and the Law. In Rom 14:5–6 the "weak" "observe the day," a possible reference to Jewish Sabbaths, feasts, and fast days. A regular weekly insistence on Sabbath observance by a part of the congregation would certainly have caused some friction with those not honoring the Sabbath.[81] Although non-Christian Gentiles certainly observed special days as well, the special days of pagans would not likely be a point of contention between two factions within the church. In Rom 14:14 the "weak" see certain foods as "common" or "unclean" (κοινός), a classification derived from the Mosaic Law (see Mark 7:15–23; Acts 10:14, 28; 11:8). The word Paul uses for "unclean" (κοινός) is never used in a Greek writing to express purity concerns apart from Judaism. The "weak" in 14:14 are therefore reckoning purity and impurity in accordance with the Mosaic Law.[82] In Rom 14:20 Paul declares all things "clean" (καθαρά), a term likewise used for ritual cleanliness in the Mosaic Law (see Acts 10:15; 11:9). The "weak" are avoiding meat and wine in favor of a diet consisting of vegetables and water (14:21; cf. 14:17).

Historically those observing Jewish customs would abstain from meat and wine in hostile circumstances where they had no control over their diet.[83] Some have theorized that the avoidance of meat on the part of these Roman church members reflected the same Neopythagorean influence as may have been impacting the Colossian congregation.[84] The problem with

---

[80] Ambrosiaster (ca. 375 C.E.) (PL 17:46). Citation from A. J. M. Wedderburn, *The Reasons for Romans* (Studies of the New Testament and Its World; Edinburgh: T&T Clark, 1988), 51; see also Raymond E. Brown and John P. Meier, *Antioch and Rome: New Testament Cradles of Catholic Christianity* (New York: Paulist, 1983), 110–111. See also the additional evidence cited by Mason, "'For I Am Not Ashamed of the Gospel'," 262.

[81] Barclay, "'Do We Undermine the Law?'" 292; again, the Jews were known in Rome for their practice of the Sabbath. See ibid., 296–99, for a discussion of the primary sources.

[82] Dunn, *Romans 9–16*, 818–20, Ulrich Wilckens, *Der Brief an die Römer* (3 vols.; 2d ed.; EKKNT 6; Neukirchener-Vluyn: Neukirchener, 1989), 3:112–13.

[83] Dan 1:8–16; Jdt 12:1–14; Esth 14:7, 17 LXX; Josephus, *Ant.* 4.6.8 §137; *Life* 13–14 (on captive Jewish priests' diet of "figs and nuts" in Rome). The Jews were known in Rome for their abstention from certain meats; see Barclay's discussion of the primary sources in "'Do We Undermine the Law?'" 294–95. On Jewish abstention from pagan, likely idolatrous meat and wine, see Esler's excellent discussion in *Galatians*, 92–116.

[84] Col 2:15–23; Heinrich Schlier, *Der Römerbrief* (HTKNT 6; Freiburg: Herder, 1977), 403–6; Wilckens, *Brief an die Römer*, 3:111–12.

a Neopythagorean rationale for the avoidance of meat and wine at Rome is that the "weak" are observing these practices "for the Lord" (14:6) and could lose their faith if forced to drop their customs (14:20). "It is hard to imagine Pythagorean vegetarianism being so closely wedded to Christian faith as to be an issue on which believers could feel their loyalty to God depended."[85] Pythagorean asceticism was a matter of personal choice. Why, then, would the "weak" consider their lifestyle a universal mandate for all and judge the "strong" in 14:2? Paul would certainly not be very accommodating of the "weak" if their views were the result of Gentile or pagan convictions (cf. the far less friendly approach in Colossians).[86]

Romans 15:7–13 provides additional evidence that the "weak" of whom Paul has spoken in the immediately preceding verses are observing Jewish customs. Paul urges Jews and Gentiles to welcome one another as Christ has welcomed them. This explicit return to Jews and Gentiles in Christ maintains the thread that has dominated the letter from its beginning in 1:16.[87] The "weak" appear, then, to be observing the Jewish customs addressed at length earlier in the letter.[88]

The most difficult problem with identifying the "weak" as those who have adopted a Jewish lifestyle is that the Jews in Rome were not in a situation that would have required complete abstinence from meat or wine. They were not being forced to consume unclean Gentile foods or wine that had been offered to the gods. On the contrary, the Jews were known for their use of wine (Plutarch, *Quaest. conv.* 4.6.2; Persius, *Sat.* 5.179–184). The large Jewish population in Rome guaranteed that kosher foods were readily available for their community. Why would those practicing Jewish customs refrain from meat and wine in Rome? The problem Paul addresses, however, had arisen as Law-observant and non-Law-observant Gentile Christians came together for their common meals.[89] Long-standing Jewish custom prevented the Law-observant from sharing the same meat and drink with non-Law-observant Gentiles at a meal. Most likely this was due to an abiding concern that the meat and wine had been sacrificed to the pagan deities.[90]

---

[85] As John M. G. Barclay has observed (" 'Do We Undermine the Law?' " 292).

[86] Ibid., 293.

[87] Paul has been explicitly discussing the relationship between Jews and Gentiles throughout Romans 2–3 and 9–11, and the same sorts of issues dominate the rest of the letter as well. In fact, Romans 14–15 builds on the preceding discussions. Paul's reprisal of "weak in faith" applies the notion of "faith" (πίστις) expounded throughout the letter.

[88] Many would conclude that the "weak" must be themselves Jews. Law-observant Gentile God-fearers may be a more viable option since Paul addresses the Romans as Gentiles.

[89] As Barclay has rightly pointed out (" 'Do We Undermine the Law?' " 291).

[90] See Esler's discussion of this point (*Galatians,* 93–116) and his interaction with E. P. Sanders, *Jewish Law from Jesus to the Mishnah: Five Studies* (Philadelphia: Trinity Press International, 1990), 272–83, and "Jewish Association with Gentiles and Galatians 2.11–14," in *The Conversation Continues: Studies in Paul and John in*

Law-observant Gentile Christians who had enjoyed relations as God-fearers with non-Christian Jews likely were accustomed to abstaining from eating the meat and wine of those who did not practice the Law, even though the non-Law-observant Gentiles in question were Christians with similar scruples with respect to meat and drink sacrificed to idols.[91]

Perhaps the key to unlocking the riddle of abstention from meat and wine in a locale where kosher food was available to Jews is the due recognition that Paul has identified the congregation explicitly as Gentiles. The Law-observant in the Roman congregation were the Gentiles who formerly associated and worshiped with the Jews. If the Jews in Rome were distancing themselves from the emerging Christ movement, difficulties may have arisen for Law-observant Gentile Christians. Cut off from their relationships with the Jewish quarter, Law-observant Christian Gentiles would have experienced difficulty obtaining the necessary kosher food items. They may have been forced to avoid pagan meat and wine in the same way as Law-observant Jews deprived of access to kosher nourishment throughout Jewish history. As an increasing number of non-Law-observant Gentiles joined a Christian movement that had been forced to meet apart from the synagogues, the Law-observant Gentiles would have felt increasingly threatened. The Law-observant would have faced social pressures to relinquish their practices as they found themselves in the minority, the "weak."[92] Newer converts likely shared their society's disdain for Jewish customs. Paul therefore includes in his letter instructions on how Jews and Gentiles are to relate to each other as well as on the role of the Mosaic Law in Christian existence in order to facilitate a healthy relationship between the non-Law-observant and Law-observant Gentiles in the Roman Christian congregations.

GENTILE CHRISTIANS STILL WITHIN THE JEWISH SYNAGOGUES?

Mark Nanos has offered a vigorous challenge to a supposed split between the Roman Christians and the synagogues. Nanos argues for a very different audience for the letter. Even more important, he has touted the results of his proposal as providing a richer and more accurate understanding of Paul's relationship with Judaism. Nanos believes that as Paul wrote to the Romans, the Roman Christian believers were not yet meeting in their own churches but were still gathering amid non-Christ-believing Jews for worship. Nanos points to the jealousy motif in Romans as proof of his thesis. Paul writes in Rom 11:22 that he hopes by his ministry to make the Jews jealous of his

---

Honor of J. Louis Martyn (ed. R. T. Fortna and B. R. Gaventa; Nashville: Abingdon, 1990), 170–88.

[91] Or perhaps not if 1 Corinthians 8–10 is any indication, but Paul does not identify meat sacrificed to idols as an issue in Rome as he had in Corinth.

[92] Horace (*Sat.* 1.9) offers an instance of a Gentile seeking to observe the Jewish Sabbath. The Gentile then describes himself as a "weaker brother."

success as a missionary among the Gentiles. If the Christians were already meeting apart from the synagogues and if the Christian and Jewish worshiping communities had already gone their separate paths, why would the Jews be jealous of what was happening elsewhere away from the synagogues and perhaps even apart from their full (or even partial) knowledge?[93] On the other hand, if Paul had been attracting more Gentile worshipers into the synagogues through his message about Christ, then non-Christ-believing Jews may have been jealous of Paul's ministry. If Nanos is right, when Paul wrote Romans, he realized that the letter would be read in the context of a synagogue subgroup of those who recognized Jesus as the Messiah amid those who did not. What Paul wrote in Romans is therefore directly relevant to the apostle's opinion of Judaism per se since Paul's Gentile Christian audience would be interacting directly with Jews within synagogue communities.

Not all of Nanos's arguments carry the same persuasive force. For instance, he argues that the Christians would not have been permitted to assemble apart from synagogues because of the official ban on unapproved religious associations in Rome.[94] The only way Christians could gather would have been in the officially sanctioned synagogues. But Gentile Christians were able to assemble apart from synagogues elsewhere (e.g., in Thessalonica). One can conceive of a similar situation in Rome. Nanos does not offer evidence that the local ban on unauthorized religious meetings in Rome was rigorously enforced against religious groups as his theory would require. Rome generally tolerated illicit religious groups "by default."[95] Either Rome lacked the means to stamp out all of these new movements among the foreign population or it lacked the resolve to do so.[96] The sheer number of such groups hindered enforcement unless a particular movement happened to draw attention to itself by its behavior.[97]

Perhaps the most crucial evidence for Nanos's approach is his exegesis of Rom 14:1–15:6. When Paul offered direction to the strong and the weak at Rome, Nanos identifies the weak as non-Christian Jews within the Jewish worshiping communities where the Christians are also gathering. Nanos asks a series of questions for those who think that the "weak in faith" must be Law-observant Christian Jews: Why doesn't Paul encourage these Christians to abandon the Law in order to mature and grow "strong" in their faith? Why would Paul encourage the strong not to judge the weak if he has already implicitly judged them by calling them weak? And if Paul is urging the strong to

---

[93] Mark D. Nanos, "The Jewish Context of the Gentile Audience Addressed in Paul's Letter to the Romans," *CBQ* 61 (1999): 303.

[94] Ibid., 286–88.

[95] See Walters's discussion in *Ethnic Issues*, 40–45 (relying on Waltzing and Garnsey).

[96] On general Roman tolerance of foreign religious movements, see again ibid., 40–45.

[97] Ibid., 16.

accommodate the weak, would that not endanger the strong since the strong might likewise be ensnared by the attractions of Law observance and thus be led to stumble? Why would Paul urge the weak to be convinced that their observance of the Law is "for the Lord" (14:5)?[98] These questions and others lead Nanos to question whether the weak are really Christian Jews after all. It makes better sense to consider the weak non-Christian Jews. Certainly the strong are admonished as Christ-believers in 14:15: "Do not destroy with your food him for whom Christ died." Paul as a believer in Christ numbered himself among the strong in 15:1. The strong were not observing Jewish practices since they ate all things (14:2) and did not regard the days (14:5) and drank wine.[99] The weak, on the other hand, are never identified as Christians, nor do their practices depart from Jewish customs. Paul never mentioned Christ in connection with the weak as he did with the strong (cf. 14:15). Nanos also observes that Paul never calls the Roman gathering a "church." The apostle calls the weak ones brothers and sisters in 14:10, and yet he clearly identified non-Christian Jews earlier in the letter as brothers and sisters (9:3–5).[100] Nanos concludes that Paul's audience is still assembling within the synagogues.[101] The "faith" of the weak must have been faith in God quite apart from any reference to Christ (14:1).[102] If Nanos's reconstruction is correct, the Gentile Christian strong in Rom 14:1–15:6 were being urged to respect non-Christian Jews as a people of faith. The Jews would not have recognized the full significance of Jesus Christ as Israel's Lord and Messiah. They would not have recognized that God was now including Gentiles in salvation, but they were still a people of faith even if "weak" in that faith.

Nanos's book won the 1996 National Jewish Book Award in the category of Jewish-Christian relations. The implications of Nanos's thesis for Paul's view of the Jews would be historic in changing the direction of thinking in Pauline scholarship and could help heal the long-standing rift between Jews and Christians. Nanos's Paul would be urging the Gentile Christian strong to be respectful of non-Christ-believing Jews. Although Christ is the full revelation of God, non-Christ-believing Jews are still "brothers and sisters" "in faith." The Gentiles, in the presence of non-Christian Jews, should adopt a Law-respecting way of life. They should live as "righteous Gentiles" in deference to those "weak in faith" in order that they might not cause the non-Christ-believing Jews to stumble and fall from their faith in the same God and Lord. Far from excluding non-Christ-believing Jews, Paul would be urging their inclusion with Christian Gentiles in one united people. The Christian Gentiles should even submit to the non-Christian Jewish synagogue

---

[98] Nanos, *Mystery of Romans,* 94–95.
[99] The weak are not pagans since they act "in honor of the Lord" in 14:6–7 and are accepted by God.
[100] Nanos, *Mystery of Romans,* 111.
[101] Ibid., 114–15.
[102] Ibid., 118–19.

leadership. Nanos's thesis in the context of a discussion of Paul and the Jews certainly deserves further exploration.

Nanos's identification of the weak in Romans as non-Christian Jews and the strong as Gentile Christians presents several insurmountable problems in the interpretation of Romans. In Rom 14:1–15:13 the non-Law-observant strong stand in the dominant position. Paul places the onus of the relationship with the weak on the strong. The strong are faulted for causing disunity. But non-Law-observant Gentile Christians would not have been in a strong position within the synagogues. They would have been subordinate to the Jewish synagogue leadership (who, according to Nanos, exercise the power of the sword in Rom 13:4). On the other hand, if Paul is addressing Christian house churches that are meeting separately from the synagogues and their authority structures, then these instructions to a Gentile Christian majority as the strong would make better sense.[103]

Nanos fully recognizes that the intended audience in Romans consisted almost exclusively of Gentile Christians. He also maintains that the Gentile Christians were not meeting apart from the synagogues. The question, then, is, Where would Paul's letter to the Gentile Christians be read? The very fact that the audience is identified as Gentile indicates that Paul assumed his letter would be read in a meeting context other than a synagogue. Indeed, Paul explicitly greeted a "church" (ἐκκλησία) meeting in a home (16:5).[104] Nanos's claim that Paul did not identify the Roman addressees as a church at the beginning of the letter is not a compelling argument since Paul's other letter openings do not consistently identify the recipients as a church. The apostle did not greet the Philippians with the term.[105] Neither the Ephesians nor the Colossians were greeted as "churches."[106]

---

[103] Robert A. J. Gagnon, "Why the 'Weak' at Rome Cannot Be Non-Christian Jews," *CBQ* 62 (2000): 64–82. Gagnon thinks Paul is urging the strong to welcome Noahide Gentiles, since Paul has already criticized fully Law-observant formerly Gentile Christians for their adoption of circumcision.

[104] Contra Nanos's claim that Paul does not address a "church" (ἐκκλησία) in Rome.

[105] For further discussion, see Chrys C. Caragounis, "From Obscurity to Prominence: The Development of the Roman Church between Romans and *1 Clement*," in *Judaism and Christianity in First-Century Rome* (ed. Karl P. Donfried and Peter Richardson; Grand Rapids: Eerdmans, 1998), 253; Caragounis claims (pp. 254–55) that although Christianity may have begun in some locations within synagogues, there is no evidence that the Christians continued to meet in the synagogues. Further, Caragounis argues that whenever Paul uses the singular "church," he always refers to Christianity as located within a city as a whole. He uses the plural "churches" for the Christians in regions larger than a single city. So while there may be individual house groupings in Rome, when "the church" gathered in Aquila and Prisca's home, it would be the entirety of the Roman congregation (pp. 255–60). And if this is a gathering at Prisca and Aquila's home, then it would be a *Christian* gathering.

[106] If Ephesians and Colossians are deemed to be from the hands of the Pauline school, the earliest Pauline interpreters did not consider the identification of churches at the beginning of the letter as normative and deserving of imitation.

Although Paul calls non-Christian Jews his brothers and sisters (τῶν ἀδελφῶν μου) in 9:3, Rom 14:21's expression ὁ ἀδελφός σου need not be interpreted as a similar reference to non-Christian Jews. Elsewhere Paul uses the same term to refer to fellow Christians as his brothers and sisters. In 1 Cor 7:12–14 he speaks of a "brother" who has an unbelieving wife. Romans 9:3 is the only instance where he speaks metaphorically of non-Christian Jews as fellow siblings, and this unusual verse is not without the qualification one would expect on the basis of Paul's ordinary usage. He calls them "*my* kindred," and they are brothers and sisters "*according to the flesh.*" As the discussion progresses, he clarifies that Israel apart from Christ lies outside the sphere of salvation (Rom 9:1–3, 22; 10:1; 11:17–24).[107] Israel's stumbling in Rom 14:21 should be understood in the same way as the stumbling in 1 Cor 8:7–13: one should not cause one's (Christian) "brother or sister" to stumble and thereby jeopardize his or her status as a Christian.[108]

Nanos highlights the omission of any mention of Christ in Rom 14:1–8. He points out that the diet and calendar customs discussed in those verses would match the customs of non-Christian Jews. But Gentile Christians might very well be attracted to such Jewish customs as God-fearers. The reference to "the Lord" in 14:5–6 proves that Christ is not entirely absent in these verses and that the weak are Christians and not non-Christian Jews. Romans 14:6 differentiates the Lord from God since the Lord gives thanks to God. Verse 9 then clarifies that "Christ died and lived . . . that he might be Lord of both the dead and the living." In all twenty unambiguous uses of "Lord" in Paul apart from citations of the Greek OT, the LXX, "Lord" refers to Christ. The two ambiguous instances in Rom 10:12–13 and 12:1 likely also refer to Christ.[109] Christ is Lord in Rom 14:14 and 15:6. In 14:18 the Romans serve Christ as slaves. Christ is therefore the master all throughout this passage, and if Christ is the master, then the weak in 14:1–8 are believers in Christ the Lord.

The phrase "weak in faith" in Rom 14:1 likewise argues strongly against a reference to non-Christian Jews. Whenever Paul speaks of non-Christian Jews elsewhere in the letter, he never refers to them as if they possess faith. Hardly "weak in faith," non-Christian Jews in 11:20, 23 are "without faith" (ἀπιστία). They stand in contrast to an Abraham who did not waver "with unbelief in the promise of God." Rather Abraham was strengthened in his faith or trust in God's promises (4:20). As Paul describes the "weak" throughout Romans 14, he never faults them for failing to believe in Christ. Repeatedly the "weak" are those who have adopted a certain stance

---

[107] See also 1 Cor 1:18; 2 Cor 4:3; Gal 4:21–31; and the extensive discussion of this point in ch. 4, below.

[108] Gagnon, "Why the 'Weak' at Rome," 68.

[109] Ibid., 69–70. For further discussion of Rom 10:12–13, see ch. 4, below; and C. Kavin Rowe, "Romans 10:13: What Is the Name of the Lord?" *HBT* 22 (2000): 135–73.

with respect to *food*—thus 14:2. Similarly in a different context in 1 Cor 9:22, when Paul becomes "weak to the weak," he does not become as someone who has faith in God but not Christ. Rather he abstained from idol meat when in the presence of others who were abstaining. Weakness in both contexts is defined by reference to food.

First Corinthians 9:22 with its reference to the "weak" is not the only parallel to Romans 14:1–15:6 in the Pauline corpus. Paul is writing to the Romans from Corinth and using language that he has already employed extensively in his other writings, language that he has applied to believers and the church. Paul speaks of the "weak" in 1 Cor 8:11 as those "for whom Christ died."[110] A word Paul uses, "upbuilding" (οἰκοδομή), in Rom 14:19, he uses with reference to Christ's body, the church, in the Corinthian correspondence.[111] Romans 15:1's "put up with [or bear] the failings of the weak" (ἀσθενήματα τῶν ἀδυνάτων βαστάζειν) parallels Gal 6:2's admonition to the Galatian Christians to "bear one another's burdens" (Ἀλλήλων τὰ βάρη βαστάζετε). Romans 15:5's "live in harmony" is literally "have the same mind-set" (τὸ αὐτὸ φρονεῖν); Paul employs such language for Christians in Rom 12:16; 2 Cor 13:11; and Phil 2:2; 4:2.

Paul's closing admonition in Rom 15:7 suggests that the apostle has had Gentile and Jewish Christians in mind all along: "Welcome *one another, therefore, just as* Christ has welcomed you, for *the glory of God*." "One another" (ἀλλήλοις) is used also in v. 5. Likewise the christological example in v. 7 parallels that of Christ employed throughout 15:1–6. The reference to receiving one another "just as" (καθώς) Christ received them echoes Christ's actions in vv. 3 and 5. The "glory of God" in v. 7 alludes to the glorifying of God in v. 6. "Therefore" (Διό) connects v. 7 to what precedes. The admonition to welcome in v. 7 flows naturally out of the reference to living in harmony in v. 6. Romans 15:7 thus concludes and summarizes what immediately precedes it, a section that began at least as early as 14:1, and admonishes both groups, whether weak or strong, to welcome each other even as Christ welcomed all of them.[112] Such a modeling of Christ's welcome makes little sense for the weak if they are non-Christian Jews.

---

[110] Note how in 1 Cor 8:6 Jesus is again Lord.

[111] 1 Cor 3:9–14; 8:1, 10; 10:23; 14:3–5, 12, 17, 26; 2 Cor 10:8; 12:19; 13:10; 14:12, 26; so also 1 Thess 5:1.

[112] There are numerous other connections as well. Romans 15:7 uses the word προσλαμβάνεσθε ("receive") as does 14:1 (cf. 14:3). The reciprocal "one another" (ἀλλήλους) in 15:7 parallels 14:13. Romans 15:7–12 even parallels 15:1–6 in form: a. exhortation (vv. 1–2, 7), b. christological support for the exhortation (vv. 3a, 8–9a), c. Scripture quote regarding Christ's work (vv. 3b, 9b–12), d. benediction (vv. 5–6, 13); Leander E. Keck, "Christology, Soteriology, and the Praise of God (Romans 15:7–13)," in *The Conversation Continues: Studies in Paul and John in Honor of J. Louis Martyn* (ed. Robert T. Fortna and Beverly R. Gaventa; Nashville: Abingdon, 1990), 86; Miller, *Obedience of Faith*, 75. Romans 15:7–13 therefore concludes at least 14:1–15:6. Some would go so far as to argue that it summarizes from 12:1, or even the letter as whole; see Miller, *Obedience of Faith*, 75–89.

ROMANS 14:1–15:6 REVISITED

The strong are the non-Law-observant, and the weak are Law-observant Christians. Paul has much to say in Romans 14–15 about how these two groups should relate to one another. He urges the non-Law-observant strong to accommodate and tolerate those who practice Jewish customs, whether in food and wine or in the celebration of special days. Paul appeals to the Romans not to judge one another (14:13). When they gather together, the strong should yield to the scruples of the weak (14:21). If some wish to honor a certain day, no one should judge such individuals for the practice as long as it is "in honor of the Lord" (14:6). Presumably when they gathered to eat, the strong were to be open to the weak bringing their own food and wine. Perhaps the weak would proffer the wine for the celebration of the Lord's Supper or the meat for a shared meal (14:21). The strong should put no stumbling block in the path of the weak (14:13). Anything that could result in injury or destruction of the faith of the weak should be avoided (14:15). Paul describes the weak as occupying an inferior position that could be critically influenced by the more dominant social group. The strong should not "despise" the weak and thereby pressure them to abandon their customs (14:3). To commit an act that one thinks is a sin, even if one acts on a false view of reality, is to sin (14:14b, 23). The strong must not pressure the weak to stumble. In his advice Paul is protecting the Law-observant within Christianity.

Paul permits people to hold differing opinions with respect to the Law. Food is unclean to the person who considers it such in Rom 14:14. Likewise each individual may observe days according to his or her own conviction (14:5). Whether one eats or abstains, it is to the honor of God (14:6). These are all private matters left to the individual. Thus Rom 14:22: "The faith that you have, have as your own conviction before God." Food and drink do not, then, define the boundaries of the Christian community. In this respect Paul's Christian community is very different from the Jewish community. To be Jewish meant that one obeyed the Law of Moses. Whereas Law observance was expected and required among Jews, such practices were acceptable in the church as well but were no longer expected or required, at least from Paul's point of view. The Law-observant, in fact, must "welcome" the non-Law-observant (15:7). As much as Paul accommodates Jewish practices within the Christian congregation, he counts himself among the strong who are convinced that a believer may eat anything (14:2; 15:1): "I know and am persuaded in the Lord Jesus that nothing is unclean in itself" (14:14). "Everything is indeed clean" in 14:20. Paul completely denies any sort of objective distinction between clean and unclean foods as articulated in the regulations of the Mosaic Law. The weak are simply wrong if they think certain foods are categorically unclean (14:14a, 20). "For the kingdom of God is not food and drink" (14:17). The strong are correct to "believe in eating everything" (14:2). Paul presents this position as his knowledge or conviction in Christ (14:14). "The certainty and candour with which Paul here expresses his freedom from the law is thus quite breathtaking."[113] In the context of first-century Judaism, Paul's position is a radical one. "This constitutes nothing less than a fundamental rejection of the Jewish law in one of its most sensitive dimensions."[114] From a Jewish standpoint, such an indifference to these cultural practices amounts to an eradication of Judaism itself.[115] By relativizing Jewish practices, Paul has relativized Judaism.

Paul's advice may even be considered condescending. He calls the weak "weak *in faith*" (Rom 14:1; cf. 4:19). This downgrading of their level of faith would certainly signal the possibility in his mind of a more mature position, and this more mature position would include an indifference toward the strictures of the Law. John M. G. Barclay rightly recognizes that Paul is effectively undermining Jewish social integrity. Weakness in this first-century culture is a "sickness of the soul," "an intense belief [in which someone] regards a thing that need not be shunned as though it ought to be shunned." Weakness is an "act of judging that one has knowledge where one has shunned."[116] If so, then the law would simply be irrelevant. God's salvation is "apart from the Law" and "without the works of the Law." When Paul observes the Law according to 1 Cor 9:20, it is strictly out of pragmatic reasons and not because of any sort of necessity. Paul ultimately opposes any imposition of circumcision (Gal 5:7; 1 Cor 7:19; Phil 3:3), dietary laws (Rom 14:14, 20; 1 Cor 8:4–6), or a religious calendar (Gal 4:10; Rom 14:5–6a). He even speaks of the Law as an enslaving power that confines people under sin apart from Christ (Romans 7).[117]

What may salvage Paul's discussion, from a Jewish standpoint, at least to some extent, is that he appears to be addressing an intra-Christian matter. If Nanos is correct that Paul was writing to Gentile Christians engaged in synagogue worship with non-Christian, Jewish "weak," then Paul's comments would be pointed against Judaism and its practitioners. Nanos's theory of mixed worship in the synagogues actually indicts Paul of worse anti-Semitism than Nanos had hoped to avoid. Traditionally, scholars have viewed Paul's letter as written to Christians who were observing Jewish customs. In Christ, Jewish observances were a matter of indifference. In Nanos's scheme, Paul would be intimating that Jewish observances were a matter of indifference for the synagogue Jew as well![118] According to

---

[113] Barclay, " 'Do We Undermine the Law?' " 301.

[114] Ibid., 300.

[115] Daniel Boyarin, *A Radical Jew: Paul and the Politics of Identity* (Berkeley: University of California Press, 1994), 9–10, 290 n. 10.

[116] Clarence E. Glad, *Paul and Philodemus: Adaptability in Epicurean and Early Christian Psychagogy* (NovTSup 81; Leiden: E. J. Brill, 1995), 285, citing Cicero, *Tusc.* 4.26. See also Gagnon's discussion ("Why the 'Weak' at Rome," 76).

[117] See ch. 6, below.

[118] Should this be labeled "the Nanos trap"? And is this not a worse trap than Nanos's dreaded "Luther's trap"? Ultimately, what cripples Nanos's reasoning, in

Nanos's Paul, should not the non-Christian Jews identified as the weak become strong by maturing beyond their need for Jewish customs? In the process the Jewish person would realize that the Mosaic Law, the heart of Jewish identity, was a matter of indifference.[119] Although the Christian Gentile might observe the requirements of a "righteous Gentile" living in the midst of Israel and the Jews, the practice would be strictly one of respect in what would otherwise be a matter of freedom. In other words, Gentiles as Gentiles were under no Mosaic obligation at all. On the other hand, even if Paul were addressing an entirely Christ-believing congregation, one cannot avoid implications vis-à-vis Judaism. In his reasoning, Paul was still implying that Jewish practices, indeed Judaism itself, were essentially a matter of indifference and of no saving value. What was implied by Paul's discussion at the end of Romans was stated more clearly earlier in the letter. The gracious aspects of Judaism were inoperative in the apostle's thinking and had been replaced by Christ as the agent of salvation and redemption. Our following chapters will explore the logic at work earlier in Romans that formed the basis for Paul's indifference toward Law observance in Romans 14 and 15.

Although Paul ultimately relativizes Law observance and implies that a mature Christian should not feel compelled to observe the Law's strictures, the apostle nevertheless urges the Christian Gentiles in Rome to treat each other with respect and tolerance. Paul is still respectful of those who observe the Mosaic Law in part or in its entirety. When Christians gather together, the non-Law-observant should not despise or be impatient with those who prefer to abide by the Law's ritual aspects. And if one is respectful of the Law-observant within the Christian community, should there not also be a respect for those who are Law-observant outside the community? Paul could even contemplate living as a Jew in order to win the Jew (1 Cor 9:20, 22). Many tragedies in the history of Jewish-Christian relations might have been avoided had more Christians heeded the apostle's advice. Paul would be incensed to hear of Christian intolerance or persecution of the Law-observant.

---

my opinion, is that he reasons exclusively from the positive statements about the Law in Romans and almost never considers Paul's negative comments. This limitation in his analysis seriously skews his overall interpretation of the letter. Perhaps he will address these weaknesses in a more global interpretation of Romans at a later date.

[119] What does the Jew gain by observance of the Law before God that the Gentile Christian does not already have apart from it?

~ 4 ~

THE MESSIAH AND ISRAEL'S ELECTION
IN ROMANS

> But not all have obeyed the good news; for Isaiah says, "Lord, who has believed our message?" So faith comes from what is heard, and what is heard comes through the word of Christ. (Rom 10:16–17)

SOME OF the members of the Christian community in Rome had adopted Jewish customs regarding food and drink. Where kosher sustenance was unavailable, the Jews preferred to avoid meat and wine lest they consume what had been offered to pagan deities. In Romans 14–15 Paul considers these practices acceptable for the Roman Christians but ultimately unnecessary. The apostle aligned himself with the "strong" and viewed food and drink as matters of individual freedom as long as no "weak" Christian was present for whom food and drink might be a stumbling block. To render a practice that was so central to Jewish identity ultimately unnecessary implies a similar judgment regarding that identity itself.

Romans 14–15 is not an isolated passage. Paul has prepared for his conclusions in these chapters throughout all that has preceded in the letter. The apostle's judgment regarding food and drink is a natural and consistent extension of his belief that Jewish identity in and of itself offers no saving benefit to the Jew. Whereas the Mishnah could celebrate that "all Israelites have a share in the world to come" with the exception of only the most egregious sinners in their history (*m. Sanh.* 10:1–4), Paul denies this virtually automatic inclusion of people into a saving relationship with God on the basis of mere ethnic identity. At the heart of these differences between the apostle and his religious confreres is disagreement over whether and how the Jewish people enjoy God's grace. If Christians, even Gentile Christians who place their faith in Christ, may be called God's elect as Paul contends, the question emerges whether God's historic people enjoy the same status. This is the question that Paul must answer for himself in Romans 9–11. The apostle's Christology forces him to speak both positively and negatively about Israel.

THE ELECTION OF CHRISTIANS

Paul does not raise the subject of Israel's election as an ethnic people until Romans 9, but the discussion is almost inevitable after some strong claims in the preceding chapter. In Romans 8 the apostle speaks at length about the blessings that God has given to those who place their faith in Jesus Christ. Paul begins Romans 8 by responding to the dilemma in the prior chapter caused by sin's commandeering of the Mosaic Law to bring about death: "There is therefore now no condemnation for those who are in Christ Jesus" (8:1). The dire situation of the individual who stands under the Mosaic Law can be resolved only in Christ: "For God has done what the law, weakened by the flesh, could not do; by sending his own Son in the likeness of sinful flesh, and to deal with sin, he condemned sin in the flesh." (v. 3).What God has done in Christ creates the opportunity for a new way of life:

> But you are not in the flesh; you are in the Spirit, since the Spirit of God dwells in you. Anyone who does not have the Spirit of Christ does not belong to him. But if Christ is in you, though the body is dead because of sin, the Spirit is life because of righteousness. If the Spirit of him who raised Jesus from the dead dwells in you, he who raised Christ from the dead will give life to your mortal bodies also through his Spirit that dwells in you. (vv. 9–11).

Verse 12 concludes that Christians must live according to the Spirit and not according to the flesh. "For all who are led by the Spirit of God are children of God" (v. 14).

When Paul calls those who possess "the Spirit of Christ" "the children [υἱοί] of God," he is drawing upon the language of the people of Israel as the Lord's elect in the Hebrew Scriptures. In Exod 4:22–23 God instructed Moses to tell Pharaoh, "Thus says the LORD: 'Israel is my firstborn son. I said to you, "Let my son go that he may worship me." But you refused to let him go; now I will kill your firstborn son.'" In Deut 14:1 Moses reminded the people of Israel, "You are the children of the LORD your God." In Deut 32:5–6 Moses lamented how God's rebellious "children" have dealt with him. Nevertheless, God remained their "father." Similarly in Jer 3:19 God will be the people's father. Jeremiah 31:9 says, "For I have become a father to Israel, and Ephraim is my firstborn," and Hosea 11:1 says, "When Israel was a child, I loved him, and out of Egypt I called my son."[1] The people of Israel were God's "children."[2] Paul now applies this title to Christians. In

---

[1] See also Sir 36:12 and *4 Ezra* 6:58.

[2] Isa 43:6; Hos 2:1 LXX (quoted in Rom 9:26); Wis 5:5; Brendan Byrne, *"Sons of God"— "Seed of Abraham": A Study of the Idea of the Sonship of God of All Christians in Paul against the Jewish Background* (AnBib 83; Rome: Biblical Institute Press, 1979), 9–70; James M. Scott, *Adoption as Sons of God: An Exegetical Investigation into the Background of* ΥΙΟΘΕΣΙΑ *in the Pauline Corpus* (WUNT 2:48; Tübingen: J. C. B. Mohr [Paul Siebeck], 1992).

the next verse, Rom 8:15, Paul continues, "For you did not receive a spirit of slavery to fall back into fear, but you have received a spirit of adoption [υἱοθεσίας]." Christians are beneficiaries of God's "adoption" (NRSV) or "sonship." Before Paul, Jewish writings expressed the view that such sonship was limited to members of ethnic Israel. Paul is appropriating the Hebrew Scriptures' language for ethnic Israel as God's elect, and he is applying these Jewish appellations to believers in Christ.[3]

Romans 8:18 speaks of the "glory" (δόξαν). In Jewish history the ultimate expression of "glory" took place at Mount Sinai. Thunder, lightning, a cloud, and trumpet blasts all accompanied the giving of the Law at Mount Sinai (Exod 19:16). Likewise in Deut 5:24: "Look, the LORD our God has shown us his glory [δόξαν] and greatness, and we have heard his voice out of the fire." Yet even before Mount Sinai, the Lord had manifested "glory" in striking down Pharaoh (Exod 14:4, 17, 18). The giving of manna revealed God's "glory" (Exod 16:7) as well as the divine presence amid the people (Exod 16:10, 24:16–17; 33:18, 22; 40:34–35). "From these origins, it is used across all the many books and different literary forms of the Old Testament to speak of a revelation of God the people could experience. It is never a *notion* about a saving God, but the *experience* of that God" (thus Ps 19:1).[4] The "glory of God" is God as experienced in saving acts on behalf of the Jewish people: "I will put salvation in Zion, for Israel my glory" (Isa 46:13). Isaiah 60:1–3 speaks of Zion (cf. 59:20): "And the glory of the LORD has risen upon you. . . . the LORD will arise upon you, and his glory will appear over you. Nations shall come to your light, and kings to the brightness of your dawn" (similarly 62:2–3; Jer 13:11). In Rom 8:18 Paul is drawing upon this rich tradition of the divine glory throughout the Hebrew Scriptures and applying it to Christian experience. Elsewhere in his writings, the apostle speaks of the even greater glory of the "new covenant" in Christ in contrast with the lesser glory of the giving of the Mosaic Law (see 2 Cor 3:1–18).

By appropriating ethnic Israel's "glory" and sonship for Christians in Romans 8, Paul has extended Israel's historical privileges to Gentile Christians. He reasons similarly elsewhere.

> [Abraham] received the sign of circumcision as a seal of the righteousness that he had by faith while he was still uncircumcised. The purpose was to make him the ancestor of all who believe without being circumcised and who thus have righteousness reckoned to them, and likewise the ancestor of the circumcised who are not only circumcised but who also follow the example of the faith that our ancestor Abraham had before he was circumcised. (Rom 4:11–12)

---

[3] Byrne, *"Sons of God,"* 215–19.
[4] Francis J. Moloney, "Telling God's Story: The Fourth Gospel," in *The Forgotten God: Perspectives in Biblical Theology* (ed. A. Andrew Das and Frank J. Matera; Louisville: Westminster John Knox, 2002), 116–18.

Paul explains that Abraham was the father not only of ethnic Israelite believers in Christ but also of uncircumcised Gentile believers. Uncircumcised Gentile believers have become the "descendants" or "seed" of Abraham.

> For this reason it depends on faith, in order that the promise may rest on grace and be guaranteed to all his descendants, not only to the adherents of the law but also to those who share the faith of Abraham (for he is the father of all of us, as it is written, "I have made you the father of many nations"). (Rom 4:16–17a)

Believers in Christ are the true circumcision: "For it is we who are the circumcision, who worship in the Spirit of God and boast in Christ Jesus and have no confidence in the flesh" (Phil 3:3). In 1 Cor 10:1 Paul speaks to his Gentile audience of "our ancestors" at the time of Moses (also vv. 6, 9, 11; 12:2). Gentile Christians are thereby placed in relationship with the patriarchs as "*our* ancestors."

Paul concludes Romans 8 in vv. 28–35 with yet another series of appellations traditionally limited to ethnic Israel:

> We know that all things work together for good for those who love God, who are called according to his purpose. For those whom he foreknew he also predestined to be conformed to the image of his Son, in order that he might be the firstborn within a large family. And those whom he predestined he also called; and those whom he called he also justified; and those whom he justified he also glorified.

> What then are we to say about these things? If God is for us, who is against us? He who did not withhold his own Son, but gave him up for all of us, will he not with him also give us everything else? Who will bring any charge against God's elect? It is God who justifies. Who is to condemn? It is Christ Jesus, who died, yes, who was raised, who is at the right hand of God, who indeed intercedes for us. Who will separate us from Christ?

In this passage Paul speaks of God's foreknowledge of Christians (v. 29, προέγνω), his election of them (v. 33, ἐκλεκτῶν θεοῦ), and their predestination (v. 29; προώρισεν). The foreknowledge Paul speaks of is not just advance knowledge but includes a relationship between God and a special people.[5] For instance, in Gen 18:19 God's foreknowledge of Abraham implied that his offspring would enjoy the special blessing of God. In Amos 3:2 God proclaimed of Israel, "You only have I known of all the families of the earth." God's knowing of a people implies their election:[6] "Therefore my people shall know my name; therefore in that day they shall know that it is I who speak; here am I" (Isa 52:6); "I will give them a heart to know that I am the Lord; and they shall be my people and I will be their God, for they shall

---

[5] Dunn, *Romans 1–8*, 482.

[6] In Deut 4:39, 7:9, and 29:6, conversely, as part of the covenant relationship, Israel is to "know" God.

return to me with their whole heart" (Jer 24:7). Those who by their actions have abandoned the covenant relationship with God no longer "know" him (e.g., Jer 4:22; 9:3). In Jer 31:34 God promised to create a new covenant in which the people will all know God. Likewise "predetermination" (Rom 8:29) is the language of a special relationship with God. Certainly the strongest term in Romans 8 is that Christians are the "elect of God." This most basic element of Jewish self-understanding is now applied to those who believe in Christ. In Ps 105 (LXX 104):6 the children of Jacob were God's "chosen ones." In LXX Isa 42:1 Israel is God's own "elect" people (see also Isa 43:20; 65:9).[7] The sectarian Qumran community at the Dead Sea saw themselves as God's "elect" people of Israel.[8] Christian believers are the "beloved of God" (Rom 1:7) and a community of brothers and sisters (Rom 1:13; 8:29), but the claim that Christian believers are God's elect fully appropriates the advantage of Jewish ethnic identity.

The closing verses of Romans 8 shower upon Christian believers appellation after appellation previously applied only to the elect people of Israel. Paul claims in 8:28 that all things work for good for those who love God and who are called according to his purpose. Such individuals God "foreknew" (προέγνω) and "predestined" (προώρισεν, v. 29). Those he predestined he then called, which in turn led to their justification and glorification. Paul closes by concluding "that neither death nor life, nor angels, nor rulers, nor things present, nor things to come, nor powers, nor height, nor depth, nor anything else in all creation, will be able to separate" God's people in Christ from that love. Yet Paul cannot avoid a crucial problem. If God is so faithful to the elect in Christ, of what value is God's prior election of ethnic Israel? Were not all these blessings originally Israel's? Romans 9–11 is a natural extension, then, of Romans 8. How can Christians find solace in their special place and election by God when God's historic, elect people are not benefiting from their blessings? "How much comfort is there in being told that nothing can separate us from God's love when there is apparently something quite capable of separating the chosen people from God's love?"[9] Or "if God is not faithful to Israel, how can Paul proclaim his faithfulness to the Gentiles?"[10] If Christians are to experience any sense of comfort or joy in their election in Christ, the apostle must address

---

[7] For a helpful survey of this central motif within the Hebrew Scriptures and throughout Judaism, see G. Schrenk, "ἐκλεκτός," *TDNT* 4:182–84.

[8] E.g., CD 4:3–4; 1QpHab 10:13.

[9] Paul J. Achtemeier, *Romans* (IBC; Louisville: John Knox, 1985), 153–54.

[10] Dunn, *Romans 9–16*, 530. Susan Eastman ("Whose Apocalypse? The Identity of the Sons of God in Romans 8:19," *JBL* 121 [2002]: 263–77) has demonstrated that Paul's use of language and imagery from the Hebrew Scriptures in Romans 8 (such as "adoption," "sons of God," and "creation") is laying the foundation and implicitly anticipating the inclusion of ethnic Israel in the apostle's reasoning in Romans 9–11. Nevertheless, the explicit application of Israel's prerogatives as the elect to Gentiles in Romans 8 remains troubling—thus 9:1–5.

the question of another elect people of God, the Jews who have not placed their faith in Jesus as the Messiah.

AN ELECT PEOPLE NOT BENEFITING FROM THEIR ELECTION

Paul turns to his brothers and sisters according to the flesh at the beginning of Romans 9. Stunningly, he applies to them many of the same titles and descriptions he has been employing up to this point in the letter for believers in Christ: "They are Israelites, and to them belong the adoption [υἱοθεσία], the glory, the covenants, the giving of the law, the worship, and the promises; to them belong the patriarchs" (vv. 4–5). The apostle insists that ethnic Israel still enjoys at least some of the privileges of being God's elect people. In 11:2 Paul calls ethnic Israel those whom God "foreknew." They are "beloved" in 11:28. These terms, which Paul applied earlier in the letter to Christians, are once again being applied to ethnic Israel. Even the apostle's calling his "kindred according to the flesh" Israelites is a departure from his preference for the term "Jews" earlier in the letter. "Israelites" is a much stronger term, evoking their election as an ethnic people.[11]

As surprisingly positive as this turn is in 9:4–5, Paul's prior discussion in the letter qualifies the praise. For instance, what Paul says regarding Abraham as "our ancestor according to the flesh" in Romans 4 undercuts the advantage of the patriarchs here in Rom 9:4. Abraham is the father in Romans 4 of those *who believe*. Circumcision is a sign of faith "to make [Abraham] the ancestor of all who believe without being circumcised and who thus have righteousness reckoned to them, and likewise the ancestor of the circumcised who are not only circumcised but who also follow the example of the faith that our ancestor Abraham had before he was circumcised" (4:11–12). The type of faith Paul has in mind is clear in 4:24–25 when he speaks of Jesus "our Lord." The reasoning of Romans 4 thus anticipates Romans 9: having Abraham as one's forefather does not offer saving benefits in and of itself.

Whereas Paul described Christians as the elect in Romans 8, he does not apply this title in Romans 9 to ethnic Israel apart from qualification. He does speak of an elect within Israel in 9:6–29, but he refrains from using this term in the list of Israel's blessings as a people in vv. 4–5. So, although he readily grants several of the privileges of historical Israel's election to his fellow Israelites according to the flesh—they remain in some sense an elect people—he is nevertheless driven by an anguish for them. At the climactic position within the list of Israel's blessings in vv. 4–5, Paul states, "from [ethnic Israel], according to the flesh, comes *the Messiah,* who is over all, God

---

[11] See Dunn, *Romans 9–16,* 526.

blessed forever. Amen."[12] This powerful christological climax to ethnic Israel's privileges drives Paul's anguish in vv. 1–3:

> I am speaking the truth in Christ—I am not lying; my conscience confirms it by the Holy Spirit—I have great sorrow and unceasing anguish in my heart. For I could wish that I myself were accursed and cut off from Christ for the sake of my own people, my kindred according to the flesh.

The solemn "I am not lying" strikes a deep chord. The apostle is burdened with "great sorrow" (λύπη μεγάλη) and "unceasing anguish" (ἀδιάλειπτος ὀδύνη) in his heart because his fellow Jews are not in Christ. Paul genuinely desires (ηὐχόμην)—in what is virtually a mirror image of Christ's own actions for the sake of a lost humanity—that he could exchange places with his own people and be "accursed" and "cut off from Christ" in their stead. Such is the utter seriousness of their predicament. To be "cut off from Christ" is to place oneself outside the benefits of God's election and under the curse (ἀνάθεμα).

Certainly it is tragic, from Paul's standpoint, that his fellow Israelites have failed to recognize their own Messiah. Their plight is even more alarming if Paul in v. 5 is identifying the Christ, the Messiah, as God-blessed forever. It is more natural to maintain an identity of subject from "the Messiah" (ὁ Χριστός) to the immediately following clause, which begins, "who is" (ὁ ὤν). The immediate antecedent of "who" would be the Messiah. It is also hard to see Paul's mention of his pain and grief (λύπη, ὀδύνη) over the Jews' unbelief leading, surprisingly, to an ascription of praise to God without some sort of adversative to highlight a contrast. Further, Paul's wording makes better sense as an ascription to Christ rather than to God the Father. In the LXX "blessed" (εὐλογητός) always *precedes* the name of God in independent doxologies, and the NT follows this pattern (see, e.g., Gen 14:20; 2 Cor 1:3). An ascription to God the Father here and not to Christ would violate the syntactical pattern.[13] Finally, Paul's doxologies are always linked to a preceding subject, which in this case would be the Messiah. For instance, the "he" of the doxology in Rom 11:36 finds its preceding subject in the "Lord" mentioned in v. 34. Likewise the ascription of praise in 1:25 to the one "who is blessed forever" finds its subject in the immediately preceding words "the Creator" (τὸν κτίσαντα).[14] If the Messiah Christ is "God

---

[12] Wright, *Climax of the Covenant,* has demonstrated that Paul sees Christ as Israel's Messiah. For a more recent expression of this viewpoint, see Christopher G. Whitsett, "Son of God, Seed of David: Paul's Messianic Exegesis in Romans 1:3–4," *JBL* 119 (2000): 661–81.

[13] The Greek construction ὁ ὤν ("who is") is equivalent to ὅς ἐστιν if referring to Christ, but the ὤν is superfluous if referring to God (see the parallel construction in 2 Cor 11:31).

[14] See, for further discussion, Murray J. Harris, *Jesus as God: The New Testament Use of Theos in Reference to Jesus* (Grand Rapids: Baker, 1992), 143–72; Cranfield, *Romans,* 2:464–70; and Bruce Metzger, "The Punctuation of Romans 9:5," in *Christ*

blessed forever," as is the most likely reading, Israel's tragedy would be accentuated. Non-Christian Israel would not only have failed to recognize their own Messiah; they would have failed to recognize the very presence of their God.

Romans 9:5 is not the only place where Paul identifies Christ with God. In Phil 2:5–11 the apostle speaks of Christ existing "in the form [μορφῇ] of God" and as equal to God (τὸ εἶναι ἴσα θεῷ). Paul then applies to Christ the words of Isa 45:23: "To me [God] every knee shall bow, every tongue shall swear." This section of Isaiah is perhaps the staunchest expression of monotheism in the Hebrew Scriptures: "I, I am the LORD, and besides me there is no savior" (43:11); "I am the first and I am the last; besides me there is no God" (44:6); "I am the LORD, and there is no other; besides me there is no god" (45:5); "'God is with you alone, and there is no other; there is no god besides him.' Truly, you are a God who hides himself, O God of Israel, the Savior" (45:14–15); "There is no other god besides me, a righteous God and Savior; there is no one besides me" (45:21); "For I am God, and there is no other" (45:22). Isaiah 45:23 follows directly after these oft-repeated and powerful affirmations of the one God of Israel as the sole Savior. Yet in Philippians 2 Paul applies Isa 45:23 to Christ.[15] Similarly in 1 Cor 8:6 Paul redefines the Shema of Israel ("Hear, O Israel: The LORD is our God, the LORD alone" [Deut 6:4]) to include Christ; Christ is the "one Lord" of whom Deut 6:4 spoke.[16] Even though Paul's authorship of Colossians is a matter of debate, Col 1:15–20 reflects Pauline thinking: "in [Christ] all things in heaven and on earth were created, things visible and invisible . . . all things have been created through him and for him. . . . For in him all the fullness of God was pleased to dwell." As does Col 2:9: "In him the whole fullness of deity dwells bodily."[17] Such affirmations elsewhere in the Pauline literature lend credibility to the similar expression of deity in Rom 9:5.[18]

Whether or not one identifies the Messiah or Christ with God in Rom 9:5, the Messiah certainly occupies the climactic position and is the key to unlocking ethnic Israel's benefits in the preceding verses. Faith in the Messiah is essential in order to benefit from Israel's historical blessings. Christ remains central to Paul's reasoning. Israel's failure to believe in the Messiah is the reason their situation is desperate from the apostle's standpoint. Gentile Christian believers, by contrast, are benefiting from Israel's prerogatives and blessings. What value would there be in God's election of a Christian

and the Spirit in the New Testament (ed. Barnabas Lindars and Stephen S. Smalley; Cambridge: Cambridge University Press, 1973), 95–112.

[15] For a more thorough treatment of Phil 2:5–11 and its implications for Christology and monotheism, see Wright, *Climax of the Covenant,* 56–98.

[16] See ibid., 120–36.

[17] See ibid., 99–119.

[18] On the early Christian identification of Christ and God against the backdrop of Second Temple Judaism, see esp. Richard Bauckham, *God Crucified: Monotheism and Christology in the New Testament* (Grand Rapids: Eerdmans, 1998).

people—where nothing can separate a person from the love of God in Christ—if there were another elect people who are not benefiting from God's election? If the Israelites, as an elect people, are separated from their God because of a failure to believe in Christ, how could Christians place any confidence in their own election? This difficult question will occupy Paul for three more chapters of his Letter to the Romans. Out of anguished concern, Paul keeps returning to the plight of ethnic Israel in Romans 9–11 and proposes three very different answers to the problem (9:6–29, 9:30–10:21, 11:1–32). Romans 9–11 may very well, then, be the climax of Paul's letter. Paul already broached the fate of ethnic Israel in Romans 2–3, and what he wrote in those chapters paves the way for his attempt at a solution in Romans 9–11. Any review of the apostle's reasoning in Romans 9–11 must remain conscious of this foundation.

GOD'S IMPARTIALITY AND ISRAEL'S ADVANTAGE

In Romans 1:16 Paul boldly proclaims, "For I am not ashamed of the gospel; it is the power of God for salvation to *everyone* who has faith, to the Jew first and also to the Greek." The Jew and the Greek are both saved by faith. In 1:18 the apostle continues, "For the wrath of God is revealed from heaven against *all* ungodliness and wickedness,"[19] and in 2:9–11, "There will be anguish and distress for everyone who does evil, the Jew first and also the Greek, but glory and honor and peace for everyone who does good, the Jew first and also the Greek. For God shows no partiality." God does not treat the Jew one way and the Gentile another.

Romans 2:12–16 addresses an obvious objection to this thesis. If God gave the Jewish people the Law of Moses, which would impart knowledge of the divine will, certainly the Jew would have an unfair advantage, and God would be less than impartial in judgment. Paul responds that the Gentile is not at a disadvantage in God's judgment since what the Law requires is written on the heart. The Gentile possesses a comparable knowledge of God's will and is therefore equally accountable alongside the Jew, who possesses the Law. Both groups, Jews and Gentiles, will be judged and repaid according to their works (2:6) "on the day when, according to my gospel, God, through Jesus Christ, will judge the secret thoughts of *all*" (2:16). God's judgment of all people through Jesus Christ will be impartial.

On the other hand, if God treats all people impartially, would this not eliminate the special privileges of God's historical election of the people of Israel? Romans 2:17–29 presses the point that God will not treat the Jews differently because of their membership in an ethnic people. They too must produce the works that are in keeping with their Jewish identity. Jews who

---

[19] That God's condemnation in 1:18–32 is not to be limited just to the Gentiles, see Das, *Paul, the Law, and the Covenant*, 171–77.

steal, commit adultery, and rob temples will be accountable for their actions. Precisely because God deals with all humanity impartially, the uncircumcised Gentile who does what the Law requires will be regarded as circumcised (v. 26). The true Jew is not one outwardly but inwardly (vv. 28–29), and the obedient Gentile will serve to condemn the disobedient Jew (v. 27).[20] Jewish ethnic identity is no exception to the rule that God will treat all people impartially.

Romans 3 maintains the focus on God's impartiality. Paul charges all people, whether Jew or Greek, as being under the power of sin in 3:9. He continues in vv. 19–20,

> Now we know that whatever the law says, it speaks to those who are under the law, so that *every mouth* may be silenced, and *the whole world* may be held accountable to God. For "*no human being* will be justified in his sight" by the deeds prescribed by the law, for through the law comes the knowledge of sin.

The question emerges, then, how anyone will be justified in God's sight. The answer comes in the following verses (vv. 21–24) and exemplifies God's impartiality once again:

> But now, apart from law, the righteousness of God has been disclosed, and is attested by the law and the prophets, the righteousness of God through faith in Jesus Christ for all who believe. For *there is no distinction,* since *all* have sinned and fall short of the glory of God; they are now justified by his grace as a gift, through the redemption that is in Christ Jesus.

Even as all people will be held accountable and judged impartially on the basis of their works, whether Jew or Gentile, God acts impartially to save all on the basis of redemption in Christ, whether Jew or Gentile.

So, if God judges all people impartially and saves both Jew and Gentile through redemption in Jesus Christ, "What advantage has the Jew? Or what is the value of circumcision?" (3:1). Paul responds in v. 2: "Much, in every way. For in the first place the Jews were entrusted with the oracles of God." No sooner has Paul identified a benefit in being a Jew—to be entrusted with the oracles of God—he changes tack and speaks in v. 3 of the Jews' "faithlessness" (ἀπιστία). In v. 9 he concludes that both Jews and Greeks are all under the power of sin. The question lingers how the oracles of God are of any value to the elect people. The apostle presents a partial answer in vv. 21–26 when he speaks of that to which the oracles testify. The oracles of God, "the law and the prophets," testify to "the righteousness of God through faith in Jesus Christ for all who believe. For there is no distinction, since all [Jew and Gentile] have sinned and fall short of the glory of God; they are now justified by his grace as a gift, through the redemption that is in Christ Jesus." In other words, the oracles of God possessed by the Jewish people do offer them an advantage. The advantage is God's testimony

---

[20] For a discussion of the potential identity of these Gentiles, see ibid., 180–82.

to them of God's righteousness, that is, God's faithfulness to his covenant promises embodied in the person and work of Jesus Christ. Earlier, in 3:3–4, Paul asks another question: "What if some were unfaithful? Will their faithlessness nullify the faithfulness of God? By no means!" These questions—the advantage of the Jew, or the lack thereof, and the faithlessness of Israel—tower over the letter and compel further discussion and elaboration in Romans 9–11. Paul's conscious revisiting in Romans 9–11 of his earlier truncated answer forces the reader to view the later chapters as a further response to the questions of 3:1–9: does it not challenge God's election and faithfulness to the people of Israel if the Jews do not believe?[21]

ETHNIC ISRAEL—GOD'S ELECT, OR GOD'S ELECT WITHIN ISRAEL

Paul's first attempt to resolve the problem of an elect people not benefiting from their election is the very plain statement of Rom 9:6: "For not all Israelites truly belong to Israel." Paul redefines Israel as a subgroup within ethnic Israel as a whole. In vv. 7–13 Paul explains that the word of God has not failed since God has distinguished between the ethnic people of Israel and an elect people within that larger group from the very beginning. God had determined that the children of Isaac and not Ishmael would be Abraham's "true descendants," the "children of the promise." Then, when Isaac's wife Rebecca bore twins, "Even before they had been born or had done anything good or bad . . . she was told, 'The elder shall serve the younger'" (v. 11). God's distinguishing within Israel is therefore consistent with these earlier precedents. The "children of the flesh" were never identical with "the children of God" (v. 8). God had never privileged ethnic Israel with a salvation that could be taken for granted. God's elect were never coterminous with a people of a particular race by their membership in that race alone. In effect, Paul is denying that the "adoption" and the "patriarchs" offer saving benefits in and of themselves to ethnic Jews. As the Jewish scholar Alan Segal recognizes, "The effect is that Paul's discourse in Romans comes painfully close to apostasy and would certainly have angered any Jew who was not already angered by his antinomianism."[22] For Paul, natural descent and human striving do not determine God's plan. Divine election remains a sovereign matter. God is a potter who can fashion the clay in whatever way he deems fitting, whether to have mercy or to harden. Paul cites Pharaoh as an instance where God acted sovereignly to harden. Segal notes the remarkable conclusion: "Paul puts the non-Christian Jews of his time on the same level as Ishmael and Esau and also with Pharaoh."[23]

---

[21] See Michael Cranford, "Election and Ethnicity: Paul's View of Israel in Romans 9.1–13," *JSNT* 50 (1993): 32–33.

[22] Segal, *Paul the Convert,* 277.

[23] Ibid. Although many have noted that Paul does not directly equate the vessels of wrath with the Jews of Israel according to the flesh, a hint perhaps of what is

If Rom 9:6–29 were the entirety of the discussion, the natural conclusion would be that Paul has simply denied that ethnic Israel is the elect people of God. God's elect have always been a people *within* Israel. From the larger perspective of Romans 9–11 in its entirety, such a conclusion may require qualification.[24] Paul returns to the matter of ethnic Israel as a whole in 11:25–32, where he reaches a very different conclusion. Even in Romans 9, however, Paul hints of another conclusion. The apostle is in anguish because of his fellow Israelites "according to the flesh" (9:3). He still boldly applies several of the categories of an elect Israel to them (9:4–5). If Paul ultimately feels that Israel's election only pertains to a subgroup within Israel, why does he express pain and anguish over all ethnic Israel, and why does he ascribe elect privileges to the very people prompting his pain? It appears that Paul genuinely ascribes to ethnic Israel as a whole—and not in part—at least some of the benefits of an elect people. The apostle is not concerned in 9:6–29 with Israel's failure to recognize the Messiah but is addressing God's faithfulness and sovereign right to act as the Creator.[25] Paul has created a tension in the discussion of Israel's election between vv. 1–5 and vv. 6–29 revolving around the climax of the list in v. 5, the Messiah. The apostle distinguishes Israel's election as an ethnic people, which never automatically brought about a right relationship with God and salvation, from an elect within Israel that is benefiting from that election. These two distinct concepts of election are related since it was precisely to the ethnic people that God initially granted the saving promises (vv. 6–13).[26]

---

to come later in Romans 11, Charles H. Cosgrove rightly notes that the contrast between vessels of wrath and vessels of mercy prepared for glory, including "us whom he has called, not from the Jews only but also from the Gentiles," suggests to the reader "that the vessels of wrath comprise an analogous and opposing group of people, those to whom God will not be merciful and who have *not* been fashioned for glory" ("Rhetorical Suspense in Romans 9–11: A Study in Polyvalence and Hermeneutical Election," *JBL* 115 [1996]: 271–87). As Jews and Gentiles comprised the vessels of mercy, so also Jews and Gentiles would be included in the vessels of wrath. "Moreover, in the context of the argument, the mass of Israelites according to the flesh who have not accepted the gospel message spring to mind as the obvious candidates for inclusion in this group, along with the Gentile world as a whole" (272).

[24] Cranford's extremes in this regard are rightly corrected by Jan Lambrecht, "Paul's Lack of Logic in Romans 9:1–13: A Response to M. Cranford's 'Election and Ethnicity,'" in *Pauline Studies* (Leuven: Leuven University Press, 1994), 55–60.

[25] Paul W. Meyer notes that the Christ has been completely absent in the discussion since Rom 9:5 ("Romans 10:4 and the 'End' of the Law," in *The Divine Helmsman: Studies in God's Control of Human Events, Presented to Lou H. Silberman* [ed. J. L. Crenshaw and Samuel Sandmel; New York: Ktav, 1980], 64). But he misses the strong shadow, created by 9:5 over the following discussion, that forces Paul's return to the matter of faith in Christ in 9:30–10:21.

[26] As Cranford rightly points out: "In his distinction between children of the flesh and children of the promise, Paul is not arguing that the boundaries are disjunctive. As the analogy with Abraham suggests, a common natural heritage is

ETHNIC ISRAEL'S STUMBLING OVER THE MESSIANIC STONE

Paul surprisingly does not discuss Israel's failure to believe in the Messiah in Rom 9:6–29, especially in light of the Messiah's prominence in v. 5. Once Paul has offered his initial response to ethnic Israel's plight, that it is God's right as the potter to shape the clay, the apostle finally addresses the matter of faith in the Messiah in 9:30–10:21. Placing Christ on the center stage of his argument in 9:30–10:21 is also necessary because the apostle has left a glaring gap in Romans 9 between Israel as the elect people and Israel as the elect within the people. In other words, 9:30–10:21 in many ways answers the expectations and tension that Paul left unanswered in 9:6–29 after his climactic announcement of the Christ in 9:5. On the other hand, Paul does not explicitly mention Christ until 10:4, and not all agree on the centrality of Christ in this section of Romans. A careful review of Paul's Christ-centered reasoning is in order.

In Rom 9:25–26 Paul quotes Hos 2:23: "Those who were not my people I will call 'my people,' and her who was not beloved I will call 'beloved.' And in the very place where it was said to them, 'You are not my people,' there they shall be called children of the living God." Whereas Hosea spoke these words to give the people of Israel hope as the elect, Paul applies these words to the Gentiles (note the contrast with Israel as the recipient of revelation in Rom 9:27). In 9:30 he continues the paradoxical contrast of Jew and Gentile that he raised in vv. 25–26. A more literal translation of vv. 30–32a than the NRSV offers is crucial to understanding Paul's rhetoric: "What then shall we say? Although the Gentiles were not pursuing righteousness, they attained righteousness, namely a righteousness which is on the basis of faith. But Israel, although they were pursuing a law of righteousness [διώκων νόμον δικαιοσύνης], did not attain the law. Why? Because they pursued it not on the basis of faith but as (if) on the basis of works."[27]

The puzzling phrase "law of righteousness" is central to the passage's meaning. After introducing this phrase, Paul explains that this "law" is based on faith rather than on works in v. 32 (ἐκ πίστεως and ἐξ ἔργων). He juxtaposed faith and works earlier in the letter when discussing the Law in 3:27–31: the Law may be understood from the perspective of the works that it demands (thus 4:4–5) or from the perspective of the faith to which it bears witness (e.g., 3:21 and the testimony to Abraham's faith in Romans 4).[28] The way Paul phrases 9:31–32a suggests that the apostle is playing on the same two perspectives on the Law as in 3:27 (the Law from the perspective of the works that it demands and the Law as a witness to righteousness and faith).

---

shared by both, though a non-fleshly criterion distinguishes between them" ("Election and Ethnicity," 39).

[27] On the text-critical and grammatical issues regarding these verses, see Das, *Paul, the Law, and the Covenant*, 242–43 n. 31; and ch. 6, below.

[28] See Das, *Paul, the Law, and the Covenant*, 192–214.

He creates a parallelism of elements in 9:31–32a: the Gentiles did not pursue; the Jews did pursue. The Gentiles attained where the Jews did not attain.[29] Although the activities of pursuing and attaining are parallel for both Jews and Gentiles, Paul disrupts the parallelism by means of a series of contrasts. The Gentiles did not pursue a righteousness based on faith whereas the Jews pursued the Law of righteousness. After mention of the Gentiles' nonpursuit of the "*righteousness* which is on the basis of faith," the reader would have expected a contrast with Israel's pursuit of a "*righteousness* on the basis of the law" (δικαιοσύνην τὴν ἐκ νόμου). Instead, Paul speaks of Israel's pursuit of the *Law* of righteousness. In yet a second contrast, whereas the Gentiles do not pursue and yet attain righteousness, the Jews pursue and yet do not attain the Law. In each case where Paul breaks from the parallelism created by pursuing and attaining, he directs his readers' attention to the role of the Law.

Consider again the first disruption of parallelism in 9:31: Paul's use of "law of righteousness" (νόμον δικαιοσύνης) where the reader would have expected "righteousness which is based on law" (δικαιοσύνην τὴν ἐκ νόμου). Paul uses the latter wording in Rom 10:5 while quoting Lev 18:5 to the effect that the righteousness of the Law is based on doing its precepts. He could have used this in 9:31 in order to say that the Jews did not attain righteousness where the Gentiles did. By using instead the phrase "law of righteousness" (νόμον δικαιοσύνης) in 9:30–31, Paul is signaling a play on terms. In other words, had Paul wished to speak unequivocally of the Law from the perspective of the works that it demands, he could have used the same phraseology as in 10:5. He chooses instead to disrupt the parallelism with conspicuously different wording in order to lead his readers to consider a different understanding of "law" (νόμος). Paul has already contrasted two very different ways of understanding the Law in 3:27–4:25: the Law from the perspective of its works is very different from the Law as a witness to righteousness. To incorporate this earlier insight into 9:30–32a, the Jews are pursuing a Law that witnesses to righteousness as if it were based on their active pursuit and performance of its works. The Jews do not realize that the Law is pointing toward a righteousness based on faith rather than on the works that it prescribes.

Paul stresses through his use of racing imagery that the Jews misunderstood the Law when they pursued it through their active pursuit and performance of its works. The Jews pursued in 9:32a much as an athlete pursues the prize in a race. The Jews did not attain the Law in v. 31b much as an athlete does not attain a prize, and they did not attain that prize because they "stumbled" (v. 32b) even as an athlete might stumble during a race.[30] To restate the line of thought:

---

[29] Although Paul uses synonyms for "attain" (κατέλαβεν, ἔφθασεν) in 9:30–31.

[30] Paul often speaks of his life as a race to the finishing line of salvation (e.g., Phil 3:12).

v. 31b: Israel did not attain the Law.

v. 32a: Why? Because they did not pursue it on the basis of faith but as if on the basis of works.

v. 32b: They stumbled on the stone of stumbling.

In pursuing the Law as if it were based on human activity or works, the Jews stumbled on the stone of stumbling and did not attain the law. The Greek word for "as if" (ὡς) in v. 32a is an important clue that the Jews pursued the Law from a false perspective. They had pursued the Law as if its righteousness were based on human effort rather than on faith.[31] Because the Jews were so engrossed in doing the Law, they failed to believe. They understood the Law from the perspective of its demands rather than from the perspective of faith. The irony is that the Jews failed to attain their own special possession, a Law that was intended for righteousness, whereas the Gentiles without the Law attained righteousness. The Jews missed out on the inner meaning of the Law in its testimony to righteousness because of their rush to pursue the Law's demands. Consequently, they stumbled over the stone of stumbling that God placed in Zion (v. 32b).

If this stone of stumbling, as many think, refers to Jesus Christ, then the Jews did not attain to righteousness because they did not place their faith in Jesus the Messiah. Scholars, however, have debated the identity of the "stumbling stone" in Rom 9:33. Some interpreters have proposed that this stone refers to God.[32] Paul is quoting and conflating Isa 8:14 and 28:16. In Isa 8:13 the prophet identified the Lord of hosts as the subject, a subject maintained in v. 14. There is no question, then, as to the identity of the stone. Although v. 14 referred to God as the stone of stumbling, Paul inserts v. 14's reference to the stone into a citation from Isa 28:16, where it is no longer the prophet but God who is speaking. Since God ("I") is distinguished as the one who placed the stone in Rom 9:33 and who is speaking, faith "in him" (the stone) cannot be faith in God. Nor can the stone be the Mosaic Law. According to Rom 9:32, Israel did not attain to the Law because they did not pursue it on the basis of faith but as if on the basis of works and because they stumbled over the stumbling stone. If Israel had been focused on the Law as an object of pursuit, that is, if the people's eyes had been on the Law, then how could the people have stumbled over it? The Law was precisely what Israel pursued. Paul's stumbling stone must therefore be something else.[33] Paul uses the same prepositional construction

---

[31] See the additional support for this conclusion in Das, *Paul, the Law, and the Covenant*, 234–49. This does not deny a nationalistic dimension to Paul's reasoning; his language is simply more encompassing.

[32] E.g., Paul W. Meyer, "Romans," in *Harper's Bible Commentary* (ed. James L. Mays; San Francisco: Harper & Row, 1988), 1157.

[33] It stretches the limits of Paul's imagery to suggest that the Jews pursued a Law that was in their sights and at the same time located beneath them as a stumbling stone (when considered from a different perspective, of course).

for "faith *in*" (πιστεύων ἐπ' αὐτῷ) the God who raised Jesus from the dead earlier in 4:24. The prepositional construction requires a personal object. One does not believe "in" the Mosaic Law. Paul never says that. And if God is not the object, then the reader would likely suspect that the object of faith over whom the Jews stumble must be the Messiah of 9:5. Surely the Law that calls for faith in 9:30–32 must relate in some way to Jesus Christ.

In a reprise of the athletic imagery of 9:30–32, Paul says in 10:4 that Christ is the goal/end (τέλος) of the Law. Paul relieves the reader's expectations from 9:30–33. Jesus Christ, the "goal" of the Law, is the one to whom it had pointed all along (thus also 3:21). At the same time, if Christ is the goal of the Law, then a double entendre may be at work.[34] If Christ is the goal of the Law, then when that goal is realized, the Law would come to an end as an object of human pursuit. Christ would be both the goal and the end of the Law. The non-Christian Jews of Paul's day have therefore shockingly failed to recognize the true meaning and fulfillment of their own Law in the person of Jesus Christ.

As if to emphasize the Law's witness to Jesus Christ more forcefully, in 10:6–8 Paul takes a passage from Deuteronomy that had originally referred to the nearness and attainability of the Law and asserts that the passage was actually speaking of Christ. Verse 8 concludes in the words of the Torah (Deut 30:14): "The word (ῥῆμα) is near you, on your lips and in your heart." This witness of the Law in Rom 10:8 turns out to be "the word of faith that we proclaim." Verses 9–10 then draw out the ramifications regarding Christ: one must confess with the lips that Jesus Christ is Lord, and one must believe that God raised him from the dead. By v. 17 what began as the "word" (ῥῆμα) of Deut 30:14 is clearly the "word of Christ" (ῥήματος Χριστοῦ). Paul's gospel message is therefore that proclaimed already in the Torah, the very point of vv. 6–8. The Torah itself witnesses to faith in Christ. This is why the Jews stumbled over the stone in 9:33 when they pursued the Law's works and were ignorant of its testimony to faith.

Paul calls Jesus Lord in Rom 10:9–10: "if you confess with your lips that Jesus is Lord and believe in your heart that God raised him from the dead, you will be saved. For one believes with the heart and so is justified, and one confesses with the mouth and so is saved." Salvation is only possible through faith and the recognition of Jesus Christ as the risen Lord.

---

[34] Τέλος is ambiguous. Paul primarily employs this word to mean a termination point, an end (see 1 Cor 1:8; 10:11; 15:24; 2 Cor 11:15; Phil 3:19); see Dunn, *Romans 9–16*, 589, who strikes the right balance; and Das, *Paul, the Law, and the Covenant*, 90 n. 69. An end may also include the notion of reaching a goal, as is the case here in Rom 10:4. Romans 10:3–4 returns to the language of 9:30–33 and revives the athletic imagery; see Das, *Paul, the Law, and the Covenant*, 247–48. Paul plays on this ambiguity in the following verses by juxtaposing and contrasting the Law in 10:5 from the point of view of its works, an approach to God that has *ended* for those in Christ, and the Law in 10:6–8 from the point of view of its goal, Christ; see ibid., 253–65.

After the rhetorically powerful identification of Christ as Lord in v. 9, Paul repeatedly invokes the Lord in the ensuing verses: "the same Lord is Lord is of all and is generous to all who call on him. For, 'Everyone who calls on the name of the Lord shall be saved'" (vv. 12–13). Romans 10:9–13 forms a tight unit of thought, as the confession of the lips that Jesus is Lord (vv. 9–10) corresponds to the calling on the name of the Lord in vv. 12–13, and the belief in the heart of vv. 9–10 corresponds to the scriptural citation in v. 11: "No one who believes in him [ὁ πιστεύων ἐπ' αὐτῷ] will be put to shame." In other words, vv. 10–13 are building on the identification of Jesus Christ as Lord in v. 9. In a unit so carefully focused upon Jesus as Lord, the most natural (and nearest) antecedent for "him" (αὐτῷ) in the scriptural quote of v. 11 is the Lord Jesus of v. 9 (αὐτόν).[35] Such an identification conforms to the apostle's regular employment of "Lord" (κύριος) elsewhere in his writings as a designation for Jesus Christ rather than for God the Father.[36] Paul also confirms for his readers that he was referring to Jesus Christ by the "stumbling stone" in 9:33. After such strongly Christ-centered reasoning in 10:4 (Christ is the goal of the Law) and in v. 9 (Jesus is Lord), in v. 11 the apostle quotes Isa 28:16 again, the very same passage he had quoted in 9:33. Now the identity of the stumbling stone is indisputable.

Paul in Rom 10:11 deliberately adds the word "everyone" (πᾶς) to his quotation of Isa 28:16 (cf. Rom 9:33). This word does not occur in the manuscripts for the Greek translation of the original Hebrew of Isa 28:16.[37] Paul maintains this emphasis on universality in Rom 10:12–13 (γάρ): "For there is no distinction between Jew and Greek; the same Lord is Lord of *all* and is generous to *all* who call on him. For, '*Everyone* who calls on the name of the Lord shall be saved.'"[38] Paul has used a form of the word πᾶς four times in vv. 11–13. Jesus Christ as Lord (v. 9) is therefore God's operative path to salvation for all people, whether Jew or Greek.[39]

In Rom 10:14–15 Paul contends that this saving message of Christ must be preached in order for it to be heard and effective. In v. 17 he adds, "So faith comes from what is heard, and what is heard comes through the word of Christ." Saving faith comes through the message about Christ. The

---

[35] If the same phrase in 9:33 cannot refer to God (since God is the one speaking), the reader would not expect the object of faith to be the God who raised Jesus from the dead in 10:11. The phrase "trust in" (πιστεύω ἐπί) requires a personal object, which rules out the Law as object, even a Law that has as its goal Jesus Christ.

[36] Paul employs "Lord" for God the Father generally only when he is constrained by a quotation from the Scriptures.

[37] The NRSV unfortunately translates the word in the negative ("no one").

[38] On Paul's christological adaptation of Joel 2:32 (Heb. 3:5) in this passage, see Rowe, "Romans 10:13."

[39] As Günter Wasserberg recognizes, "There is no question for Paul that Jews need Jesus as their savior as much as Gentiles do (10:13)" ("Romans 9–11 and Jewish-Christian Dialogue," in *Reading Israel in Romans: Legitimacy and Plausibility of Divergent Interpretations* [ed. Cristina Grenholm and Daniel Patte; Romans through History and Culture Series; Harrisburg, Pa.: Trinity Press International, 2000], 182).

emphasis in vv. 9–13 on all people being saved only by confession of Christ as Lord draws attention to non-Christian Israel. What can be said of Israel's unbelief? The remaining verses in Romans 10 return to the question of Israel. Paul's initial response is that the message about Christ, which went out to all the earth, would have reached those of Israel. Indeed, the message about Christ must be preached to the Jewish people as well. So the apostle rhetorically asks in v. 19, "did Israel not understand?" and in v. 21 gives the parting shot: "But of Israel he says, 'All day long I have held out my hands to a disobedient and contrary people.'" Israel has remained disobedient in its failure to believe the message about Christ, which went out to all the earth. Israel's election as an ethnic people does not therefore avail to them apart from faith in Christ.

What Paul concludes in Romans 10 regarding the necessity for Israel to believe in Christ coincides with what he has said in the first three chapters of the letter. Even as Romans 10 repeatedly emphasizes that all people are saved on the basis of faith in Christ, Romans 1–3 likewise emphasized humanity as a whole. And even as 10:12 asserts that "there is no distinction between Jew and Greek," Paul is quoting verbatim what he has already said in 3:22. Whereas in 3:22 all people are sinful, in 10:9–12 the only path to salvation for all people is through the person of the Lord Jesus Christ. Paul is doubly emphasizing in Romans 10 the point he made in Romans 1–3: God acts to judge and to save human beings the same way, whether Jew or Gentile.

The failure of the Jews to believe in Jesus as the Messiah in Romans 10 therefore prevents them from benefiting from God's impartial plan of salvation. Israel is a "disobedient and contrary people" (10:21; citing Isa 65:1–2) quite in contrast with the Gentiles: God has been found by those (Gentiles) who were not seeking. God has made those who are not a nation a source of jealousy for Israel. Isaiah 65:1–2's context treated Israel's sin of idolatry. Ironically it is precisely such idolatry and disobedience that the Jews in Paul's day sought to avoid by their faithful observance of the Torah. They would be as incensed about idolatry as the prophet. But by denying the end/goal of the Law in Christ (10:4), Paul's fellow Jews have fallen away from the true and proper observance of that Law. Jewish failure to follow the Law to Christ is, from the apostle's standpoint, tantamount to the idolatry of old. So Paul can apply Isaiah's condemnation of a disobedient, idolatrous people to non-Christian Jews as the conclusion of a chapter affirming faith in Christ as the only hope of salvation for all people. Isaiah's message held out hope for Israel as does Paul himself, but the apostle articulates this hope in terms of Christ and not of traditional Judaism (v. 21).

Paul seems to realize finally where his thinking has led him. Far from resolving the plight of his fellow brothers and sisters in the flesh, he has only exacerbated the problem in Rom 9–10. The apostle must engage yet again the question with which he began in 9:1–5: "I ask, then, has God rejected his people? By no means!" (11:1). From all that Paul has said up to this point, it appears that God has rejected ethnic Israel as such. Even after raising the question of God's rejection, he surprisingly resumes his negative commentary about unbelieving Israel: God has chosen a remnant within Israel. Ominously paralleling the hardening of Pharaoh in Romans 9, Paul says, "What then? Israel failed to obtain what it was seeking. The elect obtained it, but the rest were hardened" (11:7). Paul then quotes the Hebrew Scriptures: "God gave them a sluggish spirit, eyes that would not see and ears that would not hear, down to this very day" (v. 8; Deut 29:3; Isa 29:10). The quotation from Ps 68:23 in Rom 11:9–10 is even more disturbing: "Let their table become a snare and a trap, a stumbling block and a retribution for them; let their eyes be darkened so that they cannot see, and keep their backs forever bent." The elect of Israel, as in the times of Elijah, are once again a faithful remnant and distinct from ethnic Israel as a whole. The pronouncement of judgment upon the unbelieving majority of Israel is unmistakable.

By Rom 11:11 Paul's thinking has finally taken a new turn. He explains that Israel's stumbling and defeat resulted in riches for the Gentiles: "and if [Israel's] defeat means riches for the Gentiles, how much more will their full inclusion mean!" (v. 12). The apostle views his ministry to the Gentiles as a means of making his own people jealous (vv. 13–14). Israel is analogous to an olive tree (v. 17), and the Gentiles have been grafted where natural branches were broken off on account of unbelief (vv. 19–20). Since God has grafted the Gentiles onto a tree that represents the promises and relationship with Israel, the Gentiles have no room for boasting. God's ultimate plan is to graft the natural branches back in (v. 24). As Paul climactically states, "I want you to understand this mystery: a hardening has come upon part of Israel, until the full number of the Gentiles has come in. And so all Israel will be saved" (vv. 25b–26a). Verse 28 appeals to the election of Israel, and v. 29 maintains that God's gift and calling are irrevocable. Even as God has had mercy on the disobedient Gentiles, so he will have mercy on disobedient Israel (vv. 30–31). Paul has finally found an answer for the people of Israel.

THE SALVATION OF "ALL ISRAEL": THREE APPROACHES

Scholars have long grappled with this sudden and powerful reversal of the course of Paul's argument, especially with the claim in Rom 11:26 that "all Israel will be saved." One school of thought holds that there are "two covenants." Adherents to this position note that Romans 11 never speaks of any sort of preaching to ethnic Jews and that nothing in the chapter suggests that "all Israel" will place their faith in Jesus Christ.[40] Paul does not even mention Christ in Rom 10:17–11:36.[41] The "Deliverer coming from Zion" in Rom 11:26 is best taken as referring to God rather than to Jesus Christ ac-

---

[40] Lloyd Gaston, *Paul and the Torah* (Vancouver: University of British Columbia, 1987), 147–48.

[41] Krister Stendahl, *Paul Among Jews and Gentiles* (Philadelphia: Fortress, 1976), 4.

cording to the two-covenant proponents.[42] Ethnic Israel bears no blame for not recognizing Christ as the Messiah. The fault of Israel is that the people resisted the inclusion of Gentiles into God's salvation as equal partners. Paul says in Romans 11 that the Jews will become jealous of his ministry not because of the Gentiles' faith in Christ but rather because of the inclusion of Gentiles into the plan of salvation. Such jealousy of Gentile inclusion into God's riches will encourage the Jew to be more faithful as a Jew to the Torah of Moses.[43] While a remnant in Israel may be saved on the basis of God's activity in Jesus Christ, the "all Israel" of Rom 11:26 will be saved on the basis of the "Torah covenant." Israel will come to recognize that the Gentiles have through Christ what the Jews have through the Torah, and thus the Jews will be moved to greater faithfulness to God's unique and special plan for them. Paul's divine call to be an apostle required a recognition of God's inclusion of and love toward the Gentiles quite apart from the Jews' ethnic identity. His call did not involve any necessity for Jews to convert to Christ in order to experience redemption.[44] The "two covenant" theory, if correct, would offer an appealing approach to Jewish-Christian dialogue. While Christians would be saved through the Jewish Messiah, the Jews would be "saved" as members of a special and elect people on the basis of their fidelity to the Law God gave to Moses.

The two-covenant approach posits that Paul's conversion consisted primarily of a dawning recognition of Christ's significance for the Gentiles. According to the two-covenant theory, Paul in Gal 1:16 was called on the Damascus Road in a revelation of God's Son to be the apostle to the Gentiles. Yet Paul speaks of the "Lord Jesus Christ" as the one "who gave himself for our sins to set *us* free from the present evil age," a few verses earlier (1:4).[45] He includes himself, as a Jewish Christian, among those set free in Christ from the present evil age. If Paul, prior to his conversion, were not likewise enslaved, then his inclusion of himself would be incomprehensible. Elsewhere in the letter he regularly speaks of "you" (Gentile) Galatians when it suits his purpose, but Paul's "you" is noticeably absent in Gal 1:4. In Phil

---

[42] Gaston, *Paul and the Torah*, 33, 148. See on this point Christopher D. Stanley, " 'The Redeemer Will Come ἐκ Σιων': Romans 11.26–27 Revisited," in *Paul and the Scriptures of Israel* (ed. Craig A. Evans and James A. Sanders; JSNTSup 83; Sheffield: Sheffield Academic Press, 1993), 118–42.

[43] Gaston, *Paul and the Torah*, 148.

[44] Ibid., 33; John G. Gager *Reinventing Paul* (Oxford: Oxford University Press, 2000), 52–66, 86. If the Jews are guilty of anything, they have stumbled in their failure to recognize what God is doing in Christ for the Gentiles.

[45] Gaston (*Paul and the Torah*, 112, 114) cites this verse as evidence for the thinking of the Jewish Christian community prior to Paul but does not realize the difficulties the verse would then pose for his own position. If this is Jewish Christian material, Paul adapts it (e.g., "the present evil age," "liberates") and applies it to his *Gentile* audience. In other words, he affirms the inclusion of the Gentiles into Christ's benefits for *Jewish* Christians. Paul, by his use and adaptation of such material, signals his approval of its contents even if his own formulations may vary in wording.

3:4–6 Paul catalogs his accomplishments and premier lineage as a Jew by birth—including an angst-free "blamelessness" with respect to the righteousness of the Law—only to claim in 3:7–9 that his Jewish privileges are a "loss" and "rubbish" (lit. "dung," "refuse"—a vulgarity) for the sake of Christ. He contrasts a righteousness of his own "that comes through the law" with a righteousness "from God based on faith." The elements in this contrast are parallel: "of my own" versus "from God," and "through the law" versus "based on faith." In other words, the righteousness of the Law does not, in fact, come from God. Paul seeks in 3:10–11 resurrection from the dead by sharing in *Christ's* sufferings, death, and resurrection.[46] He realizes that the Jewish Christ is God's path to salvation for all people, for both Gentiles and Jews (as Paul himself). For Paul, as a Jew, this realization would require abandonment of any prior conviction that the Mosaic Law offered a path to salvation in and of itself, even for a legally "blameless" person as he describes himself. If so, non-Law-observant Gentiles could enjoy salvation in Christ, and Paul in good conscience could be an emissary of that message.

The two-covenant theory denies that Law-observant Jews as such need Christ as their Savior from sin. They enjoy salvation through their faithfulness to the Law of Moses. If they are guilty of any failure, they should have recognized and rejoiced in God's salvation of the Gentiles in Christ.[47] When Paul writes in Gal 3:10 that "all who rely on the works of the law are under a curse," the two-covenant proponents maintain that this statement refers only to the Galatian Gentiles. They point to the key phrase "works of the Law" as proof that Paul has Gentiles and not Jews in mind since the phrase refers to the curse the Law works among the Gentiles who neither possess nor observe it. Therefore it is *Gentiles* who are redeemed from the curse of the Law and not the Jews in Gal 3:13. The first person plural pronouns in 3:13, however, suggest that Paul includes himself among those redeemed by Christ from the curse of the Law. The first person pronouns are not a rhetorical device, nor does Paul temporarily lay aside his own Jewish identity.[48] Where Paul explicitly identifies himself with a particular people in his letter to the Galatians, he numbers himself among "Jews by birth and *not* Gentile sinners" (Gal 2:15). Since the initial appeal by two-covenant theorists to the phrase "works of the Law" as applicable to Gentiles only, specialists have

---

[46] Paul's desire as a Jew to be resurrected through Christ as well as his contrast of a righteousness from the Law with a righteousness based on faith renders incomprehensible Gager's conclusion from Phil 3:7 that "contrary to the traditional view of Paul's conversion and its consequences, what changed was not his view of the law as such, or of the law in relation to Israel, but only as it concerned Gentiles!" (*Reinventing Paul*, 26–27).

[47] Gaston undermines this assertion when he claims from what he understands to be traditional material that the Jerusalem Christians held that Jesus' "death means the supersession and replacement of the temple and its sacrifices as the means of expiation" and that "Jesus' death was 'for our sins' " (*Paul and the Torah*, 114).

[48] As Gaston (*Paul and the Torah*, 29) suggests.

uncovered parallels for the phrase in other Jewish writings of the period. In the Dead Sea scrolls, such language referred to the works that the Law required, including those works that distinguished one Jewish sect from another. Performance of these requirements rendered one a member of the community. Likewise for Paul in Rom 3:28–29, a person is not justified by the works of the Law lest "God [is] the God of Jews only." Performance of the "works of the Law" incorporates the Gentile into the Jewish community. Whereas two-covenant theorists argue that the phrase refers to the curse that *the Law* "works" among the Gentiles, Paul speaks of the works that *individuals* must do according to the Law. Thus he shifts from speaking of the "works of the Law" in Rom 3:28–29 to "works" as a matter of human effort and exertion with due wages in Rom 4:4–5.[49] Paul quotes Deut 27:26's curse against those who do not "do" all that is written in the book of the Law (τοῦ ποιῆσαι αὐτά) and concludes that those who rely on "the works of the Law" (ἐξ ἔργων νόμου) are under its curse. If "works of the Law" were referring to the Law's own "work" of wrath and not to the works required by the Law (of people), "why then Paul should bother to deny that justification comes through wrath (Rom 3:20) becomes rather baffling."[50] "Works of the Law" therefore refers to the works demanded by the Law.[51] When Paul speaks of the "works of the Law" in Gal 3:10, he does not single out the Gentiles but remains indefinite with "whoever" (ὅσοι). He supports his assertion with a quotation from Deut 27:26, which, in its context, threatens the covenantal curses *upon the Jews* should they fail to observe all that the Law requires of them.[52] Similarly in v. 11 Paul states, "*no one* is justified before God by the law." Once again the apostle supports his assertion with a biblical passage that had originally addressed the Jewish people (Hab 2:4). In Gal 3:12 Paul quotes Lev 18:5: "*whoever* does the works of the law will live by them." He is grounding his conclusions for *all people* in biblical passages that employ *universal* language. At a minimum, the Jewish Scriptural passages he provides in support require the *inclusion* of the Jews. Two-covenant theorists assert that Gal 3:10–12 concerns only the Gentiles, but they do not disqualify the more likely alternative that Paul's reasoning with respect to the Gentiles and the Law flows out of his conclusions about the Law *as such*.[53]

---

[49] Westerholm, *Israel's Law and the Church's Faith,* 116–117.

[50] Dunn, *Romans 9–16,* 154; contra Gaston.

[51] So also Hans Dieter Betz (*Galatians,* 144) and N. T. Wright (*Climax of the Covenant,* 144–48). See also the very detailed case of Joseph B. Tyson, "'Works of Law' in Galatians," *JBL* 92 (1973): 423–31. This does not deny that the apostle speaks of the agency of the Law elsewhere, as Gaston has shown. Paul simply does not employ the phrase "works of the Law" for that purpose.

[52] Gaston (*Paul and the Torah,* 32–31) refers to various Jewish texts where the Law was offered to the Gentiles and they refused to accept it and thus fell under its curse, but Paul drew his language of curse from biblical texts addressing *Israel* as the covenant community.

[53] For example, Gager (*Reinventing Paul,* 52) faults Sanders for reasoning from what appears to be a universal claim in Gal 3:10 to its application to the Gentiles.

Two-covenant champions grant the awful, oppressive burden of being "under the Law," but they limit this phrase to a description of the Gentiles' relationship to the Law and not the Jews'.[54] In Gal 4:4 "God sent his Son, born of a woman, born under the law." If "under the Law" were describing Gentile existence, as two-covenant proponents contend, then how could Jesus be born "under the Law" if he was born a Jew? As a Law-observant Jew he could not be "under the Law" in the same way as the Gentile. What Paul writes in Gal 4:4 underscores the error in limiting "under the Law" to a description of the Gentiles. According to the Jewish author Josephus, *the Jews* accepted the threatened curse of the Law for nonfulfillment (*Ant.* 4.8.44 §§302, 307)—a curse two-covenant theorists limit to the Gentiles—and in *Ag. Ap.* 2.28 §210 he invited Gentiles: "To all who desire to come and live under the same laws with us (ὑπὸ τοὺς αὐτοὺς ἡμῖν νόμους), he [Moses] gives a gracious welcome, holding that it is not family ties alone that constitute relationship, but agreement in the principles of conduct." Josephus invited Gentiles who were *not* currently living under the laws of Moses but who desired to live "under the same laws" with us [Jews] through Moses, even as Paul addresses Gentiles in Gal 4:21 who "desire" to be "under the Law."

The Galatians had been freed from their former status as Gentiles "under the Law" through faith in Christ. Two-covenant theorists contend that the Gentile Christians, in entertaining Law-observance in Gal 4:21, are going to revert effectively to their *pagan* state under the Law's curse. This reasoning offers a convoluted approach to the verse. Paul does not say that the Gentiles want to return to their prior status under the Law's curse apart from Christ. Rather he says that they are desiring to be under the Law, in the sense of observing it, in order to *avoid* the Law's curse. According to two-covenant advocates, Galatians 4:21–31 contrasts Gentiles "under the Law" with Gentiles in Christ, who are freed from the Law's curse. If this passage were indeed a contrast of two distinct groups of Gentiles, it would not implicate the Jews in any way. Such a reading, however, ignores Paul's choice of language, which contrasts *the present Jerusalem,* which is in slavery with Hagar at Mt. Sinai, with the Jerusalem above, which is free and associated with Isaac.[55] Gaston tries to circumvent this problem by claiming that the present Jerusalem and the Jerusalem above are *not* being contrasted as opposites: "That election, into which the Galatians have now been called, is spoken of in terms of Sarah and Mount Zion, *the heavenly Jerusalem, from*

Gager believes that Sanders has, in effect, wrongly universalized a passage that is specifically targeted toward Gentiles. Merely asserting that Sanders is in error (even repeatedly) does not demonstrate one's own position.

[54] Gaston, *Paul and the Torah,* 29.

[55] Gager (*Reinventing Paul,* 96) contrasts in parallel columns Ishmael/slave/born according to the flesh/Sinai covenant/birth into slavery/[Gentiles before Christ] and Isaac/free/[Abrahamic covenant]/[Gentiles after Christ], but he never mentions the Jerusalem language!

which the present Jerusalem really cannot be detached."[56] He then translates
Gal 4:25: "It [Sinai] is in the opposite column [συστοιχέω] from the present
Jerusalem, for she [Hagar] serves [as a slave] with her children." If, however,
Paul had intended for Sinai/Hagar and Jerusalem to be in *opposite* columns,
he would have used ἀντιστοιχέω.[57] The Greek word he actually employs
(συστοιχέω) links Sinai and Hagar to the present Jerusalem, and the present
Jerusalem remains the immediate antecedent and subject for the following
words: "she [*Jerusalem*] is in slavery with her children." Even if one were to
grant that Paul is including Gentiles on both sides of his contrast, the Jerusalem language would not permit the exclusion of Jews (or Jewish Christians)
from the contrast. The Galatian Gentiles, in their desire to observe the
Mosaic Law, are therefore on the verge of becoming enslaved with the present Jerusalem at Mt. Sinai.

According to the two-covenant theory, the Jews enjoy God's favor
through the Law. So why would God curse, condemn, and censure the
Galatian Gentile congregations for practicing the Jewish Law? While the
Galatians may be shortchanging Christ's significance for them as Gentiles,
they are nevertheless joining, as full proselytes through circumcision, a
covenant community that likewise enjoys God's favor. Paul, on the other
hand, is categorical that *all* people have sinned. In Rom 3:23 "all have
sinned and fall short of the glory of God." Two-covenant proponents would
limit the "all" to Gentiles, but such a reading would violate the immediate
context in Rom 3:9 where Paul asserts that "all" are "under the power of sin,
both Jews and Greeks." Two-covenant theorists attempt to sidestep the clear
implications of this verse by appealing to the Scriptural passages cited in
Rom 3:10–18. These passages are culled from Jewish polemic against Gentiles and Israel's enemies.[58] Even this sidestep is ineffective since Paul also
quotes Isa 59:7–8 in Rom 3:15–17, and Isaiah *does* challenge the Jewish
people with their sin and failure.[59] To restrict Paul's categorical statement in
Rom 3:20 to Gentiles stretches the limits of credulity: "For '*no human being*
(lit. "no flesh") will be justified in his sight' by deeds prescribed by the law,
for through the law comes the knowledge of sin."[60] Again in Rom 3:20, Paul
is drawing on a Scriptural text that was addressed to and included the Jew
(Ps 143:2). "Since *all* have sinned and fall short of the glory of God," the Law
itself attests to righteousness through faith in Jesus Christ/the faithfulness of

---

[56] Gaston, *Paul and the Torah,* 91; emphasis mine.
[57] Rightly Dunn, *Galatians,* 252. Gaston himself concedes: "It is doubtful that I
have completely demonstrated that Paul does not use the figure of Hagar to desig-
nate contemporary Israel" (*Paul and the Torah,* 91).
[58] Gaston, *Paul and the Torah,* 121. So Gager concludes, contrary to Rom 3:9,
that only "*some* Jews have sinned" (*Reinventing Paul,* 118).
[59] Gager again mistakenly appeals to "under the Law" in Rom 3:19 as a description of Gentile existence.
[60] Contra Gager, *Reinventing Paul,* 121–22. See Dunn's very helpful analysis of
the Scriptural citations in Rom 3:10–20 (*Romans 1–8,* 157–160).

Jesus Christ "for *all* who believe" (Rom 3:22–23). Paul nowhere limits his repeated emphasis on "all" to a particular group such as Gentiles.

The plight of Jews outside of Christ is precisely what motivates Paul's
pathos in Rom 9:1–5. At the climax of *Israel's* blessings is the Messiah or
Christ (9:5).[61] Paul expresses a genuine anguish in 9:1–5 about his own
people. He wishes himself "cursed" (ἀνάθεμα) and cut off from Christ (ἀπὸ
τοῦ Χριστοῦ). His wish implies that his own people must be "in a plight as
serious as the one he is willing to enter for their sake."[62] If the only problem
for Israel were a mere lack of recognition of God's plan for the Gentiles in
Christ, why would this move the apostle to desire to be "accursed" and "cut
off from Christ" for their sake? Paul even calls his fellow Jews "enemies of
God" in Rom 11:28. "Enemies" is hardly a description of a people who
enjoy a right relationship with God through the Law apart from Christ. If
the Jews are suffering a serious plight apart from faith in Christ, then the necessity for Peter to take the *same* gospel message to the circumcised which
Paul is taking to the Gentiles makes sense (Gal 2:7–9). The word "gospel" is
used once in Gal 2:7 for both the preaching of Peter and Paul, even as Paul
denies the existence of "another gospel" and recognizes only "the gospel of
Christ" in Gal 1:6–7.[63] Far from merely taking a message to the Jews that the
Christ has come for the Gentiles, Peter is taking to the Jews a message directly relevant to them. Jesus is the *Jewish* Messiah. If the Gentiles need to
place their trust in the Jewish Messiah, how much more would the Jews
themselves need to place their trust in the Jewish Messiah!

Abraham's "seed" is not the ethnic, collective Israel as understood in
the Genesis texts to which Paul refers in Gal 3:15–18, but rather Abraham's
"seed" is Christ alone and collectively those who are one "in Christ"—there
"is no longer Jew or Greek" (3:28–29). The Jew as well as the Greek must be
"in Christ" in order to be Abraham's Seed.[64] The differences between Jews

---

[61] Dunn writes (*Romans 9–16*, 528): "I find astonishing Gaston's claim [*Paul,* 7]
that 'Jesus is for Paul not the Messiah.'"

[62] John Piper, *The Justification of God: An Exegetical and Theological Study of
Romans 9:1–23* (2d ed.; Grand Rapids: Baker, 1993), 45. Heikki Räisänen comments: "Why the *deep sorrow* expressed by Paul in 9:1–2; 10:1? A lot of Paul's statements make little sense if it was not Israel's failure to *believe in Jesus as the Christ* that
was his problem" ("Paul, God, and Israel: Romans 9–11 in Recent Research," in *The
Social World of Formative Christianity and Judaism* [ed. Jacob Neusner, Peter Borgen,
Ernest S. Frerichs and Richard Horsley; Philadelphia: Fortress, 1988], 190; see also
p. 180). Dunn writes: "Gager's thesis that the Torah remains the path of righteousness for Israel "makes no sense . . . of Paul's anguish in 9:1–3" (*Romans 9–16*, 528).

[63] Bradley H. McLean, "Galatians 2.7–9 and the Recognition of Paul's Apostolic Status at the Jerusalem Conference: A Critique of G. Luedemann's Solution,"
NTS 37 (1991): 67–76. Cf. Gager (*Reinventing Paul,* 147) who distinguishes Peter's
"gospel" from Paul's "own gospel."

[64] Gager (*Reinventing Paul,* 88–89) incomprehensibly ignores this line of reasoning in the apostle's thought. Is there a degree of ironic truth in the title of his
book? Is this not after all a reinvention of Paul?

and Gentiles are not erased, but Gentiles do not need to become Jewish nor do the Jews need to become Gentile in order to be a part of Abraham's Seed. *All* are included by faith and by being "baptized into Christ" (Gal 3:27).[65] Paul affirms with his fellow Jews in Gal 2:15–16: "We ourselves are Jews by birth and not Gentile sinners; and yet we know that a person is justified not by the works of the law but through faith in Jesus Christ." Paul does not say "we Jews know that *the Gentiles* are justified not by works of the Law but through faith in Christ." He then adds in the very next part of v. 16: "And we have come to believe in Christ Jesus, so that we might be justified by faith in Christ, and not by doing the works of the law, because no one will be justified by the works of the law." Two-covenant theorists suppose that the "we" of the second half of v. 16 must be different from the "we Jews" of the first half. Nothing in the verse would indicate such a radical change of referent.[66] Galatians 2:16 is emphatic that "even we [Jews] have come to believe in Christ Jesus."[67] Paul concludes, drawing on the language of Ps 143:2 addressed originally to a *Jewish* audience: "*no one* will be justified [οὐ δικαιοῦται ἄνθρωπος] by the works of the law." He has interpreted Ps 143:2 to apply not only to the Jews but also to the Gentiles.[68] Two-covenant theorists are wrong, then, to deny that the apostle insists that the Jews place their faith in Christ.

Paul claims that the Jews have stumbled in Rom 9:32–33. Two-covenant proponents contend that the stone of stumbling in Rom 9:30–10:8 is not Christ but the Torah.[69] Whereas Paul says that Jews stumbled by pursuing the Mosaic Law on the basis of its works (Rom 9:32; see also 9:16), the two-covenant theorists argue that the Jews stumbled by not recognizing what God was doing for *the Gentiles* in Christ. An identification of the stone of stumbling with the Torah is unlikely.[70] "We proclaim Christ crucified, a stumbling block to Jews" (1 Cor 1:23). While some scholars have argued that the apostle is attacking Jewish ethnic presumption in Rom 9:30–10:8,

---

[65] Baptism incorporates both Jew and Greek into "the body *of Christ*" in 1 Cor 12:12–13, 27.

[66] Paul emphatically identifies himself with the Jews in 2:16a, and yet Gaston (*Paul and the Torah,* 70) claims that he is identifying himself with the Gentiles in the latter half of the verse. Gaston is trying to force a text, which says the exact opposite of what he claims, to fit into a preconceived theory.

[67] Nor is there any reason to suppose that the "we" group has changed with v. 17; see Das, *Paul, the Law, and the Covenant,* 169–70 n.71.

[68] By applying these words exclusively to the Gentiles, as Gaston does (*Paul and the Torah,* 70), he ironically ignores the Jewish setting of the allusion. From the use of "man" in Lev 18:5 (ἄνθρωπος in the LXX), R. Meir concluded that the verse applied to *all* human beings, and *not just* the Jew. In other words, the use of "man" struck R. Meir as a marker of universal reference (*b. Sanh.* 59a; see also Martyn, *Galatians,* 249 n. 120).

[69] Gager, *Reinventing Paul,* 12, 133; note the lack of argumentation for this assertion.

[70] See the discussion of the identity of the stone earlier in the chapter.

others have concluded that he is opposing a salvation based on "works" and merit. *Both* positions have strengths and are not exclusive of each other. If Jewish righteousness in the Law is a matter of empty "works" because grace and mercy have been reconceptualized in terms of Christ, then the Messiah is crucial for the Jews' salvation as well.[71] In "being ignorant of the righteousness that comes from God, and seeking to establish their own, [the Jews] have not submitted to God's righteousness" (Rom 10:3). The Jews' refusal to submit to God's righteousness will change one day when the Jews, along with all Creation, submit to *Christ,* who will in turn submit to God (1 Cor 15:24–28). On that day no one will be subject to God apart from Christ.[72] John Gager emphasizes that God is the sole object of faith for Paul but misses the fact that the apostle has redefined the *Shema* in his writings to include reference to Jesus Christ alongside God the Father.[73] As Paul writes in Rom 10:9: "If you confess with your lips that *Jesus is Lord* and believe in your heart that God raised him from the dead, you will be saved." Paul adds in vv. 12–13: "For there is *no distinction between Jew and Greek;* the same Lord is *Lord of all* and is generous to *all* who call on him. For, '*Everyone* who calls on the name of the Lord shall be saved.' "[74] God is impartial in salvation for Paul since all are saved on the same basis (see also 1:16; 3:21–31).[75] The language in 10:9–13—universality ("all"), salvation, and the Jewish people—recurs in 11:26 (all, Israel, saved). This recurrence suggests that all Israel's salvation must be understood in terms of the universality of 10:9–13 with faith in Christ. Likewise, the most natural understanding of the Jews' "disobedience" in 11:11–12, 19, 28a and "unbelief" (or "unfaithfulness"— ἀπιστία) in 11:20–23 is by reference to the faith in Christ spoken of throughout the letter, especially in 10:9–13 (πίστις *and* πιστεύω). Israel will be restored "if they do not persist in unbelief." "By the time one arrives at chapter 11, then, Paul has established a christocentric semantic range for the key vocabulary of this seemingly nonchristological discourse."[76]

---

[71] For a detailed exposition of Rom 9:30–10:8 that balances these two strands of thought in the passage, see Das, *Paul, the Law, and the Covenant,* 234–67. The failure of the Jews in these verses paves the way for the emphasis on faith in Christ for *all* people in Rom 10:9–13 (with the Jew singled out in v. 12).

[72] Gager (*Reinventing Paul,* 60) emphasizes that this is a monotheistic passage but ignores the fact that no one can be subject to God apart from a prior submission to Christ's Lordship.

[73] See the discussion of this point earlier in the chapter with reference to Rom 9:5.

[74] Tellingly, Gager (*Reinventing Paul,* 135) ignores this emphasis in Rom 10:8–13 on universal applicability.

[75] In her thorough critique of the two-covenant approach, E. Elizabeth Johnson notes that the mixed group of Jews and Gentiles that is the subject of vv. 12–13 remains the grammatical subject through the end of v. 18. Paul will single out Israel in v. 19. Therefore *for both Jews and Greeks* "faith comes from what is heard, and what is heard through the word of Christ" (10:16).

[76] Terence Donaldson, *Paul and the Gentiles: Remapping the Apostle's Convictional World* (Minneapolis: Fortress, 1997), 233.

Advocates of a two-covenant approach often translate πίστις in Paul's letters as "faithfulness" to the Law rather than "faith"/"belief" in Christ. Romans 1:16, for example, is a classic passage for proponents of faith in Christ, but this passage from the two-covenant perspective would refer to faithfulness (for the Jew to the Law) since it does not actually mention Christ.[77] Romans 4 likewise does not mention anything about faith in Christ in connection with Abraham's "faith(fulness)."[78] Certainly Abraham's faith rested on God's promises of what was still to take place (4:13). Paul is careful, though, to note that in the wake of Christ's crucifixion and resurrection a similar faith must now include recognition of what God has done *in Christ* (4:24–25). If πίστις were translated as "faithfulness," Rom 3:21–22 would be claiming that the Law and prophets witness to "the righteousness of God through the faithfulness of Jesus Christ (πίστις Ἰησοῦ Χριστοῦ) for all who believe" rather than "the righteousness of God through faith in Jesus Christ for all who believe."[79] These verses would no longer support the traditional emphasis on faith in Christ for all people, including the Jews. In spite of the two-covenanters' brash insistence on the incontestability of taking πίστις Χριστοῦ as Christ's own faithfulness, leading Pauline specialists continue vigorously to debate this translation.[80] Even if one were to grant the "faith/fulness of Christ" translation, "we Jews" confess, according to Gal 2:16, that faith in Christ incorporates the individual *into* the faithfulness of Christ.

Paul simply does not treat God's salvation of Israel separately from the salvation of the Gentiles. In Rom 11:31 he writes: "by means of the mercy shown to you [Gentiles], they, the Jews, will now receive mercy" (see also 11:13–16). The Jews' reception of mercy *by means of* the Gentiles' reception of mercy demonstrates that the two-covenant thesis of separate paths to salvation is simply wrong. The "two-covenant" approach does not explain why the Gentiles must experience mercy in order for the Jews to experience mercy. Paul speaks of *one* olive tree representing Israel's heritage as the same tree on which the Gentiles are grafted. He does not speak of two separate trees. Since a single tree represents their respective paths to salvation, the Jews must likewise place their faith in the Jewish Messiah as the fulfillment to which the Mosaic Law had pointed all along.

As a two-covenant theorist, Gager is candid in admitting that the burden of proof lies with him to demonstrate that all of Paul's negative

---

[77] For the Jew that faithfulness would express itself in a recognition of the gospel message of a Christ who has come on behalf of the Gentiles; Gager, *Reinventing Paul,* 110.

[78] Gaston, *Paul and the Torah,* 60–61, 123–26.

[79] Ibid., 12.

[80] For a recent, spirited defense of the "faith in Christ" translation, see R. Barry Matlock, "'Even the Demons Believe': Paul and πίστις Χριστοῦ," *CBQ* 64 (2002): 300–18; cf. Gaston, 12: "The correctness of the translation of *pistis Iesou Christou* as the 'faith or faithfulness of Jesus Christ' has by now been too well established to need any further support."

statements regarding the Law apply only to the Gentiles since such an interpretation did not emerge in the history of Christianity until these last few decades.[81] Pauline interpreters historically claimed that the apostle reasons about the Law in general and has applied those conclusions to the concrete situations of Gentiles in his letters. In advancing their "new perspective," two-covenanters often ignore evidence that would contradict their thesis that Paul offers no critique of the Law as such. For instance, Gager rewords Gal 3:19: "The law was added—*to Gentiles*—because of their transgressions" (emphasis mine). In this instance, Gager is able to justify the alteration by relying on a prior essay by Lloyd Gaston that angels were associated with the Gentile nations at the giving of the Law. The proponents of a two-covenant approach overlook Jewish texts that speak of angels participating in the giving of the Law at Mt. Sinai *to the Israelites* (e.g., Deut 33:2 [LXX]; Josephus, *Ant.* 15.5.3 §136; Philo, *Somn.* 1.141–143).[82] In other words, the allusion to angels pertains to the giving of the Law itself, whether to Jew or Gentile. The historic approach—that Paul is applying to the Gentiles universal conclusions with respect to the Law and salvation—simply makes much better sense of the evidence.[83] What Rosemary Radford Ruether wrote a generation ago would apply equally today: "Contemporary ecumenists who use Romans 11 to argue that Paul does not believe that God has rejected the people of the Mosaic covenant speak out of good intentions, but inaccurate exegesis."[84]

A very different approach to "all Israel will be saved" understands "all Israel" to be an "Israel of faith," all people who believe in Jesus Christ whether Jewish or Gentile. Paul would be speaking in Rom 11:26 of the Christian Church as Israel. The problem with this reading is that while the apostle certainly does apply the term "Israel" with different senses throughout Romans 9–11, he never uses the term in a way that includes Gentiles. By "Israel" he always means either the Jewish people as an entire ethnic group or a believing remnant within that people. For example, in Rom 9:4–5 Paul

---

[81] Gager, *Reinventing Paul,* 74.

[82] Ibid., 89; Gaston, *Paul and the Torah,* 35–44; Martyn, *Galatians,* 135 n.145.

[83] Frank Thielman has belabored the faulty logic among two-covenant theorists:

> So in Phil. 2:11 when Paul says "every knee shall bow, whether heavenly, earthly, or subterranean, and every tongue shall confess that Jesus Christ is Lord to the glory of God the Father" we should not infer that he means every *Gentile* knee shall bow and tongue confess, even if he is addressing a predominantly Gentile church. The scene is the eschaton and the language is cosmic and all-encompassing, even though the problem at hand is probably the mundane squabbles of the Philippian congregation (see 4:2). When Paul does not *say* "every Gentile" we should not understand him to *mean* "every Gentile" unless the context of the argument itself demands that meaning (*From Plight to Solution: A Jewish Framework for Understanding Paul's View of the Law in Galatians and Romans* [NovTSup 61; Leiden: E. J. Brill, 1989], 126–27).

[84] Rosemary Radford Ruether, *Faith and Fraticide: The Theological Roots of Anti-Semitism* (New York: Seabury, 1974), 106.

speaks of Israelites as his kindred according to the flesh to whom belong the covenants, the giving of the Law, and the fathers. He is speaking of ethnic Israel as a whole (so also 11:1–2). The entity of Israel is therefore contrasted with the Gentiles (9:30–31). In 11:28 he likewise speaks of ethnic Israel as the object of hope: they are beloved for the sake of the fathers as regards election, even though they are enemies of God as regards the gospel. Paul also distinguishes in Romans 9 between ethnic Israel per se and a believing remnant as a subgroup within ethnic Israel. Romans 9:6's statement that "not all Israel is Israel" is not, then, a reference to Gentiles. Likewise the contrast in Romans 11 is between all ethnic Israel and a remnant within ethnic Israel (11:1–7, esp. v. 7). Even when Paul speaks of the grafting of the Gentiles onto the olive tree representing Israel, he maintains a strict distinction in language between "you [Gentiles]" and "those [Israelites]." Paul continues to speak consistently of "Israel" as a group *distinct* from the Gentiles in v. 25. Nothing in v. 26's use of "Israel" signals a change from Paul's practice earlier in the chapter. Paul has maintained a consistent distinction between Jew and the Gentile throughout the letter, e.g., 1:16; 3:1–2; 4:11–12; 15:8–9. Further, the logic of Romans 11 requires that "Israel" remain exclusive of the Gentiles. In the olive branch imagery, the imagery shifts from Israel as God's chosen, to their rejection and the grafting in of the Gentiles, to the restoration of the Jews, i.e. Israel—Gentiles—Israel. Verses 25–26 are drawing conclusions based on what preceded in Romans 11, and the progression remains the same: Israel—Gentiles—Israel. The "all Israel" of v. 26 is the restoration promised in vv. 12 and 24, the "full inclusion" of ethnic Israel as distinct from the Gentiles.[85] To understand the word "Israel" in the "all Israel" phrase of v. 26 as inclusive of the Gentiles, again, would depart from Paul's limitation of "Israel" to ethnic Jews throughout Romans 9–11.[86] Paul is absorbed in these chapters with the fate of his own people.

A third approach interprets "all Israel" as another term for the believing Jewish remnant referred to in Romans 9:1–23 and 11:1–10.[87] This

---

[85] "All Israel" is a corporate expression and therefore does not mean every Israelite who ever lived, nor even every Israelite at the time when "all Israel" is saved. It has the same meaning as the "full number" in 11:12 and is parallel to the "full number" of the Gentiles in the previous verse; Joseph A. Fitzmyer, *Romans* (AB 33; New York: Doubleday, 1993), 623.

[86] Some have pointed to Paul's reference to "the Israel of God" in Gal 6:16 as proof that the apostle has used "Israel" to include Gentile Christian believers, in this case the Gentile Galatians. This is certainly a legitimate possibility, but a strong case can be made that "the Israel of God" refers to ethnic Jews who have believed the gospel message. Even if one grants that "the Israel of God" in Gal 6:16 is the church, Paul need not use "Israel" in the same sense in Romans 9–11: he may be backing off from his prior identification in a more nuanced and focused discussion. Galatians 6:16 is therefore of little help in deciding Rom 11:26's "all Israel." See the discussion in chapter 2 above.

[87] The most recent defense of this position is by Ben L. Merkle, "Romans 11 and the Future of Ethnic Israel," *JETS* 43 (2000): 709–21.

approach takes seriously the categorical statement in Rom 9:6b that "not all Israel is Israel," a distinction Paul maintains in 11:7. In light of 9:6 Rom 11:26's "all Israel" would not need to be all or even the majority of ethnic Israel. Romans 11:26 would be talking about Jewish Christians as the elect remnant throughout the world. Non-Christian Israelites would not be included. The problem that has motivated Paul's concern for Israel in 9:1–5 and throughout his discussion in Romans 9–11, however, is precisely that the vast majority of Israel does not currently believe in Christ. Only a tiny remnant has become Christian. Paul continues to speak of the small number of Jewish Christians in Romans 11 as a "remnant" (λεῖμμα in 11:5–7), "some" (τινές in 11:17), or a "part of Israel" (ἀπὸ μέρους τῷ Ἰσραήλ in 11:25). In Rom 11:26, on the other hand, Paul speaks instead of "all Israel" (πᾶς Ἰσραήλ) or the "full number" (πλήρωμα of 11:12). The contrast in language is striking: the whole of Israel (πᾶς Ἰσραήλ) stands juxtaposed with a portion (ἀπὸ μέρους τῷ Ἰσραήλ) in 11:25–26.[88] The apostle is struggling to show that God remains faithful to all Israel even though Israel has to a great extent become hardened and disobedient. A people currently characterized by "rejection" will be characterized by their "acceptance" (v.15).[89] Paul envisions his grand solution to this problem as a "mystery" in 11:25. It would hardly be a mystery if all Paul meant were that a few, elect Jews would believe in Christ.[90] If by speaking of "all Israel" being saved, Paul means nothing more than an elect group of Israelites, then v. 26 would say nothing beyond the preceding discussion.

Seeing "all Israel" as coterminous with the remnant within Israel does not do justice to the Hebrew Scriptures' concept of a remnant. Throughout the Hebrew Scriptures the remnant within Israel was always a sign of hope for Israel as a whole (Gen 7:23; 2 Kgs 19:30–31; Isa 11:11–12, 16; 37:31–32; Mic 2:12; 4:7; 5:7–8; Zech 8:12). In Romans 11 Paul speaks of the "remnant" in Elijah's day. The 7,000 in Elijah's day functioned in a preserving capacity for the wicked majority of Israel. The continuing existence of a

---

[88] It is the numerical contrast between the part of Israel in v. 25 and "all Israel" in v. 26 that poses a problem for Merkle's reading. He reverses Paul's train of thought, which moves from the vast majority of unbelieving Israel in his day as the portion to the even greater number included when "all Israel" is saved. Is it really likely that the "remnant" *within* Israel should be *the same as* "*all* Israel"?

[89] Merkle (p. 718) is forced by his interpretation to distinguish the Jews who failed to believe in Christ (thus the "rejection") from "the full number of the elect" who accept. The positing of two *different* groups ruins the contrast between a rejection and subsequent acceptance—two contrasting receptions—by *the same* people, the majority of ethnic Israel.

[90] Raymond E. Brown (*The Semitic Background of the Term "Mystery" in the New Testament* [FBBS 12; Philadelphia: Fortress, 1968]) explains that a "mystery" in biblical literature refers to God's hidden plan, which has not yet been revealed, or to a partial revelation that has not yet been fully understood. God had already revealed the existence of a Jewish remnant in Paul's own day. A believing remnant therefore would not constitute the mystery of Romans 11.

remnant proved that God had not abandoned or rejected Israel. God always promised to restore and rebuild the people around the nucleus of the remnant. What was happening with an elect portion within Israel proffered hope for the entirety of the people.[91] In Rom 9:29 when he quotes Isa 1:9, Paul says: "If the LORD of hosts had not left us a few survivors, we would have become like Sodom, and become like Gomorrah" (cf. Gen 18:26–32). In Rom 11:26 Paul envisions the blossoming of a hope that remains as a bud embodied for the moment in the believing few.

PAUL'S VISION OF ETHNIC ISRAEL'S FATE

Romans 9–11 remains riveted on the fate of ethnic Israel. Paul nowhere describes Gentiles as Israel in these chapters. On the contrary, the apostle has been moved to such great depths of emotion because of the tragic fate of his own people. They have missed the significance of Jesus Christ as the Messiah. The path to salvation for Israel will be the same as the path for the Gentiles. God is impartial both in judgment and in salvation. Israel's benefits as an ethnic people do not guarantee an automatic place in the world to come. The most satisfactory understanding of 11:26 takes the verse as an anticipation of the day when all Israel will be saved. Once the full number of the Gentiles has entered into the ranks of believers in Christ, the Jewish people will come to faith in Christ en masse.[92] The remnant of Israel that believes in Christ is a promise of what is to come. God has not abandoned the Jewish people and will graft ethnic Israel back onto its own olive tree before the end of the age (11:23).

Some have proposed that the conversion of Israel will take place with the return of Christ from the heavens.[93] Since Israel is hardened, the people will not be able to respond with faith to the message of Christ until his second coming overwhelms that hardening to create the necessary faith (cf. Rom 11:23). In other words, Israel will come to faith not through any sort of spread of Christ's message during the era of the earthly church but rather through Christ's appearance at his return. If, however, God is sovereignly and powerfully able to overcome Israel's unbelief at the point of Christ's

---

[91] And if the remnant is such because of faith in Christ, then the hope is that "all Israel" will similarly believe.

[92] Paul employs "all Israel" parallel to the "full inclusion" of Israel in 11:12. Even as the "full inclusion" of Israel refers to the bulk of the people at that time and not every Jewish person who ever lived, the same applies also to "all Israel." The apostle is focused on the whole of humanity within the course of God's saving plan and not on individuals as such.

[93] Franz Mußner, *Tractate on the Jews: The Significance of Judaism for Christian Faith* (trans. Leonard Swidler; Philadelphia: Fortress, 1984), 32–34; idem, *Die Kraft der Wurzel: Judentum—Jesus—Kirche* (Freiburg: Herder, 1989), 48–54; Otfried Hofius, "Das Evangelium und Israel: Erwägungen zu Römer 9–11," *ZTK* 83 (1986): 319–20.

return, surely God is equally able to do so during the era of the earthly church. In 9:6–23 Paul maintains God's sovereign power to harden *and* to have mercy. In 10:9–17 he emphasizes that God will save all people, whether Jews or Gentiles, through the message about Christ that human intermediaries proclaim. The gospel message comes with the divine power to evoke faith. Paul does not say in Romans 11 anything that would set aside or qualify the impartial approach to the salvation of all people that he belabored in Romans 10. In 11:13–14 he certainly hopes to win his fellow Jews through his own ministry (see also 1 Cor 9:19–23). The impression he leaves is that if "some" are saved through his ministry, the hope of salvation remains for the rest through a comparable evangelizing activity.[94] Nowhere in Romans 11 does Paul connect the salvation of all Israel to Christ's Parousia or second coming. Paul does not even refer to the Parousia of Christ in Romans 9–11. In 11:26–27 he certainly speaks of the Deliverer who "will come" out of Zion, drawing upon the language of Isa 59:20; 27:9 and Ps 49:1 LXX, but for Paul those prophecies have already been fulfilled. Christ came from Zion as the Jewish Messiah (9:5). God has already placed in Zion the stumbling stone (9:33). Christ has already become a servant of the circumcised "in order that he might confirm the promises given to the patriarchs" (15:8). The prophecies Paul cites in 11:26–27 were therefore fulfilled in Christ's *first* coming. Furthermore, the promise to take away sin in 11:27 parallels the covering of sins by faith in 4:7, and the banishment of ungodliness in 11:26 is reminiscent of the God of 4:5 "who justifies the ungodly [τὸν ἀσεβῆ]" by the same faith in the promises (now fulfilled) that Abraham possessed. The connections between 11:26–27 and 4:5, 7 suggest that the banishment of ungodliness and the removal of sins will not have to wait for the arrival of the very end of the age.[95] Paul's hopes for Israel in Romans 11 should therefore be construed in light of what he has said throughout Romans 9–11, especially the impartial preaching of the message about Christ to both Jews and Gentiles in 10:9–17.[96] Perhaps Paul views his planned missionary activity in Spain as part of a divine scheme that will trigger God's ultimate salvation of ethnic Israel once the fullness of the Gentiles has come to faith. The salvation of the Gentiles will somehow provoke the Jews to a jealousy that will lead to their salvation.[97] This is the great mystery

---

[94] The πλήρωμα ("full inclusion") of Israel verbally echoes and is linked to the πλήρωμα ("full number") of the Gentiles (11:11–12, 25).

[95] Reidar Hvalvik, "A 'Sonderweg' for Israel: A Critical Examination of a Current Interpretation of Romans 11.25–27," *JSNT* 39 (1990): 96.

[96] For a more detailed critique of a mass conversion of the Jews at Christ's second coming, see ibid., 87–107; and, more recently, Michael G. Vanlaningham, "Should the Church Evangelize Israel? A Response to Franz Mussner and Other *Sonderweg* Proponents," *TJ* 22 NS (2001): 197–217.

[97] On a temporal understanding of καὶ οὕτως in 11:26, although not necessarily to the exclusion of a modal sense, see Pieter W. van der Horst, " 'Only Then Will All Israel Be Saved': A Short Note on the Meaning of καὶ οὕτως in Romans 11:26,"

for Paul (11:25). In spite of their apparent present lack of faith, all Israel—the Jewish people—will be saved at some point in the future. The hardened lack of faith or "disobedience," to use Paul's language, will give way to Christian faith.[98]

The apostle may not have envisioned Israel's salvation in the distant future. The Living Bible's "and then" (καὶ οὕτως) in 11:26 may also be translated "and *so* all Israel will be saved" (NRSV). The realization of the full number of the Gentiles could be in motion at the very same time as the divine promise to save all Israel. Paul certainly hopes to bring about the salvation of the Jews in his own missionary activity to the Gentiles (11:14). In 11:30–31 Paul uses "once" (ποτέ) only for Gentile disobedience; he uses "now" (νῦν) for the Gentiles' present mercy, Israel's present disobedience, and also Israel's obtaining of mercy.[99] Paul saw the time in which he was living as the "now" of hardened Israel's conversion. Although the hardening will be completely removed only with the "fullness" of the Gentiles, God is already in motion to fulfill the promise.

In a neglected essay from 1981 that deserves further consideration, John Battle suggested that this climactic conclusion with respect to the Jewish people was foreshadowed already in Romans 9.[100] The apostle quotes Hos 2:23 and 1:10 in Rom 9:25–26, and Battle contends that Paul is applying these words, as had Hosea, to the fate of ethnic Israel: those who were not God's people shall be God's people. Rejected and exiled Israel will experience God's restoration and salvation; in the words of 11:26, "all Israel will be saved." Battle notes that in 9:19–29 almost all of Paul's quotations from the Scriptures refer to the fate of national Israel.[101] In Rom 9:20 Paul quotes Isa 29:16 and 45:9 (Isa 45:9 is an exception to the pattern); in Rom 9:25, Hos 2:23; in Rom 9:26, Hos 1:10; in Rom 9:27–28, Isa 10:22–23; and in Rom 9:29, Isa 1:9. In each instance the prophets were looking forward to

---

JBL 119 (2000): 521–25. Merkle's claim that καὶ οὕτως never has a temporal sense is simply wrong.

[98] As Ruether recognized years ago: "The 'conversion of the Jews,' then, becomes in Paul the last event in the historical economy of salvation. It shows that God has not cast off his people ultimately, but has reserved them in their present state of apostasy until the final ingathering of the elect" (*Faith and Fratricide,* 106).

[99] See νῦν in the Greek codices ℵ B D, and the copyists' dissatisfaction with Paul's text in the later change to ὕστερον; Michael G. Vanlaningham, "Romans 11:25–27 and the Future of Israel in Paul's Thought," *MSJ* 3 (1992): 166–67 n. 83.

[100] John A. Battle Jr., "Paul's Use of the Old Testament in Romans 9:25–26," *Grace Theological Journal* 2 (1981): 115–29. Apparently independently William S. Campbell has come to a similar reading in "Divergent Images of Paul and His Mission," in *Reading Israel in Romans: Legitimacy and Plausibility of Divergent Interpretations* (ed. Cristina Grenholm and Daniel Patte; Romans through History and Culture Series; Harrisburg, Pa.: Trinity Press International, 2000), 198–200. Battle's essay is more thorough in its argumentation.

[101] Battle also lists Rom 9:33 (Isa 8:14; 28:16) as fitting into the pattern, but that verse functions in a new section of Paul's thought from 9:30 through 10:21.

the Assyrian siege of Jerusalem in 701 B.C.E. (Hos 1:6–11; 2:9–14, 19–23; 3:4–5; Isa 1:5–9; 5:20–30; 7:17–20; 8:4; 10:5–27) and its impact on the people. Further, the "objects of wrath" of which Hosea spoke, according to Paul in Rom 9:22, cannot be equated with non-Christian Jews since the "objects of wrath" were the instruments of oppression employed against Israel and were themselves ultimately destroyed. Thus Pharaoh oppressed Israel for a time and then was destroyed. Romans 9:22–24 forms a single sentence in the Greek original, and the main clause of the sentence states that God "endured with much patience the objects of wrath that are made for destruction." According to the subordinate clauses of the sentence, God's enduring of these objects shows God's wrath, makes known his power, and makes "known the riches of his glory for the objects of mercy, which he has prepared beforehand for glory." How would God's enduring the Jewish people with patience demonstrate his wrath and power? "Would it not be better to say: he *judges, punishes,* or *oppresses* vessels of wrath?"[102]

> On the other hand, if Israel's oppressors are the "vessels of wrath," the statement makes perfect sense: God *bears with much longsuffering* heathen, godless nations, by allowing them to rule over Israel and the world, in order that he might use them as instruments to convey his wrath and power against unbelieving Israel, and in the end his glory and mercy to repentant Israel (along with believing Gentiles), when he destroys those wicked nations.

Such an interpretation of the "vessels of wrath" finds support in the use of the term "vessel" (σκεῦος; Heb. כְּלִי). The same Hebrew word translated as "vessel" in the Greek may also be translated as "weapon" (ὅπλον). The Medes were God's instrument in Isa 13:5 to destroy the Babylonians. Assyria was God's instrument or weapon against Israel, and God would ultimately destroy Assyria as well. After that point a remnant within Israel would be delivered and return (Isa 10:5–34).[103] The advantage of this interpretation is that it maintains a tighter focus upon the fate of ethnic Israel as the subject of Rom 9:6–29. Although Paul mentions Gentiles briefly in 9:24, he will not develop this point until 9:30–10:21. If Battle's exposition were correct, then by citing these particular prophetic passages in 9:19–29, Paul would already be hinting at the final solution to come in 11:25–26. Israel will return from its exile.

The crucial problem that remains to be resolved for Battle's approach lies in Rom 9:25–26. Paul cites the words of Hosea originally concerning the unworthy people of Israel. The prophet had proffered these words as hope to the people of Israel for a future restoration of the nation, which conforms nicely to Battle's reading, but Paul does in the end appear to apply these words to the Gentiles. The Hosea quote justifies the claim in v. 24 that God is right to call not only the Jews but also the Gentiles, and the application of

[102] Battle, "Paul's Use of the Old Testament," 126.
[103] Ibid., 126–27.

Hosea to the Gentiles in vv. 24–26 stands in contrast (δέ) to Paul's explicit application of Isa 10:22–23 to Israel in v. 27 (ὑπὲρ τοῦ 'Ισραήλ). The same pattern recurs at the end of Romans 10 as Gentiles benefit from the blessings of Israel (10:19–21). To put the matter differently, if Paul were applying the Hosea quote to Israel already in 9:25–26, he would not have needed to specify in v. 27 that the Isaiah prophecy refers to Israel. Such a qualification of v. 27 (and 10:21) only makes sense if the referent of the prior quotation had not been Israel. Paul applies the Hosea passage, a passage that in its original context had referred to Israel, to believing Gentiles alongside the elect remnant of Christian Jews.[104] As promising as Battle's thesis initially appears, Paul reserves the "mystery" regarding his people until Romans 11.

To summarize: A Christ-centered pattern of thought reverberates throughout Romans 9–11. He is the Messiah (9:5). The repeated emphases on a salvation for all people, including ethnic Jews, through Christ as Lord in Romans 10 color the surrounding discussion even when Christ is not actually mentioned. One simply cannot read 9:6–29 or Romans 11 in isolation apart from what the apostle says elsewhere in his discussion. Consequently, stubborn, unbelieving, ethnic Israel, insofar as the Jews remain in unbelief, stands allied with Pharaoh, Esau, and Ishmael. The Jews do not automatically enjoy salvation on the basis of their ethnic identity and election apart from faith in the Jewish Messiah. Paul's argument does not end with Romans 9 and 10. He holds out hope for Israel in Romans 11 when he claims that "all Israel will be saved." Throughout Paul's reasoning God has always had a plan for ethnic Israel. The apostle firmly maintains Israel's election (11:25–26) while he at the same time also emphasizes the necessity of faith in Christ. The coming of Jesus Christ as the Messiah has considerably altered Paul's conception of Israel's historical election as the people of God. The apostle is forced to look toward the future. Hope is on the horizon.

---

[104] See also 1 Pet 2:10, which adapts Hos 2:23 for a Gentile Christian audience. Romans 9:24, however, rules out the possibility that the application of Hosea to the Gentiles in v. 25 is to Israel's detriment; see Richard B. Hays, *Echoes of Scripture in the Letters of Paul* (New Haven: Yale University Press, 1989), 66–67.

∿ 5 ∾

ISRAEL'S PRIORITY AMONG THE NATIONS

> For I am not ashamed of the gospel; it is the power of God for sal-
> vation to everyone who has faith, to the Jew first and also to the
> Greek. (Rom 1:16)

> Now if their stumbling means riches for the world, and if their de-
> feat means riches for Gentiles, how much more will their full in-
> clusion mean! (Rom 11:12)

IF JEWS and Gentiles are both saved by faith in Jesus the Christ and are both
judged impartially by God, "what advantage has the Jew?" (Rom 3:1). What
God is doing in Christ appears entirely severed from the history of Israel.
Why not ignore Israel's heritage and focus entirely on Christ? Some in the
Roman church certainly took that approach, but the apostle's climactic pronouncement in 11:26 that "all Israel will be saved" forces a reconsideration
of Israel's place in God's plan. Ironically, after emphasizing throughout his
letter up to this point that God treats both Jew and Gentile impartially, Paul
shifts gears in Romans 11 and may suggest a privileged position for Israel
after all. Their history and heritage are not irrelevant, nor should these be
ignored. Although Paul is adamant that the salvation of all people, whether
Jew or Gentile, requires faith in Christ, the failure of the Jews to believe in
the Messiah is by no means the end of their story. Romans 11 has figured
prominently in contemporary discussions of Paul and the Jews because he
refused to concede the rights of his people before God. Paul insists that the
Jews maintain a priority in God's eschatological drama. Hints of Israel's priority may very well lie elsewhere in his writings as well. For instance, some
interpreters remain convinced that as strong as Paul's statements in Galatians appear at first sight against the Mosaic Law and perhaps also against
the Jewish people, he maintains that the Gentiles owe their salvation in no
small measure to the Jews. Interpreters remain perplexed, however, by
some of the apostle's strong statements against the Jews. One of the most difficult of these pronouncements is in his First Letter to the Thessalonians.
Paul claims in 1 Thess 2:14–16 that the Jews are guilty of murdering Jesus
and the prophets and are "filling up the measure of their sins." The apostle

claims that the Jews deserve "God's wrath," which has "overtaken them at last." If Paul can make such a bold claim against the Jews in First Thessalonians, the same Paul certainly cannot believe Israel has any priority in God's plan for all humanity.

Again: Israel's Privilege (Rom 11:11–26)

Echoing through Romans 11 is Paul's thunderous declaration from his opening page: "I am not ashamed of the gospel; it is the power of God for salvation to everyone who has faith, to the Jew *first* and also to the Greek" (1:16). Although it is a "mystery" for Paul, God reserves a priority of position for the Jewish people in the future. Addressing his Gentile readers in 11:17, Paul envisions an olive tree that represents Israel as God's own: "some of the branches were broken off, and you, a wild olive shoot, were grafted *in their place* [ἐν αὐτοῖς] to share the rich root of the olive tree." The NRSV's translation of the verse suggests that the Gentiles occupy places on the olive tree that once belonged to Israelites and that since Israel rejected the gospel message, their life-giving spots were granted to others. The NRSV translators are following a venerable tradition of interpretation that can be traced to John Chrysostom, an early church father who reasoned similarly about Israel. "There is almost a spatial analogy here. Only if some Israelites are cleared out will there be room for gentiles."[1] God rejected many in Israel in order to make room for the Gentiles. Although a displacement has taken place, Paul is wary lest the Gentiles boast that they have supplanted Israel on the olive tree of salvation.

A number of problems beset an extreme displacement reading of Rom 11:17 that sees no future at all for the branches that have been broken off. "In their place" is not the most natural translation of the Greek prepositional phrase ἐν αὐτοῖς. If Paul had intended to say that the wild olive branches have been grafted "in the place of" the excised natural branches, he would have used a different Greek prepositional phrase, such as ἀντὶ αὐτῶν. "Among them" makes a better translation within this context. As some of the natural branches were broken off, wild shoots were grafted in among them, that is, among the (remaining?) natural branches. Quite apart from the translation, it is difficult to imagine spatial limitations on God's own olive tree.[2] Paul himself explicitly raises the possibility of a displacement understanding in v. 19: "You will say, 'Branches were broken off so

---

[1] Paul J. Achtemeier, *Romans,* 180, specifically in relation to Rom 11:11.

[2] Donaldson, *Paul and the Gentiles,* 217–19. Donaldson opposes any sort of displacement reading or spatial metaphor in favor of a temporal understanding. But to accept both a spatial and a temporal dimension to Paul's imagery does not automatically grant the legitimacy of a radical displacement reading where there is no future for ethnic Israel.

that I might be grafted in.' " The NRSV once again translates Paul's response to the idea in a manner that permits a radical displacement reading: "That is true" (καλῶς). But the Greek word καλῶς is ambiguous, with a range of meanings from full approval ("Well said") to ironic concession to polite refusal ("No, thank you").[3] When Paul writes in v. 17 that the wild olive branches will be grafted in among "them," the referent to "them" (αὐτοῖς) is also ambiguous. Although the context of Paul's reasoning clearly favors the remaining natural branches as the referent for "them," or Christian Jews, the pronoun's referent may also be the cut-off branches (non-Christian Jews). Paul's ambiguity on the point appears deliberate: he is deftly leaving the door open to imagine the cut-off branches being grafted back into the olive tree alongside the wild olive shoots and the remaining natural branches.[4]

As Paul writes a few verses later in Rom 11:23–24:

> And even those of Israel, if they do not persist in unbelief, will be grafted in, for God has the power to graft them in again. For if you have been cut from what is by nature a wild olive tree and grafted, contrary to nature, into a cultivated olive tree, how much more will these natural branches be grafted back into their own olive tree.

Far from being permanently displaced, the natural branches will eventually be restored. The pattern of reasoning should be familiar from vv. 11–12:

> So I ask, have they (Israel) stumbled so as to fall? By no means! But through their stumbling salvation has come to the Gentiles, so as to make Israel jealous. Now if their stumbling means riches for the world, and if their defeat means riches for Gentiles, how much more will their full inclusion mean!

In contrast to their current stumbling, Paul foresees the ultimate blessings that will result when the fullness (πλήρωμα) of Israel benefits from God's plan.[5] The apostle continues, "For if their [the Jews'] rejection is the reconciliation of the world, what will their acceptance be but life from the dead!" (v. 15). Whereas vv. 11–12 do not specify what the benefits would be from Israel's "full inclusion," Paul concludes in v. 15 that it will be "life from the dead" (ζωὴ ἐκ νεκρῶν), resurrection.

The current rejection of the Jews has permitted a time for the Gentiles; nevertheless, Paul looks forward to a time when the Jews will again benefit from God's riches. The return of the Jews will trigger the resurrection of the dead (v. 15). In vv. 25–26 Paul identifies the plan for the salvation of all Israel:

> So that you may not claim to be wiser than you are, brothers and sisters, I want you to understand this mystery: a hardening has come upon part of

---

[3] LSJ 870.

[4] Dunn, *Romans 9–16,* 661.

[5] This is another problem for the belief that Paul is talking about only a believing remnant in 11:26. The majority ("Israel") that are currently rejecting, unlike the believing remnant, will be the ones included.

Israel, until the full number of the Gentiles has come in. And so all Israel will be saved; as it is written,

"Out of Zion will come the Deliverer;
    he will banish ungodliness from Jacob."
"And this is my covenant with them,
    when I take away their sins."

The mystery is that the hardening that has come upon part of Israel is only for a time, until the full number of the Gentiles has come in. "And so all Israel will be saved." The NRSV follows the majority of modern commentators in translating the first Greek phrase of the sentence "and so" (καὶ οὕτως). This is a modal (or logical) translation, but a temporal translation is equally plausible: "*and [only] then* all Israel will be saved."[6] Certainly the preceding words suggest a temporal sequence since the hardening of a part of Israel is only "until" (ἄχρι οὗ) the full number of the Gentiles has come in.

Israel's sinfulness has delayed the end of the world and the culmination of the ages. Their rejection has opened a window for the Gentiles that will close once Israel repents and is restored. With the repentance of Israel, the end will come. Other Jewish sources offer ample parallels for Paul's temporal logic. According to *T. Dan* 6:4 from the first or second century B.C.E., Satan knew "that on the day in which Israel trusts, the enemy's kingdom will be brought to an end."[7] Similarly in *T. Sim.* 6:2–7, the end would come "*if* you divest yourselves of envy and every hardness of heart" (emphasis mine).[8] In the *Testament of Moses* (first century B.C.E.), the deaths of Taxo and his sons triggered the end. *Fourth Ezra* 4:39 at the end of the first century C.E. responded to such beliefs: "And it is perhaps on account of us that the time of threshing is delayed for the righteous—on account of the sins of those who dwell on earth."[9] In *2 Bar.* 78:6–7 God promised "that he will never forget or forsake our offspring, but with much mercy assemble all those again who were dispersed."[10] Within the NT corpus, Peter's speech to the Jewish people in Acts 3:19–21 reflects this view of the end:

Repent therefore, and turn to God so that your sins may be wiped out, so that times of refreshing may come from the presence of the Lord, and that he may send the Messiah appointed for you, that is, Jesus, who must remain in heaven until the time of universal restoration that God announced long ago through his holy prophets.

---

[6] Horst, " 'Only Then Will All Israel Be Saved' "; see also Karl Olav Sandnes, *Paul—One of the Prophets?* (WUNT 2/43; Tübingen: J. C. B. Mohr [Paul Siebeck], 1991), 172–75. For other temporal instances of this construction in the NT, Horst points to Acts 7:8; 20:11; 27:17; 1 Thess 4:16–17.

[7] *OTP* 1:810.

[8] *OTP* 1:787.

[9] *OTP* 1:531.

[10] *OTP* 1:648.

And the author of 2 Pet 3:11–12 writes,

> Since all these things are to be dissolved in this way, what sort of persons
> ought you to be in leading lives of holiness and godliness, waiting for and has-
> tening the coming of the day of God, because of which the heavens will be set
> ablaze and dissolved, and the elements will melt with fire?[11]

The future of the cosmos and all humanity appears dependent upon the fate
of Israel.

Paul views Israel's impending restoration as potentially imminent:
"Just as you were *once* disobedient to God but have *now* received mercy because of their [Israel's] disobedience, so that they have *now* been disobedient in order that, by the mercy shown to you, they too may *now* receive
mercy" (Rom 11:30–31). "Now" is the day of Israel's salvation. Paul speaks
of Israel's present obtaining of mercy. He hopes, by his own missionary activity to the Gentiles, to bring about the salvation of the Jews (11:14). Perhaps this may explain why he wanted to travel to Spain, the western end of
the known (Gentile) world (15:22–24). He may have viewed the creation of
a Gentile Christian community in Spain as the final step in completing the
"fullness" of Gentile salvation, thereby triggering all Israel's salvation.[12] By
reaching the entire Gentile world, Paul believes he will see the day when
God's plan for Israel will be finally and fully realized.

In Rom 11:28–29 Paul makes a paradoxical claim: "As regards the
gospel they are enemies of God for your sake; but as regards election they
are beloved, for the sake of their ancestors; for the gifts and the calling of
God are irrevocable." The Jewish people are currently "enemies of God for
your sake" with respect to the gospel.[13] The qualification "As regards the
gospel" is crucial. Because the bulk of Israel has rejected the gospel of Jesus
Christ (1:16–17), they are "enemies of God." But God has not given up on
them, "for the gifts and the calling of God are irrevocable." God will bring
about a change in their condition. In other words, God's eschatological plan
revolves entirely around Israel. They remain the cultivated olive tree. The
Gentiles, for their part, remain a distinct, engrafted group. They are the wild
olive branches. The Gentiles are currently benefiting from the temporary
delay of Israel's salvation, but Paul leaves absolutely no room for Gentile

---

[11] Dale C. Allison Jr., "Romans 11:11–15: A Suggestion," *PRSt* 12 (1985):
23–25; "The Background of Romans 11:11–15 in Apocalyptic and Rabbinic Literature," *Studia biblica et theologica* 10 (1980): 229–34.

[12] For the classic expression of this position, see Roger D. Aus, "Paul's Travel
Plans to Spain and the 'Full Number of the Gentiles' in Rom. XI 25," *NovT* 21
(1979): 232–62. I have stated this view rather minimally, since I am convinced that
several of Aus's arguments tend to detract from, rather than support, his case; see
Vanlaningham's critique ("Romans 11:25–27," 164–65).

[13] This dark phrase poses difficulties for both Nanos's reading (see ch. 3 above)
and the *Sonderweg*/two-covenant theorists (see ch. 4, above). The phrase is also problematic for the view that Paul is only referring in these verses to the Jewish Christian
remnant and not the majority of non-Christian Israel.

presumption or superiority. Although the Gentiles certainly benefit from being grafted onto Israel and from sharing in Israel's blessings, the distinction between Israelite and Gentile remains. That the two groups remain separate is borne out by the consistent distinction between "you Gentiles" (cf. 11:13) and "they" (Israel) in 11:28–31. Paul rules out Gentile Christian arrogance or boasting.

Although Gentile Christians are also members of the elect people and are benefiting from Israel's prerogatives as the chosen throughout Romans 8, Paul's final view is not one of supersession and replacement. The bulk of the Jewish people will eventually benefit from the promises as well.[14] Nevertheless, this interim period on behalf of the Gentiles is the reason Paul can call Abraham "our ancestor" in 4:1 even though he is addressing a Gentile Christian audience. The same logic is at work outside Romans when Paul sees the Scriptures of Israel addressing a church inclusive of the Gentiles. In 1 Cor 10:1, 6 he draws upon the biblical accounts of "our ancestors" faltering in the wilderness and considers them events that took place as "examples for us": "These things happened to them to serve as an example, and they were written down to instruct us, on whom the ends of the ages have come" (1 Cor 10:11). Paul draws freely upon the Scriptures of Israel in his instructions to Gentile Christian churches. The words of Moses in Deut 17:7 apply in 1 Cor 5:13 to the Christian church with no further qualification, and yet Hays, in his insightful comments on the apostle's ecclesiocentric application of Israel's Scriptures, has cautioned, "It is no accident that Paul never uses expressions such as 'new Israel' or 'spiritual Israel.' There always has been and always will be only one Israel. Into that one Israel Gentile Christians such as the Corinthians have now been absorbed."[15] He also remarks, "Christology is the foundation on which [Paul's] ecclesiocentric counterreadings are constructed."[16] Faith in Christ functions as the basis for enjoying the benefits of Israel's heritage. The apostle points out in Gal 3:15–18, 29 that there is really only one true beneficiary of Abraham's promises, and only those who are incorporated into Christ can share with him in those promises. Israel's Scriptures thus prefigured the church, and yet it is a church rooted and engrafted into the history and heritage of Israel, the Jewish people. So Gentiles have become in Christ "the circumcision" (Phil 3:3; cf. Col 2:11–13). They are to live no longer as the Gentiles (1 Cor 5:1; 10:20; 1 Thess 4:5). They have a new identity in Christ that binds them to Israel's heritage and separates them from the remaining Gentiles.

---

[14] As Susan Eastman put it so well, "Paul's anguished reflections in chs. 9–11 make clear that he believes his fellow Jews will never attain righteousness apart from Christ, but he is equally clear that the church will never come to full redemption apart from Israel" ("Whose Apocalypse?" 276).

[15] Hays, *Echoes of Scripture,* 96–97.

[16] Ibid., 120–21.

The priority of Israel in the divine plan does not negate in any way what Paul has said elsewhere in Romans about God's impartiality. God impartially judges and saves within a universal plan oriented around the Jewish people. Jew and Gentile are both saved by faith in the Jewish Messiah (Rom 3:22; 10:12; Gal 3:28), and yet the categories of Jew and Gentile retain fundamental significance for Paul. "While there may be no distinction between Jew and Gentile with respect to the basis of membership [in the Christian community of salvation] (see Rom 3:22; 10:12), there certainly is with respect to the origin and progression of the gospel community of which they are both members: the Gentiles are in a position of indebtedness vis-à-vis the Jews . . . , to whom the blessings first were given and who then shared them with the Gentiles."[17] This pattern of thought is not limited to Romans 11 but is also at work in 15:25–27 when Paul discusses his collection for the Jewish Christians in Jerusalem:

> At present, however, I am going to Jerusalem in a ministry to the saints; for Macedonia and Achaia have been pleased to share their resources with the poor among the saints at Jerusalem. They were pleased to do this, and indeed they *owe it to them;* for if *the Gentiles have come to share in their spiritual blessings,* they ought also to be of service to them in material things.

The Gentiles, though fully sharing in Israel's blessings and spiritual heritage, remain ethnically distinct from the Jewish people. "For I am not ashamed of the gospel; it is the power of God for salvation to everyone who has faith, *to the Jew first* and *also to the Greek*" (1:16). The Gentiles will always take second place to the Jewish people among those who believe in Jesus Christ.

ISRAEL AS MEDIATOR OF GOD'S BLESSINGS IN GALATIANS

The Gentiles are benefiting from Israel's current rejection, according to Romans, but God has not abandoned Israel. They remain an elect people and occupy a place of priority in God's plan for the end of time. Similar reasoning may very well be at work elsewhere in Paul's letters. Several scholars have pointed to his Letter to the Galatians and the manner in which he appears to be distinguishing Jews from Gentiles throughout the letter. What Paul says forthrightly in Romans may already be implicit in this earlier writing.

In Gal 3:13–14 Paul writes, "Christ redeemed us from the curse of the law by becoming a curse for us . . . in order that in Christ Jesus the blessing of Abraham might come to the Gentiles, so that we might receive the promise of the Spirit through faith." In the Greek, Paul places the first-person pronoun "us" (ἡμᾶς) toward the beginning of v. 13 for emphasis, even as "the Gentiles" (τὰ ἔθνη) is thrust forward to the beginning of v. 14. He appears to be distinguishing and contrasting the Gentiles from the group he identifies in the first-person plural, a group that he assumes his readers will recognize.

---

[17] Donaldson, *Paul and the Gentiles,* 180.

The "curse of the law" to which he refers in v. 13 (in relation to the first-person-plural group) is first mentioned in v. 10: "For all who rely on the works of the law are under a curse; for it is written, 'Cursed is everyone who does not observe and obey all the things written in the book of the law.'" Christ alone relieves the curse pronounced by the Mosaic Law upon its adherents. Since those who rely on the Law are typically Jews and not Gentiles, the "we" group in v. 13 appears to be Jewish. Paul openly identifies a first-person-plural group as Jewish earlier in 2:15: "We ourselves are Jews by birth and not Gentile sinners." Paul's reasoning in 3:13–14, then, is that the redemption of the Jews from the curse of the Law has taken place in order that the blessing of Abraham might consequently come to the Gentiles as well. In other words, Gentile enjoyment of Abrahamic sonship in Christ (v. 29) is dependent upon the priority of the Jews in God's saving plan.

In Gal 3:23–29 the "we"/"all" contrast continues: "*we* were imprisoned and guarded under the law until faith would be revealed. Therefore the law was our disciplinarian until Christ came, so that we might be justified by faith. But now that faith has come, we are no longer subject to a disciplinarian, for in Christ Jesus you are *all* children of God through faith." As was the case in vv. 13–14, Christ has redeemed the "we" group under the Mosaic Law, the Jews, with the result that all people share in God's blessings. The final instance of the "we"/"all" ("you") contrast is in 4:3–7. Donaldson has outlined this pattern as follows:

   a) *The Group and Its Plight*

> "we" were under the "curse of the law" (3:10, 13)
> "we" were "confined under the law," our "pedagogue" (3:23–24)
> "we" were "under law," slaves of the "elemental spirits" (4:3, 5)

   b) *Identification of Christ with Plight*

> he became "a curse for us" (3:13)
> faith/Christ "came" (3:23–25)
> "born under the law" (4:4)

   c) *Redemption of the Group*

> "Christ redeemed us" (3:13)
> "now that faith has come, we are no longer under a pedagogue" (3:25)
> "to redeem those under the law" (4:5)

   d) *Saving Blessings for All Believers* (3:14, 3:26–29, 4:5b–7).[18]

Jewish and early Christian literature provides precedent and parallels for Paul's reasoning in these passages, especially for God's deliverance of the people of Israel with the subsequent benefits for the Gentiles—for example, Isa 2:2–4:

---

[18] Donaldson, "'Curse of the Law,'" 95.

In days to come the mountain of the LORD's house shall be established as the highest of the mountains, and shall be raised above the hills; all the nations shall stream to it. Many peoples shall come and say, "Come, let us go up to the mountain of the LORD, to the house of the God of Jacob; that he may teach us his ways and that we may walk in his paths. For out of Zion shall go forth instruction, and the word of the LORD from Jerusalem. He shall judge between the nations, and shall arbitrate for many peoples; they shall beat their swords into plowshares, and their spears into pruning hooks; nation shall not lift up sword against nation, neither shall they learn war any more.

Gentiles would therefore benefit from God's blessings to Israel. Isaiah responded to Israel's plight in exile with a bold offer for the "survivors of the nations" to assemble and draw near from "all the ends of the earth" to the Lord, the only God and Savior (45:20–23; see also 45:1).[19] Tobit 14:4–7 likewise expanded on the events that would happen after the exile and the rebuilding of the temple: "Then the nations in the whole world will all be converted and worship God in truth. They will all abandon their idols." The author of Acts 15:14–19 recalls James's quote of Amos 9:11–12: "On that day I will raise up the booth of David that is fallen, and repair its breaches, and raise up its ruins, and rebuild it as in the days of old; in order that they may possess the remnant of Edom and all the nations who are called by my name, says the LORD who does this." James interprets these words from the prophet to apply not to a physical temple but rather to the eschatological people of God, composed of both Jews and Gentiles.[20] Paul recognizes that Peter, James, and John were considered the "pillars" (Gal 2:9). The Jerusalem church with its supporting "pillars" would therefore be the restored, eschatological temple of Israel. The Gentiles would have to be grafted into that community.[21] The Jewish community, which had suffered the Law's curse, needed to be redeemed before it could function as God's eschatological people whom the Gentiles would finally join. Jewish believers in Christ were the core of a new humanity. Israel thus functioned as a subgroup of humanity with whom God chose to act for the sake of all humanity. God concentrated human sin upon his people Israel with the intent to concentrate it still further in Israel's representative, the Messiah Jesus Christ.[22] For this reason, Christ came from ethnic Israel according to the flesh (Rom 9:5) and was "born under the law" (Gal 4:4) entrusted to Israel. He became "a curse for us" (3:13), that is, for Israel's sake, in order to save all humanity. Galatians 3–4 is therefore exemplary of a pattern of thought common in Judaism and early Christianity. God's plan for the nations is centered upon the Jewish people.

---

[19] Ibid., 99–100.

[20] Richard Bauckham, "James and the Gentiles," in *History, Literature, and Society in the Book of Acts* (ed. Ben Witherington III; Cambridge: Cambridge University Press, 1996), 154–84.

[21] Witherington, *Grace in Galatia,* 143, 238.

[22] Wright, *Climax of the Covenant,* 196.

Although a prioritization of the Jewish people remains an attractive approach to Galatians 3–4, difficult problems remain. Terence Donaldson, who proposed this pattern, has since become more skeptical of his earlier position that Galatians 3–4 should be understood against the background of the promised pilgrimage of the nations to a restored Israel.[23] Paul nowhere cites the eschatological pilgrimage texts of the Hebrew Scriptures. In his former life as a Jew, he was not content to wait for an end-times influx of Gentiles but aggressively proselytized. Paul the Jewish proselytizer had likely drawn upon Abraham as the model Gentile convert, to judge by his repeated interest in Abraham in both Galatians 3 and Romans 4. When Paul outlines the final days, he does not envision Israel's salvation and a subsequent Gentile conversion but rather the reverse: it will be the blessing of the Gentiles that triggers Israel's restoration (Rom 11:11–32). In fact, the Gentiles will be converted because of Israel's stumbling, hardening, and *defeat* (11:12), not because of Israel's salvation; that salvation would be still to come.

Certainly Paul is often careful in his use of pronouns. He clearly distinguishes his Galatian addressees by second-person pronouns from their Jewish Christian teachers for whom he employs third-person pronouns. On the basis of this consistent distinction between second- and third-person pronouns, one might expect a similarly careful distinction of the first-person-plural Jewish Christians from the Gentiles who are benefiting from God's blessings. Unfortunately, several passages do not conform to these expectations. In Gal 3:14 Paul would be explaining, if the distinctions were neat and tidy, that whereas the Gentiles receive the blessing of Abraham, *the Jews* receive the promised Spirit. Galatians 3:14, however, forms an *inclusio,* or bookend, with vv. 1–5's mention of the Spirit, and in vv. 1–5 it is the Galatian *Gentiles* who have received the promised Spirit. The pairing of vv. 3:1–5 and 3:14 would be even stronger if these verses were part of a larger chiasm:

> A—v. 2: The Spirit received by faith
>   B—vv. 6–9: The blessing of Abraham to the nations
>   C—v. 10: The curse of the law
>   D—vv. 11–12: Living by faith vs. doing the law
>   C'—v. 13: The curse of the law
>   B'—v. 14a: The blessing of Abraham received by the nations
> A'—v. 14b: The Spirit received by faith[24]

After Paul harshly reminds the "foolish Galatians" in v. 3 that they have received the Spirit, surely his Gentile readers would understand the "we" who

---

[23] Donaldson, *Paul and the Gentiles,* 103–104, 192–97.

[24] For a useful caution on the need for greater methodological control in the identification of chiastic patterns, particularly with respect to larger macro-chiasms, see Stanley E. Porter and Jeffrey T. Reed, "Philippians as a Macro-Chiasm and Its Exegetical Significance," *NTS* 44 (1998): 213–21.

receive the Spirit in v. 14 as at least inclusive of themselves. The "we" of this verse refers to Gentile Christians and may refer also to Jewish Christians. Certainly Paul is not *excluding* Gentiles in v. 14 from the Spirit, as would be the case if the first-person-plural pronouns were consistent references to the Jews!

Even Paul's use of first-person-plural pronoun in Gal 3:13 likely does not exclude the Gentiles. He warns the Galatians in v. 10 of the curse that comes upon all who are under the Law, in order to deter their consideration of a Law-observant lifestyle. Certainly the Jewish people are "under the law." Nevertheless, the Law pronounces a curse upon all who do not obey it (Deut 27:26). Paul's language regarding the Law's curse in Gal 3:10 is inclusive: "all who" (ὅσοι; literally, "whosoever"). Paul normally employs this construction (ὅσοι; "whosoever") open with respect to its referent (see Rom 6:3; 8:14; Gal 3:27; 6:12, 16; Phil 3:15). The curse of the Law thus stands over all humanity and not just the Jews.[25] Although the Gentiles do not possess the Law, what the Law says of God's will applies to them as well: they are accountable before God's judgment (Gal 5:5, 7–9). Paul's reasoning is expressed more fully and clearly elsewhere in Rom 2:6–16, esp. 14–16, where the Gentiles are accountable for the Mosaic Law insofar as it has been written in their hearts.[26] Although the curse that falls upon the non-Law-observant would have been a consideration for the Gentiles (under the influence of Paul's rivals) to obey the Law, Paul points out that Christ has already redeemed "us" from the curse of the Law (Gal 3:13).[27] In other words, because of Christ's redeeming work, Gentiles (or Jews) need not fear the curse for not obeying all that the Law demands. Had Paul intended to limit those redeemed from the curse of the Law to the Jews or ethnic Israel, he could have identified the redeemed as "the Jews" or "Israel" rather than the more ambiguous "us."[28] A possible objection to an inclusion of Gentiles into the "us" of Gal 3:13 is that Paul explicitly identifies Gentiles in the next clause as the recipients of Abraham's blessing in v. 14. This has suggested to a majority of interpreters a contrast between the first-person-plural group of v. 13 and the Gentiles of v. 14a. On the other hand, Paul likely had to emphasize the Gentiles' reception of Abraham's blessing since those blessings were assumed to belong to the Jews, the physical descendants of Abraham, whereas such a singling out of Gentiles in the other clauses of 3:13–14 would have been unnecessary after the strong statements in vv. 1–5 on the Gentiles' pos-

---

[25] See the discussion in Norman H. Young, "Pronominal Shifts in Paul's Argument to the Galatians," in *Early Christianity, Late Antiquity, and Beyond,* vol. 2 of *Ancient History in a Modern University* (ed. T. W. Hillard, R. A. Kearsley, C. E. V. Nixon, and A. M. Nobbs; Grand Rapids: Eerdmans, 1998), 210–13.

[26] Das, *Paul, the Law, and the Covenant,* 180–82.

[27] On the opponents' use of Deut 27:26 to encourage Gentile Law observance, see ch. 2, above.

[28] Charles B. Cousar, *A Theology of the Cross: The Death of Jesus in the Pauline Letters* (OBT; Minneapolis: Fortress, 1990), 116–17.

session of the Spirit and after the rhetoric to discourage the Gentile Galatians' consideration of a Law-observant lifestyle in vv. 10–12.

Paul does not distinguish Jewish Christians from Gentile Christians by the pronouns "we" and "you" in Gal 4:3–7. In these verses the "we" group are former slaves to the elements of the cosmos, and yet he warns the "you" group of returning again to those elements in v. 9. The two groups appear to be the same former adherents of the elements of the cosmos. Those who are returning again in v. 9 must be the same ones as those who were initially released in v. 3. In Gal 4:5b *"we"* received adoption as children, and yet v. 6a concludes, on the basis of v. 5b, "And *because you* are children, God has sent the Spirit of his Son into *our* hearts." The line of reasoning in vv. 5 and 6 requires an identification of the "we" and "you" groups. The repeated indiscriminate alternation of first- and second-person-plural pronouns is so difficult for the theory of separate groups of Jews and Gentiles that one scholar has desperately resorted to emending the text from the more strongly attested "our" (hearts) of v. 6 within the manuscript tradition to a weakly attested "your."[29] The problem is that the first person is the more difficult reading and therefore, according to the canons of textual criticism, more likely the original reading since scribes would have wanted to eliminate the jarring contrast between first- and second-person pronouns. Furthermore, a scribal emendation from the awkward "our" in v. 6 to "your" would render the pronoun consistent with the second-person verb at the beginning of the verse ("you are [ἐστε] sons"). Paul freely shifts between pronouns. In 3:26–29 "you" are sons and heirs. In 4:3 and 5, "we" were "minors" enslaved to the elements and received "adoption." In v. 6 "you" are sons and the Spirit of his Son was sent into "our" hearts. In v. 7 "you" are no longer a slave but a son. "[Paul] gives his hearers no signal at all that in 4:3, 6 he is speaking exclusively of (Christian) Jews. The view that he has only Jews in mind leads to chaos, particularly in verses 5–6. In that case, Paul would be saying, 'God sent his son so that we Jews might receive sonship [a status long claimed by Israel!]. And because you Gentiles are sons, God has sent the Spirit of his son into the hearts of us Christian Jews . . . so that you (Gentile) are no longer a slave but a son.'"[30] Ironically, the Jews receive a sonship (v. 5) that the Gentiles *already* possessed (v. 6). Far from being in a position of priority, if a distinction of pronouns is to be maintained, the Jews are actually at a disadvantage. The best reading of vv. 3–7 therefore takes the first-person pronouns as referring to all believers, whether Jew or Gentile, and the second-person pronouns as similarly inclusive but perhaps rhetorically pointed toward the Gentile recipients of the letter. Paul does not appear to be speaking exclusively of Jewish or Gentile Christians.[31] Paul's chain of reasoning builds from the Son's work of redemption in vv. 4–5a to the reception of sonship in v. 5b, which itself leads

---

[29] Witherington, *Grace in Galatia*, 289.

[30] Sam K. Williams, *Galatians* (ANTC; Nashville: Abingdon, 1997), 110–11.

[31] Charles B. Cousar, *Galatians* (IBC; Louisville: John Knox, 1982), 91–92.

to the reception of the Spirit by *the same group* (v. 6). The believers' reception of sonship in 4:5 undergirds the premise for v. 6's climactic conclusion: "Because you are sons, God has sent the Spirit of his Son into our hearts."

The same phenomenon of pronominal shifting also takes place at the end of the chapter (Gal 4:26–5:1). Any attempt to distinguish between the "we" group and the "you" group leads to contradictory results. If one were to insist on such distinctions, 5:1 would read, "For freedom Christ has set us [Jewish Christians] free. Stand firm [you Gentile Christians], therefore, and do not submit again to a yoke of slavery." The conclusion to "Stand firm" ("therefore") rests more likely upon the freedom enjoyed by the *same* group or at least a group included among those in the prior clause. The "you" may again be pointed toward the addressees. Since Christ has set Christians free, the Galatians should stand firm upon their freedom.

Galatians 4:21–5:1 is marked by a series of opposing pairs. Spirit stands in opposition to flesh, [Sarah] to Hagar, freedom to slavery, and the Jerusalem above to the present Jerusalem. Paul also distinguishes between children born through the promise and children born according to the flesh. These distinctions are clearly parallel and mutually interpretive. Spirit must be categorized with promise and the Jerusalem above, whereas flesh is equated with Hagar and the present Jerusalem. In establishing these parallel groups, Paul is also contrasting them as opposing each other. Paul does not, however, discriminate by his use of pronouns. In 4:23, 26 the Jerusalem above who bears children through the promise is *"our"* mother, and yet in 4:28 "Now *you,* my friends, are children of the promise." If Paul *were* distinguishing between first- and second-person pronouns, what are clearly two parallel groups in opposition throughout this paragraph of the letter would disintegrate into three groups with nonsensical results. The first-person-plural pronouns, if consistently referring to Jews, would identify the Jewish Christian offspring of the Jerusalem above, whereas the second-person-plural pronouns would be identifying Gentile offspring of the Jerusalem above. Then alongside these two groups would be a third: the offspring of the present Jerusalem, who are either Jewish Christians or non-Christian Jews and who are forcing the Gentiles to observe the Law. Paul's intent is otherwise clear in this series of pairs of opposites: he is contrasting two groups and not three.

The strongest hypothesis to account for Paul's pronominal shifting in the letter would be one that does not conclude at Gal 4:7 but includes the instances of the same pattern later in the letter. Proponents of a distinction between first- and second-person pronouns in Galatians do not, however, carry their analysis forward to 4:21–5:1, perhaps because such a distinction in these verses seems too unlikely.[32] Nor do these proponents take into account the pronominal switching in the paraenetic section of the letter

---

[32] Witherington, e.g., does not discuss the pronouns in this paragraph at all.

(Gal 5 and 6): "If we live by the Spirit, let us also be guided by the spirit. Let us not become conceited, competing against one another, envying one another" (5:25–26); then in 6:1: "My friends, if anyone is detected in a transgression, you who have received the Spirit should restore such a one in a spirit of gentleness." Paul has just identified the recipients of the Spirit in 5:25–26 in the first person, and yet he speaks of the recipients of the Spirit in 6:1 by using the second person. One scholar who has advocated that the first-person pronouns refer to Jewish Christians in 3:1–4:7 thinks (incredibly) that the "we" in 5:25–26 clearly refers to both Paul and the Gentile Galatian congregation "for the first time in Galatians."[33] A far more plausible reading, which would avoid the problems posed by attempting to identify the first- and second-person pronouns as Jews and Gentiles respectively, would be to treat the first-person pronouns from 3:1 through the end of the letter as inclusive of Jewish and Gentile Christians, and the second-person pronouns as likewise inclusive but rhetorically pointed toward the addressees. Paul's pattern of pronominal shifting between the first and the second person, as one commentator has noted, appears to be a deliberate stylistic device.[34] The apostle is thereby underscoring the point that all people, whether Jew or Gentile, are under the same plight from the Mosaic Law with its curse for disobedience. Paul signals this all-inclusive emphasis in the very first verses of the letter when he speaks of the Lord Jesus Christ as the one "who gave himself for our sins to set us free from the present evil age" (1:4). Many scholars believe that Paul is drawing upon traditional Jewish Christian language in these verses, and yet he clearly includes his Gentile audience within this new era inaugurated by Christ's rescue.

Some passages in Galatians appear even to contradict the prioritization of the Jewish people in this letter. Although Paul is combating Jewish Christian teachers, he at times makes statements with very strong implications for Jews in general. Galatians 3:10, for instance, pronounces a curse upon all whose existence is characterized by the Law and who have not yet been released in Christ from the Law's curse (3:13), that is, non-Christian Jews. Galatians 3:28 boldly proclaims that there is "no longer Jew or Greek" in Christ. Baptism erases the old distinction and unites Jew and Gentile into a new family that is no longer Jewish or pagan. According to 4:25, "the present Jerusalem . . . is in slavery with her children."[35] These are the children "born according to the flesh" (4:23). It is difficult to escape the conclusion

---

[33] Witherington, *Grace in Galatia*, 413.

[34] See Martyn's discussion in his *Galatians,* esp. 334–36.

[35] Although Martyn ("Covenants of Hagar and Sarah," 181–83) has argued persuasively that Jerusalem throughout Galatians refers to the Jerusalem church or the city itself and never the non-Christian Jewish inhabitants, these verses remain difficult for his reading, since Paul would surely not label as enslaved a "present Jerusalem" constituted by Peter and James and other Jewish Christians who had *supported* his circumcision-free mission to the Gentiles.

that the non-Christian Jew is still in bondage in the era of the flesh and the Law with its curse.[36]

So is there no advantage for the Jew at all? Is Paul's line of thought in Romans 9–11 a recoil from the complete erasure of Jewish advantage in Galatians? Not necessarily. Throughout Gal 4:21–5:1 Paul speaks of Christians, whether Jewish or Gentile, as a people born of the "Jerusalem above." Members of the heavenly Jerusalem do not require the physical mark of circumcision as do members of the present Jerusalem. Members of the heavenly Jerusalem all place their faith in Christ, and this faith alone sufficiently marks them as a special people. They are the legitimate children of Abraham and share in Abraham's blessing and promise (3:6–7, 14). At the same time, Paul's Gentile audience should take due note that it is the heavenly *Jerusalem* that is their mother. Jerusalem is still the locus of God's saving activity. Paul never advocates the complete erasure of all differences between Jews and Gentiles. Peter was to take the gospel to the circumcised even as Paul to the uncircumcised (2:7–9). Although Paul and the other apostles agreed that circumcision played no role in entering into a right relationship with God, the Jerusalem apostles did not abandon the rite, nor did Paul expect them to do so. He envisions Jew as Jew and Gentile as Gentile bound into a new people, born of the heavenly Jerusalem, by their faith in Christ. Or more precisely, Gentiles have come to join the Jewish offspring and beneficiaries of the heavenly Jerusalem. Although the Gentiles need not be circumcised as Christians, they have not become members of just *any* heavenly city. Their ancestor is not just *any* man; it is Abraham, the forefather of the Jews. In other words, even if the priority of Israel in Galatians cannot be bolstered through the apostle's use of differing pronouns throughout the letter, Israel's priority is by no means jeopardized. Jewish Christians maintain a position of priority in God's plan as the Gentiles flock to join their heavenly city on the basis of a common faith in Christ. Paul concludes the letter by affirming an "Israel of God" (Gal 6:15–16), a people who "follow this rule," that "neither circumcision nor uncircumcision is anything; but a new creation is everything!"[37] For by faith in Christ, those who are of this Israel have died to the world (Gal 6:14).

PAUL'S CENSURE OF THE JEWISH PEOPLE (1 THESS 2:14–16)

The evidence in Paul's letters to the Romans and Galatians favors the position that he believes ethnic Israel still enjoys a special place in God's plan for humanity. Despite Paul's seemingly negative comments, his overall view of the Jews remains positive. But critics of the position that Paul maintains a special place for ethnic Israel in God's plan need only point to his First Letter to the Thessalonians as clearest evidence to the contrary. One passage alone,

---

[36] Of course, these verses are problematic for the two-covenant theory as well.
[37] See also Gal 5:6.

1 Thess 2:14–16, appears to dispel any favoring of ethnic Israel in God's plan. Paul in Rom 11:26 writes: "All Israel will be saved." Paul in Rom 9:3: "For I could wish that I myself were accursed and cut off from Christ for the sake of my own people, my kindred according to the flesh." Paul in 1 Thess 2:14–16: "The Jews killed both the Lord Jesus and the prophets." "[The Jews] displease God." "[The Jews] have constantly been filling up the measure of their sins; but God's wrath has overtaken them at last." Indeed, in the second century Christians continued to label Jews "Christ-killers."[38] More vicious labels and actions against the Jewish people followed during darker chapters in the history of the Christian church. In 1 Thessalonians Paul appears to erase any positives about the Jewish people.[39]

In the nineteenth century the NT scholar Ferdinand Christian Baur identified 1 Thess 2:14–16 as a major reason for his denial of Paul's authorship of 1 Thessalonians. The verses bear a "thoroughly un-Pauline stamp," especially when considered alongside Romans 9–11.[40] Most scholars of his day (and since) disagreed with Baur's conclusion that 1 Thessalonians, as a whole, is non-Pauline. The events narrated in the letter are similar to, but sufficiently divergent from, the history in Acts to guarantee that 1 Thessalonians is an independent account and a genuine letter. The expectations of an imminent return of Christ in 1 Thessalonians do not match the situation of the Church after Paul's lifetime, when it had become clear that Christ would not be imminently returning (1 Thess 4:15–17). The letter must therefore come from the time of Paul. Although other nineteenth-century biblical scholars viewed 1 Thessalonians as a genuine Pauline letter, doubts about 2:14–16 persisted. The statement in v. 16 that "God's wrath has overtaken [or come upon] them at last" seemed to refer to the catastrophic events of 70 C.E. when the Jewish temple was destroyed and Palestine lay devastated by the Romans. By that time the apostle was already dead and could not have authored such statements. Also, during Paul's own lifetime and before 70 C.E., the Jews and Christians were not yet distinct groups, and so a comment about Christians' suffering at the hands of the Jews would have been inconceivable. Only after the destruction of the temple were Jews and Christians identified as distinct religious traditions.[41]

---

[38] E.g., *Acts Pil.* 4:1; 9:4; 12:1; *Gos. Pet.* 1–2; 6; 21; 25 and the precedent established by Matt 27:24–25 and Luke 23:20–26.

[39] For a thorough bibliography of research on these controversial verses in 1 Thessalonians, see Jeffrey A. D. Weima and Stanley E. Porter, *An Annotated Bibliography of 1 and 2 Thessalonians* (NTTS 26; Leiden: Brill, 1998), 161–73.

[40] Ferdinand Christian Baur, *Paul the Apostle of Jesus Christ: His Life and Work, His Epistles, and His Doctrine* (ed. Eduard Zeller; trans. A. Menzies; 2 vols.; 2d ed.; London: Williams & Norgate, 1875–1876), 2:87.

[41] For a more detailed review of the nineteenth-century reasoning against the passage's authenticity, see Carol J. Schlueter, *Filling up the Measure: Polemical Hyperbole in 1 Thessalonians 2.14–16* (JSNTSup 98; Sheffield, England: Sheffield Academic Press, 1994), 16–19.

On the other hand, not all nineteenth-century scholars were convinced of these verses' non-Pauline character. Some reasoned that the wrath that had come upon the Jews might have been some event other than the destruction of the temple in 70. Perhaps Paul was referring to the famine in 46–47 (mentioned also in Acts 11:28) or to a series of persecutions under one of the harsher Judean governors in the decades preceding the Jewish war against Rome. Perhaps the "wrath" referred to the killing of twenty to thirty thousand Jews in 49 (Josephus, *Ant.* 20.2.5 §51, 20.5.3 §112; *J.W.* 2.12.1 §§224–227; even with inflated figures it was a major disaster) or to the quashing of Theudas's insurrection in 44–46. Perhaps the apostle is referring to a divine judgment quite apart from a specific, identifiable historical event. Another possibility put forth was that the past (aorist) tense of the wrath's having "overtaken them" was prophetic or proleptic in the sense that God's impending judgment was as certain as if it had already taken place (see also 1 Thess 1:10). Paul does use this verb (φθάνω) in Phil 3:16 to refer to the heavenly prize toward which he was striving as if in a sense it were already attained; and he also uses it in 1 Thess 4:15 regarding events at the end of the age. Matthew (12:28) and Luke (11:20) used the same verb to describe the arrival of God's kingdom in Jesus' ministry.[42] The unresolved debate over the authenticity of 1 Thess 2:14–16 continued into the twentieth century, when new evidence was set forth to decide the matter.

Several twentieth-century scholars—Karl-Gottfried Eckart, Birger A. Pearson, and Daryl Schmidt—buttressed the nineteenth-century case against Paul's authorship of these verses. They too were troubled by how the verses seemed at odds with the Paul of Romans.[43] The twentieth-century argu-

---

[42] An interpretation of the past (aorist) verb in which Paul saw the coming wrath as if in a sense already present, has been contested. A. T. Robertson (*A Grammar of the Greek New Testament in the Light of Historical Research* [Nashville: Broadman, 1934], 846–47) contends that a proleptic use of the aorist (past) tense may only occur in the NT within conditional sentences (Matt 12:26, 28; 18:15; John 15:6; 1 Cor 7:28; Rev 10:7). Daniel B. Wallace, on the other hand, lists several potential instances: Matt 18:15; Mark 11:24; John 13:31; John 15:6; Rom 8:30; 1 Cor 7:28; Heb 4:10; Jude 14; Rev 10:7. Many of Wallace's examples are not in conditional sentences (*Greek Grammar beyond the Basics: An Exegetical Syntax of the New Testament* [Grand Rapids: Zondervan, 1996], 563–64). Stanley E. Porter has demonstrated a perfective aspect to the aorist as well as "a few possible instances" of future reference (*Verbal Aspect in the Greek of the New Testament, with Reference to Tense and Mood* [Studies in Biblical Greek; New York: Peter Lang, 1989, 1993], 182–88, 232–33). Because of the rarity of the aorist with future reference, the context of 1 Thess 2:14–16 must offer decisive support for such an identification. Chrys C. Caragounis, in a discussion with implications for the interpretation of 1 Thess 2:14–16 ("Kingdom of God, Son of Man and Jesus' Self-Understanding," *TynBul* 40 [1989], 20–23), has demonstrated that the verb φθάνω is often employed with a futuristic sense.

[43] Karl-Gottfried Eckart, "Der zweite echte Brief des Apostels Paulus an die Thessalonicher," *ZTK* 58 (1961): 32–34; Birger A. Pearson, "1 Thessalonians 2:13–16: A Non-Pauline Interpolation," *HTR* 64 (1971): 79–94; and Daryl Schmidt,

ments may be classified into four categories: difficulties with the pattern of imitation, difficulties of linguistic construction, structural difficulties, and historical difficulties.

First, regarding the pattern of imitation, twentieth-century scholars noted that Paul quite often urges his readers to imitate either Christ or himself as apostle (1 Cor 4:16; 11:1; Phil 3:17; 1 Thess 1:6), but 1 Thess 2:14 encourages the Thessalonians to imitate the Judean churches. Although Paul regularly calls for imitation, he does not elsewhere suggest that his congregations model themselves on the Jewish church at Jerusalem, or so the critics have contended. Paul does, however, often support his exhortations with the example of other churches (see 1 Cor 11:16; 14:33; 16:1–2; 2 Cor 8:1–7; cf. Rom 15:26–27).[44] Paul opened the letter by urging his readers to become imitators of himself and his coworkers because of their example in suffering (1 Thess 1:6–9). First Thessalonians 2:13–16 then amplifies these references to suffering and imitation: such an imitation of suffering leads to salvation. This amplification of an idea raised in 1 Thessalonians 1 is typical of what the apostle is doing in the letter. He likewise refers to hope early in the letter, in 1:3, and expands on that motif in 1 Thessalonians 3 and 4.[45] The imitation motif in 2:14 thus functions well within the letter as the development of a key idea signaled at the beginning. On the other hand, Paul is not *exhorting* the Thessalonians to live like the Judean Christians; they already are. This difference in itself may account for the departure from other imitation statements where Paul is admonishing Christians.[46] The argument from imitation is therefore not compelling against the Pauline authorship of the passage.

Second, a number of linguistic constructions in 1 Thess 2:13–16 have been cited as proof against Pauline authorship. Daryl Schmidt found troubling the joining of two main clauses by the conjunction καί ("and")[47] since this was not Paul's normal style earlier in vv. 1–12. Also, vv. 14–16 have more dependent clauses than any sentence up to this point in the letter: seven dependent clauses are subordinated to the same main clause, compared with only five at most elsewhere in the letter. In addition, the words "Lord" (κύριον) and "Jesus" (Ἰησοῦν) in v. 15 are separated by a participle, a construction that is unusual elsewhere in Paul's writings. Finally, although Paul elsewhere employed the phrases "of God" (τοῦ θεοῦ), "that are in Judea"

"1 Thess 2:13–16: Linguistic Evidence for an Interpolation," *JBL* 102 (1983): 269–79 (Schmidt advanced the case against authenticity on linguistic grounds).

[44] Wayne A. Meeks, "The Circle of Reference in Pauline Morality," in *Greeks, Romans, and Christians: Essays in Honor of Abraham J. Malherbe* (ed. David L. Balch, Everett Ferguson, and Wayne A. Meeks; Minneapolis: Fortress, 1990), 307, 312.

[45] Karl P. Donfried, "Paul and Judaism: I Thessalonians 2:13–16 as a Test Case," *Int* 38 (1984): 245–47.

[46] Charles A. Wanamaker, *The Epistles to the Thessalonians: A Commentary on the Greek Text* (NIGTC; Grand Rapids: Eerdmans, 1990), 32.

[47] Schmidt, 273.

(τῶν οὐσῶν ἐν τῇ 'Ιουδαίᾳ), and "in Christ" (ἐν Χριστῷ), the combination of these phrases is unprecedented. In response to the first linguistic argument, "and" (καί) does join independent clauses elsewhere in Paul, for example, 2 Cor 1:15.[48] Regarding the high number of dependent clauses, Paul uses more in Rom 4:16–17 (nine) and Phil 1:27–30 (eight), and he uses seven in Phil 1:12–15. Schmidt also miscounted seven in 1 Thess 2:14–16 since one instance is not dependent on the same main clause as the others. First Thessalonians 2:14–16 would have, then, only one more subordinate clause than the instances of five elsewhere in the letter.[49] Regarding the combination of phrases, Paul does quite often separate a noun from a modifying adjective by means of an intervening verb form; see, for example, 1 Cor 7:7, 12; 10:4; 2 Cor 7:5; Phil 2:20; 3:20.[50] The syntactical pattern is therefore typically Pauline. The final argument, on the basis of unprecedented phrases, collapses when one recognizes the importance of each of these admittedly Pauline elements to the thought that is being expressed. For instance, "in Christ Jesus" unites the Thessalonians with the Judean churches ("in Judea") with respect to their suffering.[51]

First Thessalonians 2:14–16 includes several words that are atypical for Paul, such as "compatriot" (συμφυλέτης), "kill" (ἀποκτείνω), "drive out" (ἐκδιώκω), and "hostile [to someone]" (lit.; ἐναντίος [τινί]).[52] But the value of this evidence against Pauline authorship is questionable. For instance, regarding the Greek word for "kill," Jewish tradition had long held that the people had murdered the prophets.[53] Since Paul views himself as a persecuted prophet, he may very well be drawing upon traditional biblical language employed against the Jewish people for rejecting the prophets.[54] Elijah complained in 1 Kgs 19:10–14 that the prophets were being killed, and Paul quotes this reference to the murder of the prophets in Rom 11:3. Also, the early Christians were already applying traditional Jewish language derived from apocalyptic writings (e.g., Matt 23:29–38; Mark 12:1–9; Acts 7:52).[55] The use of non-Pauline vocabulary is not a compelling argument

---

[48] See also Rom 1:28; 2:27; 3:8; 5:16; 1 Cor 5:2; 6:2; 2 Cor 1:7, 15; 2:3; Gal 6:16; Phil 1:9, 25; 1 Thess 1:6; Jon A. Weatherly, "The Authenticity of 1 Thessalonians 2.13–16: Additional Evidence," *JSNT* 42 (1991): 91–93.

[49] Ibid., 93–94.

[50] Ibid., 94–95.

[51] Ibid., 95–97.

[52] Earl Richard, *First and Second Thessalonians* (SP 11; Collegeville, Minn.: Liturgical Press, 1995), 125.

[53] See 2 Chr 36:15–16; Neh 9:27, 30; Jer 2:20; also 1 Kgs 19:10 in Rom 11:3; cf. Matt 23:27–24:3b; Luke 13:34–35; Acts 7:52. By using the word "kill," Paul would also be distinguishing between the Jews and the Romans, whom he says were responsible for crucifying Jesus.

[54] Malherbe, *Thessalonians,* 174.

[55] R. Schippers, "The Pre-Synoptic Tradition in I Thessalonians II 13–16," *NovT* 8 (1966): 232–34; Christopher M. Tuckett, "Synoptic Tradition in 1 Thessalonians?" in *The Thessalonian Correspondence* (ed. Raymond F. Collins; Leuven:

against Pauline authorship if the apostle was drawing upon earlier Jewish and Christian traditional language as he wrote.

A third line of reasoning has questioned the authenticity of 1 Thess 2:13–16 on structural grounds. First Thessalonians 2:1–16 appears misplaced since v. 13 begins an unexpected second thanksgiving section after Paul has already provided a thanksgiving section in 1:2–3, where a first-century listener would have expected one. Deleting vv. 13–16 from the text would offer a much smoother transition from v. 12 to v. 17.[56] On the other hand, Paul quite often employs an ABA' pattern in his letters. For instance, in 1 Corinthians 8 and 10 he discusses meat sacrificed to idols. In between these chapters is a discussion of his nonexercise of apostolic rights. Similarly in 1 Corinthians 12 and 14 Paul regulates the Corinthians' expression of spiritual gifts whereas in 1 Corinthians 13 he digresses to compare the spiritual gifts to love. A similar ABA' pattern is at work in 1 Thessalonians where 2:13–16 closely parallels 1:2–10:

1. *We give thanks to God* (1:2; 2:13)

2. *always / constantly* (1:2; 2:13)

3. has chosen you / you received (1:4; 2:13)

4. *our message of the gospel came* to you / the *word of God* that *you* heard from us (1:5; 2:13)

5. *not* in *word* only / you accepted it *not* as a human *word* (1:5; 2:13)

6. *but* also in power / *but* as what it really is, God's word (1:5; 2:13)

7. and in the Holy Spirit and with full conviction / which is also at work in you believers (1:5; 2:13)

8. And *you became imitators* of us and of the Lord / For *you*, brothers and sisters, *became imitators* of the churches (1:6; 2:14)

9. for in spite of *persecution* you received the word / you *suffered* (1:6; 2:14)

10. [the success of the missionaries] / [the suffering of the missionaries] (1:7–8; 2:14–15)

11. you turned to God from idols / hindering us from speaking to the Gentiles (1:9; 2:16)

12. to serve a living and true God, and to wait for his Son / that they may be saved (1:9–10; 2:16)

13. who rescues us from the *wrath* that is coming / but God's *wrath* has overtaken them at last (1:10; 2:16)

Leuven University Press, 1990), 160–63, 165–67, 182; Malherbe, *Thessalonians,* 174–75.
[56] Pearson, "1 Thessalonians 2:13–16," 88–90.

First Thessalonians 2:13–16 mirrors 1:2–10, with both paragraphs speaking of the divine word, which comes through the apostolic intermediary and works to create a perseverance in the midst of suffering that ought to be imitated. Paul expresses concern for the Thessalonians in 2:1–12, and he continues to express that concern in 2:13–16. They are an elect people (1:4; 2:13). If 1:2–10 and 2:13–16 form the outside of the pattern (A–A'), then the center portion of the pattern (B) would be 2:1–12.[57] Also, Paul's sharp remarks about those opposing his gospel ministry in 2:16 may reflect the opposition and perhaps the slanderous charges lurking behind his defense in 2:1–12, esp. 2, 5. A repeated thanksgiving should not be surprising since thanksgiving is a motif that runs throughout the letter (see also 3:9). First Thessalonians 2:14–16 is therefore structurally plausible within the letter. These verses offer a digression that provides the necessary background to understanding Paul's anxious desire to visit the Thessalonians in the immediately following verses (2:17–20).[58] The emphatic "we" (Ἡμεῖς) at the beginning of v. 17 signals the conclusion of the digression and a return to the discussion of Paul and his associates prior to v. 13. The emphasis on "we" would have been unnecessary had v. 17 followed on the heels of the first-person plurals throughout vv. 1–12.[59]

Perhaps the strongest case against the Pauline authorship of 1 Thess 2:14–16 is the lack of historical evidence for Jewish persecution of Christians in Judea to the extent that Paul's dark description appears to warrant. In these verses the Christians at Thessalonica are suffering similarly to the Christians in Judea. Although the Thessalonians were suffering a certain level of persecution for their beliefs—thus the references to tribulation (θλῖψις and θλίβω, 1:6; 3:3–4, 7; ἀγῶνι, 2:2), suffering (προπαθόντες, 2:2; ἐπάθετε, 2:14), persecution (ἐκδιωξάντων, 2:15), distress (ἀνάγκη, 3:7), and endurance (ὑπομονῆς, 1:3)—the Thessalonians had no fear for their lives. Paul never mentions anyone being martyred at Thessalonica. Had a martyrdom taken place at Thessalonica, the apostle would surely have mentioned it since such a death would have paralleled the death of Jesus and dovetailed with Paul's imitation motif.[60] Nevertheless, by juxtaposing the Thessalonians' suffering with the Jews' killing of Jesus and the Judean Christians' suffering, Paul at least evokes a sense of violence even if he does not say that the Judean Christians were being martyred. Evidence for a violent persecution of Christians in Judea at this time is lacking. When the Sadducean high priest killed Jesus' brother James in 62 C.E., the Pharisees, angered by the

[57] John C. Hurd, "Paul Ahead of His time: 1 Thess. 2:13–16," *Paul and the Gospels,* vol. 1 of *Anti-Judaism in Early Christianity* (ed. Peter Richardson with David Granskou; Waterloo, Ont.: Wilfrid Laurier University Press, 1986), 28–30.

[58] Wanamaker, *Thessalonians,* 32, 108–9.

[59] Weatherly, "Authenticity," 81.

[60] John M. G. Barclay, "Conflict in Thessalonica," *CBQ* 55 (1993): 514; Schlueter, *Filling up the Measure,* 40.

death, managed to have the high priest deposed (Josephus, *Ant.* 20.9.1 §200). The reaction of the Pharisees to James's death would suggest that relations between the Jerusalem church and the Jewish community may not have been that tense. Josephus, a contemporary, made no mention of a widespread persecution or martyrdom of Christians in this period. The conflicts in Galatians 2 and Acts 15 revealed a preference by many Jerusalem Jews for Gentile circumcision in order to join the church (cf. Acts 16:3, 21). Adherence to circumcision would have reduced the pressure against Jewish Christians by other Jews whereas Paul's refusal to circumcise Gentiles would have aroused Jewish indignation. Paul admits in Gal 5:11 that he would not have suffered as much had he circumcised the Gentiles. Since so little evidence is available that the Judean church experienced persecution during this period prior to 70 C.E., many scholars have concluded that 1 Thess 2:14–16 must reflect a situation *after* the destruction of the temple.

Paul does not literally state that the Judean Christians were suffering violence at the hands of their fellow Jews in 1 Thess 2:14–16, but he says that the Judean Christians have suffered the same things as the Thessalonians. If the Thessalonians, by all accounts, were suffering social harassment and ostracism for their beliefs, one need conclude no more about the situation of the Judean Christians. They too must have suffered social harassment. If that were all, this crucial historical objection to Pauline authorship of 2:14–16 would collapse. One would not have to posit a violent physical persecution of either the Thessalonian or the Judean churches. Thus scholarly objections to the Pauline authorship of 1 Thess 2:14–16 on the basis of the lack of historical support for a violent persecution of Judean Christians are without merit.

The NT documents do suggest a pattern of at least occasional persecution of the early Christians at the hands of non-Christian Jews not only in Judea (e.g., Acts 6–9 [esp. 8:1]; 22:4; 26:9–11) but also elsewhere (e.g., Thessalonica in Acts 17:5). Paul speaks in 2 Cor 11:24 of his own hardships, which included multiple whippings by Jewish authorities. He says in Gal 1:13 that he, as a non-Christian Jew, persecuted (ἐδίωκον) and pillaged (ἐπόρθουν) the Christian church violently or to the extreme (καθ' ὑπερβολήν), and alludes in 6:12 to the persecution that his rivals would experience if they did not also promote circumcision. When mentioned together, persecution and pillaging indicate violence. In 1:23 Paul again speaks of persecuting and pillaging the church.[61] Paul may have mentioned

---

[61] Some have questioned Paul's persecuting activity since in Gal 1:22 he says that he was unknown "by sight" (ἀγνούμενος τῷ προσώπῳ) to the churches of Judea. Had he persecuted those people, they would have recognized his face. The objection carries little force since Paul distinguishes the churches (plural) of Judea, to whom he was unknown, from his persecuting activity in the urban center of Jerusalem ("church" singular in 1:13); Witherington, *Grace in Galatia,* 124–25. Paul's plan to persecute Christians in a second urban center, Damascus, would neatly parallel his later evangelizing activity in urban centers. He would perhaps have been recognized at Jerusalem, where he had persecuted, but would have been unknown outside the city.

the Judean Christians' suffering in 1 Thessalonians 2 because he himself had personally been engaged in similar persecutions, at least in Jerusalem. He had ironically been one of the perpetrators of such persecution.[62] Luke narrates an early persecution (in which the pre-Christian Paul took part) of the Jerusalem church (Acts 8:1–3). The apostles managed to escape the Jerusalem persecution and were able ultimately to remain in the city, even if they were forced out for a brief period. By Acts 9:31 the Christians in Judea, Galilee, and Samaria appear to be enjoying peace and serenity again. Paul's use of the past (aorist) tense in 1 Thess 2:14–16 for the Judean Christians' sufferings suggests that the period of persecution was in the past and not continuing. This would dovetail with the fact that the Judean persecutions described by Luke in Acts must have been intense but only sporadic and perhaps limited to the early years of the church prior to the death of Herod Agrippa in 44 C.E. Violent persecutions had occasionally taken place early in the history of the church, and Paul's letter may be his reflection on those events.

Although there is a historical grain of truth to what Paul is claiming in 1 Thess 2:14–16—the Christians did experience an intense period of persecution in Judea—it is possible that the apostle exaggerates the situation in Judea. He may have characterized the Judean Jews in terms of isolated, perhaps less representative incidents. He speaks of their opposition against all humanity (καὶ πᾶσιν ἀνθρώποις ἐναντίων) and of their killing the prophets, although the list of martyred prophets is not particularly long. The ancient rhetoricians often described and employed exaggeration or hyperbole as a formal device in epideictic speeches of praise and blame.[63] First Thessalonians 2:14–16 would thus conform to what is typical for censure or rebuke in antiquity.

Jewish writers typically employed polemical hyperbole in their characterizations of opponents within eschatological contexts. Paul's First Letter to the Thessalonians is certainly characterized by an apocalyptic, eschatological viewpoint. Since apocalyptic speech often employed hyperbole, the eschatological elements of the letter deserve review. Paul views the world as a persecuted prophetic figure and so draws upon the rhetoric of the murder of the prophets as he looks forward to a future vindication. Jesus not only "died for us" (1 Thess 5:10) and was raised (4:14) but is also imminently returning again, an event for which Paul and his Thessalonian audience should all remain eagerly expectant (1:10). Jesus will return like a thief in the night with all his saints (3:13; 5:1–11). At that point God's wrath will descend upon the rest of humanity. Paul explains in 5:2–3 that although those others outside the Christian community imagine that there is "peace and security," they will soon be overtaken by a sudden and inescapable destruction. Paul's converts, however, will be rescued from such a disastrous fate (1:10; 5:9). God has called them from their former lives of idolatry and

---

[62] Malherbe, *Thessalonians*, 173.
[63] Schlueter, *Filling up the Measure*, 75–88.

its dreadful consequences to the worship of the only true and living God (1:9; 2:12, 14).

Nevertheless, for the moment the Thessalonian converts remain in a world that is divided into "us" versus "them," the elect versus the lost, those who will be saved and those who will be destroyed. Non-Christians are "outsiders" (4:12), "others" (4:13; 5:6). They are children of darkness who do not know God (4:5; 5:7) and who have no hope (4:13). From a normal social perspective, Paul ironically is himself an outsider to the Thessalonians, as are the Christian believers elsewhere in Macedonia, Achaia, and Judea. Paul redraws the social map in order to bind his converts to these remote and unknown Christian people and to loosen the Thessalonian Christians' ties to their own "compatriots" nearer at hand (1:7, 2:14–15; 4:10). Paul thus encourages the Thessalonians to accept suffering as something to be expected. The entire universe is caught up in a massive power struggle between God and Satan (2:18), and anyone outside the circle of believers in Christ is an actual or potential aggressor.

Paul reminds the Thessalonians of the conflict and "great opposition" that he himself had experienced at Thessalonica (2:2). He speaks approvingly of the Thessalonian Christians' own endurance of suffering at the hands of their fellow Thessalonians as imitating his own and the Lord's sufferings (1:6; 2:14). Paul even sends Timothy to Thessalonica out of a concern that they might be shaken by the persecution (3:3–4). The Thessalonians, as a result of Paul's preaching, had abandoned the traditional deities of their land to adopt an exclusive, foreign Savior deity. The exclusiveness of this foreign, alien cult would have aroused resentment from others who would chafe at being labeled outsiders and children of darkness who do not know God (5:4–5). So Paul urges the Thessalonian Christians not to return evil for evil (5:15) and to mind their own business and behave in a proper fashion toward outsiders (4:11–12). The style of rhetoric in 2:14–16 thus conforms well to the apocalyptic message one confronts elsewhere in the letter. The apostle is binding the Thessalonians into a solidarity with fellow believers in Christ elsewhere who are suffering, and he characterizes the persecutors in dark language as those who will suffer wrath and be lost.[64] The exaggerated statements of 2:14–16 would serve well the apostle's apocalyptic purpose in dividing the world into those who are lost and those who are saved. It strengthens the boundaries between "us" and "them."

Alongside this lack of firm evidence on internal grounds that 1 Thess 2:14–16 should be excised from the letter as non-Pauline stands the overwhelming witness of all the extant ancient manuscripts, corroborating the

---

[64] For further development of the correlation between the Thessalonians' social situation and their apocalyptic worldview, see Barclay, "Conflict in Thessalonica," 512–30; and "Thessalonica and Corinth." For application of apocalyptic motifs throughout 1 Thessalonians to the authenticity of 2:14–16, see Hurd, "Paul Ahead of His Time," 33–36.

authenticity of these verses. Since 2:14–16 appears to be genuinely Pauline, the inevitable question is how to interpret these verses alongside the positive statements regarding the Jews in Romans 11. Perhaps one might read the wrath of God come upon the Jews in 1 Thess 2:16 alongside the divine decision to harden the Jews and express wrath against them in Rom 9:17–22 and 11:7–12.[65] An expression of wrath εἰς τέλος, as in 1 Thess 2:16, means "right to the end" or "completely."[66] Such wrath is an expression of God's final, eschatological judgment, but in Rom 9:22 God exercises patience toward the hardened and ultimately will change their hearts according to Romans 11.[67] The wrath expressed in 1 Thess 2:14–16 is a specific consequence of the persecution of Christians whereas God's hardening in Rom 9:18 is not in response to human actions, whether judged to be good or bad. What Paul is saying in 1 Thess 2:14–16 thus appears to be distinct from the line of reasoning in Romans 9–11. A better approach would exhaust 1 Thess 2:14–16 on its own terms before making a comparison with Romans.

In Romans 11 Paul specifically addresses the fate of unbelieving Judaism as a whole. Paul's comments are of a more limited nature in 1 Thess 2:14–16 since he identifies the churches "that are in Judea" before referring to the Jews. "The Jews" is likely a geographical term for those who live in Judea. "Jews" in this passage does not necessarily refer to a whole ethnic or religious group. Paul refers to "the Jews" (τῶν Ἰουδαίων) in 1 Thess 2:14–16 parallel to the Thessalonians' "compatriots" (τῶν συμφυλετῶν). Even as "your own compatriots" refers to the other Thessalonians persecuting the Thessalonian Christians, so other Judeans or "Jews" are persecuting the Judean Christians.[68] Paul further specifies the objects of wrath by censuring the Jews who had personally prevented him and his companions from speaking the gospel of Christ to the Gentiles that they might be saved. At the same time, he is complimenting Judean *Jewish* Christians.[69] He praises the Judean Christians for standing within a line of succession from Israel's prophets.[70] The apostle's harsh comments represent intra-Jewish polemic necessitated by a particular situation. Paul is simply responding to the resistance to his message and the persecution of his converts in the polemical language of the apocalypses, a language that tends toward exaggeration, vituperation, and starkness. He even employs such language elsewhere (see, e.g., 2 Cor 10–13; Gal 1:6–8; Phil 3:2, 18–19).

---

[65] Johannes Munck, *Christ and Israel: An Interpretation of Romans 9–11* (Philadelphia: Fortress, 1967), 62–66. See also the expression of wrath in Rom 1:18.

[66] Schlueter, *Filling up the Measure,* 57–58. On the ambiguity of the expression, see I. Howard Marshall, *1 and 2 Thessalonians* (NCB; Grand Rapids: Eerdmans, 1983), 16. The NRSV prefers "at last."

[67] Dunn, *Romans 9–16,* 566–67.

[68] Weatherly, "Authenticity," 84–89.

[69] Malherbe, *Thessalonians,* 170.

[70] Donaldson, *Paul and the Gentiles,* 227–28.

When Paul says that God's wrath has come upon the Jews resisting his ministry, he is not anachronistically referring to the events of 70 C.E. after his lifetime or even to an earlier, more plausible period of time. "Wrath" in Paul is always an eschatological concept referring to God's judgment of humanity (1 Thess 1:10; 5:9; Rom 2:5, 8; 3:5; 4:15; 5:9; 9:22; 12:19; 13:4–5). It is precisely from this wrath that Jesus has delivered those who trust in him: "For God has destined us not for wrath but for obtaining salvation through our Lord Jesus Christ" (1 Thess 5:9); this Jesus is the one "who rescues us from the wrath that is coming" (1 Thess 1:10). Paul says much the same in Rom 5:8–9: "But God proves his love for us in that while we were still sinners Christ died for us. Much more surely then, now that we have been justified by his blood, will we be saved through him from the wrath of God." The future, eschatological wrath from which faith in Christ saves can also include a present dimension (Rom 1:18; 9:22). God's eschatological wrath may erupt proleptically into the present. Again, the only escape is by faith in Christ.[71] Paul's dark statements regarding the Jews' opposing his Gentile mission in 1 Thess 2:14–16 conform neatly to the statements of God's wrath in Romans. The apostle's world is divided into those who are now or will be suffering from God's wrath and those who have been rescued from that wrath by God's salvation in Christ.[72] Romans is equally harsh against the "disobedient and contrary" people of Israel (Rom 10:21) who "have not submitted to God's righteousness" (10:3). Paul calls the "disobedient" in 11:28–30 "enemies of God" "as regards the gospel." They remain under God's curse (9:3). These negative ascriptions are the equal of Paul's pronouncement in 1 Thess 2:14–16. Indeed, the very same charge of killing the prophets in 1 Thess 2:15 is leveled against unbelieving Jews in Rom 11:3 as well.

Unbelieving Israel is experiencing God's eschatological wrath apart from Christ, and yet those who are "enemies" will one day be reconciled to God (Rom 5:10). The positive solution that Paul envisions in Romans is a "mystery" that remains hidden until the eschaton, when God proves his final faithfulness to Israel. At that point "all Israel will be saved." Although the Jewish people who are apart from Christ are experiencing wrath at the moment, the final chapter has not yet been written. Ironically, by hindering Paul from preaching the message of salvation to the Gentiles (1 Thess 2:14–16), the Jews have temporarily delayed that final chapter since Paul views the salvation of Israel as dependent upon the success of his mission to the Gentiles (Rom 11:25–32).[73] Paul nevertheless remains supremely confident that the end of the ages and the salvation of all Israel will prove this current hardening to be have been only a temporary situation.

---

[71] Donfried, "Paul and Judaism," 249–52.

[72] G. E. Okeke reasons similarly in "I Thessalonians 2. 13–16: The Fate of the Unbelieving Jews," *NTS* 27 (1980/1981): 127–36.

[73] Scott, "Paul's Use of Deuteronomic Tradition," 656–57.

ISRAEL'S PRIORITY IN SUMMARY

The Jews remain an elect people, but Paul has reconceptualized this sense of election. The benefits as God's chosen may only be realized through faith in the Jewish Messiah, Jesus Christ. The genuinely elect of Israel remain a subset within Israel. They are a heavenly Jerusalem in contrast to the present Jerusalem, which remains in slavery as "enemies of God." The presence or absence of faith in the Jewish Messiah (Rom 9:5) determines the Jewish individual's fate as well as the fate of all people. Paul makes similar comments in 2 Corinthians 3: the Mosaic covenant—glorious and of divine origin, a sign of Jewish privilege—leads to death apart from the new covenant in Christ and the Spirit (cf. Gal 5:6).

At the same time, God's mark uniquely remains upon the Jewish people even apart from faith in Christ. Gentiles are being grafted into Israel's unique heritage. The people of Israel maintain a position of priority in God's plan. The same God who cut the natural branches off will one day graft them back in. Disobedience will yield to obedience and faith. In that sense, Israel continues to occupy a privileged place in God's plan in spite of unbelief and disobedience. This dual sense of election can only be resolved within a temporal framework that encompasses the future. To look exclusively toward an unbelieving Israel in the present would belie the full plan.

The counterpart to Jewish ethnic identity and election was the Mosaic Law. The Law was given as a gift to a chosen people in order to help them live in a manner pleasing to God. If Paul believes that the Jews maintain priority among God's people in Christ and if he believes that the Gentiles are joining a heavenly *Jerusalem,* why did he not teach that the Gentiles need to become proselytes to a *Jewish* Christianity? This would certainly express more vividly and concretely the priority of the Jewish people in God's plan. In other words, why not also urge acceptance of the Mosaic Law alongside faith in the Jewish Messiah? Other Jewish Christians had adopted this position with respect to the Gentiles. Any discussion of Israel's election, even when considered from the point of view of faith in Christ, inevitably leads to a consideration of Israel's Law. While chapter 1, above, broached some of these matters in a preliminary fashion, several questions yet remain about the precise role of the Law as it defines and characterizes God's special people, the Jews, and their Gentile beneficiaries.

⌁ 6 ⌁

THE CURSE OF THE MOSAIC LAW

> Now before faith came, we were imprisoned and guarded under
> the law until faith would be revealed. Therefore the law was our
> disciplinarian until Christ came, so that we might be justified by
> faith. But now that faith has come, we are no longer subject to a
> disciplinarian. (Gal 3:23–25)

JEWISH IDENTITY was defined in Paul's day by the possession and practice of
Moses' Law. If the modern interpreter thinks that the Mosaic Law is no longer in effect for Paul with the coming of Christ, then the interpreter would
likely conclude that the apostle is negative about Judaism as well since Jewish identity is so closely intertwined with observance of the Law. But if the
interpreter sees an ongoing role for the Mosaic Law in Paul's thought, then
the interpreter may conclude that Paul's relationship to Judaism is more am-
icable. The role of the Mosaic Law in the apostle's thinking has proven pe-
rennially difficult for interpreters to unravel, and yet the approach one takes
will necessarily impact one's opinion of what Paul thinks about the Jews and
Judaism.

Several Pauline pronouncements on the Law appear contradictory. In
places he suggests that the Law was only a temporary measure that has
ceased to function with the coming of Christ. In Gal 3:19: the Law "was
added because of transgressions, *until* the offspring would come to whom
the promise had been made." A few verses later the apostle continues, "Now
before faith came, we were imprisoned and guarded under the law until
faith would be revealed. Therefore the law was our disciplinarian until
Christ came" (vv. 23–24). In other places, Paul asserts that the Law's voice is
still active. In 1 Cor 9:8–9 he appeals to the Mosaic Law as a basis for paying
ministers of the gospel their due wages. He regularly quotes from the Torah
in support of his reasoning (e.g., Rom 10:6–8). His attitude toward the Law
thus appears to differ from passage to passage, sometimes within a span of
verses. In Rom 8:2 Paul speaks of being freed from "the law of sin and
death." Yet in Romans 7 the apostle mourns sin's derailing of the Law's be-
neficent purpose to bring about death instead. This death-dealing Law remains God's with its "holy and just and good" commandment (7:12; 8:7).
These contradictory assertions puzzle and pose difficulties for modern

scholars. One commentator has thrown up his hands and suggested that we should not expect the ancient apostle to reason with the same sense of consistency as a modern thinker.[1]

Interpreters agree that Paul's writings include several harsh statements about the role of the Mosaic Law. Not all interpreters agree, however, that Paul has anything positive to say about the Law. Some interpreters affirm an ongoing role for the Mosaic Law in the life of the Christian. Others deny that Paul allows for this possibility. At the heart of these differences is debate over which passages in Paul pertain to the Mosaic Law and which do not. Those skeptical of an ongoing positive role for the Law stress that Paul's use of the word νόμος may not always refer to the Mosaic Law and that the passages critiquing Law observance exhaust the legitimate references to Moses' Law. This chapter will therefore explore what Paul finds wrong about the Mosaic Law and whether interpreters are right to limit reference to the Mosaic Law.

WHAT PAUL FINDS WRONG ABOUT THE LAW: PERFECT OBEDIENCE

Among Paul's negative statements regarding the Law, one passage has dominated scholarly attention. In Gal 3:10 he says that anyone who attempts to do what the Mosaic Law requires falls under its curse. Implied in his logic is the premise that no one actually does (or can do) all that the Law requires. Galatians 5:3 echoes 3:10: "Once again I testify to every man who lets himself be circumcised that he is obliged to obey the entire law." The most serious obstacle to this reading of 3:10 is that Paul labels his own observance of the Mosaic Law "blameless" in Phil 3:6. So which verse represents the apostle's true opinion: Gal 3:10 or Phil 3:6? The apostle appears to make contradictory statements. Many scholars today opt in favor of Phil 3:6 since the Jews, they claim, never maintained that an individual had to obey the Law perfectly.

In the enthusiasm of the last several decades over the "new perspective" on Paul and the Law, specialists have often overlooked the fact that perfect obedience to the Law as one finds it expressed in Gal 3:10 *does* figure as a motif within Jewish literature of the period. Galatians 3:10's reference to perfect obedience may not be so surprising after all. Perfection of conduct always remained the ideal within Judaism. The book of *Jubilees,* dated by most scholars to the second century before Christ, categorically states, "All of [God's] commands and his ordinances and all of his law" are to be carefully observed "without turning aside to the right or left" (23:16). "[God]

---

[1] Heikki Räisänen, *Paul and the Law* (2d ed.; WUNT 29; Tübingen: J. C. B. Mohr [Paul Siebeck], 1986).

did not show partiality, except to Noah alone . . . because his heart was righteous in all of his ways just as it was commanded concerning him. And he did not transgress anything which was ordained for him" (5:19). Noah, while the recipient of God's mercy (10:3), did "just as it was commanded" and was "righteous in all of his ways"; "He did not transgress." Jacob was also "a perfect man" (27:17). Leah "was perfect and upright in all her ways," and Joseph "walked uprightly" (36:23; 40:8). God told Abraham in 15:3 to "be pleasing before me and *be perfect*" (emphases here mine). Abraham was then praised in 23:10 since he "was *perfect in all of his actions* with the Lord and was pleasing through righteousness all of the days of his life." The author looked forward to the day when Israel would be *perfectly* obedient (1:22–24; 5:12; 50:5).[2] Although God offered provision for sin and failure, the ideal remained strict and perfect obedience to the Law. Although God granted mercy to the elect, the requirement of right conduct "in all things" (21:23) is still upheld and admonished through these exemplary models. The Law must be obeyed (1:23–24; 20:7).

A similar perspective has emerged from the literature of the Qumran community. The community admonished its members to be perfect in their obedience of the Law. One of their hymns speaks of perfection of way (1QHᵃ 9 [=1]:36). The demand of the Law is strict and absolute (1QS 1:13–17; 5:1, 8, 20–22; CD 2:15; 15:12–14; 16:6b–8; 20:2, 5, 7). According to the *Rule of the Community,* an individual must "steady his steps in order to walk with perfection on all the paths of God, conforming to all he has decreed concerning the regular times of his commands and not turn aside, either left or right, nor infringe even one of his words" (1QS 3:9–11). Although the Qumran members availed themselves of divine mercy and provision for sin, they nevertheless expressed an intense self-awareness of sin in their hymnic material. Far from finding perfect obedience a matter of due course, they struggled individually with living in a fully righteous manner before God. The author of one hymn laments falling short of the "perfect path" required by God (1QHᵃ 12 [=4]:29–33). Community members looked forward to the last days when they would be "cleansed" of this tendency toward sin (1QS 3:21–23; 4:18–22; 11:14–15; 1QHᵃ 14 [=6]:8–10; 7 [=15]:15–17). Although God was indeed merciful, the *Rule of the Community* emphasized that God would reward those who were obedient in their works: "And the visitation of those who walk in it [the counsels of the spirit] will be for healing, plentiful peace in a long life, fruitful offspring with all everlasting blessings, eternal enjoyment with endless life, and a crown of glory with majestic raiment in eternal light" (1QS 4:6–8). God is a God of compassion and mercy, but he still "pays man his wages" (1QS 10:17–18). "Man is

---

[2] Sanders, *Paul and Palestinian Judaism,* 381, on the basis of these passages, concedes, "Perfect obedience is specified." He adds, "As we have now come to expect, the emphasis on God's mercy is coupled with a strict demand to be obedient" (p. 383).

examined according to his path, each one is rewarded according to his deeds" (4QPs^f 8:4–5). "[God] shall carry out justice by . . . truthful judgment on every son of man" (1QM 11:14).

Philo, an Alexandrian Jewish thinker and contemporary of Jesus, says that to hear or profess the precepts of God's Law is not enough; one actually has to do them (*Praem.* 79–83, esp. 79 and 82, citing Deut 30:10). Individuals will be weighed in the scales (e.g., *Congr.* 164; *Her.* 46). One must not deviate to the right or to the left from the path God has prepared for humanity in the Law (*Deus* 162; *Abr.* 269; *Post.* 101–102; cf. *Leg.* 3.165; the "middle road" of *Migr.* 146). Philo praises Abraham since "he had not neglected any of God's commands" (*Abr.* 192). One's "whole life" should be one of "happy obedience to law" (*Abr.* 5–6). At the same time, God "ever prefers forgiveness to punishment" (*Praem.* 166). God granted to the Jews several means by which they could rectify the situation created by sin and violation of God's Law. Philo affirms atoning sacrifice (*Spec.* 1.235–241; 1.188–190; 2.193–196). Only God can be sinless (*Fug.* 157; *Virt.* 177; *Leg.* 3.106, 211). The possibility of repentance flows out of God's recognition of the human tendency to sin (*Fug.* 99, 105). It is as if one were ill, with repentance being the only hope for a return to health (*Fug.* 160; *Abr.* 26; *Spec.* 1.236–253). Sincere repentance blots out the effects of sin as if the sin had never occurred (*Abr.* 19; *Spec.* 1.187–188; *QG* 1.84; *Mut.* 124; *Somn.* 1.91). God will bestow rewards and blessings "in honor of their victory" (*Virt.* 175), but those who repent will still bear the scars of their misdeeds (*Spec.* 1.103).

Although Philo affirms the Jews' special status as recipients of God's mercy and repentance as a means to remedy the situation caused by sin, he nevertheless commends those whose conduct is perfect. Those who remain sinless and unblemished are superior to those who must repent and be healed of their illness (*Abr.* 26; *Virt.* 176). Abraham achieved perfect obedience of the Law (*Migr.* 127–130; *Abr.* 275–276; *Her.* 6–9). The following passage is representative as an admonition to strive toward perfect obedience as well as an expression of Abraham's attainment of that goal:

> When, then, is it that the servant speaks frankly to his master? Surely it is when his heart tells him that he has not wronged his owner, but that his words and deeds are *all* [πάντα] for that owner's benefit. And so when else should the slave of God open his mouth freely to Him Who is the ruler and master both of himself and of the All, *save when he is pure from sin* and the judgements of his conscious are loyal to his master. . . . The loyalty of Abraham's service and ministry is shewn by the concluding words of the oracle addressed to Abraham's son, "I will give to thee and thy seed all this land, and all the nations of the earth shall be blessed in thy seed, because Abraham thy father hearkened to My voice and kept My injunctions, My commands, My ordinances and My statutes" (Gen. xxvi. 3–5). It is the highest praise which can be given to a servant that *he neglects none* [μηδενός] *of his master's commands.*[3] (emphasis mine)

---

[3] Philo, *Her.* 6–9 (Colson and Whitaker, LCL).

Noah was "perfect" in virtue (*Deus* 117, 122, 140; *Abr.* 34, 47). Still, Philo immediately qualifies the attribute of perfection for Noah (*Abr.* 36–39). Noah only attained a perfection relative to his generation; he was "not good absolutely" (οὐ καθάπαξ). Philo then compares Noah's "perfection" with that of other sages who possessed an "unchallenged" and "unperverted" virtue. Noah therefore won the "second prize." Although Noah is to be praised for his achievement, Philo clearly commends the "first prize" of unqualified virtue to his audience. Moses, for instance, fell into this highest category. The lawgiver exemplified the attainment of the highest place of all (*Mos.* 1.162; 2.1, 8–11; *Leg.* 3.134, 140; *Ebr.* 94; *Sacr.* 8); he was a model of the perfection toward which Philo's readers were to strive (*Mos.* 1.158–159). Obviously, perfect obedience and sinlessness remained the ideal for Philo. Philo maintains that the Jews, as an elect people, are to strive to live as virtuously and as perfectly as possible, as difficult as this might be.[4] Even Enoch and Enosh were not able to live perfectly and without sin. On the other hand, God, a merciful God, recognizes humanity's difficulty with sin and offers abundant grace and mercy to the repentant. Although the balance certainly weighs heavily toward mercy and forgiveness of sin in Philo, the Law still enjoins a perfect obedience toward which all people should strive.

Jewish literature from Paul's era typically balanced the demand of God's Law for perfect obedience alongside God's gracious election and mercy toward a special people, whether the Jewish people as a whole or a remnant within this people (as the Qumran community viewed itself). Although scholars have debated where the emphasis may lie in a particular writing or genre, the tension was almost universal. No one earned a place in the world to come by works apart from God's grace, mercy, and forgiveness. A few Jewish writings did depart from this pattern and, in questioning God's grace and mercy, leaned exclusively toward works as the basis for one's status and relationship with God. In the immediate aftermath of Jerusalem's fall to the Romans, a few Jewish authors wrote apocalypses in which an individual's destiny depended entirely upon their deeds. *Fourth Ezra* and *2 Baruch* describe God's strict weighing of deeds on the scale. The authors of these pseudonymous works struggled to make sense of why the gracious God of Israel would have permitted the people to be conquered. They began to question whether the people's deeds must have in some way warranted such events, and they began to wonder openly whether God was at all merciful and forgiving of sin apart from a strict scale of justice. The people must not have perfectly obeyed God's Law and thus were experiencing the curse

---

[4] On the other hand, Philo does not limit God's grace to the Jewish people. In fact, he distinguishes the "Jews" from "Israel." "Israel" includes those Jews who "see God" as well as Gentiles with a similar vision; see David M. Hay, "Philo of Alexandria," in *The Complexities of Second Temple Judaism*, vol. 1 of *Justification and Variegated Nomism* (ed. D. A. Carson, Peter T. O'Brien, and Mark A. Siefrid; Grand Rapids: Baker, 2001), 369–70, 372.

of judgment. Such writings snapped the tension normally present in Jewish writings in favor of strict judgment. Such literature may offer a useful parallel for Paul since he too questions the efficacy of God's grace and mercy for the Jewish people apart from what God is doing in Christ. Paul too finds the Law's demand for perfect obedience problematic.[5]

Scholars have typically pointed to Phil 3:6 as proof that Paul does not believe that perfectly obeying the Law is difficult for human beings. The apostle speaks of his blamelessness with respect to the righteousness of the Law. Sanders has offered important background on how terms such as "righteous" and "blameless" were employed in Jewish literature. Regarding the views of the Jewish rabbis after 70 C.E., "although the term 'righteous' is primarily applied to those who obey the Torah, the Rabbis knew full well that even the righteous did not obey God's law perfectly."[6] The biblical commandments "are nevertheless difficult or even impossible fully to obey."[7] "Human perfection was not considered realistically achievable by the Rabbis."[8] The rabbinic *Sipra,* a commentary on Leviticus, relates the incident of Nadab and Abihu in the Hebrew Scriptures as an example of human imperfection (Lev 10:1–3; also Num 3:4; 26:61). Nadab and Abihu were killed by fire for an unholy offering to the Lord, and yet they were not exposed or humiliated in death.[9] The *Sipra* comments on this story: "How much the more so [will God show pity to] *other righteous persons*" (emphasis mine). Abihu and Nadab were considered among the righteous even though their sin warranted punishment by death. Righteousness for a Jew never meant that one had been sinless and had perfectly done all that God commanded in the Law. The righteous were those who attempted to obey the Law in its entirety and sought atonement for their sin or failure.[10] The ultimate criterion was faithfulness to the relationship.

The Dead Sea Scrolls present a similar view of righteousness. To walk perfectly is never to transgress (1QS 3:9–11). The Qumran hymns continually implore God for the forgiveness of sins and lament that no one is "righteous" or follows the "perfect path" (e.g., 1QH[a] 12 [=4]:29–32). Such righteousness belongs only to God, but God graciously conferred a divine

---

[5] For a more thorough discussion of these Jewish writings, see Das, *Paul, the Law, and the Covenant,* 45–69.

[6] Sanders, *Paul and Palestinian Judaism,* 203.

[7] Ibid., 115; see also 137.

[8] Ibid., 137.

[9] *Sipra Shemini Mekhilta deMiluim* 22–27 (on Lev 10:1–5).

[10] "The *righteous are those who obey the Torah and atone for transgression*" (Sanders, *Paul and Palestinian Judaism,* 204). "Righteousness, in the conception of it which Judaism got from the Scriptures, had no suggestion of sinless perfection. Nor are the sins of the righteous all venial; the gravest moral lapses may befall them, as they did David. What distinguishes the righteous man who has fallen into sin is his repentance" (George Foot Moore, *Judaism in the First Centuries of the Christian Era: The Age of the Tannaim* [3 vols.; Cambridge: Harvard University Press, 1927], 1:494–95).

righteousness on community members (e.g., 1QH^a 19 [=11]:29–32; 1QS 11:12). Because of God's mercy, the community member could be called righteous as well. Sanders has concluded from the Qumran documents that "from the point of view of the halakah [legal strictures], one is required to walk perfectly. From the point of view of the individual in prayer or devotional moments, he is unable to walk perfectly and must be given perfection of way by God's grace."[11]

The righteous were typically sinners who availed themselves of God's mercy and election even while falling short of the perfect measure toward which they were striving. Biblical figures were often characterized as "blameless" even when the biblical text admitted their sins (2 Chr 15:17 [cf. 2 Chr 16's catalog of sins]; Luke 1:6, 18–20). Paul could admonish his own audience, while it struggled against sin, to be blameless (Phil 2:15; see also 1 Thess 3:13; 5:23; and 1 Cor 1:8). So blamelessness with respect to the Law ought to be distinguished from perfect obedience. Whereas perfect obedience was unerring success in doing all that God commanded in the Law, blamelessness included the broader context of the Law: God's election and mercy upon the people. Paul reflects the same tension in his writings: he could call himself blameless with respect to the righteousness of the Law and yet still affirm that all people are sinners (Rom 3:23). Although Paul describes his prior status as blameless, he nowhere says that he was without sin as a Pharisee.

The demands God articulated within the Mosaic Law were never divorced from God's gracious mercy, forgiveness, and favor. Although a Jewish person may have evaluated him- or herself with Paul in Phil 3:6 as "blameless," the blamelessness that Paul urges upon Christians is quite different since the gracious elements of the Law have been crucially altered in Paul's thought. He does not think that Israel can benefit from its election apart from Christ. The Sinaitic covenant does not mediate God's promises to Abraham as the Jews thought it did. God's promises to Abraham are mediated through the seed, Christ (Gal 3:15–18). If Jesus Christ mediates the promises of Abraham and Israel's election, then a much more pessimistic view of the Law in God's plan emerges in Paul's reasoning.

The Jews had typically associated the Law with God's grace. Some of Paul's peers apparently thought that he was rejecting this grace when he claimed that one cannot be saved through the Mosaic Law. He responds to this potential objection in Gal 2:21: "I do not nullify the grace of God; for if justification comes through the law, then Christ died for nothing." Or later in 3:21: "For if a law had been given that could make alive, then

---

[11] Sanders, *Paul and Palestinian Judaism*, 288. "On the one hand, there is the sense of human inadequacy before God . . . ; no one can be righteous or perfect before God; no one, on his own, has 'righteous deeds.' On the other hand, there is the consciousness of being elect; thus some are righteous *(tsaddiq, yitsdaq)*, but only by the grace of God" (pp. 311–12).

righteousness would indeed come through the law." For Paul the Law is an enslaving power since no one can accomplish what it requires.

In Romans 7 Paul laments human inability to do what the Mosaic Law requires of its adherents. Although the Law is indeed "spiritual" (Rom 7:14) and "good" (v. 16; see also vv. 22 and 25), the power of sin turns out to be far stronger than the desire to do what the Law commands. People under the Law find themselves in the "wretched" position of being unable to do good. They do what they hate instead because of the tyranny and power of sin (vv. 14, 15, 17, 20, 24). Three times Paul cycles through an admission that the "I" is unable to accomplish what the Law demands (vv. 15–16, 18–20, 21–23). Paul finds one commandment epitomizing the futile struggle to obey the Law: "Do not covet." Of all the commandments, the prohibition against coveting most exposes the problem of a sinful heart. The battle against sin penetrates to the inner core of human existence, to secret desires and motives that stand in the way of obedience to God's holy Law.[12]

Paul describes the plight under the Law in Romans 7 as a failure to obey "the commandment" (ἐντολή, vv. 7–11). The varied terminology that Paul uses to express the same point makes it clear that *doing* the Law is the key issue. He uses three distinct synonyms eleven times in vv. 15–21: πράσσω (vv. 15, 19), ποιέω (vv. 15, 16, 19, 20, 21), and κατεργάζομαι (vv. 15, 17, 18, 20). The "problem" or "plight" of the Law according to Rom 7:14–25 is that those who know what the Law demands are unable to do it. Whereas a Jew would ordinarily turn to repentance, sacrifice, and atonement as the solution for such failure, Paul turns instead to Christ as the solution to fleshly humanity's inability (τὸ ἀδύνατον) to do what God requires in the Law (8:3–4). Through Christ "the just requirement of the law" (τὸ δικαίωμα τοῦ νόμου) is fulfilled in believers. The same dynamic is at work in 10:6–8. Paul takes a passage from Deuteronomy about the possibility for people to observe the precepts of the Mosaic Law and reinterprets Deut 30:11–14 as an expression of what takes place in Christ.[13]

---

[12] "Do not covet" in 7:7 is the most private and interior of the commandments. Philippians 3 says little or nothing about the possibility of an internal struggle with sin and desire and remains at the level only of a public, observable blamelessness. The only characteristic distinguishing the tenth commandment from the others is its unique focus on interiority. Whereas most Jews would have no problem keeping the other commandments (murder, adultery, robbery, the Sabbath), it is the command not to covet that exposes the extreme difficulty of keeping the Mosaic Law; J. A. Ziesler, "The Role of the Tenth Commandment in Romans 7," *JSNT* 33 (1988): 48. As Ziesler points out, Paul "almost certainly generalizes from it [the command not to covet]." Philo calls desire the fountain of iniquity from which all sinful actions flow (*Decal.* 142–153, 173); for this reason, God prohibited coveting. Fourth Maccabees 2:5–6 (in its context) claims that if one can control and limit sinful desires through reason, then one will be able to obey the Law in other ways as well. The tenth commandment could therefore epitomize the entirety of the Law (even as in Romans 7).

[13] See Das, *Paul, the Law, and the Covenant,* 234–67, for a thorough review of these verses in context.

WHAT PAUL FINDS WRONG ABOUT THE LAW: ETHNIC EXCLUSIVITY

The problem with the Law, according to the apostle, is simply that sin renders human observance of its precepts impossible. Interpreters through the centuries have often cited Romans 7 in support of the conclusion that perfect obedience to the Law is impossible. Absolutely nothing in Romans 7 indicates that Paul's problem with the Law is that it leads to national righteousness or ethnic pride.[14] Jewish possession of the Law is good as long as the Jew can also do what that Law demands. The problem with the traditional approach, as more recent interpreters have recognized, is that *other* passages in Paul *do* fault the ethnic exclusivity that characterizes those who possess the Mosaic Law.

When the apostle specifically addresses Jewish ethnic identity in Romans 2, he sees absolutely nothing wrong in this identity provided one actually does all that the Law requires. Just to obey those aspects of the Law that distinguish a person as Jewish is not enough. Paul's rhetorical charges in Rom 2:17–29 assume the difficulty of doing all that the Law requires even for Jews. He makes that assumption explicit later in Romans 7.[15] Nevertheless, the Jewish individual possesses the Law, not the Gentile. Some live "apart from the law" (ἀνόμως) in 2:12 even while others "sinned under the law" (or better, *with* the law [ἐν νόμῳ]). Those "apart from the law" are further defined in v. 14 as Gentiles (ἔθνη) who do not possess the Law (μὴ νόμον ἔχοντα). Lest it appear that the Jew has a special advantage at the judgment by virtue of his or her possession of the Mosaic Law, Paul replies that Gentiles "do instinctively what the law requires," since they are "a law to themselves" (vv. 14–15): "what the law requires is written on their hearts." Although the Gentiles do not possess the Mosaic Law in its entirety, the Law is sufficiently available in a form that is written on their hearts. The Gentile will be just as accountable before God's judgment seat as will the Jew who has the Mosaic Law. God shows no partiality (v. 11).[16] In vv. 17–24 Paul explicitly turns to the Jew who possesses the Law. He claims, in relation to the commands of the Decalogue, that the Jew too has violated the

---

[14] Dunn (*Romans 1–8*, 352) inexplicably thinks that Paul's problem with the Law in Romans 7 must be understood in terms of the sin of "national righteousness," "national self-righteous judgment on others," or the "unself-critical presumption of God's favor." The eschatological Spirit has liberated humanity "from that too narrowing understanding of the law's role" in terms of "pride in national identity" (p. 387). Where does Paul address a mistaken *understanding* of the Law in Romans 7?

[15] For a detailed exposition of Romans 1 and 2, see Das, *Paul, the Law, and the Covenant,* ch. 7.

[16] See ibid., ch. 7.

Mosaic Law.[17] The Law, contrary to Jewish sentiments of the day, offers no viable provision for sin. Circumcision will not be of any benefit to the individual who transgresses the Law (v. 25). The uncircumcised (Gentile) who does what the Law requires will be reckoned at the judgment as circumcised. Such an individual will also judge the circumcised who transgress the Law. Paul's line of reasoning in Romans 2 critiques any presumption of Jewish ethnic advantage by virtue of mere possession of the Law.

Paul continues his critique of Jewish ethnic advantage in Romans 3. The strong affirmation in 3:28 that "a person is justified by faith apart from works prescribed by the law" is quickly followed by this query: "Or is God the God of Jews only? Is he not the God of Gentiles also? Yes, of Gentiles also, since God is one; and he will justify the circumcised on the ground of faith and the uncircumcised through that same faith" (v. 29). In other words, if a person were justified by the works of the Mosaic Law, then God would be God of the Jews alone and not of the Gentiles. God would be partial after all, contrary to the apostle's claims in Romans 2. Since, however, God saves on the basis of faith rather than on the works of the Law, God is truly impartial and just in salvation. All people are saved on the same basis, faith.

Even within a passage riveted on the ethnic exclusivity of the Law, Paul's critique shifts gears within verses to "the works prescribed by the law" (3:28). In 4:4–5 he asserts, "Now to the one who works, wages are not reckoned as a gift but as something due. But to one who without works trusts him who justifies the ungodly, such faith is reckoned as righteousness." The Law's works entail due wages, but God justifies the ungodly by faith apart from works. In 4:4–5 he expands on his important claim in 3:27 that "a person is justified by faith apart from the works prescribed by the law."[18] The contribution of 4:4–5 to Paul's overarching logic would be as follows: God saves by his free grace through faith rather than by works, which are based on human accomplishment. Thus the Mosaic Law must be excluded from God's justifying activity since the Law requires accomplishment or works on the part of the observant. But if the Mosaic Law is excluded from a role in God's justifying activity, then the Gentiles are no longer excluded by that Law from salvation. Whereas the Law had divided the world into Jews and Gentiles on the basis of the works that it prescribed, the elimination of the criterion of works would eliminate the distinction itself, at least with respect to salvation. Paul's critique of the Law is therefore two-pronged: the Mosaic Law is not God's path to salvation since it is based on human activity, and at the same time, the Mosaic wall, which had divided the world into Jews and Gentiles before God's judgment, has been torn down.

---

[17] This focus on the Decalogue makes no sense if the Jews were guilty only of ethnic presumption. The problem has to do with a failure to do *all* that the Law requires.

[18] On the various linguistic and logical connections between 4:1–8 and 3:27–31, see Das, *Paul, the Law, and the Covenant,* ch. 8.

Recent scholarship has become polarized on whether Paul's problem with the Law was the inability of people to obey its demands or its exclusion of the Gentiles—whether by a misunderstanding or by ethnic pride. The modern "new perspective" approach to Paul has rightly highlighted the ethnic aspect of his reasoning, but the pendulum perhaps swung too far in the direction of the "new perspective" in the latter part of the twentieth century. "New perspective" interpreters did not always recognize that the Law not only distinguishes the Jewish people from the other nations but also places a burden of obedience upon them. Traditional interpreters were right to assert a Pauline critique of works. Both sides in the debate did not always recognize that it is a both-and relationship.[19]

WHAT PAUL FINDS WRONG ABOUT THE LAW: AN ENSLAVING POWER

In Rom 5:12 Paul writes, "Therefore, just as sin came into the world through one man, and death came through sin, so death spread to all because all have sinned." All humanity suffers the consequences of the sin of one man, Adam. Due to Adam's falling prey to the power of sin, "death exercised dominion from Adam to Moses" (v. 14). With the arrival of Christ on the stage of human existence, for Paul a new era has dawned with equally universal implications: "Therefore just as one man's trespass led to condemnation for all, so one man's act of righteousness leads to justification and life for all" (v. 18). In vv. 20–21 he identifies the forces that dominate existence under the old and new ages: the Law, Sin, and Grace. As Paul continues, he will

---

[19] I argued this complementary approach at length in Das, *Paul, the Law, and the Covenant.* Although the book was released in 2001, I had concluded my research and writing early in 1998. Bruce W. Longenecker independently came to similar conclusions in *The Triumph of Abraham's God: The Transformation of Identity in Galatians* (Nashville: Abingdon, 1998), 139–42, 179–83. I had noted in *Paul, the Law, and the Covenant,* 212, hints in his earlier research in this direction. Seyoon Kim attacks Longenecker's approach (and hence also my own) in *Paul and the New Perspective,* 144. Kim does not see how Paul could have argued against his "Jewish opponents" if his own view of Judaism had been influenced by the shift in perspective caused by his newfound christological convictions. But Kim does not recognize the crucial importance that Paul is opposing a Jewish *Christian* perspective. Jewish Christians, of all people, should recognize that salvation is in Christ and not the Law. As for the continuity that Kim seeks in Paul's position as apostle and his former position as a non-Christ-believing Jew, the answer is simply that Paul had always held Christ and the Law as competing approaches to salvation. After the Damascus Road experience, he simply realized he had been wrong about the Law as an approach to salvation and that it did not posses the gracious elements that he had assumed as a Jew. All of these benefits are located in Christ. I develop the argument in *Paul, the Law, and the Covenant* in much more detail than Longenecker since my study is devoted exclusively to these matters.

structure his argument around these three entities (see 6:1, 15; 7:7).[20] As Adam brought the powers of Sin (and Death) into the world, another man, Jesus Christ, brought the power of Grace.

The apostle's apocalyptic worldview is on display from 5:12 through the end of Romans 8. Supernatural forces are dueling for control of the world. On the one side stand the personified powers of Sin, the Law, and Death. The powers of Sin and Death exercise "dominion" (6:9, 12, 14). They enslave (e.g., vv. 6, 18). Sin "makes you obey [the mortal bodies'] passions" (v. 12). In opposition to these nefarious entities is the power of Grace. For those participating by baptism in Christ's death (vv. 3–4, 7), a change of lordship has taken place with a corresponding deliverance from bondage. Death's rule is broken (v. 9). Believers in Christ are released from the powers and effects of one age into another. The Christian must therefore take advantage of the powers of this new age by presenting his or her body to God rather than to the personified power of Sin (v. 13).[21]

In Rom 8:14–15 Paul ominously introduces the Law into his progressing argument in contrast with being under Grace. The Law thus appears to be a negative, enslaving power from which one must be liberated, much as had been the case with Sin a few verses before. By 7:1–6 Paul's focus is exclusively on the Law—clearly an enslaving power. Even as one must die to Sin (6:2), so also one must die to the Law (7:4). As death frees a person from Sin (6:7, 18), likewise death frees from the Law (7:2–3, 6). This freedom from Sin and the Law permits the Christian to serve in the newness of life (6:4) and the Spirit (7:6).[22] Paul offers the analogy of a woman bound to her husband by the Law until his death frees her from the legal obligation. A death must take place in order to liberate from the enslaving power of the Law. This death took place when the Christian was buried with Christ in baptism (6:3–13). Dying permits the believer to live!

Paul is sensitive to the negative direction toward which his reasoning has turned. He asks in Rom 7:7 if the Law is itself Sin. "By no means!" he answers. The virus of Sin has simply commandeered the Law and its commandment, originally intended to produce life, in order to multiply itself and bring about death instead (vv. 8, 10–11). The Law is holy, just, and good (v. 12), but Sin took hold of the Law and brought about a totally different result (v. 13). The power of Sin is far stronger than the desire to do what the "spiritual" Law commands (v. 14). People find themselves in the "wretched" position of being unable to do what is good; they do what they hate instead

---

[20] I am indebted to Achtemeier for this insight. See his *Romans,* 102.

[21] For an attempt to reconstruct the background to Paul's apocalyptic personification of Sin, Law, and Grace, see Chris Forbes, "Paul's Principalities and Powers: Demythologizing Apocalyptic?" *JSNT* 82 (2001): 61–88, and "Pauline Demonology and/or Cosmology? Principalities, Powers, and the Elements of the World in Their Hellenistic Context," *JSNT* 85 (2002): 51–73.

[22] Anders Nygren, *Commentary on Romans* (Philadelphia: Fortress, 1949), 268.

because of the tyranny and power of Sin (vv. 14, 15, 17, 20, 24). The Law then holds captive those infected by Sin by pronouncing upon them the sentence of death. Jesus Christ offers the only deliverance and escape from this horrible bondage and oppression (vv. 24–25).

In Galatians 3 Paul presents a similar critique of the Law. While assuming that people simply do not do all that the Law requires, Paul describes those reliant upon the Law as "under the curse" (3:10: ὑπὸ κατάραν). The phrasing parallels Romans 6 and 7's bondage "under the law" (ὑπὸ νόμον). The Law is once again an enslaving power from which a person must be delivered. In Gal 3:13 Paul responds to v. 10's pronouncement of curse: "Christ redeemed us from the curse of the law by becoming a curse for us." The next paragraph advances the critique as Paul severs the Mosaic Law from the much earlier Abrahamic covenant and promise. By v. 19 Paul realizes that it is necessary to explain why there had been a Mosaic Law at all. He explains that the Law "was added *because of* transgressions." The prepositional phrase (παραβάσεων χάριν) is ambiguous: the Law may have been added in order to produce or provoke transgressions, or the Law was added in order to deal with, stop, or prevent transgressions. Nothing in the immediate context of v. 19 suggests that the Law is capable in any way of addressing the problem of sin. In v. 21 Paul says, "For if a law had been given that could make alive, then righteousness would indeed come through the law." If the Law had been able to curb or prevent sin, then the Law would have been capable of leading people to righteousness. More likely, then, the Law *increases* transgressions, but unfortunately Paul never clarifies in what sense the Law produces transgression, at least in the Letter to the Galatians. Perhaps the apostle assumes in his reasoning what he will later explain more fully in Romans: the Law legally declares sin to be a transgression and thereby produces transgressions (Rom 4:15; 5:13–14).[23] In any case, Paul has not escaped the negative contours of his reasoning in Gal 3:19, which leads to his musing in v. 21 whether the Law is actually opposed to the promises. Such a question is hardly comprehensible if Paul had been speaking positively of the Law in v. 19 as curbing and/or preventing sin.

The following paragraphs maintain the negative focus on the Law as an enslaving power. In 3:23–4:7 Paul contrasts sonship "in Christ" with the slavery that exists "under the law" (ὑπὸ νόμον, 3:23; 4:4–5). The notion of being "under" the Law parallels being "under" several other enslaving entities in these verses, the first of which is in 3:22: "The scripture has imprisoned all things under the power of sin [ὑπὸ ἁμαρτίαν; literally, 'under sin']." The negative phrase "under sin" prompts an evaluation of "under the law" in the very next verse similarly in terms of oppression and bondage. Even as the Scriptures "imprisoned" in v. 22, so also the Law

---

[23] Jeffrey A. D. Weima, "The Function of the Law in Relation to Sin: An Evaluation of the View of H. Räisänen, *NovT* 32 (1990): 227–31; In-Gyu Hong, *The Law in Galatians* (JSNTSup 81; Sheffield, England: Sheffield Academic Press, 1993), 151–52.

confines (συγκλειόμενοι) in v. 23. Incarceration under the Law is hardly a positive situation.[24] The Law functions not to protect a people but to confine. Paul doubly emphasizes the notion of confinement by employing the word "guarded" (ἐφρουρούμεθα) alongside "enclosed" or "confined" (συγκλειόμενοι) and "under law." Similarly, when Paul speaks of being "under the law" in 4:4–5, release from that condition is analogous to the liberation or deliverance of a slave (ἐξαγοράσῃ). He uses the same verb as he uses in 3:13 to explain Christ's deliverance from an existence under the Law's curse (ὑπὸ κατάραν). Paul's verb usage echoes again the darker imagery of oppression and bondage.

Paul consistently employs the phrase "under the law" as a negative description later in Galatians as well. Existence "under the law" is analogous to being under (ὑπό) the "elemental spirits" of the world in 4:3, 9. To be under the "weak and beggarly elemental spirits"—the definition and meaning of the Greek phrase are disputed—is equivalent to a slavery "to beings that by nature are not gods" (4:8). Christ has delivered the believer from bondage to these cosmic forces. According to Paul in 5:16, the Christian who lives (literally, "walks" [περιπατεῖτε]) "by the Spirit" will not "gratify the desires of the flesh." He adds, "If you are led by the Spirit, you are not subject to [ὑπό] the law" (v. 18). To remain under the Law is to remain powerless against the flesh's desires. The Spirit is the only force that can effectively oppose the flesh (v. 17).

In 3:25 Paul speaks of existence under the Law as analogous to being under a pedagogue. In the Greco-Roman world a pedagogue was never a teacher or schoolmaster but rather a household slave who accompanied the young son of the master wherever the son might go, including to and from school. The pedagogue was charged with protecting and supervising the child. Many pedagogues in antiquity were beloved figures. At the same time, other pedagogues failed to measure up to the ideal. Ancient authors decried the custom of placing elderly slaves in charge of the young and active boys. Many pedagogues were even abusive figures who set poor examples. They restrained the youth through harsh, repressive measures.[25] The image of a pedagogue in antiquity is therefore ambiguous and offers little help for determining whether Paul's pedagogue imagery in v. 25 is positive or oppressive. One clue is the link between this verse's imagery and the preceding verse: even as the Law functions restrictively and oppressively in v. 24, so the Law is analogous to a pedagogue. Paul's pedagogue is an image of restraint and imprisonment in vv. 3:24–25.

---

[24] It is not a supervising influence or custodian, contra Linda L. Belleville, "'Under Law': Structural Analysis and the Pauline Concept of Law in Galatians 3.21–4.11, *JSNT* 26 (1986): 60; rightly Hong, *Law in Galatians,* 157.

[25] For ancient references and discussion, see David J. Lull, "'The Law Was Our Pedagogue': A Study in Galatians 3:19–25," *JBL* 105 (1986): 489–93; Norman H. Young, "*PAIDAGOGOS:* The Social Setting of a Pauline Metaphor," *NovT* 29 (1987): 150–76; Witherington, *Grace in Galatia,* 262–67.

In antiquity the pedagogue's role lasted only until the charge came of age. The Law's role in vv. 3:23–4:7 is likewise temporally limited. The Law "was added because of transgressions, *until* the offspring [Christ] would come to whom the promise had been made" (3:19). "Before faith came" in v. 23 is likely a reference to Christ since faith existed even in the time of Abraham (v. 6). What "came" was faith's object, with the result that the object, Christ, could be called "Faith." Similarly at the end of v. 23, "we were imprisoned and guarded under the law *until* faith would be revealed," and in v. 25, "Now that faith *has come,* we are *no longer* subject to a disciplinarian [pedagogue]." In other words, the Law enslaves and restricts within its particular, temporary place in history. Although 4:1–7 drops reference to the pedagogue, Paul begins to speak of an existence "under guardians and trustees" (ὑπὸ ἐπιτρόπους καὶ οἰκονόμους): "heirs, *as long as* [ἐφ' ὅσον χρόνον] they are minors, are no better than slaves, though they are the owners of all the property; but they remain under guardians and trustees *until* the date [ἄχρι τῆς προθεσμίας] set by the father." Once again, the situation prior to Christ's coming "under the law" (4:4–5) is compared to a condition of slavery until "when the fullness of time had come" (ὅτε δὲ ἦλθεν τὸ πλήρωμα τοῦ χρόνου). With the coming of Christ, "born of a woman, born under the law," a new era in the history of humanity has dawned for the apostle, an era in which true freedom from bondage and imprisonment under the Law is possible.

For most Jews in Paul's day, the Law's demands were held in tension with a gracious framework of election and provision for failure. But the apostle nowhere hints of anything gracious or saving about the Mosaic Law in Galatians 3 or in the first few verses of Galatians 4. Christ plays the role of gracious provision for sin in Paul's thought. If the grace of God has had to wait for the coming of his Son, then the era prior to Christ's coming under the Law must have been an era without grace, or at least insofar as the Law itself is concerned. What *has* been of saving value in the past has been faith, as that of Abraham, in the promise of a seed, the Christ to come (3:15–18). The Mosaic Law, apart from the Abrahamic promises, has become in Paul's hands an empty set of requirements and stipulations that no human being could adequately obey. Paul has discovered that the Law was never God's provision for sin (2:21; 3:21). The Law's requirements belong to the realm of imperfect human accomplishment. Nor is the Law a sign of automatic Jewish privilege vis-à-vis the Gentiles; it entails an enslaving obligation. It entails "works" (Rom 4:4–5). It entails oppression and bondage.

THE MEANING OF "LAW" (νόμος)

The Law from Paul's vantage point appears to be an entirely negative entity, which places its followers in a position of oppression and bondage. Many have concluded from Paul's temporal expressions throughout Galatians 3–4 that the Law no longer functions in the Christian life. The Law has been abolished. Language similar to Galatians 3–4 greets the reader at the end of Paul's discussion of bondage under the Law in Romans 7. Romans 8:2 further proclaims that those in Christ Jesus have been freed "from the law of sin and of death." Stephen Westerholm, an important contributor to the ongoing discussion of Paul's view of the Law, has championed the position that Christians, freed from the Law, are no longer obligated to obey it.[26] On the contrary, they independently "fulfill" the Law as a result of lives led according to the Spirit. For instance, in 8:3–4 the apostle writes, "For God has done what the law, weakened by the flesh, could not do: by sending his own Son in the likeness of sinful flesh, and to deal with sin, he condemned sin in the flesh, so that the just requirement of the law *might be fulfilled* in us, who walk not according to the flesh but according to the Spirit." Those who live in accordance with the Spirit's guidance will fulfill the just requirement of the Law. Westerholm notes that Paul never admonishes Christians to "do" or "obey" what the law requires; Christians are always to "fulfill" the Law (see also Gal 6:2): "Owe no one anything, except to love one another; for the one who loves another *has fulfilled* the law" (Rom 13:8). In other words, by charting an independent course from the Law, the path of the Spirit, the Christian will ultimately arrive at the destination toward which the Law had been pointing all along. The Mosaic Law for Westerholm, as well as for many other interpreters, has ceased to function in the Christian life. The believer has "died to the law" (Gal 2:19).

Paul does grant that the Law still speaks to the Christian as Scripture. The Law testifies in Gal 4:21 to the freedom that has come in Christ by virtue of the Spirit (cf. 3:22). The Law testifies alongside the prophets in Rom 3:21–22 to the righteousness of God "through faith in Jesus Christ for all who believe." Although a new era has dawned with the coming of faith in Jesus Christ, the Law's voice is not muted or silenced. Nevertheless, to grant that the Law witnesses as Scripture to Christ's coming is quite different from granting that the Mosaic Law somehow continues to be the norm and guide by which the Christian walks. The crucial question is whether Paul ever speaks of the Mosaic Law as normative or applicable to the Christian life. Some scholars have pointed to expressions such as "the law of faith" in Rom 3:27, "the law of the Spirit of life" in 8:2, "the law of God" in 7:22, and "the law of Christ" in Gal 6:2. These phrases are striking when considered alongside expressions such as "[the law] of works" (Rom 3:27), "the law of sin" (7:23), and "the law of sin and death" (8:2). One set of modifying genitive nouns—"of faith," "of the Spirit of life," "of God," and "of Christ"—may suggest a favorable view of the Mosaic Law even as the other set—"of works," "of sin," "of sin and death"—suggests a contradictory, less praiseworthy evaluation. Many scholars have resolved the potential contradictions by ex-

---

[26] Westerholm, *Israel's Law and the Church's Faith,* 198–216.

plaining that positive expressions such as "the law of the Spirit," "the law of faith," and "the law of Christ" do not in fact refer to the Mosaic Law at all. These metaphorical turns of phrases contrast the Mosaic Law with a different law, "*another* law" (ἕτερον νόμον) to use the language of 7:23. The Greek word for "law" (νόμος) had a wide range of meanings in the first-century world. The apostle, no doubt, would reflect this diversity of usage himself.[27] On the other hand, if Paul is referring to the Mosaic Law by these more favorable expressions, then expressions such "the law of faith" and "the law of the Spirit of life" suggest that Paul believed the Mosaic Law plays an ongoing role with respect to Christian conduct. The scholarly debate over the meaning of "law" (νόμος) is well worth pursuing because the meaning of the word may resolve the question of the Law's continuing validity and value within the Christian life. Romans 3:27–31; 7:7–8:11 and Gal 6:2 (see ch. 7, below) are the key passages in the debate.

When Paul asks in Rom 3:27, "By what law [is boasting excluded]?" the question could very well be a play on words. Since there was only one Law given to Moses on Mount Sinai, Paul would make no sense if he were comparing two different Mosaic laws in the question "By what law?" He must thus be comparing something else. Perhaps he is comparing the *principle* ("law") of works with that of faith. Only a few verses earlier, in vv. 21–22, Paul claimed that God's righteousness "through faith in Jesus Christ for all who believe" has been revealed "apart from the law." Faith and the Law stand "apart" from each other. If "By what law?" is taken as a reference to two diametrically opposed principles—and the position certainly has merit—Paul has again excluded the Law from the realm of justification and faith in v. 27. The key problem with reading v. 27 as "principle" is that Paul used the word "law" (νόμος) eleven times in 3:19–31, and the count would be much higher if one were to include all the instances of the word in Romans 2 and 3. In each case prior to 3:27, without exception, the apostle has employed the Greek word with reference to the Mosaic Torah. A departure from the pattern, with no contextual clue to signal the departure, would take the reader completely by surprise.

Nor does his 3:27 question, "By what [Mosaic] law?" necessarily lead to the absurd conclusion that he is positing the existence of two different Mosaic laws. He need not be asking "which" law. In 1 Cor 15:35 Paul uses the same Greek word (ποῖος) to introduce a different sort of question: "With *what kind of* body" will the dead be raised? In Rom 3:27 he could be asking "what kind of Law" or, better, from which perspective is the Law to be understood. The Law could be viewed from the perspective of the works that it prescribes (ἐξ ἔργων) or from the perspective of the faith to which it bears witness (ἐκ πίστεως). Paul already set up a tension in vv. 21–22 between two

---

[27] Heikki Räisänen, "Paul's Word-Play on νόμος: A Linguistic Study," in *Jesus, Paul, and Torah: Collected Essays* (trans. David E. Orton; JSNTSup 43; Sheffield, England: JSOT Press, 1992), 69–94.

different perspectives on the Mosaic Law: one is saved "apart from the Law," and yet "the Law" (along with the prophets) can testify to God's righteousness and faith in/of Christ. Paul is likewise viewing the Mosaic Law in v. 27 from different angles: negatively, as salvation is apart from its works, and positively, as a witness to the righteousness that comes through faith. The advantage of understanding νόμος in v. 27 as the Mosaic Law from differing perspectives is that the meaning of the word would remain consistent all through this section (vv. 21–31). The genitive case of the nouns modifying νόμος is flexible enough in usage in the Greek to permit reference to the Mosaic Law.[28] The context of v. 27 must ultimately decide whether Paul is referring to *the Mosaic law* from differing vantage points or to the *principles* of faith and works.

The twofold use of "Law" in vv. 21–22 referencing the Law from the point of view of its demands and from its witness to Christ is not the only consideration in favor of taking the word "law" in v. 27 as uniformly referring to the Mosaic Torah. The "[Law] of works" in v. 27 stands alongside the notion of boasting. In 2:17 and 2:23 Paul speaks of the Jews' pride in their special relationship to God. The basis for this "boast" is their possession of the Torah, the Mosaic Scriptures (ὃς ἐν νόμῳ καυχᾶσαι, 2:23). The Jew "relies on the Law" (ἐπαναπαύῃ νόμῳ, v. 17), is instructed by the Law (κατηχούμενος ἐκ τοῦ νόμου, v. 18), and has the embodiment of knowledge and truth in the Law (τῆς γνώσεως καὶ τῆς ἀληθείας ἐν τῷ νόμῳ, v. 20). Since Paul has already related Jewish *boasting* to their possession of the Mosaic *Law* in Romans 2, the appearance of the two terms together in 3:27 must carry the same meaning unless he signals a departure from the prior precedent. Had he desired to avoid a reference to the Mosaic Law in 3:27, he need only have deleted the word "law" (νόμος): "Where then is boasting? It is excluded. Through works? No, through faith."[29] Since he does clearly refer to "[the Mosaic Law] of works" in v. 27, he can pose the ques-

---

[28] Nigel Turner, *Syntax,* vol. 3 of *A Grammar of New Testament Greek* by James Hope Moulton and Nigel Turner (Edinburgh: T&T Clark, 1963), 207. C. F. D. Moule, "Justification in Its Relation to the Condition κατὰ πνεῦμα (Rom. 8:1–11)," in *Battesimo e giustizia in Rom 6 e 8* (ed. L. de Lorenzi; Rome: St. Paul Abbey, 1974), 181, calls the use of the genitive "notoriously flexible and pregnant"; contra Michael Winger, "Meaning and Law," *JBL* 117 (1998): 108–9. "The words in the genitive are not incidental 'add-ons' for Paul, but often carry as much or more force than the noun they qualify. When Paul asks 'What kind of law?' the options he offers are 'law characterized by works' and 'law characterized by faith.' I do not think that we can avoid a reference to the Torah with these expressions" (Klyne R. Snodgrass, "Spheres of Influence: A Possible Solution to the Problem of Paul and the Law," *JSNT* 32 [1988]: 101).

[29] Bruce W. Longenecker, *Eschatology and the Covenant: A Comparison of 4 Ezra and Romans 1–11* (JSNTSup 57; Sheffield, England: JSOT Press, 1991), 208. On this point, Longenecker is following Snodgrass, "Spheres of Influence," 101; so also Peter von der Osten-Sacken, *Die Heiligkeit der Tora: Studien zum Gesetz bei Paulus* (Munich: Chr. Kaiser, 1989), 23–24.

tion in v. 29 whether God is the God only of the Jews. Since only the Jews possess the Mosaic Law, the Law is the source of the distinction between Jew and Gentile. Romans 3:29 thus offers conclusive proof that Paul is thinking in terms of the Mosaic Law and not of some "principle" of works in v. 27.[30]

Some scholars have granted that the phrase "[law] of works" in v. 27 clearly refers to the Mosaic Law but have contended that "the law of faith" in the same verse does not. Paul would be contrasting the Mosaic Law with the principle of faith. The apostle would not, however, suddenly alter the meaning of this word within the span of a half verse, especially when each of his other ten uses of "law" in vv. 21–31 has consistently referred to the Mosaic Law (including the instance just a few words earlier within the same verse). An isolated exception in v. 27b would be both unexpected and unlikely. Either one should treat both instances of "law" as "principle" or as "Mosaic Law." Interpreters who have taken "law" as "principle" all through v. 27 at least have recognized the need for consistency.

One scholar who has questioned Paul's consistent use of "law" meaning the Mosaic Torah in v. 27 has asked how the Mosaic Law would have excluded boasting.[31] Since the Mosaic Law was incapable of excluding boasting in Romans 2, then Paul must not be referring to the Mosaic Law in 3:27. In vv. 21–26 Paul is speaking of *God's* activity. He is explaining what *God* is doing in Christ. The most likely agent of the passive "it is excluded" (ἐξεκλείσθη) in v. 27 is God. A more useful query would be to ask how Paul thinks God excludes boasting "by [means of]" the Law. In vv. 21–26 he indicates that God's saving action in Christ has excluded boasting; he makes no mention of the Law. Although it is true that the Mosaic Law does not exclude boasting—that is, the Law "of works"—the "Law of faith" *does* help exclude boasting. By the word "Law" in the phrase "Law of faith," Paul is referring to the Law's witness to the righteousness *of God* that is through faith. The Law, as Paul views it from the standpoint of faith, testified long ago to God's impending action in Christ.

Romans 3:31 offers further proof that Paul is speaking of the Mosaic Law through the entirety of v. 27. In vv. 21–22 he contrasted the Law as a witness to justification by faith with the Law as excluded from participation in that justification. In v. 27 he then contrasts "[the law] of works" with "the law of faith." In v. 31 he presents a similar sharp antithesis by asking whether the Law has been nullified through faith. His query assumes a fairly gloomy estimate of the Law in the preceding verses: "Is the [Mosaic] law

---

[30]James D. G. Dunn, " 'The Law of Faith,' 'the Law of the Spirit,' and 'the Law of Christ,' " in *Theology and Ethics in Paul and His Interpreters* (ed. Eugene H. Lovering Jr. and Jerry L. Sumney; Nashville: Abingdon, 1996), 65–66.

[31]Heikki Räisänen, "The 'Law' of Faith and the Spirit," in *Jesus, Paul, and Torah: Collected Essays* (trans. David E. Orton; JSNTSup 43; Sheffield, England: JSOT Press, 1992), 48–68, here 59–62; repr. from *NTS* 26 (1979/1980): 101–17.

abolished through faith?" In the latter half of the verse he responds: No, we *establish* it. The answer must match the query. Even as Paul questions whether the Mosaic Law has been abolished, he turns around and affirms that the Mosaic Law yet remains. A change in meaning between the first and second part of the verse would ruin his logic. His affirmation of the Law as *established* would be stunningly surprising and unexpected were it not for a positive reference to the Mosaic Law in v. 27. Paul's mention of "the law of faith" in v. 27 prepares the way for his discussion in v. 31 of the Mosaic Law alongside faith. Just as a negative construal of the Mosaic Law in vv. 27–28 leads to the question, so also a corresponding positive construal of the Mosaic Law alongside faith in vv. 27–28 is necessary for Paul to sustain his response. To understand "the law of faith" as referring to the Mosaic Law is therefore well grounded in the immediate context.

The very next section of Paul's letter—Romans 4—neatly supports Paul's argument in 3:21–31 that the Mosaic Law, understood in the sense of Torah/Scripture, pointed to salvation by faith all along through the example of Abraham. Paul claims in 3:21 that the Law testified in advance that justification is by faith; Abraham according to Romans 4 is the prime exhibit. In its prophetic witness, the Law remains a "Law of faith." Some scholars have noted, however, that Paul does not speak of "the Law of faith" in Romans 4. If the Mosaic Law had been so central to his reasoning, he ought to have referred to it again in the context of Romans 4. In response, the apostle is simply guided in Romans 4 by the language of the Genesis (Torah) narratives that used the word "promise." One need not expect Paul to continue using "the Law of faith" without good reason once his purpose has been served. His attention shifts to the Genesis narrative. When Paul contrasts the promise in 4:13–14 with the Law, the strong antithesis would echo the strong antitheses in 3:21–22, 27, and 31. Paul invites the reader to recognize a promising voice in the Torah that stands in opposition to its proper legislative voice.

Understanding "law" in 3:27 to mean the Mosaic Law unifies vv. 27–30 with the discussion of the Law that preceded in vv. 21–22 and with what follows in v. 31. In all three places, vv. 21–22, v. 27 and v. 31, Paul speaks of the Law both positively and negatively. The Law functions negatively when considered from the perspective of the works that it requires. The Law functions positively when considered from the vantage point of faith. In Romans 4 Paul shows in the story of Abraham precisely how the Mosaic Law testifies to faith. "The Law of faith, then, is the Law in its function of calling for and facilitating the same sort of trust in God as that out of which Abraham lived."[32] On the other hand, the notion of the Mosaic Law as a Scriptural witness to the righteousness of faith does not affirm that the various laws and

---

[32] Dunn, "'Law of Faith,'" 68–69. It is more than coincidental that Paul says in Rom 14:23, "whatever does not proceed from faith is sin," hence "the law of faith"; ibid., 69 n. 23; *Romans 9–16*, 828–29.

regulations of the Sinaitic legislation are to offer guidance for the Christian life. For evidence that Sinai guides the Christian, one must turn elsewhere.

Paul's language in Rom 7:7–8:4 is reminiscent of 3:27–31. He once again posits various genitives in relation to "law" (νόμος). Although phrases such as "the law of sin" or "the law of sin and death" do not offer much support for a continued role for the Mosaic Law in the Christian life, Paul also speaks of a "law of God" and a "law of my mind" struggling against "the law of sin." He claims in 7:12, "The law is holy, and the commandment is holy and just and good." As was the case in 3:27–31, many scholars do not believe that Paul is referring to the Mosaic Law by such crucial phrases as "law of God" and "law of my mind" in 7:7–8:4. From their standpoint, Paul is playing on the word "law" in 7:14–25 in a fashion similar to his play on the word in 3:27–31. They therefore contend that the word "law" does not always refer to the Mosaic Law. Paul could be referring at certain points in his discussion to a general "principle" and not to the Mosaic Law. The key verses cited in support of this conclusion are 7:21–23:

> So I find it to be a law that when I want to do what is good, evil lies close at hand. For I delight in the law of God in my inmost self, but I see in my members another law at war with the law of my mind, making me captive to the law of sin that dwells in my members.

"Law" in v. 21 reads well when translated as "principle": "I find it to be a *principle* that when I want to do what is good, evil lies close at hand."[33] In the immediately ensuing verses, Paul contrasts the "law of God" with "another law", the "law of sin." Douglas Moo has pointed out that the word "another" (ἕτερος [and not ἄλλος]) does not always mean "another of a different kind" but can distinguish between "two separate entities."[34] "The law of God" would be the Mosaic Law (cf. 7:7, 12, 14), and the "other" law would not be the same as the "law of God." "The other law" must be "the law of sin" or, better, the "principle" of sin's power that is waging war against the "law of my mind."

Although many scholars have been persuaded to see a play on the word "law" as meaning "principle" throughout Rom 7:7–8:4, Paul has consistently used the word "law" (νόμος) for the Mosaic Law in the preceding material in 5:12–7:7. Romans 5:12–14 defines an era from Adam until Moses prior to the Law. The entry of the Mosaic Law onto the stage of human history, according to 5:20, only increased transgressions (similarly 7:13). The elements of sin, grace, and the Mosaic Law in 5:20 then become Paul's organizing concepts for the three rhetorical questions of 6:1,

---

[33] If so, the ὅτι clause would stand in apposition to τὸν νόμον; thus Michael Winger, *By What Law? The Meaning of* νόμος *in the Letters of Paul* (SBLDS 128; Atlanta: Scholars Press, 1992), 81–82 n. 74.

[34] Moo, *Romans*, 463 n. 72.

6:15, and 7:7.³⁵ Even the "law concerning the husband" in 7:2 ought to be
understood in terms of the Mosaic Law. Verse 2 is part of a chain of reasoning leading to v. 7's question regarding the Mosaic Law (and v. 7's question
whether the Law is sin acts as a heading for the remainder of the chapter).
Verse 2 must therefore be referring to "the [Mosaic] Law with respect to the
husband," a genitive of reference (τοῦ ἀνδρός).³⁶ If the Greek word (νόμος)
has consistently referred to the Mosaic Law before 7:21–23, then a reading
that maintains focus on the Mosaic Law in vv. 21–23 would be the superior
reading apart from contextual evidence to the contrary.

To understand "the law of sin" (τῷ νόμῳ τῆς ἁμαρτίας) in v. 23 as
something other than the Mosaic Law itself in the hands of or under the control of Sin is to miss totally the point of Paul's argument in Romans 7. In
v. 10 the command, which was intended for life, has become a means of
death because of the distorting effects of Sin. According to vv. 7–12, the Law
is not Sin, but Sin used the Law to bring about death instead of life. Although the Law is "spiritual" (v. 14) and "holy and just and good" (v. 12), it
stands in tension with itself since it leads to death because of Sin.³⁷ The
Torah itself is not divided, but rather the Mosaic Torah has been used by
Sin in a way completely contrary to what God intended or even as recognized by the "inner man" (v. 22; NRSV: "my inmost self"), or the "mind."
The Law, like the "I," has been forced by Sin to act in a way contrary to
God's intended plan and is, in that sense, a "divided law."³⁸ The Law has
been so distorted under the influence of Sin that Paul can call it "another
Law." Paul Meyer, in his study of the Law in Romans 7, has concurred that
one cannot interpret the "other Law" in vv. 22–23 apart from 8:1–2: "The
phrase 'the law of sin and death' in 8:2 can only be intended as a shorthand
summary of the whole point of 7:7–25: It is the *law* that has been used by *sin*
to produce *death.* But that means that not only the 'law of God' (v. 22) but
also this 'different law' (v. 23) is the Mosaic law!"³⁹

---

³⁵Achtemeier, *Romans,* 102.

³⁶That Paul is describing the Mosaic Law and not the Roman system, see
Dunn, *Romans 1–8,* 360; Fitzmyer, *Romans,* 457; see also 1 Cor 7:39.

³⁷Wilckens, *Brief an die Römer,* 2:90. Wright says that to take νόμος in these
verses as anything other than the Mosaic Law is "to escape the deep rush of Paul's
argument and paddle off into a shallow and irrelevant backwater" (*Climax of the
Covenant,* 199).

³⁸Dunn, *Romans 1–8,* 409; contra Räisänen, "Paul's Word-Play," 89.

³⁹Paul W. Meyer, "The Worm at the Core of the Apple: Exegetical Reflections on Romans 7," in *The Conversation Continues: Essays in Paul & John in Honor of J.
Louis Martyn* (ed. Robert T. Fortna and Beverly R. Gaventa; Nashville: Abingdon,
1990), 79; contra Winger, *By What Law?* 43–44, 185–89, who is forced to see four
separate and distinct "nomoi" in Rom 7:22–23 even though Paul has been consistently discussing the Mosaic Law in the preceding verses. Winger (p. 186) summarizes well himself the problems with seeing the uses of νόμος as something other
than the Mosaic Law: "There are so many νόμοι that they can scarcely be kept
straight" (!).

If "the law of sin" phrase in Rom 7:23 and 8:2 summarizes what Paul says about Sin using the Law in 7:7–12, the path is clear for a similar understanding of the genitive modifiers employed alongside "law" (νόμος) elsewhere in Romans 7 and 8. The way the Law functions depends directly upon the sphere in which it is operating. In the realm of Sin, the Law functions very differently from the way it functions in the hands of Christ and the Spirit.[40] The disputed phrase in 8:2 ὁ νόμος τοῦ πνεύματος τῆς ζωῆς would be "the Law in the hands of the Spirit of life," a deliberate echo of Paul's assertion in 7:14 that the Mosaic Law is itself "spiritual." In Romans 7 the Spirit of life works through the Mosaic Law to resolve the "plight" under the Mosaic Law that was caused by sin. Further, the grammatical connections linking Rom 8:2 to v. 3 (γάρ) and v. 4 (ἵνα) require a reference to the Mosaic Law in 8:2 since the Mosaic Law is the clear subject of vv. 3–4, with these verses building on v. 2.[41]

One potential problem with identifying "law" in Rom 8:2 as the Mosaic Torah is that Paul would be saying that the Law is the agent that frees the individual from the Mosaic Law itself ("the Law of sin and death").[42] But Paul asserts in v. 2 that a different agent is handling the Law with very different results: the Spirit. Paul is not entirely clear at this point *how* the Spirit uses the Law to free people from "the law of sin and death." One possibility is that the Spirit uses the Law to testify to the righteousness found in Christ, as Paul stated in 3:27–4:8. In any case, the Mosaic Law stands in tension with itself here in Romans 7–8 just as it stood in tension with itself earlier in the letter, in 3:21–22 and 3:27–31 (and again in 9:30–10:8).[43] Of greater importance in Paul's genitive phrases modifying "law" (νόμος) is the power that he says is controlling the Law rather than the Law itself. With the arrival of the Spirit, the period of the Law's inability to effect anything positive has come to an end (note the imperfect tense of 8:3's "used to be weak" (lit.; ἠσθένει).[44]

Romans 7:21–22's "I find it to be a law[/principle] that when I want to do what is good . . ." may also be translated, "I find with respect to the Law that when I want to do what is good evil lies close at hand." The object of the verb "I find" (εὑρίσκω) cannot be a law or principle since the object is supplied by the ὅτι ("that") clause. What the "I" has found is that evil lies close at hand whenever the "I" wishes to do good. "Law" (νόμον) here is simply an accusative of respect. Paul makes this discovery with respect to the

---

[40] Snodgrass, "Spheres of Influence," 99–101.

[41] Osten-Sacken, *Heiligkeit,* 16; contra Räisänen, " 'Law' of Faith and the Spirit," 64–67.

[42] Räisänen, " 'Law' of Faith and the Spirit," 65.

[43] See Das, *Paul, the Law, and the Covenant,* ch. 10, for a thorough defense of a consistent usage of "law" (νόμος) as Mosaic Law in Rom 9:30–10:8.

[44] On the grammar and context of 8:3, see Jonathan F. Bayes, *The Weakness of the Law: God's Law and the Christian in New Testament Perspective* (Paternoster Biblical and Theological Monographs; Carlisle, England: Paternoster, 2000) 84–103.

Torah: "That is, whenever the ἐγώ seeks to do the good as understood and defined in the torah, the result is the opposite, namely the doing of evil."[45] The parallels between vv. 10 and 21 reinforce the conclusion that "law" in v. 21 must refer to the Mosaic Law:

v. 10—the *command* which was for *life was discovered* to be *death*

v. 21—with respect to *the law I discovered . . . good . . . evil.*[46]

Just as v. 10 refers to the Mosaic Law (see vv. 7–9 and "the commandment"), so also does v. 21. "Good" (καλόν) in v. 21 parallels "good" (ἀγαθόν) in vv. 12–13, 16, 18–19 as opposed to "evil" (κακόν) in vv. 19, 21. "Lies close at hand" (παράκειται) in v. 21 parallels v. 18. The close ties between v. 21 and the preceding verses focused on the Mosaic Law (e.g., v. 16b) indicate that v. 21 must also be referring to the Mosaic Law. Thus "in both cases what is in view is the harsh discovery through personal experience of how the law, which should be for life and should promote the good, actually helps bring about the opposite."[47] A reference to the Mosaic Law in v. 21 dovetails with the use of the article in "*the* Law" (τὸν νόμον), which renders the noun definite in the Greek; this verse is not speaking of "*a* principle."[48]

Scholars who have insisted that "Law" (νόμος) does not always refer to the Mosaic Law point to the phrase "another law" (ἕτερον νόμον) in Rom 7:23. Since "another" (ἕτερον) modifies "law" (νόμον), this "law" must not be the same entity, they claim, as "the Law [νόμος] of God" and so must be "another law or *principle.*" In the context of Paul's discussion, however, "another Law" is simply "the Torah as it has been taken over and used by sin operating through the foothold which is the flesh."[49] Paul would simply be saying that the Law has been so distorted in the hands of sin that one can speak of it as if it were actually "another Law." Paul never claims that there

---

[45] Paul J. Achtemeier, "Unsearchable Judgments and Inscrutable Ways: Reflections on the Discussion of Romans," in *SBL Seminar Papers, 1995* (ed. Eugene H. Lovering Jr.; Atlanta: Scholars Press, 1995), 532–33; repr. (with corrections) in *Looking Back, Pressing On* (ed. E. Elizabeth Johnson and David M. Hay), vol. 4 of *Pauline Theology* (SBLSymS 4. Atlanta: Scholars Press, 1997); so also Meyer, "Worm at the Core," 79; and Wright, *Climax of the Covenant,* 198.

[46] Dunn, *Romans 1–8,* 392; Wright, *Climax of the Covenant,* 198.

[47] Dunn, *Romans 1–8,* 392.

[48] Paul J. Achtemeier has noted (private correspondence with the author) that translating the phrase as "a principle" does not reflect the grammar of the original language. Winger (*By What Law?* 81, 183) agrees that τὸν νόμον is definite, since the ὅτι ("that") phrase stands in apposition, and yet he still translates τὸν νόμον "a principle." Winger is proposing a cataphoric use of the Greek article, in which case the article anticipates the defining or qualifying statement that follows. I have not been able to find an example of this syntactical construction that should be rendered in the English with the indefinite article. See Wallace, *Greek Grammar beyond the Basics,* 220–21; Wesley J. Perschbacher, *New Testament Greek Syntax: An Illustrated Manual* (Chicago: Moody, 1995), 50.

[49] Wright, *Climax of the Covenant,* 198.

are two different "laws" (νόμοι) at issue here: the "I" merely perceives (βλέπω) "another Law." The "I" does not see the Law manifested as truly the Law of God; rather the "I" sees the Law clothed in an unrecognizable shape because of Sin. Similarly, "the law of my mind" in v. 23 should be understood alongside v. 22, where the "I" delights in the "law of God according to the inner man [NRSV: 'my inmost self']." The "inner man" would be the same as the "mind" of v. 23. The "inner man," or the "mind," recognizes the Law to be spiritual, holy, just, and good, but Sin uses the flesh in order to bring about a different result (7:14; 8:7). Nothing in Rom 7:7–8:4 compels the reader to take "law" (νόμος) to refer to anything other than the Mosaic Law.

Romans 3:27–31 and 7:7–8:11 remain tightly focused upon the Mosaic Law. Although Paul is critiquing the Mosaic Law in these passages, he also speaks positively of the Law. Although the Law remains in effect after the arrival of the new age of Christ and the Spirit, Paul has not outlined in these passages a precise role for the Mosaic Law in a Christian's life beyond its testimony to a righteousness by faith (e.g., 3:21–22). How the Spirit of the apocalyptic new age in Christ employs the Law is another matter.

7

THE MOSAIC LAW IN THE LIFE OF THE CHRISTIAN

> For the law of the Spirit of life in Christ Jesus has set you free
> from the law of sin and of death. For God has done what the law,
> weakened by the flesh, could not do: by sending his own Son in
> the likeness of sinful flesh, and to deal with sin, he condemned sin
> in the flesh, so that the just requirement of the law might be ful-
> filled in us, who walk not according to the flesh but according to
> the Spirit. (Rom 8:2–4)

IN ROM 3:27–31 and 7:7–8:4 Paul maintains an ongoing role for the Mosaic
Law in the new age inaugurated by Christ and his Spirit. These two passages, when interpreted consistently in terms of the Law, stand at odds with
other Pauline texts that limit the role of the Law to a particular era in human
history that ended with the coming of Christ. The question remains how
precisely the Law is to function in the context of a Christian's life. Perhaps
the best starting point is Paul's discussion of yet another tantalizing and debated modifying genitive phrase, "the law of Christ" in Gal 6:2. To understand the "law of Christ" as a reference to Moses' Law requires grappling
with the apostle's stern insistence in Galatians 3 that the Law's reign is limited to a bygone era.

THE ABOLITION OF SLAVERY AND THE LAW OF CHRIST

To insist that the coming of Christ has totally abolished the Mosaic Law in
Paul's mind may be a premature conclusion. Whenever Paul speaks of the
temporary nature of the Mosaic Law, he is focusing on a particular aspect of
the Law. What has certainly ceased for the Christian, from the apostle's
standpoint, is the former slavery under the Law's "commandment." The
Spirit has taken hold of the Law and transformed it into a non-enslaving
body of legislation in the new age. In Rom 8:2 the "Law of the Spirit of life"
has supplanted the "Law of sin." In Rom 3:27 "the Law of faith" has done
away with "the Law of works." In both passages what has been abolished is
the Law from the narrow point of view of its enslaving obligations. The

Christian is no longer bound to obey slavishly all the Law's commandments and obligations. The presence of the Spirit and faith has apocalyptically transformed the Law. Paul describes the Law as if it were an entirely different entity, "another law." In so speaking, Paul is saying that the Law continues to function even though it has been transformed by the Spirit. Paul's Letter to the Galatians corroborates the cessation of the Law as an enslaving force. Galatians 3:23–4:7 emphasizes the temporal limitations on the Law: slavery under the Law is relegated to the apocalyptic age prior to the coming of Christ. Faith in Christ now delivers the individual from the present evil age (1:4). Christian existence and experience is so radically new and discontinuous that Paul can describe it as the dawning of a new world, a new creation (6:15). A similar transformation has taken place regarding the Mosaic Law. No longer is the Christian "under the Law." The Law can no longer curse and enslave the Christian.

If the Christian is no longer under the Law, the Mosaic Law must be serving another function for Paul if it still applies to a Christian's life. In Galatians Paul employs the Law throughout his letter as evidence for his understanding of Christ's significance, albeit in the context of responding to passages from the Jewish Scriptures cited by his opponents. Paul draws upon their texts to support his own position. For example, Gal 3:13 cites Deut 21:23 as proof that Christ's death on the "tree" of the cross bore the curse of the Law (cf. Gal 3:10). The Mosaic Torah, as Scripture, announced in advance "the gospel" "that God would justify the Gentiles by faith" (3:8). In 3:2–5 Paul laments that in order to complete for themselves what the Spirit began, the Galatian Christians who had begun with the Spirit were returning to the flesh in doing the works of the Law. The teachers at Galatia, whom Paul was rebuking, were supplementing the gospel message with guidance from the Mosaic Law.[1] The Law would have been attractive for recent converts who had abandoned their pagan way of life for the sake of faith in Christ. They would have yearned for a new lifestyle and new customs. The Mosaic Law would offer a structured alternative to the religious world that they had abandoned. One must be circumcised. One must observe the new faith's special days, months, seasons, and years (4:8–11). An enthusiastic advocacy of the Law on the part of Paul's rivals may explain why he couches his own positive construal of the Christian life within two polemical thrusts against the Mosaic Law (5:2–12; 6:11–16). Paul is clear that the Law cannot justify (2:15–16), nor is the Christian simply to "do" the Law (3:10). A legitimate conclusion from his argument, which many have drawn, would be that the Mosaic Law does not function as a guide or norm for the Christian life at all.

Galatians 5:2–12 is perhaps the center of Paul's argument within this letter. This paragraph echoes the language Paul had used at the very beginning

---

[1] See the discussion of the Teachers' use of the Law in ch. 2, above.

of the letter, and the echoes suggest that this is the climactic moment of his argument. His tone is once again severe. Paul claims that the Galatians are deserting the one who called them (5:8, echoing 1:6). They are falling away from Christ's "grace" (5:4, echoing 1:6). Paul feels compelled to reiterate his grave concerns ("again" in 5:3 echoing 1:9). The doubled invective against those who will "pay the penalty" in 5:10 and who should "castrate themselves" in 5:12 evokes the doubled curse of 1:8–9.[2] For the first time, in 5:2–12 Paul confronts the Galatians' consideration of the rite of circumcision. His concern about the Galatians' potential circumcision is so important that he repeats it, at times verbatim, within the conclusion of the letter, in 6:11–17. In 5:6 Paul maintains that "neither circumcision nor uncircumcision counts for anything"; likewise in 6:15: "For neither circumcision nor uncircumcision is anything." Circumcision is linked with the possibility of persecution in 5:11 even as it is in 6:12. The apostle in 5:3 claims that those who are circumcised must obey the entire Law even as in 6:12 those who advocate the Law and are circumcised themselves do not obey it. These two sections urging the Galatians not to adopt the path of circumcision and the works of the Mosaic Law enclose a section from 5:13 to 6:10 that, as will be clear in a moment, offers the apostle's own approach to the Christian life.[3]

In Gal 5:3 Paul warns anyone who would seek circumcision that everyone is "obliged to obey the entire law." Verse 4 clarifies that the Law does not offer a viable path to justification before God. In other words, the Law is unnecessary insofar as a right relationship with God is concerned. "Neither circumcision nor uncircumcision counts for anything; the only thing that counts is faith working through love" (v. 6) Note that Paul does not stop with just faith. Faith is always *active* in love. Faith is never a license for sin. Verse 13 develops this thought: "For you were called to freedom, brothers and sisters; only do not use your freedom as an opportunity for self-indulgence, but through love become slaves to one another." Perhaps Paul's opponents had critiqued his "gospel" message as abandoning the concrete direction provided by the Mosaic Law. Their critique may have been similar to what people were saying about Paul's message according to Rom 3:8: "Why not say (as some people slander us by saying that we say), 'Let us do evil so that good may come'?" After all, since the Christian is justified entirely by faith in Christ apart from works, what prevents the Christian from living a life of evil? Certainly the answer for Paul's opponents at Galatia would have been the concrete guidance of the Mosaic Law. In Gal 5:4 and 13 the apostle speaks instead of a love in action. It was precisely such love that the Mosaic Law all along had been seeking to capture in its various laws and legislation. "For the whole law is summed up in a single commandment, 'You shall love your neighbor as yourself'" (5:14).

---

[2] Richard N. Longenecker, *Galatians* (WBC 41; Dallas: Word, 1990), 221–22.
[3] Frank J. Matera, "The Culmination of Paul's Argument to the Galatians: Gal. 5.1–6.17," *JSNT* 32 (1988): 79–91.

Paul's reference in Gal 5:14 to the fulfillment of "the whole law" (ὁ πᾶς νόμος) responds to the obligation to obey the entire Law in v. 3 (ὅλον τὸν νόμον). Paul speaks of Christians who *fulfill* the whole Mosaic Law by their love, even as he censures those who attempt to obey and do the entire Law. In other words, while Christians do not set out to obey the entire Mosaic Law, Christians remain obliged to fulfill it. This paradox of "fulfilling" versus "doing" reflects the changing of the ages that has taken place with Christ's coming. Believers are freed from the old obligation to do the Law, and yet are freed to fulfill it in their actions. For an audience so eager to live according to the Law, the apostle sets forth an alternate route, the path of love. And yet the path of love is not completely severed from any connection to the Mosaic Law. Galatians 5:14 does not abolish the totality of the Law when he reduces it to the one command to love. The passage Paul cites in 5:14 is Lev 19:18: "You shall love your neighbor as yourself." Jewish literature of the period typically viewed the Leviticus verse as a summary of *all* the commands of the Mosaic Law.[4] Jesus' contemporary, the great teacher of the Law Hillel, once told an aspiring convert: "What is hateful to you, do not do to your neighbor: that is the whole Torah, while the rest is commentary thereof; go and learn it" (*b. Šabb.* 31a). Whether or not Hillel actually said this, the quotation reveals the understanding of the later rabbis. A quick sideways glance at Rom 13:8–10 (and Lev 19:18)—"Love one another; for the one who loves another has fulfilled the law"—will confirm that the entire Law remains in view when Paul speaks of fulfilling the Law in Gal 5:14. After listing several of the Ten Commandments in Rom 13:8, Paul adds in vv. 9–10: "[These,] and any other commandment, are summed up in this word, 'Love your neighbor as yourself.' Love does no wrong to a neighbor; therefore, love is the fulfilling of the law." The listing from the Ten Commandments "and any other commandment" demonstrates that Paul has not eliminated the bulk of the Mosaic Law in favor of just the commandment to love one's neighbor. Instead he speaks in vv. 8–10 of *fulfilling* the Mosaic Law. He uses the same language in Gal 6:2. Christians are obliged to fulfill the stipulations of the Mosaic Law.

Many scholars have justifiably doubted whether "the law of Christ" (τὸν νόμον τοῦ Χριστοῦ) in Gal 6:2 refers to the Mosaic Law, particularly considering its position toward the end of a letter that has vigorously contrasted Christ and the Law. A person is not justified by the works of the Law but rather by faith in Christ (2:16). Christ and the Law represent opposing approaches to justification. To combine the Law and Christ within the same phrase may even seem jarring. Perhaps Paul is playing on the word "law" in 6:2 as he may have elsewhere.[5] Scholars have often sought an alternative explanation rather than admit that "the law of Christ" refers somehow to the

---

[4] Sanders, *Paul and Palestinian Judaism,* 112–114; John M. G. Barclay, *Obeying the Truth: Paul's Ethics in Galatians* (Minneapolis: Fortress, 1988), 132–33, 135–36.
[5] See the discussion of Rom 3:27–31 and 7:7–8:4 in ch. 6, above.

Mosaic Law. One possibility scholars have offered is that the phrase refers to the new "law of the messiah," a distinctively Christian law based on the words of Jesus. Jewish authors in an era long after Paul claimed that a new Torah would accompany the Messiah's coming.[6] Unfortunately, little evidence exists for such expectations in Paul's own day. The first Christians did not interpret Jesus' message as a new law in contrast with the Mosaic Law of old. Although Matthew's Jesus was adamant that not one minor point in the Law would pass away (Matt 5:17–20), this Jesus did not promote a new law but reinterpreted Moses' (e.g., Matt 5:21–48). The Jesus of Matthew's Gospel consistently opposed the Pharisees for their oral additions to the Mosaic Law (e.g., 15:3, 9). A variation of the "new law" position has been that "the law of Christ" in Gal 6:2 refers to Jesus' sayings.[7] Galatians may very well be echoing oral traditions of Jesus' teachings. "Bear one another's burdens" in 6:2 is similar to Jesus' admonition in Matt 23:4. Perhaps Paul's reference to restoring the fallen brother in Gal 6:1 alludes to Jesus' teachings in Matt 18:15–16. Paul does elsewhere quote Jesus' teachings (e.g., Rom 12:14; 13:7; 14:13–14; 1 Cor 7:10; 9:14; 11:23–26; 1 Thess 5:2, 13). On the other hand, these allusions need not imply that Paul's "law of Christ" phrase is without reference to the Mosaic Law. Christ's teachings, to which the apostle refers, may simply explicate how the Mosaic Law applies to the Christian life. Galatians 6:2 would in that case be referring to the Mosaic Law as interpreted by Christ. Others have contended that "the law of Christ" in 6:2 is identical to the command to love in 5:14 and has nothing to do with the Mosaic Law. "The law of Christ," however, cannot be the same as 5:14's command to love. The command to love is the *means* of fulfilling the whole Law, but the law of Christ in 6:2 is that which is to be fulfilled, the *object* of the fulfillment.[8] Perhaps "the law of Christ" is merely an ironic turn of phrase in response to Paul's opponents' use of such phrasing. Paul, however, employs similar language in 1 Cor 9:21: "To those outside the law I became as one outside the law (though I am not free from God's law but am under Christ's law) so that I might win those outside the law." In other words, Paul chooses to use similar language quite apart from the influence of his Galatian opponents, which suggests that this is no mere turn of phrase in reaction to his rivals' teachings.

The hesitancy to admit a reference to the Mosaic Law in Gal 6:2's "law of Christ" is understandable after Paul has repeatedly set Christ and the Law

---

[6] W. D. Davies, *The Torah in the Messianic Age and/or the Age to Come* (JBLMS 7; Philadelphia: Society of Biblical Literature, 1952), 92–93; expanded in *The Setting of the Sermon on the Mount* (Cambridge: Cambridge University Press, 1964), 109–90.

[7] C. H. Dodd, "Έννομος Χριστοῦ," in *More New Testament Studies* (Grand Rapids: Eerdmans, 1968), 134–48; repr. from *Studia Paulina, in honorem Johannis de Zwaan septuagenarii* (Bohn: Haarlem, 1953); see also "The Law of Christ," in *Gospel and Law: The Relation of Faith and Ethics in Early Christianity* (New York: Columbia University Press, 1951), 64–83.

[8] Hong, *Law in Galatians*, 176.

in opposition before this verse. A metaphorical interpretation of 6:2 would appear to many interpreters as unavoidable. A closer inspection of this verse within its context, however, actually leads to the reverse conclusion. What is unavoidable may very well be a reference to the Mosaic Law. All thirty-two instances of the word "law" (νόμος) in Paul's letter before 6:2 have referred to the Mosaic Law. Even 5:23, the most likely candidate for a break in the pattern, must be understood as a reference to the Mosaic Law. After listing the fruit of the Spirit, Paul adds, "There is no law against such things." "Such things" (τῶν τοιούτων) likely refers to the nine aspects of the fruit (singular) of the Spirit (cf. "such things" in 5:21 [τὰ τοιαῦτα]).⁹ After claiming in v. 18 that those who are led by the Spirit are not under the Law (note the juxtaposition of *Spirit* and *Law*), Paul qualifies in v. 23, lest readers draw the wrong conclusion, that the *Spirit* is not acting in opposition to the *Law*. Galatians 5:18 and 5:23 must therefore be understood alongside one another. Freedom from the bondage of the Law does not mean a complete elimination of the Mosaic Law. Paul affirms in v. 23 that the Mosaic Law is a continuing norm. To interpret "no law" in this verse in the generic sense of a denial of *any* law and without particular reference to the Law of Moses ignores the close connection between the Spirit and the Mosaic Law in both v. 18 and v. 23. Although the Christian believer is no longer under bondage to the Law, the path of the Spirit is not in any way contrary to what the Law enjoins. The fruit of the Spirit "fully satisfies the true intention of the law."¹⁰ The Law has all along dealt with matters such as the fruit of the Spirit: compare, for instance, love as a fruit of the Spirit in v. 22 with the summary of the Mosaic Law in terms of love in v. 14, a summary that itself comes from the pages of the Law (Lev 19:18).

Paul's language in Gal 6:2 parallels the language he employs regarding the Mosaic Law in 5:14. In 6:2 Paul uses alongside "law" (νόμον) the word "fulfill" (ἀναπληρώσετε), a cognate of 5:14's "fulfill" (πεπλήρωται), similarly used alongside νόμος. The NRSV's translation, "is summed up," in 5:14 unfortunately obscures the connection. It confuses the Greek word for "fulfill" (πληρόω) with another word that actually does mean "sum up" (ἀνακεφαλαιόω); since the two words are used together in Rom 13:8–9, the translator may have considered them synonyms. The Greek word used in Gal 6:2 does not elsewhere mean "sum up" in ancient Greek literature and is more precisely translated "fulfill." Paul uses the word group for "fulfill" (πληρόω) alongside the Mosaic Law also in Rom 8:4 and 13:8 (cf. 13:10). The admonition to mutuality and to Christian service in Gal 6:2, "Bear one another's burdens," also echoes Gal 5:13's "become slaves to one another."

---

⁹For the neuter interpretation of "such things" (τῶν τοιούτων), see Barclay, *Obeying the Truth,* 19–25. For a masculine interpretation as "such people," see R. A. Campbell, "'Against Such Things There Is No Law'? Galatians 5:23*b* Again," *ExpTim* 107 (1996): 271–72.

¹⁰Hong, *Law in Galatians,* 185.

The verbal ties between 6:2 and 5:13–14 necessitate interpreting 6:2 as a reference to the Mosaic Law as well. In 6:1 Paul admonishes the Christian community to help restore those guilty of "transgression" (παραπτώματι), language traditionally used by the Jews in connection with a violation of the Mosaic Law (cf. Rom 5:20). The evocation of Mosaic language in Gal 6:1 confirms the Mosaic reference in 6:2's "Law of Christ."

Galatians 5:14 and 6:2 thus offer the final clues to Paul's understanding of the Mosaic Law. The believer fulfills the Mosaic Law as it has been modified by its existence in the era of Christ; the believer fulfills "the Law of Christ." The language of "Law of Christ" in 6:2 echoes love as the fulfillment of the Mosaic Law in 5:14, which itself echoes the mention of love earlier in the letter in 2:20 regarding "the Son of God, who loved me and gave himself for me."[11] Paul has already interpreted love through Jesus' self-sacrifice for the sake of others in 2:20. So now Christians are to bear each others' burdens in 6:2. Likewise in Rom 15:1–3 Paul insists that Christians should please their neighbors even as Christ did not please himself but endured suffering for the sake of others. Christ's self-sacrificial example offers a pattern for others to follow. In other words, by following their Lord's example, the Christian will consequently be fulfilling the Mosaic Law as it has been redefined by Christ's example in love.[12] This is why the Christian believer paradoxically "fulfills" what the Mosaic Law had required even while never setting out to "do" it.[13] The Christian fulfills "the Law of Christ," the Law when viewed in the hands of Christ. By the Spirit's power the believer looks to and follows Christ's example. Then the requirements of the Mosaic Law will take care of themselves.

The Mosaic Law thus looks very different when viewed through the lens of Christ and his example. Since Christ is the Savior of all people, Jew and Gentile, circumcision no longer is necessary for Paul (Gal 5:6; 6:15). The Jews need not withdraw from table fellowship with Gentile Christians (2:11–14). Gentile Christians need not adopt the Jewish calendar (4:10). Christ's work has opened up the possibility of blessing for the Gentiles as Gentiles (3:8–9, 14). Indeed, Paul quotes the Mosaic Law itself in proving as much (Gen 12:3). The Mosaic Law witnesses to the blessing of the Gentiles in Abraham. If Paul is correct, the Gentile Christian who does not observe these ethnic boundary-marking aspects of the Law is by no means violating the Torah since the Torah had predicted this new age for the Gentiles. Paul may not, then, be redefining the Torah but urging a recognition of the new

---

[11] Gal 6:2, Christ/Law; 5:14, Law/love; 2:20, love/Christ

[12] Barclay, *Obeying the Truth,* 134.

[13] Paul in this respect departs from other Jews in his understanding of love as the fulfillment of the Law. For other Jews, the command to love was always a summary of the Law's commands, never to the exclusion of actually doing them. For Paul, to follow Jesus' example is to fulfill what the Law commanded. Also, Christians are the only people for whom Paul employs the expression "fulfill the law."

age in which the Torah is functioning. Once he has reinterpreted the Law in light of the salvation that has taken place in Christ, Paul claims that the Law can continue to function as a norm and guide for the Christian even while the Christian's focus remains primarily upon following the example of Christ.

GOD'S WILL FOR THE CHRISTIAN: CHRIST AND THE LAW

Although he grants that the Mosaic Law continues to be the norm for godly conduct, Paul is much fonder of presenting Christ as an example for believers. In Phil 2:5 he admonishes his audience, "Let the same mind be in you that was in Christ Jesus." In vv. 6–11 he describes how Christ, who was in the form of God, emptied himself, took on the form of a slave as a human, and suffered death on a cross, for which God exalted him. Verses 12–18 then draw upon Christ's example for Christian obedience ("Therefore," v. 12). Paul extols various individuals who model Christlikeness in their actions. In v. 20 Timothy, like the Lord Jesus, is "genuinely concerned for [the Philippians'] welfare." Epaphroditus in vv. 25–30 "nearly died" on behalf of the Philippians. Like the Lord, he "came close to death for the work of Christ, risking his life." Paul presents himself as yet another example of Christlikeness in 3:3–11. Even as Christ did not take advantage of his equality with God (2:6), Paul does not take advantage of his privileges as a "blameless" Law-observant Jew. Even as Jesus humbled himself to take on human form, Paul regards his "gains" as a Jew "loss because of Christ." In 3:10, "I want to know Christ and the power of his resurrection and the sharing of his sufferings by becoming like him in his death," Paul hopes to share in Jesus' own resurrection and glorification through sharing in the Lord's sufferings.[14] The Philippians should likewise live "in a manner worthy of the gospel of Christ. . . . For he has graciously granted you the privilege not only of believing in Christ, but of suffering for him as well" (1:27, 29). So the Philippians are also participating in Christ's sufferings (1:30). Jesus, Paul, and the Philippians are all bound together by their sharing of affliction. In that regard the Philippians may consciously imitate Paul's lifestyle insofar as he is imitating and following Christ (4:17; cf. 4:12).

In Rom 6:1–14 also Paul grounds Christian behavior in the unique example of Christ: "Should we continue in sin in order that grace may abound? . . . By no means!" Paul asks in vv. 3–4, "Do you not know that all of us who have been baptized into Christ Jesus were baptized into his death? Therefore we have been buried with him by baptism into death, so that, just as Christ was raised from the dead by the glory of the Father, so we too might walk in newness of life." Since the Christian has "been united with

---

[14] Garland, "Composition and Unity of Philippians," 162–72; Wright, *Climax of the Covenant,* 88.

him in a death like his," a resurrection "like his" is sure to follow, and even
as the Christian has died by baptism with Christ, so the Christian now lives
through Christ. "So you also must consider yourselves dead to sin and alive
to God in Christ Jesus. Therefore, do not let sin exercise dominion in your
mortal bodies, to make you obey their passions" (vv. 11–12). Since the
Christian shares in Christ's death, so the Christian must now live in the
power and imitation of Christ's life. Christians "suffer with [Christ]" (8:17)
and are "to be conformed to the image of [the] Son" (8:29).

Paul's statement in 1 Cor 11:1, "Be imitators of me, as I am of Christ,"
grounds his exhortations in the preceding verses not to eat anything that
would trouble the conscience of another "just as I try to please everyone in
everything I do, not seeking my own advantage, but that of many, so that
they may be saved" (10:33). Even as Christ suffered death for the advantage
of others, the same pattern now informs Christian conduct. Christians must
seek to imitate that concern for others in their own actions.

Paul expresses the same pattern of thought again in an important passage in 2 Cor 4:7–15:

> . . . We are afflicted in every way, but not crushed; perplexed, but not driven
> to despair; persecuted, but not forsaken; struck down, but not destroyed; al-
> ways carrying in the body the death of Jesus, so that the life of Jesus may also
> be made visible in our bodies. For while we live, we are always being given up
> to death for Jesus' sake, so that the life of Jesus may be made visible in our
> mortal flesh. So death is at work in us, but life in you.
>
> . . . because we know that the one who raised the Lord Jesus will raise us also
> with Jesus, and will bring us with you into his presence. . . .

In his ministry the apostle bears the marks of Jesus' suffering in his own
body and consequently can look forward to resurrection and final glory.
The language is reminiscent of Gal 6:17: "From now on, let no one make
trouble for me; for I carry the marks of Jesus branded on my body." Paul
has suffered in a similar fashion as his Lord. In 2 Cor 12:9b–10 he writes,
"So, I will boast all the more gladly of my weaknesses, so that the power of
Christ may dwell in me. Therefore I am content with weaknesses, insults,
hardships, persecutions, and calamities for the sake of Christ; for whenever
I am weak, then I am strong." Paradoxically, at the moment of greatest
weakness, the apostle mirrors most closely the power manifested in Christ's
death on the cross, "for my power is made perfect in weakness" (12:9a).
Paul's body bears the marks of beatings, stonings, torture, imprisonments,
hunger, hardship, thirst, cold, and nakedness (11:21–29); these are the
marks of which he will boast. In the words of Gal 2:19–20: "For through the
law I died to the law, so that I might live to God. I have been crucified with
Christ; and it is no longer I who live, but it is Christ who lives in me. And
the life I now live in the flesh I live by faith in the Son of God, who loved me
and gave himself for me."

Paul reminds the Galatians (in 3:27) that by baptism they "have clothed" themselves "with Christ." In Romans 13:14 Paul admonishes his addressees to "put on the Lord Jesus Christ" and "make no provision for the flesh." The Jewish Scriptures provide the necessary background to understand these expressions.[15] When Eleazar put on Aaron's priestly apparel in Num 20:25–28 LXX, he received the powers of the high-priestly office. When Elijah placed his mantle on Elisha in 1 Kgs 19:19, Elijah had anointed his successor. In 2 Kgs 2:1–3, 9, 14–15 the falling of the mantle of Elijah accompanied the transfer to Elisha of Elijah's power of the Spirit. In *2 En.* 22:8–10, when Michael clothed Enoch in the garments of glory, Enoch was transformed into an angel-like state (similarly the Christian *Ascen. Isa.* 8:14–15). Gideon was empowered by God to act as Israel's deliverer at the point when the Spirit clothed him (Judg 6:34 LXX). Joshua's mind was afire and his spirit moved when he put on, at God's command, Moses' garments of wisdom and belt of knowledge (*L.A.B.* 20:2–5). Jerusalem was to wrap around herself the double garment of "the righteousness that comes from God" (Bar 5:2, 9). *Testament of Levi* 18:14 anticipates the day when "all the saints shall be clothed in righteousness." When the Christian puts on Christ, according to Paul, the Christian enjoys the power of Christ's Spirit and is enabled to live according to God's will.[16]

Christ's self-sacrificial action for the sake of others is, according to Paul, a paradigm for Christian behavior. The Christian's mirroring of Christ's selfless concern inevitably binds the individual believer into a relationship with others as recipients of that love. Christians come together as a new community in Christ. No one can imitate Christ apart from service to others. Paul's positive admonitions in his Galatian letter begin in Gal 5:13–14 with the command to "become slaves to one another" and to "love your neighbor as yourself." This fulfills the whole Law; "If, however, you bite and devour one another, take care that you are not consumed by one another" (v. 15). Paul maintains the corporate motif in the ensuing verses. He lists the works of the flesh in vv. 19–21, several are corporate sins: enmities, strife, jealousy, anger, quarrels, dissensions, factions, and envy. After

---

[15] See Charles H. Talbert, "Paul, Judaism, and the Revisionists," *CBQ* 63 (2001): 1–22.

[16] Talbert (ibid., 20) is right that the apostle is pessimistic about the ability of those "under the Law" to avoid its curse. The empowerment of the Christian enables an obedience that would not otherwise be possible. Talbert agrees with Timo Laato that Paul's thinking at these points is directly at odds with synergistic strands in Second Temple Jewish thought that attributed "staying in" the relationship with God to human ability. This may be, but Paul nowhere actually points his finger against Jewish synergism, and Talbert recognizes that many of the apostle's Jewish peers would have rejected any credit for maintaining the covenant relationship, since good works stem from God's prior motivating activity. Paul's reasoning appears grounded in seeing God's grace and mercy in Christ rather than the Law. Any attack on synergism would be a *consequence* of his reasoning rather than a motivation for it; see Das, *Paul, the Law, and the Covenant,* 247–49.

listing the fruit of the Spirit, the apostle exhorts the Galatians in the first person plural in vv. 25–26: "If we live by the Spirit, let us also be guided by the Spirit. Let us not become conceited, competing against *one another,* envying *one another*." The concrete application of these directions in 6:1–10 alternates between individual accountability and corporate responsibility:

Corporate Responsibility—6:1a: correct a sinning church-member

Individual Accountability—6:1b: take care of oneself

Corporate Responsibility—6:2: bear one another's burdens

Individual Accountability—6:3–5: test one's own work, bear one's own load

Corporate Responsibility—6:6: support those who teach

Individual Accountability—6:7–8: whatever one sows, one will reap

Corporate Responsibility—6:9–10: do good to all, especially Christians[17]

The Christian is never an individual participating in Christ alone but is always a member of a community of those who *together* image Christ. Thus Paul can call the church Christ's own body in Romans 12 and 1 Corinthians 12. Christians must treat one another as likewise in Christ.[18]

While Paul's ethical admonitions are based especially on the example of Christ, the apostle often implicitly relies on the Mosaic Law as a norm for Christian behavior as well. In 1 Cor 5:1–5 Paul censures the Corinthian congregation for tolerating a man who is living with his stepmother. The apostle points out that this sort of behavior is sexually immoral "even among pagans." "Even among pagans" betrays the Jewish orientation of Paul's reasoning. "Fornication" (πορνεία; NRSV: "sexual immorality"), the sin of which this man is guilty (5:1), is listed as a sexual sin only in the lists of vices compiled by *Jewish* authors.[19] Paul's phrasing—that the "man is living with his father's wife"—reflects the Mosaic Law's distinction between the mother and the step-mother in Lev 18:7–9; 20:11. The later rabbis drew upon this language in their own legal discussions (e.g., *m. Sanh.* 7:4; see also Lev 20:11). Paul's ethical reasoning is therefore implicitly dependent upon the Mosaic Law and assumes his Jewish heritage.[20] In 1 Cor 5:11 he lists several

---

[17] Barclay, *Obeying the Truth,* 149–50.

[18] For further development of this strand in Paul's reasoning, see Richard B. Hays, *The Moral Vision of the New Testament: A Contemporary Introduction to New Testament Ethics* (New York: HarperCollins, 1996), 32–36.

[19] In Hellenistic, non-Jewish vice lists, sexual sins are listed under the heading ἀκολασία rather than πορνεία; Friedrich Hauck and Siegfried Schulz, "πόρνη, πόρνος, πορνεία, πορνεύω, ἐκπορνεύω," *TDNT* 6:581–84, 587–90.

[20] Peter Tomson, *Paul and the Jewish Law: Halakha in the Letters of the Apostle to the Gentiles* (CRINT 3.1; Minneapolis: Fortress, 1990), 97–103; Traugott Holtz, "The Question of the Content of Paul's Instructions," in *Understanding Paul's Ethics: Twentieth-Century Approaches* (ed. Brian S. Rosner; Grand Rapids: Eerdmans, 1995),

sins that require separation from the community: "But now I am writing to you not to associate with anyone who bears the name of brother or sister who is sexually immoral or greedy, or is an idolater, reviler, drunkard, or robber. Do not even eat with such a one." Each of these sins corresponds to sins listed in Deuteronomy that require expulsion from the holy community. Sexual immorality (πόρνος) in Paul's list corresponds to sexual promiscuity in Deut 22:21 (ἐκπορνεῦσαι, LXX). Idolatry in Paul's list corresponds to Deut 17:3, 7. Paul's "reviler" (λοίδορος) matches malicious false testimony in Deut 19:18–19. Paul's drunkard (μέθυσος) matches Deut 21:20–21's rebellious son who is also a drunkard. Finally, Paul's thief (ἅρπαξ) matches Deut 24:7. In each of these cases in Deuteronomy, the Mosaic Law cites a standard expression to signal the execution of various offenders (see also 13:5; 17:7; 19:19; 21:21; 22:21; 24:7). Deuteronomy 22:22–24 employs a version of the same formula against the man found sleeping with another man's wife. A few verses later in 22:30 a man shall not marry his father's wife.[21] So Paul closes this part of his discussion of the man sleeping with his stepmother in 1 Cor 5:13 with the Deuteronomic curse in support of his advice: "Drive out the wicked person from among you" (cf. Deut 17:7).[22] Paul considers the Mosaic Law's list of heinous sins that deserve exclusion from the Israelite community to be binding within the Christian community as well. The apostle has already identified the Christian community ("you" plural) in 1 Cor 3:16–17 as God's holy temple that must remain holy.[23]

The apostle's reasoning in 1 Corinthians 6 continues to rely upon the Mosaic Law. Paul nowhere demonstrates *why* lawsuits before pagan judges are wrong in 6:1–6, but Judaism, grounded in the Mosaic Law, maintained its own system of justice. Moses appointed judges in Exod 18 and Deut 1:16–17 and provided them directions in Deut 16:18–20 and 17:8–13. Later judges, kings, and administrators followed this pattern of appointments.[24]

56–57; trans. of "Zur Frage der inhaltlichen Weisungen bei Paulus," *Theologische Literaturzeitung* 106 (1981): 385–400.

[21] Brian S. Rosner, *Paul, Scripture, and Ethics: A Study of 1 Corinthians 5–7* (AGJU 23; Leiden: E. J. Brill, 1994), 82–83. A wide array of sources show that Judaism maintained the Deuteronomic exclusion from the community for incest (*m. Sanh.* 7:4; 9:1; *m. Ker.* 1:1; *Jub.* 33:10–14; *t. Sanh.* 10:1; CD 5; 11QT^a 66; Philo, *Spec.* 3.22–28).

[22] Paul's use of the verb ἐξαίρω ("drive out") is a *hapax legomenon* within the NT (i.e., only occurring here) and comes from the Greek of Deut 17:7; Rosner, *Paul, Scripture, and Ethics,* 63–64, 69–70.

[23] Rosner (ibid., 75–80) suggests that 1 Cor 3:16–17 anticipates the discussion in 1 Corinthians 5. Compare 3:15 and 5:5; e.g., both mention the destruction that is necessary to maintain holiness.

[24] See 1 Sam 8:1; 1 Chr 23:4; Ezra 7:25; 10:14; and esp. 2 Chr 19:5–11, which scholars have contended is dependent on Deuteronomy. Exodus 18 and Deuteronomy 1 exerted influence in the Second Temple period on 11QT^a 51:11–18; Josephus, *Ant.* 4.8.14 §§214–216; and Philo, *Spec.* 4.65–67 (Deut 16:20), 4.70–71 (Deut 1:17; 16:19).

Paul's vocabulary in 1 Corinthians 6 reflects his reliance upon the Mosaic model of establishing judges. First Corinthians 6:5b ("to decide between one believer [brother] and another" [διακρῖναι ἀνὰ μέσον τοῦ ἀδελφοῦ αὐτοῦ]) directly parallels the LXX's translation into the Greek of Deut 1:16 ("judge rightly between one person and another" [κρίνατε δικαίως ἀνὰ μέσον ἀνδρὸς καὶ ἀνὰ μέσον ἀδελφοῦ]).[25] Such phrasing only occurs in Greek literature dependent on Deut 1:16.[26] Paul is drawing upon Mosaic precedents in his advice to the Corinthian community.[27] As the Jews would categorically label pagans "unrighteous" (ἄδικοι), so too does Paul in 1 Cor 6:1.[28] Judges typically accepted bribes in the pagan courts of law, an "unrighteous" practice from a Jewish standpoint. Judges, according to Deut 16:18–20a, were to judge fairly, or righteously, by showing no partiality and by accepting no bribes.[29]

In 1 Cor 6:9–10 Paul lists various vices, including the six already mentioned in 5:11, but now he includes three matters of sexual sin. The first of these is less controversial: μοιχός refers to a married person who has engaged in sexual relations outside marriage. The Greek translation of the Mosaic Law conveyed a condemnation of this sin in Exod 20:13, Lev 20:10, and Deut 5:18. Far more controversial are the other two vices Paul lists—those practiced by the ἀρσενοκοίτης and the μαλακός. The word ἀρσενοκοίτης (an exceedingly rare compound that occurs elsewhere only where there is Jewish or Christian influence) is most likely derived from the conjunction of its component parts in both Lev 18:22 and 20:13, two passages that censure homosexual activity. Paul also censures homosexual activity in Rom 1:24–27. Again, the warrants against certain behaviors appear to derive from the Mosaic Law.[30]

In 1 Cor 6:12–20 the apostle continues, "All things are lawful for me." A variation of the same Corinthian slogan appears in 10:23 in the context of pure and impure foods. Members of the Corinthian congregation appear to have extended to the realm of sexuality the same freedom applied to the Jewish food laws.[31] Paul disagrees with the Corinthians, and in the process

---

[25] Some of the LXX manuscripts for Deut 1:16 directly support Paul's language: ἀνὰ μέσον τοῦ ἀδελφοῦ αὐτοῦ.

[26] Rosner, *Paul, Scripture, and Ethics,* 99–101, who lists a whole array of terminological parallels between 1 Cor 6:1–6 and the Mosaic legislation regarding judges. As Rosner (pp. 104–106) explains, the grammatically incorrect use of the singular "brother" (ἀδελφοῦ) in 1 Cor 6:5b merely reflects the language of Deut 1:16.

[27] Rosner, *Paul, Scripture, and Ethics,* 101–4.

[28] Holtz, "Content of Paul's Instructions," 58.

[29] Note the δικ-stem that runs all through Deut 16:18–20a; Rosner, *Paul, Scripture, and Ethics,* 106–7 (see also 107–12).

[30] See esp. the discussion of Robert A. J. Gagnon, *The Bible and Homosexual Practice: Texts and Hermeneutics* (Nashville: Abingdon, 2001), 306–32 (on the two terms in 1 Cor 6:9–10), 229–303 (on Rom 1:26–27).

[31] Hans Lietzmann, *An die Korinther I.II* (5th ed.; HNT 9; Tübingen: J. C. B. Mohr [Paul Siebeck], 1969), 27.

of opposing sexual relations with prostitutes, he reminds the Corinthians in 1 Cor 6:15 that they are members of Christ. This christological reminder as a warrant for changed behavior is then supported in v. 16 by a second warrant, a reference to Gen 2:24 from the Torah. First Corinthians 10:18 offers yet a third argument that appears to assume that fornication is sin. Amid these three lines of reasoning against sexual relations with a prostitute, the Law hovers in the background as a Pauline assumption. Indeed, the apostle's reasoning is far more dependent on Jewish practice than it may first appear to be. For example, Paul makes the blanket statement that the Christian's body is a member of Christ, and so the Christian, who is a member of Christ, should not sexually unite and become one body with someone else, namely, a prostitute. Bodily oneness with Christ precludes oneness with the prostitute. The argument from already being one body with Christ could equally apply, however, to *any* sexual union by the Christian, even between husband and wife. The unstated premise against sexual relations with prostitutes appears to derive from the Mosaic Law (see Gen 39:9; Lev 19:29).[32] The Qumran community affirmed the Law's teaching: "refrain from fornication in accordance with the regulation" (CD 7:1–2). The *Testament of Reuben,* a document probably from the first century before Christ, repeatedly urges, on the basis of the narratives of the Torah, "Accordingly, my children, flee from sexual promiscuity" (*T. Reu.* 5:5); "So guard yourself against sexual promiscuity" (6:1; similarly 1:6; 4:1–11; 6:4). For Paul, a man steeped in a Jewish upbringing and education in the Mosaic Law, some of the Corinthians' actions were inconceivable.

Paul often explicitly grounds his teachings in the words of the Jewish Scriptures and Law. Romans 12:19, with its "for it is written" and quotation of Deut 32:35, shows that the Scriptures are still authoritative. First Corinthians 5:13 appeals to Deut 17:7. Second Corinthians 8:15 cites Exod 16:18: "As it is written." In each instance, Paul refers to the OT to confirm and summarize authoritatively his exhortations. Not usually content to stop with a quotation from the Torah as his basis for Christian behavior, Paul in 1 Cor 9:7 argues for his right to receive support from the community and offers three examples from ordinary life: soldiers, winegrowers, and shepherds. Verses 8–9 then appeal to the Jewish Scriptures (Deut 25:4)—as does v. 13. In v. 14 Paul appeals to a word of the Lord. Wolfgang Schrage notes that the apostle lists these mutually supporting warrants in ascending order of strength: first, everyday life and economics; then the OT; and finally the word of the Lord.[33] First Corinthians 14:34 similarly appeals to the Law in urging women's silence in the assemblies. Once again Paul is not satisfied, however, by merely appealing to the Mosaic Law. He adds several

---

[32] Holtz, "Content of Paul's Instructions," 53–55.

[33] Wolfgang Schrage, *The Ethics of the New Testament* (trans. David E. Green; Philadelphia: Fortress, 1988), 205. Paul cites in Rom 15:3 Christ's conduct as a model for the Christians but confirms it with a passage from the Psalms.

additional warrants for his instruction in 14:35–38: honor/shame conven-
tions, Paul's prophetic authority and spiritual giftedness, and the danger of
divine judgment.[34]

Paul's handling of the Torah in 1 Corinthians 10 offers insight into
why he is not content merely to quote the Law as a norm for Christian behavior. He explains that what happened under the old age (before Christ)
were "types" for what is happening in the new age. Paul says as much in
10:11: "These things happened to them [the Israelites] to serve as an example, and they were written down to instruct us, on whom the ends of the
ages have come." When Moses drew forth water from the rock, Paul
explains, the rock was really Christ. As a type or shadow of what was to
come, the Mosaic Law offers guidance but is not in itself the sole authority
for Christians. Christ's teachings are therefore the final court of appeal
and modify the application of the OT for the new age in which the Christian lives.

Galatians 5:14 cites Lev 19:18's command to love one's neighbor as
still normative, but the twist is that Gal 5:14 echoes Christ's own self-giving
love, which Paul has already emphasized earlier in the Galatian letter. Paul
seeks to understand the Mosaic Law in light of Christ's example (2:20). Such
an interpretation of the Mosaic Law in light of Christ's loving sacrifice renders more likely the analogous interpretation of "the Law of Christ" in 6:2 as
a reference to the Mosaic Law. Paul uses a similar phrase in Rom 8:2, "the
Law of the Spirit of life," a phrase which is followed later in Romans by a reminder of the necessity for Christians to heed the Ten Commandments
from the Mosaic Law (Rom 13:9). In each case the Law functions differently
for Paul under the influence of the powers of a new age.

This prioritization of Christ's own example and teachings in the life of
the early Christian movement often led Paul to a radical reinterpretation of
the Mosaic Law. First Corinthians 7:19 distinguishes between circumcision
and uncircumcision as opposed to "the commandments of God," the aspects
of the Mosaic Law that endure. In Rom 14:14 Paul declares all foods clean
even as he promotes elsewhere a fulfillment of the Law inclusive of the Ten
Commandments (Rom 13:8–10). Schrage summarizes Paul's approach to
the Mosaic Law: "We find in Paul a dialectical attitude toward the authority
of the Old Testament. On the one hand, it is authoritative. On the other
hand, it derives its authority only from Christ and the law of love, even
though Rom. 13:8–10 maintains that the law of love, in which all the other
commandments are summed up . . . , is itself found in the Old Testament."[35]

---

[34] On the authenticity of 14:34, see the recent discussion of Anthony Thisel-
ton, *The First Epistle to the Corinthians: A Commentary on the Greek Text* (NIGTC;
Grand Rapids: Eerdmans, 2000), 1148–50; and Curt Niccum, "The Voice of the
Manuscripts on the Silence of Women: The External Evidence for 1 Cor 14:34–35,"
NTS 43 (1997): 242–55.

[35] Schrage, *Ethics of the New Testament*, 206.

GOD'S STANDARD FOR JUDGMENT

All people, even Christians, will be judged according to the standard of the Mosaic Law according to Paul. That he does not abandon the Law in his admonitions should not, then, be surprising. According to Rom 2:6–11, all people are accountable for their actions, and God will repay each person according to what he or she has done (2:6: ὃς ἀποδώσει ἑκάστῳ κατὰ τὰ ἔργα αὐτοῦ). In vv. 7–8 Paul contrasts the fate of those who do good with the fate of those who do evil. God will reward the former and will pour out wrath and anger against the latter (cf. v. 5). In vv. 9–10 Paul emphasizes that all will be judged according to their deeds, whether Jew or Gentile.[36]

Paul declares in Rom 1:16–17 that the gospel is the power of God's salvation to everyone who believes, to the Jew first and to the Greek. This tantalizingly brief mention of Jews alongside Gentiles invites further investigation, particularly in light of God's historic relationship with Israel. Paul says in 1:16–2:11 that no one has an excuse before God's judgment. God will impartially judge each individual on the basis of his or her works, whether Jew or Greek. God does not show favoritism (2:11). This leads to an obvious objection. Did God not give the Law to the Jews rather than to the Gentiles? Surely this introduces an unfair inequality into God's dealings with humanity. Paul again mentions Jews and Gentiles in 2:9–10 before he turns to the matter of possession or nonpossession of the Mosaic Law in vv. 12–16.

Paul addresses in Rom 2:12–16 a logical objection to his claim of divine impartiality in vv. 6–11. God appears to have treated humanity with partiality by providing the Law only to the Jews but not to the Gentiles. The Jews benefited from the revealed knowledge of God's will provided to Moses. God would hardly be fair if he were to judge Gentiles by the standard of a Law that they never possessed. Paul responds by saying that both Jews (those "in the Law") and Gentiles (those "apart from the Law") will be impartially judged according to the standard of whether they have done what the Law requires (v. 12). In v. 13 he proclaims, "For it is not the hearers of the law who are righteous in God's sight, but the doers of the law who will be justified."[37] Verses 14–15 then clarify how Gentiles who do not possess the law will be judged according to it:

---

[36]The twofold repetition of both πᾶς ("everyone") and Ἰουδαῖος τε πρῶτον καὶ Ἕλλην ("the Jew first and also the Greek") underscores how "each one" (ἑκάστῳ; v. 6) will be judged in the same way; Jouette M. Bassler, *Divine Impartiality: Paul and a Theological Axiom* (SBLDS 59; Chico, Calif.: Scholars Press, 1982), 126. Note also that this is not a pre-Christian situation. These verses are stating axiomatically the basis for God's judgment. God's wrath "is being revealed" (present tense; NRSV: "is revealed") against ungodliness and unrighteousness (1:18). Likewise, several passages in Paul speak of Christians being judged according to their works.

[37]"Not the expounding of the Law is the chief thing but the doing of it" (*m. ʾAbot* 1:17); see also Wis 6:18–20; Josephus, *Ant.* 20.2.4 §44; 1 Macc 2:67.

> When Gentiles, who do not possess the law, do instinctively what the law re-
> quires, these, though not having the law, are a law to themselves. They show
> that what the law requires is written on their hearts, to which their own con-
> science also bears witness; and their conflicting thoughts will accuse or per-
> haps excuse them.[38]

The Gentiles' consciences act to accuse and defend them; they are a Law to
themselves even though they do not have the Law.[39] Although the Gentiles
do not possess the Law, what they have by reason of their consciences is
comparable to the Mosaic Law, at least to the extent of rendering God's
judgment impartial. Having dispelled a potential objection, Paul returns in
v. 16 to the language of the divine tribunal that dominated vv. 1–5. Far from
saying that the Gentiles fulfill the entire Law, Paul is simply saying that the
Gentiles occasionally do things that the Law requires. By their occasional
fulfilling of the Law, the Gentiles show that the work of the Law is written on
their hearts. They are as accountable before God as the Jews with the Law.
Nonpossession of the Law is no excuse. Paul expounds in vv. 14–16 on
v. 12a: those without the Law will perish without it, since their consciences
attest that the work of the Law is written on their hearts. He builds in
vv. 17–29 on vv. 12b–13: it is not enough to hear the Law; the Jew must also
do it.[40] Paul appeals in vv. 12–13 to the Law as the criterion of God's impartial judgment. In vv. 17–29 he again returns to this impartial judgment of
what is in people's hearts. Paul shows that everyone is accountable to
God, even the Jew. People will be judged on the basis of whether they have
done what the Law requires. Mere possession of the Law is not enough
(vv. 17–24).

Jewish identity was based on possession of the Law of Moses, but that
identity was also ritually symbolized by the act of circumcision, to which
Paul turns in Rom 2:25–29. He says that circumcision is of value only if
there is a simultaneous doing of the Law (v. 25). If one transgresses the Law,
then one's circumcision has become uncircumcision. Obedience is the ultimate criterion. If the uncircumcised does the "just requirements of the
Law," he or she will be regarded as circumcised (v. 26). In v. 27 Paul asserts
that the uncircumcised individual who fulfills (τελοῦσα) the Law will judge
the outwardly circumcised Jew who transgresses. Merely to say that a hypothetical Gentile judges the Jew is not persuasive or even worthy of mention.

---

[38] The first line could be translated, "For whenever Gentiles, who do not have
by nature the law, do what the law requires."

[39] See esp. Philo, *Ios.* 29; *Mos.* 1.162; 2.12, 14, 37, 52; *Spec.* 2.13; *Prob.* 46; *Opif.*
3. Philo says that Abraham kept the "unwritten Law" that is clear even from nature
(*Abr.* 5–6, 60, 275–276).

[40] Verse 17 and what follows seems to build on v. 13: it is not the hearers of the
Law who will be justified. If so, vv. 17–29 would likewise be subordinated to the
statement of God's impartial judgment in vv. 9–11. Verses 14–16, building on v. 13,
contend that the Gentile is accountable before God even as vv. 17–29 contend that
the Jew is also accountable.

Only if the Gentile has *actually* been obedient and would *actually* judge, would the Jew be shamed. Paul concludes that outward circumcision does not make one a Jew, but rather the inward circumcision that comes through the Spirit (vv. 28–29).

Paul's entire description of the true Jew in Rom 2:28–29 draws upon language that he later uses to describe Christians. In v. 26 he speaks of "the requirements of the law" (τὰ δικαιώματα τοῦ νόμου), the same phrase he uses in the singular in 8:4, where those who walk by the Spirit fulfill the "just requirement of the Law" (cf. Gentile disobedience to God's "decree" [δικαίωμα] in 1:32). Paul's contrast in 2:29 of the spirit and the letter (of the Law) recurs in 7:5–6 (cf. 8:1–4) and 2 Cor 3:6–7. He contrasts the new eschatological situation of those in Christ who have the Spirit with those under the letter of the Law who do not have the Spirit (similarly in Phil 3:3, those who worship in the Spirit are "the circumcision"). In Rom 2:26 the uncircumcised are *"reckoned"* as circumcised. Paul is using a verb that he employs elsewhere in Romans 3 and 4 for those reckoned righteous on the basis of faith (3:28; 4:3, 4, 5, 6, 8, 9, 10, 11, 22, 23, 24; 9:8; Gal 3:6; 2 Cor 5:19). Paul will even reinterpret circumcision as a sign of Abraham's faith rather than as an observance of the Law. Finally, the uncircumcised who keep the Law in Rom 2:27 will judge (κρινεῖ) the circumcised who do not. In 1 Cor 6:2 Paul specifies Christians as those who will share in God's activity as the Judge.

If Paul has Gentile *Christians* in mind in his description of a Gentile in Romans 2, a potential objection arises as to why he doesn't identify them as such. Paul does not turn to Christ's work until 3:21–26. A precise identification at this point would disrupt his flow of thought. His point in Romans 2 is strictly that God's judgment is objective and impartial. Similarly, questions about whom Paul had in mind in 2:6–10 are irrelevant. Paul is simply laying down the criteria of God's just judgment. He does not actually identify anyone falling into the category of the "good" although his language again is suggestive of Christians. Nevertheless, as Paul proceeds, he clarifies that those Gentiles judged righteous on the final day are Gentiles in Christ. His argument, essentially, is looping back on itself. In light of what comes later, Paul's intention in 2:6–10 and 2:25–29 to include all people, even Gentiles in Christ, becomes apparent.[41] In vv. 25–29 he is preparing the reader for what he states later in Romans and for the recognition that it is the Christian Gentile who fulfills the Law.[42]

Romans 2:25–29 is thus Paul's final stage in an argument that turns on its head Jewish presumption on the basis of the Law along with circumcision.

---

[41] Romans 2:25–29 parallels and builds on vv. 6–10. E.g., the mention of eschatological praise in v. 29 parallels the reward to those who do good works in vv. 6–10.

[42] Not surprisingly, Paul speaks of *Christians* being judged according to their works throughout the rest of his letters (e.g., Gal 5:21; 6:8; 1 Cor 6:9–10; 9:24–27).

Gentiles who do what is good are circumcised in heart (vv. 7, 10, 12–16, 25–29). The Gentiles are Paul's proof that God's judgment is impartial and based on actions and not on the mere possession of the Law or circumcision. All people are accountable before God's judgment. The Gentile Christians' fulfillment of the Law will contrast at God's judgment with the Jews' non-observance of the Law. In Gal 6:7–9 Paul says, "Do not be deceived; God is not mocked, for you reap whatever you sow. If you sow to your own flesh, you will reap corruption from the flesh; but if you sow to the Spirit, you will reap eternal life from the Spirit. So let us not grow weary in doing what is right, for we will reap at harvest time, if we do not give up." For the apostle, the Law remains the standard by which God will judge all people. Gentile Christians are actually doing what the Law requires. God will be vindicated.

THE SPIRIT TAKES HOLD OF THE LAW

The Mosaic Law continues to express God's will and remains the standard for God's judgment, but the Law must be understood within the context of the new age that has come in Christ. The Law is incapable, of itself, to motivate genuine obedience, according to Paul. Only the power of the new age, the Spirit, can take hold of the Law to bring forth life instead of death (thus Rom 7:7–8:4). Paul likewise invokes the Spirit in Gal 3:3 as the only real power that can combat the flesh, which is still active in the Christian life even if in defeat. Galatians 5:24 says, "Those who belong to Christ Jesus have crucified the flesh with its passions and desires." "Have crucified" is an indicative statement expressing a fact, a current state of affairs. This indicative grounds the imperative in v. 16, the command for Christians, "Live by the Spirit, I say, and do not gratify the desires of the flesh" (literally, "Walk [περιπατεῖτε] by the Spirit").[43] Paul maintains that the flesh's passions are still active and are producing their own works and waging war against the Spirit (vv. 19–21), but the Spirit opposes the flesh (v. 17) in order to bring about a different fruit (vv. 22–23). The apostle exhorts the Christian to submit actively to the leading of the Spirit in order to maintain the state of victory over the flesh's desires. The Christian is to "walk by the Spirit."[44]

In Gal 5:17 Paul says, "For what the flesh desires is opposed to the Spirit, and what the Spirit desires is opposed to the flesh; for these are op-

---

[43] On the indicative and imperative in Paul's ethics, see especially Michael Parsons, "Being Precedes Act: Indicative and Imperative in Paul's Writing," in *Understanding Paul's Ethics: Twentieth-Century Approaches* (ed. Brian S. Rosner; Grand Rapids: Eerdmans, 1995), 217–47 reprinted from *Evangelical Quarterly* 88 (1988): 99–127.

[44] The Jews walked according to the Law (Exod 16:4; 18:20; Lev 18:4; Deut 13:4–5; Ps 86:11; Jer 44:23; Ezek 5:6–7; 1QS 3:18–4:26), but the Christian is to walk by the Spirit. Again, from Paul's perspective, the Law offers no power to curb the flesh; Dunn, *Galatians,* 295.

posed to each other, to prevent you from doing what you want." Scholars
have put forth at least three possible interpretations regarding the meaning
of "what you want." First, it could refer to both what the flesh desires *and*
what the Spirit desires. This is a grammatically feasible interpretation that
maintains the same two subjects as the prior part of the sentence (what the
flesh desires opposes the Spirit, and what the Spirit desires opposes the
flesh), but this approach suggests parity or a stalemate in the battle between
the flesh and the Spirit. Paul does not envision a stalemate between the flesh
and the Spirit (see v. 16). The believer always has the power, by virtue of the
Spirit, to choose and to act contrary to the flesh (3:3; 5:22–24). Another interpretation takes "what you want" as Spirit-prompted desires. The Spirit
moves the Christian to cry to God as Father (e.g., 4:6), but the flesh prevents
the Christian from doing what the Spirit prompts. The praiseworthy desire
created by the Spirit ("what you want") would parallel the desires in
Rom 7:15 to do what is good ("what I want" [ὃ θέλω]), which are likewise
hindered by the flesh. But Paul's Galatian context does not support the conclusion that the flesh successfully hinders the Spirit from producing its God-
pleasing fruit, i.e. "what you want." A third interpretation takes "what you
want" as referring to the flesh's negative desires: the Spirit prevents the
Christian from doing "what you want" in the flesh. This interpretation creates a problem, however: the similar expression in Rom 7:15, "what I
want," expresses God-pleasing intentions whereas Gal 5:17's "what you
want" requires a negative interpretation. Furthermore, the second and third
approaches do not account for both the Spirit *and* the flesh as the subjects of
the sentence. In a neglected study of Gal 5:17, Ronald Lutjens offers a satisfactory resolution of the verse.[45] He contends that v. 17 includes a paren-
thetical remark: "For what the flesh desires is opposed to the Spirit (and
what the Spirit desires is opposed to the flesh; for these are opposed to
each other) to prevent you from doing what you want." This punctuation
maintains the positive construal of "what I want" as well as the Spirit's pre-
eminence over the flesh and leads to a satisfactory interpretation that incorporates the strengths of the other readings. If this punctuation is correct,
Paul can barely countenance the flesh's opposition to Spirit-prompted desires without immediately qualifying in a parenthesis that the flesh's actions
are countered by the overwhelming power of the Spirit to which the
Christian has immediate access. Paul would be saying that Christians therefore have a power available to them that is not accessible through the
Mosaic Law. This power enables them to live the godly life to which
the Mosaic Law had pointed. The Spirit directs believers back to the example of Christ, who himself lived "under the law" (4:4). Consequently, in
following Christ in love, the believer will be fulfilling all that the Mosaic
Law has been urging all along.

---

[45] Ronald Lutjens, " 'You Do Not Do What You Want': What Does Galatians
5:17 Really Mean?" *Presby* 16, no. 2 (1990): 103–17.

God entrusted the divine "oracles" of the Law to the Jewish people (Rom 3:2). Paul maintains that the Gentile will be judged according to the same Law as the Jew even if the Gentile does not possess that Law in its written form. The Jews' Law remains the standard of God's will. Nevertheless, the Law itself had pointed forward to a future day, a day when the Messiah would finally come and the Gentiles would benefit from Israel's deliverance. The Gentiles need not adopt the ethnic customs of Jews to experience God's blessing in the new age. They would be included as Gentiles. That new age had finally dawned for Paul with Christ's death and resurrection. The power of the age to come, the Spirit, has grabbed hold of the Law, once powerless and enslaving, and rendered it useful. The Christian has a power available that others do not. The Spirit directs the Christian's focus to Christ. In imitating the love of Christ for others, the Christian will paradoxically fulfill what the Law prescribed without ever having set out to "do" all that the Law commands.

REFLECTIONS: PAUL,
THE APOSTLE OF HOPE

> So that you may not claim to be wiser than you are, brothers and
> sisters, I want you to understand this mystery: a hardening has
> come upon part of Israel until the full number of the Gentiles has
> come in. (Rom 11:25)

Since the publication of Sanders's monumental work, *Paul and Palestinian Judaism,* in 1977, Pauline scholarship has revisited its understanding of the apostle's relationship with the Jewish people. While scholars have debated and fine-tuned Sanders's depiction of Judaism over the past twenty-five years, almost all Jewish and Pauline specialists would agree that in the era of the birth of Christianity the Jews did not think that they earned their way into heaven merely by their good works. Although God's Law required obedience and although the Jews often spoke of being judged according to works, Jewish writers regularly spoke of God's unmerited mercy. They spoke of a God who chose a special people, whether they identified that people with ethnic Jews or with a select group among the Jews. They regularly spoke of repentance, sacrifice, and atonement for violations of God's Law. In other words, Jewish authors typically held in tension the demand of God's Law for works and the provision of God's gracious mercy and forgiveness for failure. Although the shape of this tension varied from author to author and from genre to genre, both elements were almost always present side by side. Paul himself reflected a far more gracious understanding of Judaism than had been generally recognized before Sanders. In Gal 1:14 Paul boasted that he had advanced in Judaism beyond many of his contemporaries. As a Jew he had been extremely zealous for the traditions of his ancestors. Nowhere did he ever say that he had harbored doubts about his elect status as a Jew. He was a Pharisee of Pharisees, of the tribe of Benjamin, a Hebrew born of Hebrews, a member of God's elect people. He was "blameless" (Phil 3:6). He likely viewed himself as "having in the law the embodiment of knowledge and truth"; he was "a guide to the blind, a light to those who are in darkness" (Rom 2:19). So he violently persecuted "the church of God" (Gal 1:13).

The day Jesus Christ revealed himself to Paul the Jew marked a watershed. In that moment face-to-face with God's Messiah, Paul, who had been persecuting the church, recognized that somewhere he had gone terribly wrong in his thinking. The confidence in his former way of life as a pious Pharisee lay shattered. It dawned on him that a Judaism apart from God's Messiah did not—could not—proffer God's grace and a place in the world to come. The glories of his past were now all a loss for the sake of Christ (Phil 3:8). This radical reconceptualization of grace in the apostle's reasoning sent ripples through his whole belief system. Suddenly everything revolved around Jesus Christ. Salvation was available only through faith in the Christ who suffered, died, and rose again. A Jewish way of life, including especially circumcision, Sabbath, the food laws, and Law observance, no longer marked an elect and chosen people guaranteed a place in the world to come. After his meeting with Christ, the gracious elements of Judaism were replaced in Paul's thinking by the mercy found in Jesus Christ. Henceforth Paul committed himself with single-minded determination to his prophetic calling, a mission from God among the Gentiles in the service of the Jewish Messiah.

To understand this metamorphosis from zealous Pharisee to maverick apostle is to comprehend Paul, with his seeming contradictions and ambiguities. Paul began to insist that Jesus was the Messiah promised to the Jewish people (Rom 9:5). He was the one promised by the Jewish Scriptures. Jesus was the seed God had spoken of to Abraham and the one to whom the promises were made (Gal 3:15–18). But the Messiah was also the Savior of *all* people. No longer did the Gentiles need to be circumcised or to obey the Mosaic Law in order to experience a place in the world to come. Paul fought furiously for their right to enjoy Israel's privileges without having to become Jewish. As a former Pharisaic Jew, Paul was perhaps uniquely qualified to dissuade the Gentile Galatians from following the Jewish Christian evangelists in their midst. He went on the offensive against those trying to impose the Jewish Law upon Gentiles who were enjoying God's freedom in Christ. Paul classified the Law from Mount Sinai and "the present Jerusalem" under the category of a slavery represented not by Sarah but by Hagar (Gal 4:21–31).

Although Paul was combating Jewish Christians, his rhetoric appears to lead to a condemnation of Judaism itself. He spoke of circumcision as a sort of castration (Gal 5:12). He attacked Jewish (Christian?) teachers again in Phil 3:2, calling them "dogs" and "mutilators." Although this sort of language seems to indict the Jewish people and their defining rite, readers of Paul must never lose sight of the fact that this language emerged out of situations of intense conflict among fellow Jewish Christians. This was an *inter-Christian* dispute! Paul's rhetoric against Jewish Christian evangelists insisting on circumcision was so vitriolic because they did not realize that Jewish ethnic identity and Law observance would not guarantee a place in the world to come. With the change in gracious framework, the Law could not justify—quite unlike the perspective the Jews, or even Paul himself before his conversion, would have held. Although Paul's opponents at Galatia recognized the importance of faith in Christ (Gal 2:16), they were danger-ously inconsistent in their thinking and were compromising saving faith by their stern insistence on a belief system oriented on the Law. Paul had to work back through their prooftexts and supporting material to demonstrate that faith in Christ was the sole essential element and not the doing of the Law. A powerful new world had invaded the cosmos in Christ. God through the cross of Christ was shattering the dominion of sin and the elements of this world, including slavery under the Law's impossibly difficult demands (since there is no viable means of atonement for failure). The power of the promised Spirit was in Christ and not in the Law. Paul's Galatian oppo-nents' insistence on the covenant God made with Israel and on Israel's spe-cial place did not recognize the centrality and priority of faith in Christ.

After using with respect to Gentile Christians terms that the Jewish Scriptures had applied to Israel, such as election, adoption, and glory, Paul turned around in Romans 9 and asked about his own people. If Gentiles were enjoying a status traditionally accorded to Israel, would this imply that God had abandoned the Jewish people? Were the Jews no longer God's chosen? In Romans 9–10 the apostle initially compounded the problem of ethnic Israel by noting that only a fraction within ethnic Israel was ever in-tended by God to be the elect. Then he added that the Jews stumbled over the stone, namely, Jesus Christ. They failed to benefit from God's saving promises since these promises may only be enjoyed through faith in Christ, a faith that the Word about Christ creates (Rom 10:16–17). Only a remnant of Jews were numbered among God's elect. Nevertheless, a remnant did remain.

In 1 Thess 2:14–16 Paul claimed that God's wrath has come upon the Jewish people, but the context makes clear that his comments were again pointed toward a specific group and not against Jews in general. He was speaking regarding those who had resisted his gospel ministry to the Gen-tiles. Such Jews did not yet realize that Jesus Christ is the Savior of *all* people. Never did Paul condemn the Jewish people as a whole or leave them without any hope in God's final plan. Although he insisted that they must adhere to his gospel message about Christ, as had been the case in Galatia, he did not censure them completely.

God had always proven himself faithful to the promises made to Is-rael. Paul never abandoned Israel's priority in God's plan. Although the Scriptures were written for the benefit of God's people in Christ, the new chapter of history begun with Christ and the church was never to exclude the Jewish people. Paul's slogan to the Romans remained, "to the Jew *first* and also to the Greek" (Rom 1:16; 2:9, 10). To comprehend Israel's priority in God's plan as the apostle explained it, the Letter to the Romans must be set within its historical setting in first-century Rome. The letter was targeted to the situation of the Roman audience. In the years prior to Paul's writing to the congregation, the Roman church had been based in synagogues. After a conflict over the significance of Jesus Christ, the Jewish Christians— and perhaps the more vocal Gentile Christian God-fearers within the

synagogue—were among those expelled from Rome for their role in pro-
voking the conflict. Having drawn the attention of the emperor, the synagogues would have wanted to distance themselves from the new religious
movement. By the time of Nero, the Jewish authorities, through their ties to
the imperial court, had successfully managed to impress upon the emperor
the difference between themselves and the Christians. In the meantime, the
Christians had been forced to meet separately. With the loss of their Jewish
Christian members as a result of Claudius's expulsion, the Christians in
Rome had become a largely, if not exclusively, Gentile movement. So Paul
addressed his letter to a Gentile congregation. Although the members of the
Gentile Roman congregation who had been involved in the movement
while it was still situated within the synagogues would have had an appreciation of Christianity's Jewish heritage, other Gentiles had joined the movement who were apparently less sympathetic to Christianity's Jewish roots.
Many Roman Gentiles numbered among "the strong" harbored disregard,
if not arrogance, toward Jewish customs and practices. Paul himself may
have strengthened these suppositions as he wrote earlier in Romans of the
futility of the Law as a means of salvation and leveled any Jewish advantage
before God. By the time Paul finished enlightening the Gentiles who no longer appreciated their Judaic heritage and were trampling upon God's Law,
he was boldly telling them that they dare not claim exclusive rights to God's
plan of salvation. By the first several verses of Romans 11, the problem Paul
began to tackle in 9:1–5 had become exceedingly acute. Finally he unveiled
the "mystery," God's eschatological plan to save ethnic Israel. At the end of
time, a moment the apostle believes to be fast approaching, the Jews would
come to believe in Christ and so experience salvation and the benefits of
their election. Paul may even have seen his own ministry as ushering in that
final phase of the plan. Was his plan to hurry on to Spain in 15:24, 28 an attempt to trigger God's ultimate plan for the Jews by closing the window for
the Gentiles with the gathering of their full number?

  Although Gentiles formed the majority of Christian believers in Paul's
missionary endeavors, they remained, within Paul's analogy of Romans 11,
wild olive shoots grafted artificially into an olive tree that remained properly
ethnic Israel. In other words, Israel maintained its priority and place in
God's plan in spite of its current failure to believe Paul's message about
Christ. Gentiles dared not claim exclusive rights to God's plan of salvation.
The Christian church did not completely usurp the promises of ancient Israel. The Gentiles would enjoy their place in the olive tree of Israel only for
a time at a cost to the natural shoots. Gentiles must be prepared to welcome
back the Jews as the natural olive branches. One day in the not too distant
future, the window of salvation would be closed for the Gentiles as the Jews
returned to God's fold. Should not such a perspective engender respect and
consideration for the Jewish people as those to whom the divine promises
were made? The Jews remained an elect people even though they were not,
from the apostle's vantage point, currently benefiting from that election.

God would save Israel. Israel was therefore God's elect in two very different senses: a remnant currently believing and an entirety of Israel believing at the time when God would fully reveal the fulfillment of the promises to Israel. God would prove to be faithful to the Jews even in the face of their current rejection of the Messiah (9:5).

Paul's position on the Law in many ways mirrored his ambiguity with respect to Israel's election. Even as Paul could speak negatively about the majority of Israel who had failed to believe in Christ and at the same time could speak positively about the elect remnant (or the elect people as a whole to be manifested at the end of time), so could he speak about the Law. The apostle's statements about the Law were likewise both positive and negative. Each grouping must be given its proper due if a complete picture is to emerge.[1] Negatively, Paul viewed the Law as divorced from the gracious elements in Judaism. The value of the Jewish Law lay in the foreshadowing of what would come in the age of Christ. Paul said Abraham had believed in the promises to be fulfilled in Christ in a manner analogous to Christian belief in the face of the fulfillment of those promises. The Law given at Mount Sinai, while legitimately reflecting God's will, *never* saved in and of itself and could lead only to vain and futile human striving. The Law had always pointed forward to a new day, which had arrived in Paul's time. Further, since God saved in Christ, the ethnic markers within the Mosaic Law were not necessary for Gentiles. The Gentiles did not need to become Jewish to enjoy a place in the world to come. Paul did not abandon the Mosaic Law. Apart from its ethnic boundary markers, he continued to draw upon the Law in his advice to the Christian community. The Law often remained an unstated premise in his ethical reasoning, even though he preferred first to admonish the community to embody Christlike behavior. Paul continued to reason from and explicitly cite the Mosaic Law as a continuing norm for Christian behavior. In that sense, Christianity must not abandon its Jewish roots and must continually return to the Torah, both as Scripture and as norm.

The struggle between Paul and his Christian Jewish rivals in Galatia was perhaps only a harbinger of darker times ahead. Paul's struggle against the Christian Gentiles in Rome, who were already dismissing Judaism and the value of the Mosaic Law, also presaged problems in the future. Two failed Jewish attempts to wage war on their Roman overlords further separated Jews and Christians. Soon a predominantly Gentile Christianity abandoned much of its Jewish heritage. Jewish Christians met in a separate communion and were labeled and marginalized. The seeds were sown for a struggle between religions in the centuries ahead. The author of the canonical Letter to the Hebrews, dated by scholars to the end of the first century (possibly to a Roman audience!), understood Jewish Scriptures and rites to have reached their fulfillment in Christ and his church. *The Epistle of Barnabas,*

---

[1] In his *Mystery of Romans* Nanos limits himself to Paul's positive statements on the Mosaic Law. This limitation skews Nanos's sketch of Paul on the Law.

a second-century document, offered a similar perspective. Although the epistle was not ultimately included in the Christian canon, some considered it Scripture in the second century. *Barnabas* interpreted circumcision, Sabbath, and Jewish observances as only shadows pointing to what God had done in Christ. With the arrival of Christ, the Jewish practices had become obsolete. The Christian church had superseded and supplanted Israel in God's plan. Although Paul likewise interpreted the story of Israel as instruction for a Christian church consisting predominantly of Gentiles (1 Cor 10:1–13), he never went so far as the outright supersessionism of the authors of Hebrews or *Barnabas*. Within a hundred years of Paul, Judaism and Christianity parted ways in a split that soon became dark and acrimonious.

James Carroll traces the roots of the Shoah, known by most today as the Holocaust, one of the darkest chapters in Jewish history, all the way back to the first century.[2] Carroll cites the Christian church's canonical gospels as blaming the Jewish people for the death of Christ. At first the charge was leveled within the confines of the Jewish community between the synagogue and emerging, separate Jewish Christian churches. Matthew's Gospel reflected the painful intra-Jewish family struggle and break. Matthew placed on the lips of the Jewish people at Jesus' death, "His blood be on us and on our children" (Matt 27:25). Although in Matthew's context the blood of Christ ironically possessed the power to forgive (26:28), this point was lost upon (Gentile) Christians in the ensuing centuries. Luke created the impression in his Gospel that it was not the Roman soldiers who led Jesus to be crucified, as in Mark, but rather the Jews themselves (Luke 23:18–27). Later readers soon lost sight of the powerful significance of Jesus' final words: "Father, forgive them; for they do not know what they are doing" (23:34).[3] Melito of Sardis in the second century was perhaps the first to openly label the Jews "Christ killers."

Carroll exonerates Paul as the bright spot in early Christianity, but Carroll is far too dependent on a questionable two-covenant theory, that God has a special plan for the Jewish people apart from faith in Christ.[4] The Jewish Paul did *not* share that viewpoint. Carroll rightly highlights the apostle's defense of Israel's special place as an elect people, but Paul insisted, contra Carroll, that the benefits of Jewish election must be realized by the same

---

[2] James Carroll, *Constantine's Sword: The Church and the Jews—a History* (New York: Houghton Mifflin, 2001). My exposition of the NT literature in this paragraph, however, is independent of Carroll, but in agreement with his analysis.

[3] Stephen's Christlike utterance of a similar prayer later in the story (Acts 7:60) led to the conversion of one of the early Christians' most violent persecutors, the soon-to-be-apostle Paul.

[4] Carroll is not alone in this understanding of the apostle. A recent committee meeting in 2002 of the U.S. Conference of Catholic Bishops declared that the OT covenant between the Jews and God was valid and that Jews do not need to convert to Christianity to be saved; Alan Cooperman, "Catholics No Longer Out to Convert Jews," *Houston Chronicle,* August 18, 2002, 4A.

faith in Christ as that of the Gentiles. If Paul were to preach his message of justification before God by faith in Jesus Christ to the Jew first and also to the Greek today, no doubt many Jewish listeners would be offended. Paul was maintaining that a Jew *as ethnic Jew* did not occupy a place of favor in God's sight apart from faith in Christ. One second-century Jewish Christian, who had seen the fruit that Paul's letters had in large measure produced in Gentile communities, did not hesitate to call him "the enemy man," an advocate of "lawlessness."[5]

Even as many Jews objected to Paul's insistence on faith in Jesus as the Jewish Messiah, Jewish priests at the Jerusalem temple undoubtedly did not appreciate being numbered among the "lost" by the members of the Qumran community on the shores of the Dead Sea, who had taken a similar approach toward their fellow ethnic Jews. They spoke of a "return to the Law of Moses" (1QS 5:7–9) in their writings. In joining the community, the covenanters vowed to take upon themselves not only the "revealed things" that would have been clear to everyone in Moses but also the "hidden things" that would have been clear only to the "sons of Zadok" within the sect (1QS 5:8–9). These "hidden things" were not simply concoctions of the community's imagination. Rather, they understood this revelation as having been embedded and preserved in the Scriptures all along. Now with the arrival of the Qumran community, God had seen fit to reveal the "hidden things" of the Law.[6] Since the Law, from the community's standpoint, had been fully revealed only to its members, only those within the Qumran community could fulfill the Law in all that it required.[7] This understanding of the Law as, in a certain respect, their own possession no doubt strengthened their sense of God's election. Members were to be examined on the basis of their observance of the Law.[8] Anyone who did not observe God's Law as they understood it would be destroyed.[9] Consequently, those outside the community were lost. Although God had established his covenant with the people of Israel, the rest of Israel had disobeyed God's Law and remained apostate. The covenanters were the sole rightful heirs of Israel's heritage. They were the faithful remnant of Israel.[10] They were

---

[5] *Let. Pet. Jas.* 2.3–5.

[6] God had entrusted to them the "hidden things" of his Law; Sanders, *Paul and Palestinian Judaism,* 317–18. On the distinction between the "revealed things" and the "hidden things," see also Wayne O. McCready, "A Second Torah at Qumran?" *SR* 14 (1985): 5–15.

[7] CD 14:8; 20:11, 29, 33; 1QSa 1:5–7; 1QS 1:7; 4:22; 5:10–12; 6:15; 9:17–21.

[8] 1QS 5:20–24; 6:14, 17.

[9] 1QH[a] 12 (=4):26–27; CD 2:6, 19–21; 1QS 5:10–13.

[10] Eckhard J. Schnabel, *Law and Wisdom from Ben Sira to Paul: A Tradition History Enquiry into the Relation of Law, Wisdom, and Ethics* (Tübingen: J. C. B. Mohr [Paul Siebeck], 1985), 175–77. The community was therefore structured along the biblical parameters for historical Israel. They were a community of priests, Levites, and Israelites (CD 3:21–4:4).

the elect.[11] At the end of the age, they would inherit the promises as the re-stored people of Israel. The rest of the Jews who adhered to the temple cult of their day would be marked for destruction. The Dead Sea community of-fers a prime example of sectarian rhetoric within first-century Judaism. As representatives of the true "Israel," they lashed out in polemical language against the majority of ethnic Jews. Such intense disagreement and great va-riety of perspectives have led scholars to suggest that the Judaism of the first century would be better characterized as "Judaisms." The Qumran commu-nity stood in the tradition of the Hebrew prophets, who likewise viewed their own people rather critically.

Even as the Dead Sea Scroll community represented a form of first-century Jewish thought that viewed itself as God's elect with its own distinc-tive approach to the Mosaic Law, so also was the case with the apostle Paul. Such sectarian rhetoric on behalf of the "true Israel," whether by the Qumran community or by Paul, needs to be distinguished as sharply as pos-sible from the darker chapters of history in the centuries and millennia to follow. To raise the specter of anti-Semitism in regard to the apostle Paul or fellow sectarians is largely anachronistic. Paul would have been appalled by the treatment of his fellow Jews over the course of time. He would have viewed the persecution of Jews as a flagrant violation of the Law of love ex-pressed in the Ten Commandments (Rom 13:8–10), worthy of God's con-demnation and punishment (Rom 2:6–11).

Paul's insistence that to be Jewish did not grant one membership in God's elect people, however, together with his stubborn demand for faith in Jesus as the Messiah, would have struck many of his own ethnic people as offensive. Many Jews would react similarly today. Is it possible for moderns to affirm the Pauline emphasis on Christ without at the same time affirming the Christian confession's "anti-Judaic left hand" for the vast majority of Jews who would disagree?[12] A German scholar, Günter Wasserberg, has re-flected on Rom 9—11 in the aftermath of the Shoah:

> In using Paul as a framework for their theology and reading him christo-logically—and exclusivistically—Augustine and Luther were, I believe, being true to what I have tried to outline as basic to his theology: Christ is a savior not only for the Gentiles, but also for the Jews. And that separates me from Paul. I do not regard Judaism as a deficient religion, although I am afraid that is exactly what is implicit and sometimes explicit in the New Testament. Therefore I fear that we have to admit that Paul, and the New Testament gen-erally, do not provide us with a paradigm that is useful or helpful for Jewish-Christian relations.

---

[11] E.g., 1QS 3:18–25; 11:7–8, 11; 1QH^a 6 (=14):12–13, 25–26; see for discus-sion Sanders, *Paul and Palestinian Judaism,* 257–70.

[12] "The character of anti-Judaic thinking in the Christian tradition cannot be correctly evaluated until it is seen as the negative side of its christological hermeneu-tic" (Ruether, *Faith and Fratricide,* 64).

As long as I move in Christian circles, I might perhaps feel at ease with a view of faith in Christ as savior of all and might wonder why Jews cannot see the advantages of Christianity. But as soon as I step outside and become aware of the synagogue, I come to the painful realization that not only is the New Testament perception of Jews negative and polemical but so too, by extension (or by our reading of it), is its view of Judaism today. I find that unacceptable. Jews are as much saved as are Christians, even as they are in as much need of God's love and forgiveness as are Christians. If we could perceive Judaism and Christianity as two different religious paradigms that are expressive of our human needs and strivings, I would be more at ease. But I fear that many Christians will not leave Jews in peace, because the Christian claim that Christ is the universal savior is directed also toward Jews. The Jewish "no" is a deep wound to the Christian soul. That wound contributed to what happened in Germany under National Socialism. And as long as we do not perceive the problematic and potentially explosive dynamics underlying Christian texts and discourse about Judaism, similar *Shoahs* may result. That is my fear. Maybe I am wrong. I hope I am wrong.[13]

If a modern Christian, unlike Wasserberg, maintains Paul's perspective as normative for his or her own personal worldview, then disagreement will be inevitable. If the Christian claims Paul's emphasis on faith in Christ as the sole means to salvation in the world to come, then such a Christian is as much at odds with a Jew who rejects Jesus as the Jewish Messiah as the Jewish Paul was at odds with his own brothers and sisters in the first century. May such disagreement be expressed with the mutual respect and humility that is required in this post-Shoah generation. As the Jewish scholar Daniel Boyarin has wisely written: "Paul certainly argued as a Jew for a fundamentally new interpretation of Judaism. There is nothing problematic in that. What Christians have to repent for is not Paul but the *Wirkungsgeschichte,* for which Paul is not (directly) responsible. Christians may hold any theology they wish, including supersessionism. (Why not? After all, biblical theology is supersessionist with respect to polytheists!) They just have to learn to let Jews live."[14]

A modern-day Jew who adopted Paul's message found the reaction from his Jewish peers no less vitriolic than the reaction the apostle seems to have experienced from his Jewish brothers and sisters in the first century. Moishe Rosen, founder of Jews for Jesus, told of such conflict in his spiritual autobiography. After attending a Yom Kippur service, Rosen encountered a Christian named Orville Freestone by chance at a bus stop. Freestone expressed interest in the Jewish holiday and asked Rosen if he believed his sins were forgiven. Not at all comfortable with the direction of the conversation,

---

[13] Wasserberg, "Romans 9–11 and Jewish-Christian Dialogue," 184–85.

[14] Daniel Boyarin, "Israel Reading in 'Reading Israel,' " in *Reading Israel in Romans: Legitimacy and Plausibility of Divergent Interpretations* (ed. Cristina Grenholm and Daniel Patte; Romans through History and Culture Series; Harrisburg, Pa.: Trinity Press International, 2000), 250.

Rosen nevertheless accepted Freestone's copy of the New Testament. Freestone was even conversant with the Hebrew Scriptures. Later that night Rosen reflected on the day's conversation and the New Testament on his dresser: "If I read that book, I might believe it. . . . And if I believe it, then I might believe in Christ. By believing in Christ, I will have become a Christian, according to what Orville said. And that means I will have joined the people who have persecuted us. It would amount to ethnic treason. My family would disown me, disinherit me. My friends would desert me. Other Jews would consider me a social outcast, a betrayer to my people."[15] Moishe Rosen did come to faith in Jesus as the Jewish Messiah. Subsequent events bore out his fears of that night. He goes on to narrate the conflict that his advocacy as a Jew for Christ has engendered among other Jews: "The problem we face is that not all rabbis and other Jewish leaders are willing to accept us as Jews."[16] He related how an Orthodox Jew who converted to Catholicism was denied Israeli citizenship under the law of return even though his mother was Jewish, the ordinary definition of a Jew. American Jewish leaders have vigorously opposed Rosen's group. He tells several stories of the Jewish Defense League's provocative tactics to confront, intimidate, distort, or silence the message of Jews for Jesus. For many Jews, adoption of faith in Jesus as the Messiah is tantamount to abandonment of one's Jewish identity. It is tantamount to abandoning family, ancestors, and heritage. It is an act of betrayal.

Although Paul ultimately held out hope for ethnic Israel, the christocentric focus of his hope will likely remain a stumbling block for Jewish readers. Whether or not the change that took place in Paul's life is described as a conversion, it initiated a radical departure from his former worldview. He adopted the aberrant position that ethnic Israel would not benefit from God's election or promises apart from faith in Jesus Christ. Should a Jew or Gentile follow Paul in his spiritual journey, a similar conversion would be necessary. But such a convert dare not proceed beyond faith in Christ to a presumptuous dismissal of ethnic Israel's place in God's plan. The apostle would excoriate any who do not recognize Jesus as the Messiah *of Israel*. "The gifts and the calling of God are irrevocable" (Rom 11:29).

---

[15] Moishe Rosen with William Proctor, *Jews for Jesus* (Old Tappan, N.J.: Fleming H. Revell, 1974), 23.

[16] Ibid., 95.

SELECT BIBLIOGRAPHY

Aageson, James W. "Scripture and Structure in the Development of the Argument in Romans 9–11." *Catholic Biblical Quarterly* 48 (1986): 265–89.

Achtemeier, Paul J. *The Quest for Unity in the New Testament Church.* Philadelphia: Fortress, 1987.

———. *Romans.* Interpretation: A Bible Commentary for Teaching and Preaching. Louisville: John Knox, 1985.

———. "Unsearchable Judgments and Inscrutable Ways: Reflections on the Discussion of Romans." Pages 521–34 in *SBL Seminar Papers, 1995.* Edited by Eugene H. Lovering Jr. Atlanta: Scholars Press, 1995. Repr. (with corrections), pages 3–21 of *Looking Back, Pressing On.* Edited by E. Elizabeth Johnson and David M. Hay. Vol. 4 of *Pauline Theology.* Society of Biblical Literature Symposium Series 4. Atlanta: Scholars Press, 1997.

Alexander, Philip S. "Torah and Salvation in Tannaitic Literature." Pages 261–301 in *The Complexities of Second Temple Judaism.* Vol. 1 of *Justification and Variegated Nomism.* Edited by D. A. Carson, Peter T. O'Brien, and Mark A. Siefrid. Grand Rapids: Baker, 2001.

Allison, Dale C., Jr. "The Background of Romans 11:11–15 in Apocalyptic and Rabbinic Literature." *Studia biblica et theologica* 10 (1980): 229–34.

———. "Romans 11:11–15: A Suggestion." *Perspectives in Religious Studies* 12 (1985): 23–30.

Alt, Albrecht. "The Origins of Israelite Law." *Essays on Old Testament History and Religion.* Oxford: Basil Blackwell, 1966.

Ashton, John. *The Religion of Paul the Apostle.* New Haven: Yale University Press, 2000.

Aus, Roger D. "Paul's Travel Plans to Spain and the 'Full Number of the Gentiles' in Rom. XI 25." *Novum Testamentum* 21 (1979): 232–62.

Avemarie, Friedrich. *Tora und Leben: Untersuchungen zur Heilsbedeutung der Tora in der frühen rabbinischen Literatur.* Texte und Studien zum antiken Judentum 55. Tübingen: J. C. B. Mohr (Paul Siebeck), 1996.

Bachmann, Michael. "4QMMT und Galaterbrief, התורה מעשי und ΕΡΓΑ ΝΟΜΟΥ." *Zeitschrift für die neutestamentliche Wissenschaft* 89 (1998): 91–113.

Bailey, Jon Nelson. "*Metanoia* in the Writings of Philo Judaeus." Pages 135–41 in *SBL Seminar Papers, 1991*. Edited by Eugene H. Lovering Jr. Atlanta: Scholars Press, 1991.

Barclay, John M. G. "Conflict in Thessalonica." *Catholic Biblical Quarterly* 55 (1993): 512–30.

———. "'Do We Undermine the Law?' A Study of Romans 14.1–15.6." Pages 287–308 in *Paul and the Mosaic Law*. Edited by James D. G. Dunn. Tübingen: J. C. B. Mohr (Paul Siebeck), 1996.

———. *Jews in the Mediterranean Diaspora: From Alexander to Trajan (323 B.C.E.–117 C.E.)*. Edinburgh: T&T Clark, 1996.

———. *Obeying the Truth: Paul's Ethics in Galatians*. Minneapolis: Fortress, 1988.

———. "Thessalonica and Corinth: Social Contrasts in Pauline Christianity." *Journal for the Study of the New Testament* 47 (1992): 49–74.

Barrett, C. K. *The Epistle to the Romans*. Black's New Testament Commentaries. London: Adam & Charles Black, 1957.

Barth, Markus. *The People of God*. Journal for the Study of the New Testament: Supplement Series 5. Sheffield, England: JSOT Press, 1983.

Bassler, Jouette M. *Divine Impartiality: Paul and a Theological Axiom*. Society of Biblical Literature Dissertation Series 59. Chico, Calif.: Scholars Press, 1982.

Battle, John A., Jr. "Paul's Use of the Old Testament in Romans 9:25–26." *Grace Theological Journal* 2 (1981): 115–29.

Bauckham, Richard. "Apocalypses." Pages 135–87 in *The Complexities of Second Temple Judaism*. Vol. 1 of *Justification and Variegated Nomism*. Edited by D. A. Carson, Peter T. O'Brien, and Mark A. Siefrid. Grand Rapids: Baker, 2001.

———. *God Crucified: Monotheism and Christology in the New Testament*. Grand Rapids: Eerdmans, 1998.

———. "James and the Gentiles." Pages 154–84 in *History, Literature, and Society in the Book of Acts*. Edited by Ben Witherington III. Cambridge: Cambridge University Press, 1996.

Baur, Ferdinand Christian. *Paul the Apostle of Jesus Christ: His Life and Work, His Epistles and His Doctrine*. Edited by Eduard Zeller. Translated by A. Menzies. 2 vols. 2d ed. London: Williams & Norgate, 1875–1876.

Bayes, Jonathan F. *The Weakness of the Law: God's Law and the Christian in New Testament Perspective*. Paternoster Biblical and Theological Monographs. Carlisle, England: Paternoster, 2000.

Beale, G. K. "Peace and Mercy upon the Israel of God: The Old Testament Background of Galatians 6,16b." *Biblica* 80 (1999): 204–23.

Bellefontaine, Elizabeth. "The Curses of Deuteronomy 27: Their Relationship to the Prohibitives." Pages 256–68 in *A Song of Power and the Power of Song*. Edited by Duane L. Christensen. Winona Lake, Ind.: Eisenbrauns, 1993.

Belleville, Linda L. "'Under Law': Structural Analysis and the Pauline Concept of Law in Galatians 3.21–4.11." *Journal for the Study of the New Testament* 26 (1986): 53–78.

Benko, Stephen. "The Edict of Claudius of A.D. 49 and the Instigator Chrestus." *Theologische Zeitschrift* 25 (1969): 406–18.

———. *Pagan Rome and the Early Christians.* Bloomington: Indiana University Press, 1984.

Best, Thomas F. "The Apostle Paul and E. P. Sanders: The Significance of Paul and Palestinian Judaism." *Restoration Quarterly* 25 (1982): 65–74.

Betz, Hans Dieter. *Galatians.* Hermeneia. Philadelphia: Fortress, 1979.

Bockmuehl, Markus. "1QS and Salvation at Qumran." Pages 381–414 in *The Complexities of Second Temple Judaism.* Vol. 1 of *Justification and Variegated Nomism.* Edited by D. A. Carson, Peter T. O'Brien, and Mark A. Siefrid. Grand Rapids: Baker, 2001.

Boers, Hendrikus. "The Form Critical Study of Paul's Letters: I Thessalonians as a Case Study." *New Testament Studies* 22 (1975–1976): 140–58.

Boyarin, Daniel. "Israel Reading in 'Reading Israel.'" Pages 246–50 in *Reading Israel in Romans: Legitimacy and Plausibility of Divergent Interpretations.* Edited by Cristina Grenholm and Daniel Patte. Romans through History and Culture Series. Harrisburg, Pa.: Trinity Press International, 2000.

———. *A Radical Jew: Paul and the Politics of Identity.* Berkeley: University of California Press, 1994.

Brändle, Rudolf, and Ekkehard W. Stegemann. "The Formation of the First 'Christian Congregations' in Rome in the Context of Jewish Congregations." Pages 117–27 in *Judaism and Christianity in First-Century Rome.* Edited by Karl P. Donfried and Peter Richardson. Grand Rapids: Eerdmans, 1998.

Broer, Ingo. "'Antisemitismus' und Judenpolemik im Neuen Testament— ein Beitrag zum besseren Verständnis von 1 Thess 2,14–16." *Biblische Notizen* 20 (1983): 59–91.

———. "'Der ganze Zorn ist schon über sie gekommen': Bemerkungen zur Interpolationshypothese und zur Interpretation von 1 Thess 2,14–16." Pages 137–59 in *The Thessalonian Correspondence.* Edited by Raymond F. Collins. Bibliotheca ephemeridum theologicarum lovaniensium 87. Leuven: Leuven University Press, 1990.

Brown, Raymond E. *The Semitic Background of the Term "Mystery" in the New Testament.* Facet Books, Biblical Series 12. Philadelphia: Fortress, 1968.

Brown, Raymond E., and John P. Meier. *Antioch and Rome: New Testament Cradles of Catholic Christianity.* New York: Paulist, 1983.

Bruce, F. F. "Christianity under Claudius." *Bulletin of the John Rylands Library* 44 (1961): 309–26.

Bultmann, Rudolf. *Theology of the New Testament.* Translated by Kendrick Grobel. 2 vols. New York: Charles Scribner's Sons, 1951–1955.

Byrne, Brendan. "The Problem of Νόμος and the Relationship with Judaism in Romans." *Catholic Biblical Quarterly* 62 (2000): 294–309.

———. *'Sons of God'— 'Seed of Abraham': A Study of the Idea of the Sonship of God of All Christians in Paul against the Jewish Background.* Analecta biblica 83. Rome: Biblical Institute Press, 1979.

Campbell, Douglas A. "Determining the Gospel through Rhetorical Analysis in Paul's Letter to the Roman Christians." Pages 315–36 in *Gospel in Paul: Studies on Corinthians, Galatians, and Romans for Richard N. Longenecker.* Edited by L. Ann Jervis and Peter Richardson. Journal for the Study of the New Testament: Supplement Series 108. Sheffield, England: Sheffield Academic Press, 1984.

Campbell, R. A. "'Against such things there is no law'? Galatians 5:23*b* Again." *Expository Times* 107 (1996): 271–72.

Campbell, William S. "Divergent Images of Paul and His Mission." Pages 187–211 in *Reading Israel in Romans: Legitimacy and Plausibility of Divergent Interpretations.* Edited by Cristina Grenholm and Daniel Patte. Romans through History and Culture Series. Harrisburg, Pa.: Trinity Press International, 2000.

———. *Paul's Gospel in an Intercultural Context: Jew and Gentile in the Letter to the Romans.* Studien zur interkulturellen Geschichte des Christentums 69. New York: Peter Lang, 1991.

———. "The Rule of Faith in Romans 12:1–15:13: The Obligation of Humble Obedience to Christ as the Only Adequate Response to the Mercies of God." Pages 259–86 in *Romans.* Edited by David M. Hay and E. Elizabeth Johnson. Vol. 3 of *Pauline Theology.* Minneapolis: Fortress, 1995.

———. "Salvation for Jews and Gentiles: Krister Stendahl and Paul's Letter to the Romans." Pages 65–72 in *Papers on Paul and Other New Testament Authors.* Vol. 3 of *Studia Biblica, 1978.* Edited by E. A Livingstone. Journal for the Study of the New Testament: Supplement Series 3. Sheffield, England: JSOT Press, 1980.

Caragounis, Chrys C. "From Obscurity to Prominence: The Development of the Roman Church between Romans and *1 Clement.*" Pages 245–79 in *Judaism and Christianity in First-Century Rome.* Edited by Karl P. Donfried and Peter Richardson. Grand Rapids: Eerdmans, 1998.

———. "Kingdom of God, Son of Man and Jesus' Self-Understanding." *Tyndale Bulletin* 40 (1989), 3–23, 223–38.

Carroll, James. *Constantine's Sword: The Church and the Jews—a History.* New York: Houghton Mifflin, 2001.

Carson, D. A. "Summaries and Conclusions." Pages 505–48 in *The Complexities of Second Temple Judaism.* Vol. 1 of *Justification and Variegated Nomism.* Edited by D. A. Carson, Peter T. O'Brien, and Mark A. Siefrid. Grand Rapids: Baker, 2001.

Clements, Ronald E. "'A Remnant Chosen by Grace' (Romans 11:5): The Old Testament Background and Origin of the Remnant Concept." Pages 106–21 in *Pauline Studies*. Edited by Donald A. Hagner and Murray J. Harris. Grand Rapids: Eerdmans, 1980.

Cohen, Naomi G. "The Jewish Dimension of Philo's Judaism—an Elucidation of de Spec. Leg. IV 132–150." *Journal of Jewish Studies* 38 (1987): 165–86.

Cohen, Shaye J. D. *The Beginnings of Jewishness: Boundaries, Varieties, Uncertainties*. Hellenistic Culture and Society 31. Berkeley: University of California Press, 1999.

Collins, John J., ed. *Apocalypse: The Morphology of a Genre*. Semeia 14. Missoula, Mont.: Scholars Press, 1979.

———. *Between Athens and Jerusalem: Jewish Identity in the Hellenistic Diaspora*. 2d ed. Grand Rapids: Eerdmans, 2000.

Collins, Raymond F. "Apropos the Integrity of 1 Thess." *Ephemerides theologicae lovanienses* 65 (1979): 67–106. Repr., pages 96–135 in *Studies on the First Letter to the Thessalonians*. Leuven: Leuven University Press, 1984.

Cooperman, Alan. "Catholics No Longer Out to Convert Jews." *Houston Chronicle*. August 18, 2002, 4A.

Coppens, J. "Miscellanées bibliques, LXXX: Une diatribe antijuive dans I Thess., II, 13–16." *Ephemerides theologicae lovanienses* 51 (1975): 90–95.

Cosgrove, Charles H. *The Cross and the Spirit: A Study in the Argument and Theology of Galatians*. Macon, Ga.: Mercer University Press, 1988.

———. *The Elusive Israel: The Puzzle of Election in Romans*. Louisville: Westminster John Knox, 1997.

———. "Rhetorical Suspense in Romans 9–11: A Study in Polyvalence and Hermeneutical Election." *Journal of Biblical Literature* 115 (1996): 271–87.

Cousar, Charles B. *Galatians*. Interpretation: A Bible Commentary for Teaching and Preaching. Louisville: John Knox, 1982.

———. *A Theology of the Cross: The Death of Jesus in the Pauline Letters*. Overtures to Biblical Theology. Minneapolis: Fortress, 1990.

Cranfield, C. E. B. *A Critical and Exegetical Commentary on the Epistle to the Romans*. 2 vols. International Critical Commentary. Edinburgh: T&T Clark, 1975–1979.

Cranford, Michael. "Abraham in Romans 4: The Father of All Who Believe." *New Testament Studies* 41 (1995): 71–88.

———. "Election and Ethnicity: Paul's View of Israel in Romans 9.1–13." *Journal for the Study of the New Testament* 50 (1993): 27–41.

———. "The Possibility of Perfect Obedience: Paul and an Implied Premise in Galatians 3:10 and 5:3." *Novum Testamentum* 36 (1994): 242–58.

Dahl, Nils A. "Euodia and Syntyche and Paul's Letter to the Philippians." Pages 3–15 in *The Social World of the First Christians: Essays in Honor of*

Wayne A. Meeks. Edited by L. Michael White and O. Larry Yarbrough. Minneapolis: Fortress, 1995.

———. "The Future of Israel." Pages 137–58 in *Studies in Paul.* Minneapolis: Augsburg, 1977.

Das, A. Andrew. "Another Look at ἐὰν μή in Galatians 2:16." *Journal of Biblical Literature* 119 (2000): 529–39.

———. "Oneness in Christ: The *nexus indivulsus* between Justification and Sanctification in Paul's Letter to the Galatians." *Concordia Journal* 21 (1995): 173–86.

———. *Paul, the Law, and the Covenant.* Peabody, Mass.: Hendrickson, 2001.

Davies, Philip R. "Didactic Stories." Pages 99–133 in *The Complexities of Second Temple Judaism.* Vol. 1 of *Justification and Variegated Nomism.* Edited by D. A. Carson, Peter T. O'Brien, and Mark A. Siefrid. Grand Rapids: Baker, 2001.

Davies, W. D. *The Setting of the Sermon on the Mount.* Cambridge: Cambridge University Press, 1964.

———. *The Torah in the Messianic Age and/or the Age to Come.* Journal of Biblical Literature Monograph Series 7. Philadelphia: Society of Biblical Literature, 1952.

Deines, Roland. "The Pharisees Between 'Judaism' and 'Common Judaism.'" Pages 443–504 in *The Complexities of Second Temple Judaism.* Vol. 1 of *Justification and Variegated Nomism.* Edited by D. A. Carson, Peter T. O'Brien, and Mark A. Siefrid. Grand Rapids: Baker, 2001.

Dodd, C. H. "Ἔννομος Χριστοῦ." Pages 134–48 in *More New Testament Studies.* Grand Rapids: Eerdmans, 1968. Repr. from *Studia Paulina, in honorem Johannis de Zwaan septuagenarii* (Bohn: Haarlem, 1953).

———. "The Law of Christ." Pages 64–83 in *Gospel and Law: The Relation of Faith and Ethics in Early Christianity.* New York: Columbia University Press, 1951.

Donaldson, Terence L. "The 'Curse of the Law' and the Inclusion of the Gentiles: Galatians 3.13–14." *New Testament Studies* 32 (1986): 94–112.

———. *Paul and the Gentiles: Remapping the Apostle's Convictional World.* Minneapolis: Fortress, 1997.

Donfried, Karl P. "Paul and Judaism: I Thessalonians 2:13–16 as a Test Case." *Interpretation* 38 (1984): 242–53.

———. "A Short Note on Romans 16." Pages 44–52 in *The Romans Debate.* Edited by Karl P. Donfried. Rev. ed. Peabody, Mass.: Hendrickson, 1991.

Donfried, Karl P., and Johannes Beutler, eds. *The Thessalonians Debate: Methodological Discord or Methodological Synthesis?* Grand Rapids: Eerdmans, 2000.

Dunn, James D. G. "4QMMT and Galatians." *New Testament Studies* 43 (1997): 147–53.

———. *The Epistle to the Galatians.* Black's New Testament Commentaries 9. Peabody, Mass.: Hendrickson, 1993.

————. *Jesus, Paul, and the Law: Studies in Mark and Galatians.* Louisville: Westminster John Knox, 1990.

————. " 'The Law of Faith,' 'the Law of the Spirit,' and 'the Law of Christ.' " Pages 62–82 in *Theology and Ethics in Paul and His Interpreters.* Edited by Eugene H. Lovering Jr. and Jerry L. Sumney. Nashville: Abingdon, 1996.

————. "Paul and Justification by Faith," Pages 85–101 in *The Road from Damascus: The Impact of Paul's Conversion on His Life, Thought, and Ministry.* Edited by Richard N. Longenecker. Grand Rapids: Eerdmans, 1997.

————. *Romans 1–8.* Word Biblical Commentary 38A. Dallas: Word, 1988.

————. *Romans 9–16.* Word Biblical Commentary 38B. Dallas: Word, 1988.

————. *The Theology of Paul the Apostle.* Grand Rapids: Eerdmans, 1998.

————. *The Theology of Paul's Letter to the Galatians.* Cambridge: Cambridge University Press, 1993.

————. "What Was the Issue between Paul and 'Those of the Circumcision'?" Pages 295–317 in *Paulus und das antike Judentum.* Edited by Martin Hengel and Ulrich Heckel. Tübingen: J. C. B. Mohr (Paul Siebeck), 1991.

————. "Whatever Happened to Exegesis? In Response to the Reviews by R. B. Matlock and D. A. Campbell." *Journal for the Study of the New Testament* 72 (1998): 113–20.

————. "Yet Once More—'the Works of the Law': A Response." *Journal for the Study of the New Testament* 46 (1992): 99–117.

Eastman, Susan. "The Evil Eye and the Curse of the Law: Galatians 3.1 Revisited." *Journal for the Study of the New Testament* 83 (2001): 69–87.

————. "Whose Apocalypse? The Identity of the Sons of God in Romans 8:19." *Journal of Biblical Literature* 121 (2002): 263–77.

Eckart, Karl-Gottfried. "Der zweite echte Brief des Apostels Paulus an die Thessalonicher." *Zeitschrift für Theologie und Kirche* 58 (1961): 30–44.

Elliott, Neil. *The Rhetoric of Romans: Argumentative Constraint and Strategy and Paul's Dialogue with Judaism.* Journal for the Study of the New Testament: Supplement Series 45. Sheffield, England: Sheffield Academic Press, 1990.

Elliott, Susan M. "Choose Your Mother, Choose Your Master: Galatians 4:21–5:1 in the Shadow of the Anatolian Mother of the Gods." *Journal of Biblical Literature* 118 (1999): 661–83.

Enns, Peter. "Expansions of Scripture." Pages 73–98 in *The Complexities of Second Temple Judaism.* Vol. 1 of *Justification and Variegated Nomism.* Edited by D. A. Carson, Peter T. O'Brien, and Mark A. Siefrid. Grand Rapids: Baker, 2001.

Eskola, Timo. "*Avodat Israel* and the 'Works of the Law' in Paul." Pages 175–97 in *From the Ancient Sites of Israel: Essays on Archaeology, History, and Theology.* Edited by T. Eskola and E. Junkaala. Helsinki: Theological Institute of Finland, 1998.

————. "Paul, Predestination, and 'Covenantal Nomism'—Reassessing Paul and Palestinian Judaism." *Journal for the Study of Judaism* 28 (1997): 390–412.

Esler, Philip F. *Galatians.* New Testament Readings. London: Routledge, 1998.

Evans, Craig A. "Scripture-Based Stories in the Pseudepigrapha." Pages 57–72 in *The Complexities of Second Temple Judaism.* Vol. 1 of *Justification and Variegated Nomism.* Edited by D. A. Carson, Peter T. O'Brien, and Mark A. Siefrid. Grand Rapids: Baker, 2001.

Falk, Daniel. "Prayers and Psalms." Pages 7–56 in *The Complexities of Second Temple Judaism.* Vol. 1 of *Justification and Variegated Nomism.* Edited by D. A. Carson, Peter T. O'Brien, and Mark A. Siefrid. Grand Rapids: Baker, 2001.

Fitzmyer, Joseph A. "Paul's Jewish Background and the Deeds of the Law." Pages 18–35 in *According to Paul: Studies in the Theology of the Apostle.* Mahwah, N.J.: Paulist, 1993.

———. *Romans.* Anchor Bible 33. New York: Doubleday, 1993.

Forbes, Chris. "Paul's Principalities and Powers: Demythologizing Apocalyptic?" *Journal for the Study of the New Testament* 82 (2001): 61–88.

———. "Pauline Demonology and/or Cosmology? Principalities, Powers, and the Elements of the World in Their Hellenistic Context." *Journal for the Study of the New Testament* 85 (2002): 51–73.

Friedrich, Gerhard. "Das Gesetz des Glaubens Röm. 3,27." *Theologische Zeitschrift* 10 (1954): 401–17.

Gager, John G. *The Origins of Anti-Semitism: Attitudes toward Judaism in Pagan and Christian Antiquity.* Oxford: Oxford University Press, 1983.

———. *Reinventing Paul.* Oxford: Oxford University Press, 2000.

Gagnon, Robert A. J. *The Bible and Homosexual Practice: Texts and Hermeneutics.* Nashville: Abingdon, 2001.

———. "Why the 'Weak' at Rome Cannot Be Non-Christian Jews." *Catholic Biblical Quarterly* 62 (2000): 64–82.

Gamble, Harry, Jr. *The Textual History of the Letter to the Romans: A Study in Textual and Literary Criticism.* Studies and Documents 42. Grand Rapids: Eerdmans, 1977.

Garland, David E. "Composition and Unity of Philippians." *Novum Testamentum* 27 (1985): 141–73.

Gaston, Lloyd. "Israel's Enemies in Pauline Theology." *New Testament Studies* 28 (1982): 400–423.

———. *Paul and the Torah.* Vancouver: University of British Columbia Press, 1987.

Given, Mark D. *Paul's True Rhetoric: Ambiguity, Cunning, and Deception in Greece and Rome.* Emory Studies in Early Christianity 7. Harrisburg, Pa.: Trinity Press International, 2001.

Glad, Clarence E. *Paul and Philodemus: Adaptability in Epicurean and Early Christian Psychagogy.* Novum Testamentum Supplements 81. Leiden: E. J. Brill, 1995.

Goodman, Martin. *Mission and Conversion: Proselytizing in the Religious History of the Roman Empire.* Oxford: Oxford University Press, 1994.

Gordon, T. David. "A Short Note on ΠΑΙΔΑΓΩΓΟΣ in Galatians 3.24–25." *New Testament Studies* 35 (1989): 150–54.

Gowan, Donald E. "Wisdom." Pages 215–39 in *The Complexities of Second Temple Judaism*. Vol. 1 of *Justification and Variegated Nomism*. Edited by D. A. Carson, Peter T. O'Brien, and Mark A. Siefrid. Grand Rapids: Baker, 2001.

Gräßer, Erich. "Zwei Heilswege? Zum theologischen Verhältnis von Israel und Kirche." Pages 411–29 in *Kontinuität und Einheit: Für Franz Mußner*. Edited by Paul-Gerhard Müller and Werner Stenger. Freiburg: Herder, 1981.

Grindheim, Sigurd. "The Law Kills but the Gospel Gives Life: The Letter-Spirit Dualism in 2 Corinthians 3.5–18." *Journal for the Study of the New Testament* 84 (2001): 97–115.

Grobel, Kendrick. "A Chiastic Retribution-Formula in Romans 2." Pages 255–61 in *Zeit und Geschichte: Dankesgabe an Rudolf Bultmann zum 80. Geburtstag*. Edited by Erich Dinkler. Tübingen: J. C. B. Mohr (Paul Siebeck), 1964.

Hafemann, Scott J. *Paul, Moses, and the History of Israel*. Wissenschaftliche Untersuchungen zum Neuen Testament 81. Tübingen: J. C. B. Mohr (Paul Siebeck), 1995.

———. "The Salvation of Israel in Romans 11:25–32: A Response to Krister Stendahl." *Ex auditu* 4 (1988): 38–58.

Hagner, Donald A. "Paul and Judaism: Testing the New Perspective." Pages 75–105 in *Revisiting Paul's Doctrine of Justification: A Challenge to the New Perspective*, by Peter Stuhlmacher. Downers Grove, Ill.: InterVarsity, 2001. Revised version of "Paul and Judaism: Testing the New Perspective." *Bulletin for Biblical Research* 3 (1993): 111–30.

Hahn, Ferdinand. "Zum Verständnis von Römer 11.26a: ' . . . Und so wird ganz Israel gerettet werden.'" Pages 221–36 in *Paul and Paulinism: Essays in Honour of C. K. Barrett*. Edited by M. D. Hooker and S. G. Wilson. London: SPCK, 1982.

Hall, Robert G. "Arguing Like an Apocalypse: Galatians and an Ancient *Topos* outside the Greco-Roman Rhetorical Tradition." *New Testament Studies* 42 (1996): 434–53.

Harris, Murray J. *Jesus as God: The New Testament Use of Theos in Reference to Jesus*. Grand Rapids: Baker, 1992.

Harvey, John D. *Listening to the Text: Oral Patterning in Paul's Letters*. Evangelical Theological Society Studies. Grand Rapids: Baker, 1998.

Hasel, Gerhard F. *The Remnant: The History and Theology of the Remnant Idea from Genesis to Isaiah*. Berrien Springs, Mich.: Andrews University Press, 1972.

Hay, David M. "Philo of Alexandria." Pages 357–79 in *The Complexities of Second Temple Judaism*. Vol. 1 of *Justification and Variegated Nomism*. Edited by D. A. Carson, Peter T. O'Brien, and Mark A. Siefrid. Grand Rapids: Baker, 2001.

Hays, Richard B. *Echoes of Scripture in the Letters of Paul.* New Haven: Yale University Press, 1989.

———. *The Faith of Jesus Christ: The Narrative Substructure of Galatians 3:1–4:11.* 2d ed. Grand Rapids: Eerdmans, 2001.

———. "Have We Found Abraham to Be Our Forefather according to the Flesh? A Reconsideration of Rom 4:1." *Novum Testamentum* 27 (1985): 76–98.

———. *The Moral Vision of the New Testament: A Contemporary Introduction to New Testament Ethics.* New York: HarperCollins, 1996.

———. Review of J. Louis Martyn, *Galatians. Review of Biblical Literature* 3 (2001): 59–65.

Hemer, Colin J. *The Book of Acts in the Setting of Hellenistic History.* Edited by Conrad H. Gempf. Winona Lake, Ind.: Eisenbrauns, 1990.

Hennecke, Edgar, and Wilhelm Schneemelcher, eds. *New Testament Apocrypha.* Translated by R. McL. Wilson. 2 vols. Rev. ed. Louisville: Westminster John Knox, 1989.

Hillerbrand, Hans J. "Martin Luther and the Jews." Pages 127–50 in *Jews and Christians: Exploring the Past, Present, and Future.* Edited by James H. Charlesworth. New York: Crossroad, 1990.

Hoerber, Robert G. "The Decree of Claudius in Acts 18:2." *Concordia Theological Monthly* 31 (1960): 690–94.

———. "Galatians 2:1–10 and the Acts of the Apostles." Pages 12–21 in *Studies in the New Testament.* Cleveland: Biblion, 1991.

Hofius, Otfried. "Das Evangelium und Israel: Erwägungen zu Römer 9–11." *Zeitschrift für Theologie und Kirche* 83 (1986): 297–324.

———. "Das Gesetz des Mose und das Gesetz Christi." *Zeitschrift für Theologie und Kirche* 80 (1983): 262–86.

Holtz, Traugott. "The Question of the Content of Paul's Instructions." Pages 51–71 in *Understanding Paul's Ethics: Twentieth-Century Approaches.* Edited by Brian S. Rosner. Grand Rapids: Eerdmans, 1995. Translation of "Zur Frage der inhaltlichen Weisungen bei Paulus." *Theologische Literaturzeitung* 106 (1981): 385–400.

Holwerda, David E. *Jesus and Israel: One Covenant or Two?* Grand Rapids: Eerdmans, 1995.

Hong, In-Gyu. "Does Paul Misrepresent the Jewish Law? Law and Covenant in Gal. 3:1–14." *Novum Testamentum* 36 (1994): 164–82.

———. *The Law in Galatians.* Journal for the Study of the New Testament: Supplement Series 81. Sheffield, England: JSOT Press, 1993.

Horne, Charles M. "The Meaning of the Phrase 'And Thus All Israel Will Be Saved' (Romans 11:26)." *Journal of the Evangelical Theological Society* 21 (1978): 329–34.

Horst, Pieter W. van der. " 'Only Then Will All Israel Be Saved': A Short Note on the Meaning of καὶ οὕτως in Romans 11:26." *Journal of Biblical Literature* 119 (2000): 521–25.

Howard, George. "The Beginnings of Christianity in Rome: A Note on Suetonius, Life of Claudius XXV.4." *Restoration Quarterly* 24 (1981): 175–77.

———. *Paul—Crisis in Galatia: A Study in Early Christian Theology.* 2d ed. Cambridge: Cambridge University Press, 1990.

Hübner, Hans. *Law in Paul's Thought.* Translated by James C. G. Greig. Edinburgh: T&T Clark, 1984.

Hurd, John C. "Paul ahead of His Time: 1 Thess. 2:13–16." Pages 21–36 in *Paul and the Gospels.* Vol. 1 of *Anti-Judaism in Early Christianity.* Edited by Peter Richardson with David Granskou. Waterloo, Ont.: Wilfrid Laurier University Press, 1986.

Hvalvik, Reidar. "A 'Sonderweg' for Israel: A Critical Examination of a Current Interpretation of Romans 11.25–27." *Journal for the Study of the New Testament* 39 (1990): 87–107.

Jaubert, Annie. *La notion d'alliance dans le judaïsme: Aux abords de l'ère chrétienne.* Patristica sorbonensia 6. Paris: Cerf (Editions du Seuil), 1963.

Jeffers, James S. *Conflict at Rome: Social Order and Hierarchy in Early Christianity.* Minneapolis: Fortress, 1991.

Jewett, Robert. *The Thessalonian Correspondence: Pauline Rhetoric and Millenarian Piety.* Foundations and Facets: New Testament. Philadelphia: Fortress, 1986.

Johnson, Dan. "The Structure and Meaning of Romans 11." *Catholic Biblical Quarterly* 46 (1984): 91–103.

Johnson, E. Elizabeth. *The Function of Apocalyptic and Wisdom Traditions in Romans 9–11.* Society of Biblical Literature Dissertation Series 109. Atlanta: Scholars Press, 1989.

Josephus. Translated by H. St. J. Thackeray et al. 10 vols. Loeb Classical Library. Cambridge: Harvard University Press, 1926–1965.

Judge, E. A. "The Origin of the Church at Rome: A New Solution?" *Reformed Theological Review* 25 (1966): 81–94.

Keck, Leander E. "Christology, Soteriology, and the Praise of God (Romans 15:7–13)." Pages 85–97 in *The Conversation Continues: Studies in Paul and John in Honor of J. Louis Martyn.* Edited by Robert T. Fortna and Beverly R. Gaventa. Nashville: Abingdon, 1990.

Kim, Seyoon. *Paul and the New Perspective: Second Thoughts on the Origin of Paul's Gospel.* Grand Rapids: Eerdmans, 2002.

Kjær-Hansen, Kai. "The Problem of Two-Covenant Theology." *Mishkan* 21 (1994): 52–81.

Kugler, Robert A. "Testaments." Pages 189–213 in *The Complexities of Second Temple Judaism.* Vol. 1 of *Justification and Variegated Nomism.* Edited by D. A. Carson, Peter T. O'Brien, and Mark A. Siefrid. Grand Rapids: Baker, 2001.

Laato, Timo. *Paul and Judaism: An Anthropological Approach.* Translated by T. McElwain. South Florida Studies in the History of Judaism 115. Atlanta: Scholars Press, 1995.

Lake, Kirsopp. "The Chronology of Acts." Pages 445–74 in vol. 5 of *The Acts of the Apostles.* Part 1 of *The Beginnings of Christianity.* Edited by F. J. Foakes Jackson and Kirsopp Lake. Grand Rapids: Baker, 1979.

Lambrecht, Jan. "Man before and without Christ: Rom 7 and Pauline Anthropology." *Louvain Studies* 5 (1974/1975): 18–33.

———. "Paul's Lack of Logic in Romans 9,1–13: A Response to M. Cranford's 'Election and Ethnicity.'" Pages 55–60 in *Pauline Studies.* Leuven: Leuven University Press, 1994.

———. "Why Is Boasting Excluded? A Note On Rom 3,27 and 4,2." *Ephemerides theologicae lovanienses* 61 (1985): 365–69.

Lambrecht, Jan, and Richard W. Thompson. *Justification by Faith: The Implications of Romans 3:27–31.* Zacchaeus Studies. Wilmington, Del.: Michael Glazier, 1989.

Lampe, Peter. "The Roman Christians of Romans 16." Pages 216–30 in *The Romans Debate.* Edited by Karl P. Donfried. Rev. ed. Peabody, Mass.: Hendrickson, 1991.

Lane, William L. *Hebrews 1–8.* Word Biblical Commentary 47. Dallas: Word Books, 1991.

———. "Social Perspectives on Roman Christianity during the Formative Years from Nero to Nerva: Romans, Hebrews, *1 Clement.*" Pages 196–244 in *Judaism and Christianity in First-Century Rome.* Edited by Karl P. Donfried and Peter Richardson. Grand Rapids: Eerdmans, 1998.

Lenski, R. C. H. *The Interpretation of St. Paul's Epistle to the Romans.* Lutheran Book Concern, 1936. Repr., Peabody, Mass.: Hendrickson, 2001.

Leon, Harry J. *The Jews of Ancient Rome.* Rev. ed. Peabody, Mass.: Hendrickson, 1995.

Levinskaya, Irina. *The Book of Acts in Its Diaspora Setting.* Vol. 5 of *The Book of Acts in Its First Century Setting.* Edited by Bruce W. Winter. Grand Rapids: Eerdmans, 1996.

Lietzmann, Hans. *An die Korinther I.II.* 5th ed. Handbuch zum Neuen Testament 9. Tübingen: J. C. B. Mohr (Paul Siebeck), 1969.

Lohse, Eduard. "Ὁ νόμος τοῦ πνεύματος τῆς ζωῆς: Exegetische Anmerkungen zu Röm 8,2." Pages 279–87 in *Neues Testament und christliche Existenz: Festschrift für Herbert Braun zum 70. Geburtstag am 4. Mai 1973.* Edited by Hans Dieter Betz and Luise Schottroff. Tübingen: J. C. B. Mohr (Paul Siebeck), 1973.

Longenecker, Bruce W. "Different Answers to Different Issues: Israel, the Gentiles, and Salvation History in Romans 9–11." *Journal for the Study of the New Testament* 36 (1989): 95–123.

———. *Eschatology and the Covenant: A Comparison of 4 Ezra and Romans 1–11.* Journal for the Study of the New Testament: Supplement Series 57; Sheffield, England: JSOT Press, 1991.

———. *The Triumph of Abraham's God: The Transformation of Identity in Galatians.* Nashville: Abingdon, 1998.

Longenecker, Richard N. *Galatians.* Word Biblical Commentary 41. Dallas: Word, 1990.

Lull, David J. "'The Law Was Our Pedagogue': A Study in Galatians 3:19–25." *Journal of Biblical Literature* 105 (1986): 481–98.

Luther, Martin. "On the Jews and Their Lies, 1543." Pages 137–306 in vol. 47 of *Luther's Works.* Philadelphia: Fortress, 1971.

Lutjens, Ronald. "'You Do Not Do What You Want': What Does Galatians 5:17 Really Mean?" *Presbyterion* 16, no. 2 (1990): 103–17.

Lyons, George. *Pauline Autobiography: Toward a New Understanding.* Society of Biblical Literature Dissertation Series 73. Atlanta: Scholars Press, 1985.

Macmullen, Ramsay. *Enemies of the Roman Order: Treason, Unrest, and Alienation in the Empire.* Cambridge: Harvard University Press, 1966.

Malherbe, Abraham J. *The Letters to the Thessalonians.* Anchor Bible 32B. New York: Doubleday, 2000.

Marcus, Joel. "'Under the Law': The Background of a Pauline Expression." *Catholic Biblical Quarterly* 63 (2001): 72–83.

Marshall, I. Howard. *1 and 2 Thessalonians.* New Century Bible Commentary. Grand Rapids: Eerdmans, 1983.

Martin, Troy. "Apostasy to Paganism: The Rhetorical Stasis of the Galatian Controversy." *Journal of Biblical Literature* 114 (1995): 437–61.

———. "Whose Flesh? What Temptation? (Galatians 4.13–14)." *Journal for the Study of the New Testament* 74 (1999): 87–89.

Martyn, J. Louis. "Apocalyptic Antinomies in Paul's Letter to the Galatians." *New Testament Studies* 31 (1985): 410–24.

———. "Covenant, Christ, and Church in Galatians." Pages 137–51 in *The Future of Christology: Essays in Honor of Leander E. Keck.* Edited by Abraham J. Malherbe and Wayne A. Meeks. Minneapolis: Fortress, 1993.

———. "The Covenants of Hagar and Sarah: Two Covenants and Two Gentile Missions." Pages 160–92 in *Faith and History: Essays in Honor of Paul W. Meyer.* Edited by John T. Carroll, Charles H. Cosgrove, and E. Elizabeth Johnson. Atlanta: Scholars Press, 1990. Repr., pages 191–208 in *Theological Issues in the Letters of Paul.* Nashville: Abingdon, 1997.

———. *Galatians.* Anchor Bible 33A. New York: Doubleday, 1997.

Mason, Steve. "'For I Am Not Ashamed of the Gospel' (Rom. 1.16): The Gospel and the First Readers of Romans." Pages 254–87 in *Gospel in Paul: Studies on Corinthians, Galatians, and Romans for Richard N. Longenecker.* Edited by L. Ann Jervis and Peter Richardson. Journal for the Study of the New Testament: Supplement Series 108. Sheffield, England: Sheffield Academic Press, 1994.

———. *Josephus and the New Testament.* 2d ed. Peabody, Mass.: Hendrickson, 2003.

———. "Paul, Classical Anti-Jewish Polemic, and the Letter to the Romans." Pages 181–223 in *Self-Definition and Self-Discovery in Early Christianity:*

A Study in Changing Horizons. Edited by David J. Hawkin and Tom Robinson. Studies in the Bible and Early Christianity 26. Lewiston, N.Y.: Edwin Mellen, 1990.

Matera, Frank J. "The Culmination of Paul's Argument to the Galatians: Gal. 5.1–6.17." *Journal for the Study of the New Testament* 32 (1988): 79–91.

Matlock, R. Barry. "Almost Cultural Studies? Reflections on the 'New Perspective' on Paul." Pages 433–59 in *Biblical Studies/Cultural Studies: The Third Sheffield Colloquium.* Edited by J. Cheryl Exum and Stephen D. Moore. Sheffield, England: Sheffield Academic Press, 1998.

———. "'Even the Demons Believe': Paul and πίστις Χριστοῦ." *Catholic Biblical Quarterly* 64 (2002): 300–18.

———. "Sins of the Flesh and Suspicious Minds: Dunn's New Theology of Paul." *Journal for the Study of the New Testament* 72 (1988): 67–90.

McKnight, Scot. *A Light among the Gentiles: Jewish Missionary Activity in the Second Temple Period.* Minneapolis: Fortress, 1991.

McLean, Bradley H. "Galatians 2.7–9 and the Recognition of Paul's Apostolic Status at the Jerusalem Conference: A Critique of G. Luedemann's Solution." *New Testament Studies* 37 (1991): 67–76.

McNamara, Martin. "Some Targum Themes." Pages 303–56 in *The Complexities of Second Temple Judaism.* Vol. 1 of *Justification and Variegated Nomism.* Edited by D. A. Carson, Peter T. O'Brien, and Mark A. Siefrid. Grand Rapids: Baker, 2001.

McCready, Wayne O. "A second Torah at Qumran?" *Studies in Religion* 14 (1985): 5–15.

Meeks, Wayne A. "The Circle of Reference in Pauline Morality." Pages 305–17 in *Greeks, Romans, and Christians: Essays in Honor of Abraham J. Malherbe.* Edited by David L. Balch, Everett Ferguson, and Wayne A. Meeks. Minneapolis: Fortress, 1990.

———. "Judgment and the Brother: Romans 14:1–15:13." Pages 290–300 in *Tradition and Interpretation in the New Testament.* Edited by Gerald F. Hawthorne and Otto Betz. Grand Rapids: Eerdmans, 1987.

Merkle, Ben L. "Romans 11 and the Future of Ethnic Israel." *Journal of the Evangelical Theological Society* 43 (2000): 709–21.

Metzger, Bruce. "The Punctuation of Romans 9:5." Pages 95–112 in *Christ and the Spirit in the New Testament.* Edited by Barnabas Lindars and Stephen S. Smalley. Cambridge: Cambridge University Press, 1973.

Meyer, Paul W. "Romans." Pages 1130–67 in *Harper's Bible Commentary.* Edited by James L. Mays. San Francisco: Harper & Row, 1988.

———. "Romans 10:4 and the 'End' of the Law." Pages 59–78 in *The Divine Helmsman: Studies in God's Control of Human Events, Presented to Lou H. Silberman.* Edited by James L. Crenshaw and Samuel Sandmel. New York: Ktav, 1980.

———. "The Worm at the Core of the Apple: Exegetical Reflections on Romans 7." Pages 62–84 in *The Conversation Continues: Essays in Paul &*

John in Honor of J. Louis Martyn. Edited by Robert T. Fortna and Beverly R. Gaventa. Nashville: Abingdon, 1990.

Miller, James C. *The Obedience of Faith, the Eschatological People of God, and the Purpose of Romans*. Society of Biblical Literature Dissertation Series 177. Atlanta: Society of Biblical Literature, 2000.

Mitchell, Margaret M. *Paul and the Rhetoric of Reconciliation: An Exegetical Investigation of the Language and Composition of 1 Corinthians*. Louisville: Westminster John Knox, 1991.

Moloney, Francis J. "Telling God's Story: The Fourth Gospel." Pages 107–22 in *The Forgotten God: Perspectives in Biblical Theology*. Edited by A. Andrew Das and Frank J. Matera. Louisville: Westminster John Knox, 2002.

Moo, Douglas J. *The Epistle to the Romans*. New International Commentary on the New Testament. Grand Rapids: Eerdmans, 1996.

———. "Israel and Paul in Romans 7.7–12." *New Testament Studies* 32 (1986): 122–35.

Moore, George Foot. "Christian Writers on Judaism." *Harvard Theological Review* 14 (1921): 197–254.

———. *Judaism in the First Centuries of the Christian Era: The Age of the Tannaim*. 3 vols. Cambridge: Harvard University Press, 1927. Repr. 2 vols. Peabody, Mass.: Hendrickson, 1997.

Moule, C. F. D. *An Idiom Book of New Testament Greek*. Cambridge: Cambridge University Press, 1959.

———. "Justification in Its Relation to the condition κατὰ πνεῦμα (Rom. 8:1–11)." Pages 177–87 in *Battesimo e Giustizia in Rom 6 e 8*. Edited by L. de Lorenzi. Rome: St. Paul Abbey, 1974.

Munck, Johannes. *Christ & Israel: An Interpretation oj Romans 9–11*. Philadelphia: Fortress, 1967.

Murphy-O'Connor, Jerome. "Paul and Gallio." *Journal of Biblical Literature* 112 (1993): 315–17.

Mußner, Franz. "'Ganz Israel wird gerettet werden' (Röm 11,26)." *Kairos* 18 (1976): 241–55.

———. "Heil für Alle: Der Grundgedanke des Römerbriefs." *Kairos* 23 (1981): 207–14.

———. *Die Kraft der Wurzel: Judentum–Jesus–Kirche*. Freiburg: Herder, 1989.

———. *Tractate on the Jews: The Significance of Judaism for Christian Faith*. Translated by Leonard Swidler. Philadelphia: Fortress, 1984.

Nanos, Mark D. "Challenging the Limits That Continue to Define Paul's Perspective on Jews and Judaism." Pages 212–24 in *Reading Israel in Romans: Legitimacy and Plausibility of Divergent Interpretations*. Edited by Cristina Grenholm and Daniel Patte. Romans through History and Culture Series. Harrisburg, Pa.: Trinity Press International, 2000.

———. "The Inter- and Intra-Jewish Political Context of Paul's Letter to the Galatians." Pages 146–59 in *Paul and Politics: Ekklesia, Israel, Imperium,*

Interpretation. Edited by Richard A. Horsley. Harrisburg, Pa.: Trinity Press International, 2000.

———. *The Irony of Galatians.* Minneapolis: Fortress, 2002.

———. "The Jewish Context of the Gentile Audience Addressed in Paul's Letter to the Romans." *Catholic Biblical Quarterly* 61 (1999): 283–304.

———. *The Mystery of Romans: The Jewish Context of Paul's Letter.* Minneapolis: Fortress, 1996.

Niccum, Curt. "The Voice of the Manuscripts on the Silence of Women: The External Evidence for 1 Cor 14:34–35." *New Testament Studies* 43 (1997): 242–55.

Nygren, Anders. *Commentary on Romans.* Philadelphia: Fortress, 1949.

Oberman, Heiko A. *The Roots of Anti-Semitism in the Age of Renaissance and Reformation.* Translated by James I. Porter. Philadelphia: Fortress, 1983.

Ogg, George. *The Chronology of the Life of Paul.* London: Epworth, 1968.

Okeke, G. E. "I Thessalonians 2. 13–16: The Fate of the Unbelieving Jews." *New Testament Studies* 27 (1980/1981): 127–36.

Osten-Sacken, Peter von der. *Christian-Jewish Dialogue: Theological Foundations.* Translated by Margaret Kohl. Philadelphia: Fortress, 1986.

———. *Die Heiligkeit der Tora: Studien zum Gesetz bei Paulus.* Munich: Chr. Kaiser, 1989.

Parsons, Michael. "Being Precedes Act: Indicative and Imperative in Paul's Writing." Pages 217–47 in *Understanding Paul's Ethics: Twentieth-Century Approaches.* Edited by Brian S. Rosner; Grand Rapids: Eerdmans, 1995.

Patte, Daniel. "A Post-Holocaust Biblical Critic Responds." Pages 225–45 in *Reading Israel in Romans: Legitimacy and Plausibility of Divergent Interpretations.* Edited by Cristina Grenholm and Daniel Patte. Romans through History and Culture Series. Harrisburg, Pa.: Trinity Press International, 2000.

Pearson, Birger A. "1 Thessalonians 2:13–16: A Non-Pauline Interpolation." *Harvard Theological Review* 64 (1971): 79–94.

Perkins, Pheme. *Abraham's Divided Children: Galatians and the Politics of Faith.* New Testament in Context. Harrisburg, Pa.: Trinity Press International, 2001.

Perschbacher, Wesley J. *New Testament Greek Syntax: An Illustrated Manual.* Chicago: Moody, 1995.

Philo. Translated by F. H. Colson and G. H. Whitaker et al. 10 vols. Loeb Classical Library. Cambridge: Harvard University Press, 1929–1962.

Piper, John. *The Justification of God: An Exegetical and Theological Study of Romans 9:1–23.* 2d ed. Grand Rapids: Baker, 1993.

Ponsot, Hervé. "Et ainsi tout Israel sauvé; Rom., XI, 26a." *Revue biblique* 89 (1982): 406–17.

Porter, Stanley E. "Paul of Tarsus and His Letters." Pages 533–85 in *Handbook of Classical Rhetoric in the Hellenistic Period, 330 B.C.–A.D. 400.* Edited by Stanley E. Porter. Leiden: E. J. Brill, 1997.

————. *Verbal Aspect in the Greek of the New Testament, with Reference to Tense and Mood.* Studies in Biblical Greek. New York: Peter Lang, 1989, 1993.

Porter, Stanley E. and Jeffrey T. Reed. "Philippians as a Macro-Chiasm and Its Exegetical Significance." *New Testament Studies* 44 (1998): 213–21.

Räisänen, Heikki. "Galatians 2.16 and Paul's Break with Judaism." Pages 112–26 in *Jesus, Paul, and Torah: Collected Essays.* Translated by David E. Orton. Journal for the Study of the New Testament: Supplement Series 43. Sheffield, England: JSOT Press, 1992.

————. "The 'Law' of Faith and the Spirit." Pages 48–68 in *Jesus, Paul, and Torah: Collected Essays.* Translated by David E. Orton. Journal for the Study of the New Testament: Supplement Series 43. Sheffield, England: JSOT Press, 1992. Repr. from *New Testament Studies* 26 (1979/1980): 101–17.

————. *Paul and the Law.* 2d ed. Wissenschaftliche Untersuchungen zum Neuen Testament 29. Tübingen: J. C. B. Mohr (Paul Siebeck), 1986.

————. "Paul, God, and Israel: Romans 9–11 in Recent Research." Pages 178–206 in *The Social World of Formative Christianity and Judaism: Essays in Tribute to Howard Clark Kee.* Edited by Jacob Neusner, Peder Borgen, Ernest S. Frerichs, and Richard Horsley. Philadelphia: Fortress, 1988.

————. "Paul's Word-Play on νόμος: A Linguistic Study." Pages 69–94 in *Jesus, Paul, and Torah: Collected Essays.* Translated by David E. Orton. Journal for the Study of the New Testament: Supplement Series 43. Sheffield, England: JSOT Press, 1992.

Rajak, Tessa. "Was There a Roman Charter for the Jews?" *Journal of Roman Studies* 74 (1984): 107–23.

Reasoner, Mark. "The Theology of Romans 12:1–15:13." Pages 287–99 in *Romans.* Edited by David M. Hay and E. Elizabeth Johnson. Vol. 3 of *Pauline Theology.* Minneapolis: Fortress, 1995.

Refoulé, François. "Cohérence ou incohérence de Paul en Romains 9–11." *Revue biblique* 98 (1991): 51–79.

————. "... Et ainsi tout Israël sera sauvé": Romans 11:25–32. Lectio divina 117. Paris: Cerf, 1984.

Rhyne, C. Thomas. *Faith Establishes the Law.* Society of Biblical Literature Dissertation Series 55. Chico, Calif.: Scholars Press, 1981.

Richard, Earl. *First and Second Thessalonians.* Sacra pagina 11. Collegeville, Minn.: Liturgical Press, 1995.

Richardson, Peter. "Augustan-Era Synagogues in Rome." Pages 17–29 in *Judaism and Christianity in First-Century Rome.* Edited by Karl P. Donfried and Peter Richardson. Grand Rapids: Eerdmans, 1998.

————. *Israel in the Apostolic Church.* Society for New Testament Studies Monograph Series 10. Cambridge: Cambridge University Press, 1969.

Ridderbos, Herman. *Paul: An Outline of His Theology.* Translated by John Richard de Witt. Grand Rapids: Eerdmans, 1975.

Riesner, Rainer. *Paul's Early Period: Chronology, Mission Strategy, Theology.* Grand Rapids: Eerdmans, 1998.

Robertson, A. T. *A Grammar of the Greek New Testament in the Light of Historical Research.* Nashville: Broadman, 1934.

Robinson, D. W. B. "The Distinction between Jewish and Gentile Believers in Galatians." *Australian Biblical Review* 13 (1965): 29–48.

———. "The Salvation of Israel in Romans 9–11." *Reformed Theological Review* 26 (1967): 81–96.

Roo, Jacqueline C. R. de. "The Concept of 'Works of the Law' in Jewish and Christian Literature." Pages 116–47 in *Christian-Jewish Relations through the Centuries.* Edited by Stanley E. Porter and Brook W. R. Pearson; Journal for the Study of the New Testament: Supplement Series 192. Sheffield: Sheffield Academic Press, 2000.

Rosen, Moishe, with William Proctor. *Jews for Jesus.* Old Tappan, N.J.: Fleming H. Revell, 1974.

Rosner, Brian S. *Paul, Scripture, and Ethics: A Study of 1 Corinthians 5–7.* Arbeiten zur Geschichte des Antiken Judentums und des Urchristentums 23. Leiden: E. J. Brill, 1994.

Rowe, C. Kavin. "Romans 10:13: What Is the Name of the Lord?" *Horizons in Biblical Theology* 22 (2000): 135–73.

Ruether, Rosemary Radford. *Faith and Fratricide: The Theological Roots of Anti-Semitism.* New York: Seabury, 1974.

Sampley, J. Paul. "The Weak and the Strong: Paul's Careful and Crafty Rhetorical Strategy in Romans 14:1–15:13." Pages 40–52 in *The Social World of the First Christians: Essays in Honor of Wayne A. Meeks.* Edited by L. Michael White and O. Larry Yarbrough. Minneapolis: Fortress, 1995.

Sanders, E. P. "Jewish Association with Gentiles and Galatians 2.11–14." Pages 170–88 in *The Conversation Continues: Studies in Paul and John in Honor of J. Louis Martyn.* Edited by R. T. Fortna and B. R. Gaventa. Nashville: Abingdon, 1990.

———. *Jewish Law from Jesus to the Mishnah: Five Studies.* Philadelphia: Trinity Press International, 1990.

———. *Paul and Palestinian Judaism: A Comparison of Patterns of Religion.* Philadelphia: Fortress, 1977.

———. *Paul, the Law, and the Jewish People.* Philadelphia: Fortress, 1983.

Sandnes, Karl Olav. *Paul—One of the Prophets?* Wissenschaftliche Untersuchungen zum Neuen Testament. Second Series 43. Tübingen: J. C. B. Mohr (Paul Siebeck), 1991.

Sänger, Dieter. "Rettung der Heiden und Erwählung Israels: Einige vorläufige Erwägungen zu Römer 11,25–27." *Kerygma und Dogma* 32 (1986): 99–119.

Schippers, R. "The Pre-Synoptic Tradition in I Thessalonians II 13–16." *Novum Testamentum* 8 (1966): 223–34.

Schlier, Heinrich. *Der Römerbrief.* Herders theologisher Kommentar zum Neuen Testament 6. Freiburg: Herder, 1977.

Schlueter, Carol J. *Filling up the Measure: Polemical Hyperbole in 1 Thessalonians 2.14–16.* Journal for the Study of the New Testament: Supplement Series 98. Sheffield, England: Sheffield Academic Press, 1994.

Schmidt, Daryl. "1 Thess 2:13–16: Linguistic Evidence for an Interpolation." *Journal of Biblical Literature* 102 (1983): 269–79.

Schmithals, Walter. *Paul and the Gnostics.* Translated by John E. Steely. Nashville: Abingdon, 1972. German original: *Paulus und die Gnostiker.* Hamburg: Herbert Reich Evangelischer Verlag, 1965.

Schnabel, Eckhard J. "How Paul Developed His Ethics: Motivations, Norms, and Criteria of Pauline Ethics." Pages 267–97 in *Understanding Paul's Ethics: Twentieth-Century Approaches.* Edited by Brian S. Rosner. Grand Rapids: Eerdmans, 1995.

———. *Law and Wisdom from Ben Sira to Paul: A Tradition History Enquiry into the Relation of Law, Wisdom, and Ethics.* Tübingen: J. C. B. Mohr (Paul Siebeck), 1985.

Schrage, Wolfgang. *The Ethics of the New Testament.* Translated by David E. Green. Philadelphia: Fortress, 1988.

Schreiner, Thomas R. "The Church as the New Israel and the Future of Ethnic Israel in Paul." *Studia biblica et theologica* 13 (1983): 17–38.

———. *The Law and Its Fulfillment: A Pauline Theology of Law.* Grand Rapids: Baker, 1993.

Schurb, Ken. "Luther and the Jews: A Reconsideration." *Concordia Journal* 13 (1987): 307–30.

Schürer, Emil. *A History of the Jewish People in the Time of Jesus Christ.* Part 2. Vol 2. Translated by Sophia Taylor and Peter Christie. 1890. Repr., Peabody, Mass.: Hendrickson, 1994.

Scott, James M. *Adoption as Sons of God: An Exegetical Investigation into the Background of* ΥΙΟΘΕΣΙΑ *in the Pauline Corpus.* Wissenschaftliche Untersuchungen zum Neuen Testament. Second Series 48. Tübingen: J. C. B. Mohr (Paul Siebeck), 1992.

———. " 'For as Many as Are of Works of the Law Are under a Curse' (Galatians 3.10)." Pages 187–221 in *Paul and the Scriptures of Israel.* Edited by Craig A. Evans and James A. Sanders. Journal for the Study of the New Testament: Supplement Series 83. Sheffield, England: JSOT Press, 1993.

———. "Paul's Use of Deuteronomic Tradition." *Journal of Biblical Literature* 112 (1993): 645–65.

———, ed. *Exile: Old Testament, Jewish, and Christian Conceptions.* Journal for the Study of Judaism in the Persian, Hellenistic, and Roman Periods: Supplement Series 56. Leiden: E. J. Brill, 1997.

Segal, Alan F. *Paul the Convert: The Apostolate and Apostasy of Saul the Pharisee.* New Haven: Yale University Press, 1990.

———. "Response: Some Aspects of Conversion and Identity Formation in the Christian Community of Paul's Time." Pages 184–90 in *Paul and Politics—Ekklesia, Israel, Imperium, Interpretation: Essays in Honor of Krister Stendahl.* Edited by Richard A. Horsley. Harrisburg, Pa.: Trinity Press International, 2000.

Seifrid, Mark A. *Christ, Our Righteousness: Paul's Theology of Justification.* New Studies in Biblical Theology 9. Downers Grove, Ill.: InterVarsity, 2000.

———. "The 'New Perspective on Paul' and Its Problems." *Themelios* 25 (2000): 4–18.

———. "Righteousness Language in the Hebrew Scriptures and Early Judaism." Pages 415–42 in *The Complexities of Second Temple Judaism.* Vol. 1 of *Justification and Variegated Nomism.* Edited by D. A. Carson, Peter T. O'Brien, and Mark A. Siefrid. Grand Rapids: Baker, 2001.

Sievers, Joseph. "'God's Gifts and Call Are Irrevocable': The Reception of Romans 11:29 through the Centuries and Christian-Jewish Relations." Pages 127–73 in *Reading Israel in Romans: Legitimacy and Plausibility of Divergent Interpretations.* Edited by Cristina Grenholm and Daniel Patte. Romans through History and Culture Series. Harrisburg, Pa.: Trinity Press International, 2000.

Slingerland, Dixon. "Acts 18:1–17 and Luedemann's Pauline Chronology." *Journal of Biblical Literature* 109 (1990): 686–90.

———. "Chrestus: Christus?" Pages 133–44 in *The Literature of Early Rabbinic Judaism: Issues in Talmudic Redaction and Interpretation.* Edited by Alan J. Avery-Peck. New Perspectives on Ancient Judaism 4. Lanham, Md.: University Press of America, 1989.

Smallwood, E. Mary. *The Jews under Roman Rule: From Pompey to Diocletian.* Studies in Judaism in Late Antiquity 20. Leiden: E. J. Brill, 1976.

Smiles, Vincent M. "The Concept of 'Zeal' in Second-Temple Judaism and Paul's Critique of It in Romans 10:2." *Catholic Biblical Quarterly* 64 (2002): 282–99.

———. *The Gospel and the Law in Galatia: Paul's Response to Jewish-Christian Separatism and the Threat of Galatian Apostasy.* Collegeville, Minn.: Liturgical Press, 1998.

Snodgrass, Klyne R. "Spheres of Influence: A Possible Solution to the Problem of Paul and the Law." *Journal for the Study of the New Testament* 32 (1988): 93–113.

Spilsbury, Paul. "Josephus." Pages 241–60 in *The Complexities of Second Temple Judaism.* Vol. 1 of *Justification and Variegated Nomism.* Edited by D. A. Carson, Peter T. O'Brien, and Mark A. Siefrid. Grand Rapids: Baker, 2001.

Stanley, Christopher D. "The Redeemer Will Come 'ἐκ Σιων': Romans 11.26–27 Revisited." Pages 118–42 in *Paul and the Scriptures of Israel.* Edited by Craig A. Evans and James A. Sanders. Journal for the Study of the New Testament: Supplement Series 83. Sheffield, England: Sheffield Academic Press, 1993.

Stendahl, Krister. *Paul among Jews and Gentiles.* Philadelphia: Fortress, 1976.

Stern, Menahem. *Greek and Latin Authors on Jews and Judaism.* 3 vols. Fontes ad res judaicas spectantes. Jerusalem: Israel Academy of Sciences and Humanities, 1974–1984.

Stowers, Stanley K. *A Rereading of Romans: Justice, Jews, and Gentiles.* Fontes ad res judaicas spectantes. New Haven: Yale University Press, 1994.

Strack, Hermann L., and Paul Billerbeck. *Kommentar zum Neuen Testament aus Talmud und Midrash.* 4 vols. Munich: C. H. Beck, 1924–1928.

Strelan, J. G. "A Note on the Old Testament Background of Romans 7:7." *Lutheran Theological Journal* 15 (1981): 23–25.

Stuhlmacher, Peter. *Das paulinische Evangelium.* Forschungen zur Religion und Literatur des Alten und Neuen Testaments 95. Göttingen: Vandenhoeck & Ruprecht, 1968.

———. *Revisiting Paul's Doctrine of Justification: A Challenge to the New Perspective.* Downers Grove, Ill.: InterVarsity, 2001.

Sumney, Jerry. *'Servants of Satan,' 'False Brothers,' and Other Opponents of Paul.* Journal for the Study of the New Testament: Supplement Series 188. Sheffield, England: Sheffield Academic Press, 1999.

Tacitus. *The Histories and the Annals.* Translated by C. H. Moore and J. Jackson. 4 vols. Loeb Classical Library. Cambridge: Harvard University Press, 1937.

Talbert, Charles H. "Paul, Judaism, and the Revisionists." *Catholic Biblical Quarterly* 63 (2001): 1–22.

Theon, *Progymnasmata* 3.104–109. "The 'Progymnasmata' of Theon: A New Text with Translation and Commentary." Translated by James R. Butts. Ph.D. diss., Claremont Graduate School, 1986. Ann Arbor, Mich.: University Microfilms International, 1986, 198–201.

Thielman, Frank. *From Plight to Solution: A Jewish Framework for Understanding Paul's View of the Law in Galatians and Romans.* Novum Testamentum Supplements 61. Leiden: E. J. Brill, 1989.

———. *Paul and the Law.* Downers Grove, Ill.: InterVarsity, 1994.

Thiselton, Anthony. *The First Epistle to the Corinthians: A Commentary on the Greek Text.* New International Greek Testament Commentary. Grand Rapids: Eerdmans, 2000.

Tomson, Peter. *Paul and the Jewish Law: Halakha in the Letters of the Apostle to the Gentiles.* Compendia rerum iudaicarum ad Novum Testamentum 3.1. Minneapolis: Fortress, 1990

Tuckett, Christopher M. "Deuteronomy 21,23 and Paul's Conversion." Pages 345–50 in *L'apôtre Paul: Personnalité, style, et conception du ministère.* Edited by A. VanHoye. Leuven: Leuven University Press, 1986.

———. "Synoptic Tradition in 1 Thessalonians?" Pages 160–82 in *The Thessalonian Correspondence.* Edited by Raymond F. Collins. Leuven: Leuven University Press, 1990.

Turner, Nigel. *Syntax.* Vol. 3 of *A Grammar of New Testament Greek* by James Hope Moulton and Nigel Turner. Edinburgh: T&T Clark, 1963.

Tyson, Joseph B. "'Works of Law' in Galatians." *Journal of Biblical Literature* 92 (1973): 423–31.

Vanlaningham, Michael G. "Romans 11:25–27 and the Future of Israel in Paul's Thought." *The Master's Seminary Journal* 3 (1992): 141–74.

———. "Should the Church Evangelize Israel? A Response to Franz Mussner and Other *Sonderweg* Proponents." *Trinity Journal* 22 New Series (2001): 197–217.

Verseput, D. J. "Paul's Gentile Mission and the Jewish Christian Community: A Study of the Narrative in Galatians 1 and 2." *New Testament Studies* 39 (1993): 36–58.

Wagner, J. Ross. "The Heralds of Isaiah and the Mission of Paul: An Investigation of Paul's Use of Isaiah 51–55 in Romans." Pages 193–222 in *Jesus and the Suffering Servant: Isaiah 53 and Christian Origins.* Edited by William H. Bellinger Jr. and William R. Farmer. Harrisburg, Pa.: Trinity Press International, 1998.

Wallace, Daniel B. *Greek Grammar beyond the Basics: An Exegetical Syntax of the New Testament.* Grand Rapids: Zondervan, 1996.

Wallis, Gerhard. "Der Vollbürgereid in Deuteronomium 27, 15–26." *Hebrew Union College Annual* 45 (1974): 47–63.

Walter, Nicholas. "Paulus und die Gegner des Christusevangeliums in Galatien." Pages 351–56 in *L'apôtre Paul: Personnalité, style, et conception du ministère.* Edited by A. VanHoye. Leuven: Leuven University Press, 1986.

Walters, James C. *Ethnic Issues in Paul's Letter to the Romans: Changing Self-Definitions in Earliest Roman Christianity.* Valley Forge, Pa.: Trinity Press International, 1993.

———. "Romans, Jews, and Christians: The Impact of the Romans on Jewish/Christian Relations in First Century Rome." Pages 175–95 in *Judaism and Christianity in First-Century Rome.* Edited by Karl P. Donfried and Peter Richardson. Grand Rapids: Eerdmans, 1998.

Wanamaker, Charles A. *The Epistles to the Thessalonians: A Commentary on the Greek Text.* New International Greek Testament Commentary. Grand Rapids: Eerdmans, 1990.

Wasserberg, Günter. "Romans 9–11 and Jewish-Christian Dialogue." Pages 174–86 in *Reading Israel in Romans: Legitimacy and Plausibility of Divergent Interpretations.* Edited by Cristina Grenholm and Daniel Patte. Romans through History and Culture Series. Harrisburg, Pa.: Trinity Press International, 2000.

Watson, Francis. *Paul, Judaism, and the Gentiles: A Sociological Approach.* Society for New Testament Studies Monograph Series 56. Cambridge: Cambridge University Press, 1986.

Weatherly, Jon A. "The Authenticity of 1 Thessalonians 2.13–16: Additional Evidence." *Journal for the Study of the New Testament* 42 (1991): 79–98.

Wedderburn, A. J. M. *The Reasons for Romans*. Studies of the New Testament and Its World. Edinburgh: T&T Clark, 1988.

Weima, Jeffrey A . D. "The Function of the Law in Relation to Sin: An Evaluation of the View of H. Räisänen." *Novum Testamentum* 32 (1990): 219–35.

Weima, Jeffrey A. D., and Stanley E. Porter. *An Annotated Bibliography of 1 and 2 Thessalonians*. New Testament Tools and Studies 26; Leiden: Brill, 1998.

Westerholm, Stephen. *Israel's Law and the Church's Faith: Paul and His Recent Interpreters*. Grand Rapids: Eerdmans, 1988.

Whitsett, Christopher G. "Son of God, Seed of David: Paul's Messianic Exegesis in Romans 1:3–4." *Journal of Biblical Literature* 119 (2000): 661–81.

Wiefel, Wolfgang. "The Jewish Community in Ancient Rome and the Origins of Roman Christianity." Pages 85–101 in *The Romans Debate*. Edited by Karl P. Donfried. Rev. ed. Peabody, Mass.: Hendrickson, 1991.

Wilckens, Ulrich. *Der Brief an die Römer*. 3 vols. Evangelisch-katholischer Kommentar zum Neuen Testament 6. Neukirchener-Vluyn: Neukirchener Verlag, 1978–1982.

Williams, Sam K. *Galatians*. Abingdon New Testament Commentaries. Nashville: Abingdon, 1997.

———. "The 'Righteousness of God' in Romans. *Journal of Biblical Literature* 99 (1980): 245–55.

Winger, Michael. *By What Law? The Meaning of* Νόμος *in the Letters of Paul*. Society of Biblical Literature Dissertation Series 128. Atlanta: Scholars Press, 1992.

———. "Meaning and Law." *Journal of Biblical Literature* 117 (1998): 105–10.

Winston, David. "Philo's Doctrine of Repentance." Pages 29–40 in *The School of Moses: Studies in Philo and Hellenistic Religion*. Edited by John Peter Kenney. Atlanta: Scholars Press, 1995.

Winter, Bruce. *Seek the Welfare of the City: Christians as Benefactors and Citizens*. First Century Christians in the Graeco-Roman World. Grand Rapids: Eerdmans, 1994.

Witherington, Ben, III. *The Acts of the Apostles: A Socio-rhetorical Commentary*. Grand Rapids: Eerdmans, 1998.

———. *Grace in Galatia: A Commentary on Paul's Letter to the Galatians*. Grand Rapids: Eerdmans, 1998.

Wright, N. T. *Climax of the Covenant: Christ and the Law in Pauline Theology*. Minneapolis: Fortress, 1991.

Young, Norman H. "*PAIDAGOGOS:* The Social Setting of a Pauline Metaphor." *Novum Testamentum* 29 (1987): 150–76.

———. "Pronominal Shifts in Paul's Argument to the Galatians." Pages 205–15 in *Early Christianity, Late Antiquity, and Beyond*. Vol. 2 of *Ancient History in a Modern University*. Edited by T. W. Hillard, R. A. Kearsley, C. E. V. Nixon, and A. M. Nobbs. Grand Rapids: Eerdmans, 1998.

Zeller, Dieter. "Christus, Skandal und Hoffnung: Die Juden in den Briefen des Paulus." Pages 256–78 in *Gottesverächter und Menschenfeinde? Juden zwischen Jesus und frühchristlicher Kirche.* Edited by Horst Goldstein. Düsseldorf: Patmos, 1979.

Ziesler, J. A. "The Just Requirement of the Law (Romans 8.4)." *Australian Biblical Review* 35 (1987): 77–82.

———. "The Role of the Tenth Commandment in Romans 7." *Journal for the Study of the New Testament* 33 (1988): 41–56.

INDEX OF MODERN AUTHORS

INDEX OF SUBJECTS

INDEX OF ANCIENT SOURCES